BALLADS AND VERSES

AND

MISCELLANEOUS CONTRIBUTIONS TO 'PUNCH'

Frontispiece.

W. M. THACKERAY.

From the Painting by Samuel Lawrence in the National Portrait Gallery.

BALLADS AND VERSES

AND

MISCELLANEOUS CONTRIBUTIONS TO 'PUNCH'

BY

WILLIAM MAKEPEACE THACKERAY

With Illustrations by the Author, John Leech, etc.

London

MACMILLAN AND CO., Limited

NEW YORK : THE MACMILLAN COMPANY

1904

NOTE.

THE composition of verses was a favourite amusement of Thackeray from his childhood. As a boy he loved to rhyme, and his productions edified his comrades at the Charterhouse. The late Anthony Trollope in his monograph on Thackeray in the *English Men of Letters* series quoted one of the best of his boyish effusions :—

> In the romantic little town of Highbury
> My father kept a circulatin library ;
> He followed in his youth that man immortal, who
> Conquered the French on the plains of Waterloo.
> Mamma was an inhabitant of Drogheda,
> Very good she was to darn and to embroider.
> In the famous island of Jamaica,
> For thirty years I've been a sugar-baker ;
> And here I sit, the Muses' 'appy vot'ry,
> A-cultivatin' every kind of po'try.[1]

The rhyming of "immortal who" with "Waterloo" has many parallels in Thackeray's later work. Impossible rhymes were nearly always a distinguishing feature of his humorous poetry ; and even in the exquisite *Vanitas Vanitatum*, written when the author was nearly fifty years of age, he rhymed "splendid" with "penned it." His powers of impromptu rhyming were exceptional—as witness *The Three Sailors*—and his fondness for that kind of mental exercise never waned. He was always rhyming and always fooling, from his school-days until almost the last day of his life. A lady begged him to write a verse in her album. Turning over the pages he found the following quatrain by Albert Smith :—

> Mont Blanc is the Monarch of Mountains,
> They crowned him long ago,
> But who they got to put it on,
> Nobody seems to know.

---

[1] The 'Note' to vol. ix. of this edition, *Burlesques* . . . *Juvenilia*, contains other verses written by Thackeray at Charterhouse.

Yielding to temptation, Thackeray wrote underneath :—

A HUMBLE SUGGESTION.

I know that Albert wrote in hurry—
    To criticise I scarce presume ;
But yet, methinks that Lindley Murray
    Instead of ' who ' has written ' whom.'

Mr. Herman Merivale, who, with Mr. Frank T. Marzials, has written a sympathetic appreciation of Thackeray, has related that when a neighbour, knowing the novelist to be a *gourmet*, asked at the dinner-table what part of a fowl he preferred, he replied with great gravity :—

Oh ! what's the best part of the fowl ?
    My own Anastasia cried ;
Then, giving a terrible howl,
    She turned on her stomach and died.

As a lad he wrote and illustrated half-a-dozen *Simple Melodies*, of which one may be quoted :—

Little Miss Perkins
Much loved pickled Gerkins,
And went to the cupboard and stole some ;
    But they gave her such pain
    She ne'er ate them again,
She found them so shocking unwholesome.[1]

He was always throwing off nonsense verses, such as that on Bishop Colenso and Bishop Wilberforce :—

This is the bold Bishop Colenso
Whose heresies seem to offend so,
    Quoth Sam of the Soap,
    ' Bring fagot and rope,
For we know he ain't got no friends, oh ! '

For the most part his verses were a relaxation, for he did not take himself seriously as a poet. ' It is easy enough to knock off that nonsense of " Policeman X.," ' he said to Frederick Locker-Lampson ; ' but to be able to write really good *occasional* verse is a rare intellectual feat.' Yet, as Mr. Locker-Lampson remarked, it seems that it would be indeed a triumph to write anything half so good as ' Policeman X.' Thackeray could be serious when

[1] The whole set of *Simple Melodies*, with the illustrations, and *The Bandit's Revenge, or The Fatal Sword*, a romantic drama told in fifteen drawings, are included in an article on *Thackeray as Artist* by Mr. Lewis Melville, in *The Connoisseur* (January, March, 1904).

writing verses, as in *The End of the Play*, or tender as in *Peg of Limavaddy*, or indignant as in *Jacob Homnum's Hoss :—*

> Come down from that tribewn,
> Thou shameless and unjust,

but as a rule he gave rein to his sense of humour, and burlesqued and parodied to his heart's content. Yet the man's sentiment sometimes overruled his intention, and if he wrote *The Willow Tree* only to parody it, when he sat down to compose a series of *Love Songs Made Easy*, after burlesquing the 'Mayfair' and the 'Oriental,' he wrote the sympathetic 'Domestic' love song, *The Cane-Bottom'd Chair*.

All the ballads and verses that Thackeray wrote, whether published as separate items or inserted in his stories and articles, are here represented, with the exception of *The Georges* (see vol. xvi. of this edition : *The English Humourists; The Four Georges*, etc.) and the parodies and caricatures that appeared in *The Snob, The Gownsman*, and *The National Standard* (see vol. ix. of this edition : *Burlesques . . . Juvenilia*). It happens that sometimes Thackeray practically rewrote a ballad after its appearance : when this has occurred both versions are given. Instances of this are the poems *The King of Brentford* and *Lucy's Birthday*. Translations or adaptations from French, German, and Latin poets are, for the purposes of comparison, accompanied by the original verses.

I.

(i.) *The Great Cossack Epic of Demetrius Rigmarolovicz, Translated by a Lady*, appeared in *Fraser's Magazine* (December, 1839). It was reprinted, without the prose introduction, under the title of *The Legend of St. Sophia of Kioff* in *Miscellanies* (vol. i. : *Ballads, etc. ;* 1855), in the Library edition of Thackeray's Works (vol. xviii. : *Ballads ;* 1869) ; and also in *Miscellanies* (Boston ; vol. v. : 1870).

The Introduction is now reprinted for the first time.

(ii.) *The King of Brentford's Testament, By Michael Angelo Titmarsh* (*George Cruikshank's Omnibus*, December, 1841), was reprinted in *Miscellanies* (vol. i. : *Ballads, etc. ;* 1855) ; in the Library edition of Thackeray's Works (vol. xviii. : *Ballads, etc. ;* 1869) ; and also in *Miscellanies* (Boston ; vol. v. : 1870).

At Cruikshank's request Thackeray sent him these verses for the *Omnibus*, and was rewarded by the editor with a sovereign in full satisfaction ! The author used to tell the story against himself, adding, 'You may suppose after that I did not trouble with any more of my poems.'

(iii.) *The Chronicle of the Drum* was issued in
The | Second Funeral of Napoleon : | In Three Letters | to
Miss Smith, of London, | and | *The Chronicle of the Drum* | By |
Mr. M. A. Titmarsh. | London : Hugh Cunningham, St. Martin's
Place, | Trafalgar Square. | 1841.

It was reprinted in *Miscellanies* (vol. i.: *Ballads, etc. ;* 1855) ;
in the Library edition of Thackeray's Works (vol. xviii. : *Ballads,
etc. ;* 1869) ; and also in *Miscellanies* (Boston ; vol. v. :
1870).

(iv.) *The Mahogany Tree* (*Punch*, January 9, 1847) was reprinted, with the omission of the second verse, in *Miscellanies*
(vol. i. : *Ballads, etc. ;* 1855); in the Library edition of Thackeray's
Works (vol. xviii. : *Ballads, etc. ;* 1869) ; and in *Miscellanies*
(Boston ; vol. v. : 1870).

It is now reprinted in its entirety for the first time.

In connection with these verses there is a touching incident.
To the last Thackeray would, from time to time, attend the
weekly dinners of the *Punch* staff, and when he died, it was in
the columns of this periodical that was chronicled the most sincere
regret at the great loss suffered, not by the death of the novelist,
but by the death of the comrade and friend.   On the sad Christmas
Eve Horace Mayhew brought the news to the jovial *Punch* party.
' I'll tell you what we'll do,' he said ; ' we'll sing the dear old
boy's Mahogany Tree ; he'd like it.'   Accordingly they stood up,
and with such memory of the words as each possessed, and a
catching of the breath here and there by about all of them, the
song was sung.

(v.) *The Ballad of Bouillabaisse. From the Contributor at
Paris* (*Punch*, February 17, 1849), was reprinted in *Miscellanies*
(vol. i. : *Ballads, etc. ;* 1855) ; in the Library edition of Thackeray's
Works (vol. xviii. : *Ballads, etc. ;* 1869) ; and in *Miscellanies*
(Boston ; vol. v. : 1870).

Thackeray went to Paris towards the end of 1848 and revisited
his old haunts.   He chronicled his sight-seeing in *Paris Revisited,
Two or Three Theatres in Paris, On some Dinners in Paris,* [1]
and *The Ballad of Bouillabaisse*.   His memories were sad, for
in the Rue Neuve St. Augustin, close by the Rue Neuve des
Petits Champs, in which Terrés' tavern was situated, he had spent
the first happy months of his married life, the happiness of which
was so soon to be blighted.

(vi.) *May Day Ode* (*The Times*, April 30, 1851) was reprinted
in *Miscellanies* (vol. i. : *Ballads, etc. ;* 1855) ; in the Library

[1] These articles are reprinted in vol. xvii. of this edition : *Travels in
London, etc.*

edition of Thackeray's Works (vol. xviii. : *Ballads, etc. ;* 1869) ;
and also in *Miscellanies* (Boston ; vol. v. : 1870).

As it has already been stated in the 'Note' to vol. x. of this
edition, *The Book of Snobs, etc.,* the *Ode* was intended for
publication in *Punch.* For insertion in the next issue, however,
this should have been received not later than Saturday morning,
but it was not delivered until the evening, when Mark Lemon,
the editor, either could not or would not insert it until the
following week. Thackeray was annoyed, and himself carried the
manuscript to Printing House Square : it appeared in *The Times*
on the following Monday morning.

(vii.) *The Pen and the Album,* written in Miss Kate Perry's
Album, appeared in *The Keepsake,* 1853. It was reprinted in
Miscellanies (vol. i. : *Ballads, etc. ;* 1855) ; in the Library edition
of Thackeray's Works (vol. xviii. : *Ballads, etc. ;* 1869) ; and in
Miscellanies (Boston ; vol. v. : 1876).

(viii.) *Vanitas Vanitatum* (*The Cornhill Magazine,* July,
1860) was reprinted in the Library edition of Thackeray's Works
(vol. xviii. : *Ballads, etc. ;* 1869) ; and in *Miscellanies* (Boston ;
vol. v. : 1870).

II.

(i.) *The Sick Child. By the Honourable Wilhemina Skeggs,*
appeared in *Punch,* January 14, 1843.

It is now reprinted for the first time.

(ii.) *Titmarsh's Carmen Lilliense* (*Fraser's Magazine,* March,
1844) was reprinted in *Miscellanies* (vol. i. : *Ballads, etc. ;*
1855) ; in the Library edition of Thackeray's Works (vol. xviii. :
Ballads, etc.; 1869) ; and in *Miscellanies* (Boston ; vol. v.: 1870).

Carmen Lilliense is supposed to have been founded upon an
unpleasant experience of the author.

(iii.) *Great News ! Wonderful News !* with an Illustration
by the Author (*Punch,* May 4, 1844), was reprinted in *The
Hitherto Unidentified Contributions of W. M. Thackeray to
Punch,* by Mr. M. H. Spielmann (1899).

It is now included for the first time in an edition of Thackeray's
Works.

(iv.) *Jenny Wren's Remonstrance* (*Punch,* August 24, 1844)
was reprinted in *The Hitherto Unidentified Contributions of
W. M. Thackeray to Punch,* by Mr. M. H. Spielmann (1899).

It is now included for the first time in an edition of Thackeray's
Works.

(v.) *A Doe in the City. By Frederick Haltamont de Mont-*

morency, with an Illustration by the Author (*Punch*, November 1, 1845), was reprinted in the Library edition of Thackeray's Works (vol. xviii. : *Ballads, etc. ;* 1869), and also, without the Illustration, in *Miscellanies* (Boston ; vol. v. : 1870).

(vi.) *Kitchen Melodies.—Curry*, with an Illustration by the Author (*Punch*, November 28, 1846), was reprinted in *The Hitherto Unidentified Contributions of W. M. Thackeray to Punch*, by Mr. M. H. Spielmann (1901).

It is now included for the first time in an edition of Thackeray's Works.

(vii.) *Mr. Smith and Mr. Moses*, with an Illustration by the Author (*Punch*, March 25, 1848), was reprinted in a supplementary volume of the Library edition of Thackeray's Works (vol. xxiv. : *Contributions to Punch ;* 1886).

(viii.) *The Froddylent Butler*, with a Prose Introduction by the Author (*Punch*, February 10, 1849), was reprinted in a supplementary volume of the Library edition of Thackeray's Works (vol. xxiv. : *Contributions to Punch*, 1886).

(ix.) *The Three Sailors* was issued in

Sand and Canvas. A Narrative of Adventures in Egypt, with a Sojourn among the Artists in Rome. By Samuel Bevan. London : Charles Gilpin, 5 Bishopsgate Street, Without. MDCCCXLIX.

The original manuscript, with a letter from Thackeray to Mr. Bevan, were facsimiled in *The Autographic Mirror* (November 1, 1864). These are reproduced at the end of this ' Note.'

Different versions of this song have appeared, under the title of *Little Billee*, in an article on Thackeray by Dr. John Brown (*The North British Review*, February, 1864) ; in the Library edition of Thackeray's Works (vol. xviii. : *Ballads, etc. ;* 1869) ; and also in *Miscellanies* (Boston ; vol. v. : 1870).

(x.) *Lucy's Birthday* were verses sent on April 15, 1853, to Miss Lucy Baxter, the daughter of some American friends of Thackeray. They were rewritten and printed in *The Keepsake*, 1854 ; and reprinted, with some alterations, in *Miscellanies* (vol. i. : *Ballads, etc. ;* 1853) ; in the Library edition of Thackeray's Works (vol. xviii. : *Ballads, etc. ;* 1869) ; and in *Miscellanies* (Boston ; vol. v. : 1870).

The original verses were facsimiled in *Thackeray's Friendship with an American Family* (*The Century Illustrated Magazine*, December, 1903).

(xi.) *Piscator and Piscatrix*,[1]

[1] *Piscator and Piscatrix* was reprinted in 1868, under the title of *The Anglers*, in *The Princess Alexandra Gift-Book*, edited by Mr. John Shearer.

(xii.) *The Sorrows of Werther* and

(xiii.) *The Last of May* appeared in

Miscellanies : | Prose and Verse. | By | W. M. Thackeray. | Author of ' Vanity Fair,' | ' The Newcomes,' etc. | vol. i. | Ballads. | The Book of Snobs. | The Fatal Book. | Cox's Diary. | The Tremendous Adventures of Major Gahagan. | London : | Bradley and Evans, 11 Bouverie Street. | 1855.

They were reprinted in the Library edition of Thackeray's Works (vol. xviii. : *Ballads, etc. ;* 1869) ; and also in *Miscellanies* (Boston ; vol. v. : 1870).

(xiv.) *The Idler,* signed *Essel* (*The Idler Magazine of Fiction, Essays, Belles Lettres, and Comedy ;* March, 1856), was reprinted in the Library edition of Thackeray's Works (vol. xviii. : *Ballads, etc. ;* 1869) ; and also in *Miscellanies* (Boston ; vol. v. : 1870).

III.

The . following verses are scattered throughout Thackeray's Works. They are printed in chronological order.

(i.) ' *Some Love the Matin Chimes* ' (*Friar's Song*), from *The Devil's Wager* in *The National Standard*.

(ii.) *The Almack's Adieu,* from *Our Annual Execution.*

(iii.) *The Battle-Axe Polacca* (*The Knightly Guerdon*) and

(iv.) *Song of the Violet,* from *A Shabby-Genteel Story.*

(v.) ' *Æthelfred Koning Murning Post Redinge* ' and

(vi.) *The Story of King Canute,* from *Miss Tickletoby's Lectures on English History.*

These verses were reprinted in *Rebecca and Rowena.*

(vii. and viii.) *The Willow Tree* (two versions), from *Ottilia.*

(ix.) *The Minaret Bells,* and

(x.) *Come to the Greenwood Tree,* from *The Ravenswing.*

(xi.) *Peg of Limavaddy,* from *The Irish Sketch Book.*

(xii.) *Jeames of Buckley Square : A Helegy,*

(xiii.) *Sonnick sejested by Prince Halbert,*

(xiv.) *When Moonlike ore the Hazure Seas,* and

(xv.) *Lines upon my Sister's Portrait,* from *Jeames's Diary and Letters.*

(xvi.) *The White Squall,* from *A Journey from Cornhill to Grand Cairo.*

(xvii.) *Ah ! Bleak and Barren was the Moor,* and

(xviii.) *The Rose upon my Balcony,* from *Vanity Fair.*

(xix.) *Dear Jack,* from *Phil Fogarty.*

FRENCH DITTIES.

(i. and ii.) *Imitations of Béranger :* (i.) *Il était un roi d'Yvetot. The King of Brentford*, under the heading of *The Fraser Papers for May*, appeared in *Fraser's Magazine* (May, 1834). It was reprinted in *The Early Writings of Mr. W. M. Thackeray*, by Mr. C. P. Johnson (1888) ; and in Thackeray's *Stray Papers*, by Mr. Lewis Melville (1901).

It is now for the first time included in an edition of Thackeray's Works.

This version was rewritten and published in *The Paris Sketch Book* (1840), together with

A second rendering of the same poem, entitled *The King of Yvetot*.

(iii.) *Imitations of Béranger : Le Grenier—The Garret ;* and

(iv.) *Imitations of Béranger : Roger-Bontemps—Jolly Jack*, with an Illustration by the Author.

These poems were reprinted, without the Illustration, in *The Paris Sketch Book* (New York, 1852) ; but they have been deleted from all subsequent editions of that work, and have been inserted among the Ballads. *See* the Library edition of Thackeray's Works (vol. xviii. : *Ballads and Tales ;* 1869) ; and *Miscellanies* (Boston ; vol. v. : 1870).

(v.) *Le Bon Ange—O Virgin Blest !* The translation of this poem, which appeared in Dumas's famous piece of *Don Juan de Marana*, was inserted in the article on *French Dramas and Melodramas* in *The Paris Sketch Book* (1840).

It is now for the first time included among the Ballads.

GERMAN DITTIES.

(i.) *A Tragic Story*, from *Tragische Geschichte*, by Adelbert von Chamisso.

(ii.) *The Chaplet*, from *Der Kranz*, by Ludwig Uhland.

(iii.) *The King on the Tower*, from *Der König auf dem Turme*, by Ludwig Uhland ; and

(iv.) *To a Very Old Woman*, from *Die Greisin*, by Friedrich Baron de la Motte Fouqué,

appeared in *Miscellanies* (vol. i. : *Ballads, etc. ;* 1855). They were reprinted in the Library edition of Thackeray's Works (vol. xviii. : *Ballads, etc. ;* 1869), and also in *Miscellanies* (Boston ; vol. v. : 1870).

Doctor Luther appeared in *The Adventures of Philip*. It was reprinted, under the title of *A Credo*, in the Library edition of Thackeray's Works (vol. viii. : *Ballads, etc. ;* 1869) ; and also in *Miscellanies* (Boston ; vol. i. : 1870).

IMITATIONS OF HORACE.

(i.) *To his Serving Boy—Ad Ministram*, appeared in *Memorials of Gormandising* (*Fraser's Magazine*, June, 1841), and were reprinted in *Miscellanies* (vol. i. : *Ballads, etc. ;* 1855) ; in the Library edition of Thackeray's Works (vol. xviii. : *Ballads, etc. ;* 1869) ; and also in *Miscellanies* (Boston ; vol. v. : 1870).

(ii.) *Be Happy and thy Counsel Keep—Est et fideli tuta silentio merces*, appeared in *A Pictorial Rhapsody* (*Fraser's Magazine*, June, 1840).

It is now for the first time included among the Ballads.

LOVE SONGS MADE EASY.

(i.) *Love Songs made Easy. The Genteel or Mayfair Love Song, 'What makes my Heart to Thrill and Glow ?' By Fitzroy Clarence*, with a prose Introduction and Conclusion and an Illustration by the Author (*Punch*, March 6, 1847).

(ii.) *Love Songs by the Fat Contributor. The Domestic Love Song : The Cane-Bottom'd Chair*, with a prose Introduction and two Illustrations by the Author (*Punch*, March 27, 1847) ; and

(iii.)-(v.) *Love Songs by the Fat Contributor. The Ghazul, or Oriental Love Song : The Rocks, The Merry Bard, The*

Caïque, with a prose Introduction and two Illustrations by the Author (*Punch*, June 5, 1847).

These verses were reprinted, without the Illustrations, in *Miscellanies* (vol. i. : *Ballads, etc. ;* 1855) and in *Miscellanies* (Boston ; vol. v. : 1870), and, without the Illustrations, in the Library edition of Thackeray's Works (vol. xviii. : *Ballads, etc. ;* 1869).

The verses, with the Introductions, etc., are now reprinted for the first time.

(vi.) *Ghazul to the Houri Chai-ree-toh* appeared in the *Second Turkish Letter concerning the Divertissement ' Les Houris.'* This paper was reprinted for the first time in vol. x. of this edition : *The Book of Snobs, etc.*

The verses are now for the first time included among the Ballads.

(vii.) *To Mary* appeared in *The Snobs of England*.

(viii.) *Now the Toils of Day are Over*, afterwards called *Serenade*, appeared in the revised version of *The Devil's Wager* (*The Paris Sketch Book*).

(ix.) *Ronsard to his Mistress* (*Fraser's Magazine*, January, 1846) was reprinted in *Miscellanies* (vol. i. : *Ballads, etc. ;* 1855) ; in the Library edition of Thackeray's Works (vol. xviii. : *Ballads, etc.*) ; and in *Miscellanies* (Boston ; vol. v. : 1870).

(x.) *On the Lady Emily X——*, afterwards called *My Nora*, appeared in *Fitz-Boodle's Professions*.

LYRA HYBERNICA.

(i.) *The Pimlico Pavilion. By the Mulligan of Kilbally-mulligan* (*Punch*, August 9, 1845),

(ii.) *The Battle of Limerick* (*Punch*, May 13, 1848),

(iii.) *Mr. Finigan's Lament*, afterwards called *Molony's Lament* (*Punch*, March 23, 1850),

(iv.) *Mr. Molony's Account of the Ball given to the Nepaulese Ambassador by the Peninsular and Oriental Company* (*Punch*, August 3, 1850), and

(v.) *Mr. Molony's Account of the Crystal Palace*, afterwards called *The Crystal Palace* (*Punch*, April 26, 1851),

were reprinted under the title of *Lyra Hibernica : The Poems of the Molony of Kilballymolony*, in *Miscellanies* (vol. i. : *Ballads, etc. ;* 1855) ; in the Library edition of Thackeray's Works (vol. xviii. : *Ballads, etc. ;* 1869) ; and also in *Miscellanies* (Boston ; vol. v. : 1870).

(vi.) *The Last Irish Grievance* (*Punch*, November 22, 1851) was reprinted in the Library edition of Thackeray's Works (vol. xviii. : *Ballads, etc.;* 1869); and in *Miscellanies* (Boston; vol. v. : 1870).

(vii.) *The Rose of Flora* appeared in *The Luck of Barry Lyndon*.

(viii.) *You've all heard of Larry O'Toole*, usually called *Larry O'Toole*, appeared in *Phil Fogarty*.

THE BALLADS OF POLICEMAN X.

(i.) *A Bow Street Ballad. By a Gentleman of the Force* (*Pleaceman X.*).—*The Knight and the Lady*, with an Illustration by the Author, appeared in *Punch*, November 28, 1848. It was reprinted, without the Illustration, in *Miscellanies* (vol. i. : *Ballads, etc.;* 1855); in the Library edition of Thackeray's Works (vol. xviii. ; *Ballads, etc.;* 1869) ; and also in *Miscellanies* (Boston ; vol. v. : 1870); and, with the Illustration, in the cheaper illustrated edition of Thackeray's Works (vol. xxi. : *Ballads, etc.;* 1879) ;

(ii.) *Bow Street Ballads.*—*No. II. Jacob Omnium's Hoss. A New Pallice Court Chaunt*, with an Illustration by the Author, appeared in *Punch* (December 9, 1848),

were reprinted, without the Illustrations, in *Miscellanies* (vol. i. : *Ballads, etc.;* 1855) ; and in *Miscellanies* (Boston; vol. v. : 1870); and, with the Illustrations, in the Library edition of Thackeray's Works (vol. xviii. : *Ballads, etc.;* 1869).

(iii.) *The Three Christmas Waits*, with an Illustration by the Author (*Punch*, December 23, 1848), and

(iv.). *The Ballad of Eliza Davis*, with an Illustration by the Author (*Punch*, February 9, 1850),

were reprinted, without the Illustrations, in *Miscellanies* (vol. i. : *Ballads, etc.;* 1855) ; and in the Library edition of Thackeray's Works (vol. xviii. : *Ballads, etc.;* 1869) ; and in *Miscellanies* (Boston ; vol. v. : 1870).

The Illustrations are now reprinted for the first time.

(v.) *The Lamentable Ballad of the Foundling of Shoreditch*, with an Illustration by the Author, appeared in *Punch*, February 23, 1850. It was reprinted, without the Illustration, in *Miscellanies* (vol. i. : *Ballads, etc.;* 1855), and in *Miscellanies* (Boston ; vol. v. : 1870) ; and, with the Illustration, in the Library edition of Thackeray's Works (vol. xviii. : *Ballads, etc.;* 1869).

(vi.) *Lines on a late Hospicious Event. By a Gentleman of the Footguards* (*Blue*) (*Punch*, May 11, 1850),

(vii.) *The Wofle New Ballad of Jane Roney and Mary Brown* (*Punch*, May 25, 1850), and

(viii.) *Damages, Two Hundred Pounds* (*Punch*, August 24, 1850),

were reprinted in *Miscellanies* (vol. i. : *Ballads, etc. ;* 1855) ; in the Library edition of Thackeray's Works (vol. xviii. : *Ballads, etc. ;* 1869) ; and in *Miscellanies* (Boston ; vol. v. : 1870).

(ix.) *A Woeful New Ballad of the Protestant Conspiracy to take the Pope's Life. By a Gentleman who has been on the Spot* (*Punch*, March 15, 1851), and

(x.) *The Organ Boy's Appeal* (*Punch*, October 1, 1853),

were reprinted in the Library edition of Thackeray's Works (vol. xviii. : *Ballads, etc. ;* 1869) ; and in *Miscellanies* (Boston ; vol. v. : 1870).

(xi.) *Railroad Speculators*, with an Illustration by the Author (*Punch*, May 31, 1845), was reprinted under the title of *The Speculators*, without the Illustration, in *Miscellanies* (vol. i. : *Ballads, etc. ;* 1855), and in *Miscellanies* (Boston ; vol. v. : 1870) ; and, with the Illustration, in the Library edition of Thackeray's Works (vol. xviii. : *Ballads, etc. ;* 1869).

POLITICAL AND TOPICAL VERSES.

(i.) *Daddy, I'm Hungry. A Scene in a Coach-Maker's Family*, with an Illustration by the Author, appeared in *The Nation* (Dublin), May 13, 1843. It was reprinted, without the Illustration, in *Young Ireland*, by Sir Charles Gavan Duffy (1880) ; and *Sultan Stork, etc.*, by Mr. R. H. Shepherd (1887) ; and, with the Illustration, in Thackeray's *Stray Papers*, by Mr. Lewis Melville (1901).

Thackeray contributed to *The Nation* a second drawing which has been described : A Stage-Coach—a Royal Mail—with a Highland driver and guard, in plaids, but *with no passengers*, at which the country people are jeering. Sir Charles Gavan Duffy, the editor of *The Nation*, wrote to the author of this 'Note,' 'The second drawing was not printed, because the controversy with which it was concerned was brought to a premature close by a decision of the Government. It was not accompanied by any verses, perhaps because it told its own story so effectually. The block of engraved wood lay about in *The Nation* office for a time, but was never printed anywhere. . . . This transaction happened between fifty and sixty years ago, and . . . I left Ireland between forty and fifty years ago, and *The Nation* passed into other hands. You will remember that at the time the engravings were made, Thackeray had written none of the books which will make his name immortal, and there were at least half-a-dozen unused blocks of various articles in *The Nation* office, most of them portraits of eminent men.'

(ii.) *A Rare New Ballad of Malbrook* (*Punch*, May 11, 1844) was reprinted in *The Hitherto Unidentified Contributions of W. M. Thackeray to Punch*, by Mr. M. H. Spielmann (1899).

It is now included for the first time in an edition of Thackeray's Works.

(iii.) *The Dream of Joinville* (*Punch*, June 15, 1844) was reprinted in *The Hitherto Unidentified Contributions of W. M. Thackeray to Punch*, by Mr. M. H. Spielmann (1899).

It is now included for the first time in an edition of Thackeray's Works.

(iv.) *Punch to Daniel in Prison*, with an Illustration by John Leech (*Punch*, July 20, 1844), was reprinted, without the Illustration, in *The Hitherto Unidentified Contributions of W. M. Thackeray to Punch*, by Mr. M. H. Spielmann (1899).

It is now included for the first time in an edition of Thackeray's Works.

(v.) *A Painter's Wish. By Paul Pindar* (*Punch*, April 5, 1845), was reprinted in *The Hitherto Unidentified Contributions of W. M. Thackeray to Punch*, by Mr. M. H. Spielmann (1899).

It is now included for the first time in an edition of Thackeray's Works.

(vi.) *Ode to Sibthorp. By the Poet Laureate*, with an Illustration by the Author (*Punch*, April 26, 1845), was reprinted in *The Hitherto Unidentified Contributions of W. M. Thackeray to Punch*, by Mr. M. H. Spielmann (1899).

It is now included for the first time in an edition of Thackeray's Works.

(vii.) *The Excellent New Ballad of Mr. Peel at Toledo* (*Punch*, May 3, 1845) was reprinted in *The Hitherto Unidentified Contributions of W. M. Thackeray to Punch*, by Mr. M. H. Spielmann (1899).

It is now included for the first time in an edition of Thackeray's Works.

(viii.) *The Allegory of the Fountains* (*Punch*, May 31, 1845) was reprinted in *The Hitherto Unidentified Contributions of W. M. Thackeray to Punch*, by Mr. M. H. Spielmann (1899).

It is now included for the first time in an edition of Thackeray's Works.

(ix.) *Punch's Regency* appeared in *Punch* (August 23, 1845). It is now reprinted for the first time.

(x.) *Serenade* appeared in *Punch* (September 6, 1845). It is now reprinted for the first time.

(xi.) *New Version of 'God Save the Queen'* appeared in *Punch* (September 6, 1845). It is now reprinted for the first time.

(xii.) *The Cambridge Address to Prince Albert*, with an Illustration by the Author (*Punch*, March 13, 1847), was reprinted in *The Hitherto Unidentified Contributions of W. M. Thackeray to Punch*, by Mr. M. H. Spielmann (1899). It is now included for the first time in an edition of Thackeray's Works.

(xiii.) *The Yankee Volunteers* (*Punch*, January 4, 1851) was reprinted in *Miscellanies* (vol. i. : *Ballads, etc.* ; 1855) ; in the Library edition of Thackeray's Works (vol. xviii. : *Ballads, etc.* ; 1869) ; and in *Miscellanies* (Boston ; vol. v. : 1870). It is now reprinted for the first time.

(xiv.) *The Irish Martyrs* appeared in *Punch*, April 12, 1845. It is now reprinted for the first time.

(xv.) *Father Mathew's Debts* appeared in *Punch*, May 24, 1845. It is now reprinted for the first time.

(xvi.) *The Eureka* appeared in *Punch*, July 5, 1845. It is now reprinted for the first time.

A LITTLE DINNER AT TIMMINS'S,

with eight Illustrations by the Author, appeared in *Punch*, May 27 ; June 17, 24 ; July 1, 8, 22, 29, 1848. It was reprinted, without the Illustrations, in *A Shabby Genteel Story and Other Tales* (New York, 1853) ; in *Miscellanies* (vol. iii. : 1856) ; and in *Miscellanies* (Boston ; vol. iii. : 1869) ; and, with the Illustrations, in the Library edition of Thackeray's Works (vol. xxi. : *Denis Duval . . . and Other Stories ;* 1869).

MISCELLANEOUS CONTRIBUTIONS TO PUNCH
(1851-1854).

Of the twenty prose items which Thackeray contributed to *Punch* during these four years, six are now reprinted for the first time, and five more are now for the first time included in an edition of his works.

SKETCHES, ETC.

The Sketches and Initial Letters were contributed to *Punch* from time to time throughout Thackeray's connection with the periodical. Of the twenty-nine cuts, two are now reprinted for the first time, and twenty are now for the first time included in an edition of Thackeray's Works ; while of the thirty-two Initial Letters, etc., eleven are now reprinted for the first time, and all are now for the first time included in an edition of Thackeray's Works.

L. M.

Dear Bevan

    I dont like the looks of the ballad at all in print but if you please prefer to have it in this way exactly. ' Be blowed' It would never do in a printed ballad of

        Yours very truly

          W M Thackeray

The Three Sailors.

> There were three sailors in Bristol City
> Who took a boat and went to sea
>
> But first with beef and Captains biscuit
> And peckled pork they loaded she.

There was guzzling Jack & gorging Jimmy
And the youngest he was little Billy.

Now very soon they were so greedy
They didn't leave not one split pea.

Says Guzzling Jack to gorging Jimmy
I ame confounded hung-ery.

Says Gorging Jim to guzzling Jacky
We have no wittles so we must eat we

Says Guzzling Jack to gorging Jimmy
O gorging Jim what a fool you be.

There's little Bill as is young & tender
We're old & tough so let's eat he.

O Bill we're going to kill and eat you
So undo the collar of your chemee.

When Bill he heard this information
He used his pocket hand ker chee

O let me say my Catechism
As my poor Mammy taught to me.

Make haste make haste says guzzling Jacky
Whilst Jim pulled out his snickersnee.

So Bill went up the main-top-gallant mast
When down he fell on his bended knee.

He scarce had said his Catechism
When up he jumps there's land I see

There's Jerusalem & Madagascar
And North & South Amerikey

There's the British fleet a riding at Anchor
With Admiral Napier K C B

So when they came to the Admirals vessel
He hanged fat Jack and flogged Jimmy

But as for little Bill he made him
The Captain of a Seventy three.

CONTENTS.

I.

II.

III.

FRENCH DITTIES.

GERMAN DITTIES.

IMITATIONS OF HORACE.

LOVE SONGS MADE EASY.

LYRA HYBERNICA.

THE BALLADS OF POLICEMAN X.

POLITICAL AND TOPICAL VERSES.

A LITTLE DINNER AT TIMMINS'S.

MISCELLANEOUS CONTRIBUTIONS TO *PUNCH*
(1851–54.)

CONTENTS

AUTHORS' MISERIES.

I. SOCIAL CUTS.

II. MISCELLANEOUS SKETCHES.

CONTENTS

BALLADS AND VERSES.

I.

THE GREAT COSSACK EPIC OF DEMETRIUS RIGMAROLOVICZ.[1]

Translated by a Lady.

(St. Sophia of Kioff.)

NOTICE.—This extraordinary poem is founded on the legend of St. Sophia, whose statue is said to have walked, of its own accord, up the river Dnieper, to take its station in the Church of Kiew.

We have no further proof of this fact than the consent of ages, the universal belief of enlightened Russia, and the testimony of the celebrated Rigmarolovicz.

His poem, the BUMBAROSKI-KIOFFSCHOTZCKJ (the Leaguer of Kiew) is founded on the legend.

DIMITRI-NEPOMUK MOUGIKOVITCH RIGMAROLOVICZ is himself a *native of Kiew.* He always speaks with enthusiasm of the place of his birth, and has been known to the writer of this memoir seven and twenty years and three months ; from the time when, *an humble serf,* he first attracted the notice of the Emperor Alexander, up to the present time, when he forms one of the *proudest ornaments* in the *literary galaxy* of the *Russian Hemisphere.* He is a singularly elegant-looking man, and about five and twenty.

Some amusing traits are told of him. In the year 1813 (when only a lad) he was in the Hetman Platoff's service, and first awakened public attention by a biting satire upon the Hetman's favourite poodle. For this he was sentenced to receive as many lashes of the knout as there were lines in his poem—viz. 4209 (with a double thong for the Alexandrines). Taken down from the pillar, he calmly said, 'I did not think there had been so much *sting* in my *lines.*' The epigram was spread through Europe instantly, and the *young wit* was lauded to the skies. 'They call me a *Martial,*' said he ; 'I wish I were a *field-*

[1] [*Fraser's Magazine,* December 1839.]

marshal.' Martial, I need not say, was the great foreign poet.
It was thus that Demetrius had a sally for every circumstance of
his life.

He spent very many years in Siberia. Being asked whether
he had read Madame Cotton's work on the exiles of that country,
'*Madame Cotton!'* said he at once; 'egad, when *I* was in
Siberia, I preferred *Madame Worsted,'* alluding to the coldness
of the climate. For this *bonne bouche* he was recalled to the
capital, and may truly be called the *Russian Rogers.*

He has published forty-three volumes of *jus-di-sprees* and
fiscetia, and one hundred and four epic poems. If the following
version of the shortest of them shall be acceptable to the English
reader, *my* end will be *fully* answered, and I shall feel proud at
having planted this Northern Light, or Aurora Borealis, in *our
climes.*

He lives happily with his family; and it must *never be forgotten* that, while the birthplace of DEMETRIUS RIGMAROLOVICZ
is at *Kiew* on the *Dnieper,* the dwelling of a BRITISH PRINCE and
a GERMAN SOVEREIGN is at *Kew* on the *Thames.*

A LADY.[1]

BUMBAROSKI-KIOFFSCHOTZCKJ, THE LEAGUER OF KIOFF.

BY DEMETRIUS RIGMAROLOVICZ.

An Epic Poem in Twenty Books.

I.

Rigmarolovitch
describes the city
and spelling of Kiew,
Kioff, or Kiova.

A THOUSAND years ago, or more
　　A city filled with burghers stout,
　　And girt with ramparts round about,
Stood on the rocky Dnieper shore.
In armour bright, by day and by night,
　　The sentries there paced to and fro.
　　Well guarded and walled was this town, and called
　　　By different names, I'd have you to know;

---

[1] This 'lady' gives, in confidence, her name, which is Jemima Grundy;
she says she is the *real* author of *Blundering Recollections, The Great
Necropolis, Walks and Wanderings in the Fields of,* etc. We never heard
of such works, and are inclined to believe the lady to be an impostor.
If she has any more poems, however, she may send them to us.—O. Y.[1]

[1] [O.Y., the initials of 'Oliver Yorke,' the pseudonym of Dr. Maginn, the editor of
Fraser's Magazine, in which this poem appeared.]

For, if you looks in the g'ography books,
In those dictionaries the name it varies ;
And they write it off Kieff or Kioff,
                                    Kiova or Kiow.

II.

Thus guarded without by wall and redoubt,
    Kiova within was a place of renown,
With more advantages than in those dark ages
        Were commonly known to belong to a town.
There were places and squares, and each year four
        fairs,
And regular aldermen and regular lord-mayors ;
And streets and alleys, and a bishop's palace ;
And a church with clocks for the orthodox—
With clocks and with spires, as religion desires ;
And beadles to whip the bad little boys
Over their poor little corduroys,
In service time, when they *didn't* make a noise ;
And a chapter and dean, and a cathedral-green
With ancient trees, underneath whose shades
Wandered nice young nursery-maids.
Ding-dong, ding-dong, ding-ding-a-ring-ding,
The bells they made a merry, merry ring

From the tall, tall steeple, and all the people
(Except the Jews) came and filled the pews—
        Poles, Russians, and Germans,
        To hear the sermons,
Which HYACINTH preached to those Germans and
        Poles,
        For the safety of their souls.

III.

A worthy priest he was, and a stout—
    You've seldom looked on such a one ;
For, though he fasted thrice in a week,
Yet, nevertheless his skin was sleek ;
His waist it spanned two yards about,
    And he weighed a score of stone.

IV.

and like unto the author of *Plymley's Letters.*

A worthy priest for fasting and prayer,
    And mortification most deserving,
And as for preaching beyond compare ;
He'd exert his powers for three or four hours,
With greater pith than Sydney Smith
    Or the Reverend Edward Irving.

V.

Of what convent he was prior, and when the convent was built.

He was the prior of Saint Sophia
(A Cockney rhyme, but no better I know)—
Of Saint Sophia, that church in Kiow,
    Built by missionaries I can't tell when ;
Who by their discussions converted the Russians,
    And made them Christian men.

VI.

Of Saint Sophia of Kioff, and how her statue miraculously travelled thither.

Sainted Sophia (so the legend vows)
With special favour did regard this house ;
    And to uphold her converts' new devotion
Her statue (needing but her legs for *her* ship)
    Walks of itself across the German Ocean ;
        And of a sudden perches
        In this the best of churches,
Whither all Kiovites come and pay it grateful
    worship.

VII.

And how Kioff should have been a happy city, but that

Thus with their patron-saints and pious preachers
    Recorded here in catalogue precise,
A goodly city, worthy magistrates,
You would have thought in all the Russian states
The citizens the happiest of all creatures,—
    The town itself a perfect Paradise.

VIII.

certain wicked Cossacks did besiege it ;

No, alas ! this well-built city
    Was in a perpetual fidget ;
For the Tartars, without pity,
    Did remorselessly besiege it.

Tartars fierce, with sword and sabres,
    Huns and Turks, and such as these,
Envied much their peaceful neighbours
    By the blue Borysthenes.

murdering the citizens

Down they came, these ruthless Russians,
    From their steppes, and woods and fens,
For to levy contributions
    On the peaceful citizens.

Winter, summer, spring, and autumn,
    Down they came to peaceful Kioff,
Killed the burghers when they caught 'em,
    If their lives they would not buy off.

until they agreed to pay a tribute yearly.

Till the city, quite confounded
    By the ravages they made,
Humbly with their chief compounded,
    And a yearly tribute paid ;

How they paid the tribute, and then suddenly refused it,

Which (because their courage lax was)
    They discharged while they were able ;
Tolerated thus the tax was,
    Till it grew intolerable.

to the wonder of the Cossack envoy.

And the Calmuc envoy sent,
    As before, to take their dues all,
Got to his astonishment
    An unanimous refusal !

Of a mighty gallant speech

'Men of Kioff!' thus courageous
    Did the stout Lord-Mayor harangue them,
'Wherefore pay these sneaking wages
    To the hectoring Russians ?—hang them !

that the Lord-Mayor made,

'Hark ! I hear the awful cry of
    Our forefathers in their graves ;
"Fight, ye citizens of Kioff !
    Kioff was not made for slaves."

exhorting the burghers to pay no longer.

'All too long have ye betrayed her ;
    Rouse, ye men and aldermen,
Send the insolent invader—
    Send him starving back again !'

IX.

Of their thanks and heroic resolves.

He spoke, and he sate down ; the people of the town,
    Who were fired with a brave emulation,
Now rose with one accord, and voted thanks unto the Lord-
    Mayor for his oration.

They dismiss the envoy,

The envoy they dismissed, never placing in his fist
    So much as a single shilling ;
And all with courage fired, as his lordship he desired,

and set about drilling.

At once set about their drilling.

Of the city-guard ;

Then every city ward established a guard,
    Diurnal and nocturnal ;

viz. militia, dragoons, and bummadiers, and their commanders.

Militia volunteers, light dragoons, and bombadiers,
    With an alderman for colonel.

There was muster and roll-calls, and repairing city walls,
    And filling up of fosses ;

Of the majors and captains,

And the captains and the majors, so gallant and courageous,
    A-riding about on their hosses.

the fortifications and artillery.

To be guarded at all hours they built themselves watch-towers,
    With every tower a man on ;
And surly and secure, each from out his embrasure,
    Looked down the iron cannon !

Of the conduct of the actors and clergy.

A battle-song was writ for the theatre, where it
    Was sung with vast enérgy
And rapturous applause ; and besides, the public cause
    Was supported by the clergy.

The pretty ladies'-maids were pinning of cockades
    And tying on of sashes ;
And dropping gentle tears, while their lovers blustered fierce
    About gun-shot and gashes ;

Of the ladies;   The ladies took the hint, and all day were scraping
                       lint,
                     As became their softer genders ;
                 And got bandages and beds for the limbs and for
                     the heads
                     Of the city's brave defenders.

                 The men, both young and old, felt resolute and
                     bold,
                     And panted hot for glory ;
and, finally, of the   Even the tailors 'gan to brag, and embroidered on
taylors.   their flag
                     ' AUT WINCERE AUT MORI ! '

X.

Of the Cossack   Seeing the city's resolute condition,
chief, his stratagem ;   The Cossack chief, too cunning to despise it,
                 Said to himself, ' Not having ammunition
                 Wherewith to batter the place in proper form,
                 Some of these nights I'll carry it by storm,
                     And sudden escalade it or surprise it.

and the burghers' ' Let's see, however, if the cits stand firmish.'
sillie victorie.   He rode up to the city-gates ;—for answers,
                 Out rushed an eager troop of the town *élite*,
                 And straightway did begin a gallant skirmish :
                 The Cossack hereupon did sound retreat,
                     Leaving the victory with the city lancers.

What   prisoners   They took two prisoners and as many horses,
they took,   And the whole town grew quickly so elate
                 With this small victory of their virgin forces,
                 That they did deem their privates and commanders
                 So many Cæsars, Pompeys, Alexanders,
                     Napoleons, or Fredericks the Great.

and how conceited And puffing with inordinate conceit,
they were.   They utterly despised these Cossack thieves ;
                 And thought the ruffians easier to beat
                 Than porters carpets think, or ushers boys.
                 Meanwhile a sly spectator of their joys,
                     The Cossack captain giggled in his sleeves.

'When'er you meet yon stupid city hogs
  (He bade his troops precise this order keep),
'Don't stand a moment—run away, you dogs!'
'Twas done; and when they met the town battalions,
The Cossacks, as if frightened at their valiance,
  Turned tail, and bolted like so many sheep.

They fled, obedient to their captain's order:
  And now this bloodless siege a month had
    lasted,
When, viewing the country round, the city warder
(Who, like a faithful weather-cock, did perch
Upon the steeple of Saint Sophy's church)
  Sudden his trumpet took, and a mighty blast
    he blasted.

The warder pro-
clayms the Cossacks
retreat, and the citie
greatly rejoyces.

His voice it might be heard through all the streets
  (He was a warder wondrous strong in lung),
'Victory, victory!—the foe retreats!'
'The foe retreats!' each cries to each he meets;
'The foe retreats!' each in his turn repeats.
  Gods! how the guns did roar, and how the joy-
    bells rung!

Arming in haste his gallant city lancers,
  The Mayor, to learn if true the news might be,
A league or two out issued with his prancers.
The Cossacks (something had given their courage
    a damper)
Hastened their flight, and 'gan like mad to
    scamper:
  Blessed be all the saints, Kiova town was free!

XI.

Now, puffed with pride, the Mayor grew vain,
Fought all his battles o'er again;
And thrice he routed all his foes, and thrice he
    slew the slain.
'Tis true he might amuse himself thus,
And not be very murderous;
For as of those who to death were done
The number was exactly *none*,
His Lordship, in his soul's elation,
Did take a bloodless recreation.

Going home again, he did ordain
A very splendid cold collation
For the magistrates and the corporation ;
Likewise a grand illumination,
For the amusement of the nation.
That night the theatres were free,
The conduits they ran Malvoisie ;
Each house that night did beam with light,
And sound with mirth and jollity :

But shame, O shame ! not a soul in the town,
Now the city was safe and the Cossacks flown,
Ever thought of the bountiful saint by whose care
    The town had been rid of these terrible Turks—
Said ever a prayer to that patroness fair,
    For these her wondrous works !

Long Hyacinth waited, the meekest of priors—
He waited at church with the rest of his friars ;
He went there at noon, and he waited till ten,
Expecting in vain the Lord-Mayor and his men.
    He waited and waited from mid-day to dark ;
But in vain—you might search through the whole
        of the church,
Not a layman, alas ! to the city's disgrace,
From mid-day to dark showed his nose in the place.
    The pew-woman, organist, beadle, and clerk,
Kept away from their work, and were dancing like
        mad
Away in the streets with the other mad people,
Not thinking to pray, but to guzzle and tipple
        Wherever the drink might be had.

XII.

Amidst this din and revelry throughout the city
        roaring,
The silver moon rose silently, and high in heaven
        was soaring ;
Prior Hyacinth was fervently upon his knees
        adoring :

' Towards my precious patroness this conduct sure
        unfair is ;

I cannot think, I must confess, what keeps the
   dignitaries
And our good Mayor away, unless some business
   them contraries.'

He puts his long white mantle on, and forth the
   prior sallies—
(His pious thoughts were bent upon good deeds,
   and not on malice) :
Heavens ! how the banquet lights they shone
   about the Mayor's palace !

*How the groomes
and lacqueys jeered
him.*

About the hall the scullions ran with meats both
   fresh and potted ;
The pages came with cup and can, all for the
   guests allotted :
Ah, how they jeered that good fat man as up the
   stairs he trotted !

He entered in the anterooms, where sate the
   Mayor's court in ;
He found a pack of drunken grooms a-dicing and
   a-sporting—
The horrid wine and 'bacco fumes, they set the
   prior a-snorting !

The prior thought he'd speak about their sins
   before he went hence,
And lustily began to shout of sin and of repentance ;
The rogues, they kicked the prior out before he'd
   done a sentence !

And having got no portion small of buffeting and
   tussling,
At last he reached the banquet-hall, where sate the
   Mayor a-guzzling,
And by his side his lady tall, dressed out in white
   sprig muslin.

*And the mayor,
mayoress, and alder-
men, being tipsie,
refused to go to
church.*

Around the table in a ring the guests were drinking
   heavy ;
They drunk the church, and drunk the king, and
   the army and the navy ;
In fact they'd toasted everything.   The prior said,
   ' God save ye ! '

The Mayor cried, 'Bring a silver cup—there's one
    upon the *beaufét :*
And, prior, have the venison up—it's capital *ré-
    chauffé.*
And so, Sir Priest, you've come to sup ?   And pray
    you, how's Saint Sophy ?'

The prior's face quite red was grown, with horror
    and with anger ;
He flung the proffered goblet down—it made a
    hideous clangour ;
And 'gan a-preaching with a frown—he was a
    fierce haranguer.

He tried the Mayor and Aldermen—they all set
    up a-jeering ;
He tried the common-councilmen—they too began
    a-sneering :
He turned towards the May'ress then, and hoped
    to get a hearing.

He knelt and seized her dinner-dress, made of the
    muslin snowy,
'To church, to church, my sweet mistress !' he
    cried ; 'the way I'll show ye.'
Alas, the Lady-Mayoress fell back as drunk as
    Chloe !

XIII.

How the prior
went back alone, Out from this dissolute and drunken court,
    Went the good prior, his eyes with weeping dim :
He tried the people of a meaner sort—
    They too, alas, were bent upon their sport,
      And not a single soul would follow him !
      But all were swigging schnaps and guzzling beer.
He found the cits, their daughters, sons, and
    spouses,
Spending the livelong night in fierce carouses ;
    Alas, unthinking of the danger near !

One or two sentinels the ramparts guarded,
    The rest were sharing in the general feast :
'God wot, our tipsy town is poorly warded ;
    Sweet Saint Sophia help us !' cried the priest.

Alone he entered the cathedral gate,
  Careful he locked the mighty oaken door ;
Within his company of monks did wait,
  A dozen poor old pious men—no more.
  Oh, but it grieved the gentle prior sore,
To think of those lost souls, given up to drink and
    fate !

and shut himself
into Saint Sophia's
chapel   with   his
brethren.

The mighty outer gate well barred and fast,
  The poor old friars stirred their poor old bones,
  And pattering swiftly on the damp cold stones,
They through the solitary chancel passed.
The chancel walls looked black, and dim, and
    vast,
  And rendered ghostlike, melancholy tones.
Onward the fathers sped, till coming nigh a
  Small iron gate, the which they entered quick
    at,
  They locked and double-locked this inner wicket,
And stood within the chapel of Sophia.   ·

Vain were it to describe this sainted place,
  Vain to describe that celebrated trophy,
  The venerable statue of Saint Sophy,
Which formed its chiefest ornament and grace.
Here the good prior, his personal griefs and
    sorrows
  In his extreme devotion quickly merging,
At once began to pray with voice sonorous ;
The other friars joined in pious chorus,
  And passed the night in singing, praying,
    scourging,
  In honour of Sophia, that sweet virgin.

XIV.

The   episode of
Sneezoff and Kat-
inka.

Leaving thus the pious priest in
    Humble penitence and prayer
And the greedy cits a-feasting,
    Let us to the walls repair.

Walking by the sentry-boxes,
    Underneath the silver moon,
Lo ! the sentry boldly cocks his—
    Boldly cocks his musketoon.

Sneezoff was his designation,
    Fair-haired boy, for ever pitied ;
For to take this cruel station,
    He but now Katinka quitted.

Poor in purse were both, but rich in
    Tender love's delicious plenties ;
She a damsel of the kitchen,
    He a haberdasher's 'prentice.

Tinka, maiden tender-hearted,
    Was dissolved in tearful fits
On that fatal night she parted
    From her darling fair-haired Fritz.

Warm her soldier lad she wrapt in
    Comforter and muffetee ;
Called him ' general ' and ' captain,'
    Though a simple private he.

' On your bosom wear this plaster,
    'Twill defend you from the cold ;
In your pipe smoke this canaster,
    Smuggled 'tis, my love, and old.

' All the night, my love, I'll miss you.'
    Thus she spoke ; and from the door
Fair-haired Sneezoff made his issue,
    To return, alas, no more !

He it is who calmly walks his
    Walk beneath the silver moon ;
He it is who boldly cocks his
    Detonating musketoon.

He the bland canaster puffing,
    As upon his round he paces,
Sudden sees a ragamuffin
    Clambering swiftly up the glacis.

' Who goes there ? ' exclaims the sentry ;
    ' When the sun has once gone down,
No one ever makes an entry
    Into this here fortified town ! '

How the sentrie, Shouted thus the watchful Sneezoff ;
Sneezoff, was sur-   But, ere any one replied,
prised and slayn. Wretched youth ! he fired his piece off,
    Started, staggered, groaned, and died !

XV.

Ah, full well might the sentinel cry, ' Who goes
    there ? '
But Echo was frightened too much to declare.
Who goes there ?   Who goes there ?   Can any
    one swear
To the number of sands *sur les bords de la mer*,
Or the whiskers of D'Orsay Count down to a hair ?
As well might you tell of the sands the amount,
Or number each hair in each curl of the Count,
As ever proclaim the number and name
Of the hundreds and thousands that up the wall
    came !
Down, down the knaves poured, with fire and
    with sword :

There were thieves from the Danube, and rogues
    from the Don ;
There were Turks and Wallacks, and shouting
    Cossacks ;
Of all nations and regions, and tongues and
    religions—
Jew, Christian, Idolater, Frank, Mussulman ;
Ah, a horrible sight was Kioff that night !

The gates were all taken—no chance e'en of flight ;
And with torch and with axe the bloody Cossacks
Went hither and thither a-hunting in packs :
They slashed and they slew both Christian and
    Jew—
Women and children, they slaughtered them too.
Some, saving their throats, plunged into the moats,
Or the river—but, oh, they had burned all the
    boats !

But here let us pause—for I can't pursue further
This scene of rack, ravishment, ruin, and murther.
Too well did the cunning old Cossack succeed !
His plan of attack was successful indeed !
The night was his own—the town it was gone ;
'Twas a heap still a-burning of timber and stone.
One building alone has escaped from the fires,

Saint Sophy's fair church, with its steeples and
    spires.

Calm, stately, and white,
It stood in the light ;
And, as if 'twould defy all the conqueror's power,—
As if naught had occurred,
Might clearly be heard
The chimes ringing soberly every half-hour !

XVI.

The city was defunct—silence succeeded
Unto its last fierce agonising yells ;
And then it was the conqueror first heeded
The sound of these calm bells.

How the Cossack chief bade them burn the church too. Furious towards his aides-de-camp he turns
And (speaking as if Byron's works he knew)
'Villains !' he fiercely cries, 'the city burns,
Why not the temple too ?
Burn me yon church, and murder all within !'
The Cossacks thundered at the outer door ;

How they stormed it ; and of Hyacinth, his anger thereat. And Father Hyacinth, who heard the din
(And thought himself and brethren in distress
Deserted by their lady patroness), ·
Did to her statue turn, and thus his woes out-
pour.

XVII.

His prayer to the Saint Sophia. 'And is it thus, O falsest of the saints,
Thou hearest our complaints ?
Tell me, did ever my attachment falter
To serve thy altar ?
Was not thy name, ere ever I did sleep,
The last upon my lip ?
Was not thy name the very first that broke
From me when I awoke ?
Have I not tried, with fasting, flogging, penance,
And mortified countenance,
For to find favour, Sophy, in thy sight ?
And lo ! this night,
Forgetful of my prayers, and thine own promise,
Thou turnest from us ;

C

Lettest the heathen enter in our city,
   And, without pity,
Murder our burghers, seize upon their spouses,
   Burn down our houses !
Is such a breach of faith to be endured ?
   See what a lurid
Light from the insolent invaders' torches
   Shines on your porches !
E'en now, with thundering battering-ram and
   hammer,
   And hideous clamour ;
With axemen, swordsmen, pikemen, billmen, bow-
   men,
   The conquering foemen,
O Sophy ! beat your gate about your ears,
   Alas ! and here's
A humble company of pious men
   Like muttons in a pen,
Whose souls shall quickly from their bodies be
   thrusted,
   Because in you they trusted.
Do you not know the Calmuc chief's desires—
   KILL ALL THE FRIARS !
And you, of all the saints most false and fickle,
   Leave us in this abominable pickle ! '

The Statue sud- 'RASH HYACINTHUS ! '
denlie speaks ; (Here to the astonishment of all her backers,
Saint Sophy, opening wide her wooden jaws
 Like to a pair of German walnut-crackers,
Began), 'I did not think that you had been
   thus,—
O monk of little faith ! Is it because
A rascal scum of filthy Cossack heathen
Besiege our town, that you distrust in *me*,
   then ?
Think'st thou that I, who in a former day
Did walk across the Sea of Marmora
(Not mentioning, for shortness, other seas),—
That I, who skimmed the broad Borysthenes,
Without so much as wetting of my toes,
Am frightened at a set of men like *those* ?
I have a mind to leave you to your fate :
Such cowardice as this my scorn inspires—'

but is interrupted
by the breaking in
of the Cossacks.

Saint Sophy was here
    Cut short in her words,—
For at this very moment in tumbled the gate,
            And with a wild cheer,
                And a clashing of swords,
                Swift through the church porches,
                With a waving of torches,
                And a shriek and a yell
                Like the devils of hell,
                With pike and with axe,
                In rushed the Cossacks—
In rushed the Cossacks, crying, 'MURDER THE
    FRIARS!'

Of Hyacinth, his
courageous address,

Ah! what a thrill felt Hyacinth,
    When he heard that villainous shout Calmuc!
Now, thought he, my trial beginneth;
    'Saints, O give me courage and pluck!
Courage, boys! 'tis useless to funk!'
    Thus unto the friars he began,
'Never let it be said that a monk
    Is not likewise a gentleman.
Though the patron saint of the church,
    Spite of all that we've done and we've prayed,
Leaves us wickedly here in the lurch:
    Hang it, gentlemen! who's afraid?'

and preparation for
dying.

As thus the gallant Hyacinthus spoke,
    He, with an air as easy and as free as
If the quick-coming murder were a joke,
Folded his robes around his sides, and took
Place under sainted Sophy's legs of oak,
    Like Cæsar at the Statue of Pompeius.
The monks no leisure had about to look
(Each being absorbed in his particular case),
Else had they seen with what celestial grace
A wooden smile stole o'er the saint's mahogany
            face.

Saint Sophia, her
speech.

'Well done, well done, Hyacinthus, my son!'
    Thus spoke the sainted statue.
'Though you doubted me in the hour of need,
And spoke of me very rude indeed,
You deserve good luck for showing such pluck,
    And I won't be angry at you.'

She gets on the prior's shoulders straddleback,

The monks by-standing, one and all
　Of this wondrous scene beholders,
To this kind promise listened content,
And couldn't contain their astonishment,
When Saint Sophia moved and went
Down from her wooden pedestal
And twisted her legs, sure as eggs is eggs,
　Round Hyacinthus's shoulders!

and bids him run.

'Ho! forwards!' cries Sophy, 'there's no time for
　　waiting;
The Cossacks are breaking the very last gate in:
See, the glare of their torches shines red through
　　the grating;
We've still the back door, and two minutes or
　　more.
　Now, boys, now or never, we must make for
　　the river,
For we only are safe on the opposite shore.
　Run swiftly to-day, lads, if ever you ran,—
　Put out your best leg, Hyacinthus, my man;
And I'll lay five to two that you'll carry us
　　through,—
　Only scamper as fast as you can.'

XVIII.

He runneth,

Away went the priest through the little back door,
And light on his shoulders the image he bore:
　The honest old priest was not punished the least,
Though the image was eight feet, and he measured
　　four.
Away went the prior, and the monks at his tail
Went snorting, and puffing, and panting full sail;
　And just as the last at the back door had passed,
In furious hunt behold at the front
The Tartars so fierce, with their terrible cheers;
With axes and halberds, and muskets and spears,
And torches a-flaming the chapel now came in.
They tore up the mass-book, they stamped on the
　　psalter,
They pulled the gold crucifix down from the
　　altar;

The vestments they burned with their blasphemous
    fires,
And many cried, ' Curse on them ! where are the
    friars ?
When loaded with plunder, yet seeking for more,
One chanced to fling open the little back door,
Spied out the friars' white robes and long shadows,
In the moon, scampering over the meadows,
And stopped the Cossacks in the midst of their
    arsons,

and the Tartars after him.

By crying out lustily, ' THERE GO THE PARSONS ! '
With a whoop and a yell, and a scream and a shout,
At once the whole murderous body turned out ;
And swift as the hawk pounces down on the pigeon,
Pursued the poor short-winded men of religion.

How the friars sweated,

When the sound of that cheering came to the
    monks' hearing,
    O Heaven, how the poor fellows panted and blew !
At fighting not cunning, unaccustomed to running,
    When the Tartars came up, what the deuce
    should they do ?
' They'll make us all martyrs, those blood-thirsty
    Tartars ! '
    Quoth fat Father Peter to fat Father Hugh.
The shouts they came clearer, the foe they drew
    nearer ;
    Oh, how the bolts whistled, and how the lights
    shone.
' I cannot get further, this running is murther ;
    Come carry me, some one ! ' cried big Father
    John.
And even the statue grew frightened, 'Od rat you ! '
    It cried, ' Mr. Prior, I wish you'd get on.
On tugged the good friar, but nigher and nigher
Appeared the fierce Russians, with sword and with
    fire,
On lugged the good prior at Saint Sophy's desire,—
A scramble through bramble, through mud and
    through mire.
The swift arrow's whizziness causing a dizziness,
Nigh done his business, fit to expire.
Father Hyacinth tugged, and the monks they
    tugged after :

and the pursuers
fired arrows into
their tayls.

The foemen pursued with a horrible laughter,
    And hurled their long spears round the poor
        brothers' ears.
So true, that next day in the coats of each priest,
    Though never a wound was given, there were found
        A dozen arrows at least.

How at the last
gasp

                Now the chase seemed at its worst,
                Prior and monks were fit to burst ;
                Scarce you knew the which was first,
                    Or pursuers or pursued.
                When the statue, by Heaven's grace,
                Suddenly did change the face
                Of this interesting race
                    As a saint sure only could.

For as the jockey who at Epsom rides,
    When that his steed is spent, and punished sore,
Diggeth his heels into the courser's sides,
    And thereby makes him run one or two furlongs
        more ;
    Even thus, betwixt the eighth rib and the ninth,
The saint rebuked the prior, that weary creeper ;
    Fresh strength unto his limbs her kicks im-
        parted,—

the friars won, and
jumped into Borys-
thenes fluvius.

    One bound he made, as gay as when he started ;
Yes, with his brethren clinging at his cloak,
The statue on his shoulders—fit to choke,—
    One most tremendous bound made Hyacinth,
And soused friars, statue, and all, slap dash into
    the Dnieper !

XIX.

And how the Rus-
sians saw

And when the Russians in a fiery rank,
    Panting and fierce, drew up along the shore
    (For here the vain pursuing they forbore,
Nor cared they to surpass the river's bank),
There, looking from the rocks and rushes dank,
    A sight they witnessed never seen before,
And which, with its accompaniments glorious,
Is writ i' the golden book, or *liber aureus*.

the Statue get off
Hyacinth his back,
and sit down with
the friars on Hya-
cinth his cloak.

Plump in the Dnieper flounced the friar and
     friends,—
   They dangling round his neck, he fit to choke,
   When suddenly his most miraculous cloak
Over the billowy waves itself extends.
Down from his shoulders quietly descends
   The venerable Sophy's statue of oak ;
Which, sitting down upon the cloak so ample,
Bids all the brethren follow its example !

How in this man-
ner of boat they
sayled away.

Each at her bidding sate, and sate at ease ;
   The statue 'gan a gracious conversation,
   And (waving to the foe a salutation)
Sailed with her wondering happy *protégés*
Gaily adown the wide Borysthenes,
   Until they came unto some friendly nation,
And when the heathen had at length grown shy of
Their conquest, she one day came back again to
   Kioff.

XX.

Finis, or the end.

THINK NOT, O READER, THAT WE'RE LAUGHING
   AT YOU ;
YOU MAY GO TO KIOFF NOW, AND SEE THE
   STATUE.

THE KING OF BRENTFORD'S TESTAMENT.[1]

THE noble King of Brentford
    Was old and very sick ;
He summoned his physicians
    To wait upon him quick ;
They stepped into their coaches,
    And brought their best physick.

They crammed their gracious master
    With potion and with pill ;
They drenched him and they bled him :
    They could not cure his ill.
'Go, fetch,' says he, 'my lawyer,
    I'd better make my will.'

The monarch's royal mandate
    The lawyer did obey ;
The thought of six-and-eightpence
    Did make his heart full gay.
'What is't,' says he, 'your majesty
    Would wish of me to-day ?'

'The doctors have belaboured me
    With potion and with pill ;
My hours of life are counted,
    O man of tape and quill !
Sit down and mend a pen or two,
    I want to make my will.

'O'er all the land of Brentford
    I'm Lord, and eke of Kew ;
I've three-per-cents, and five-per-cents ;
    My debts are but a few ;
And to inherit after me
    I have but children two.

[1] [*George Cruikshank's Omnibus,* December 1841.]

24

'Prince Thomas is my eldest son,
    A sober prince is he,
And from the day we breeched him
    Till now—he's twenty-three—
He never caused disquiet
    To his poor mama or me.

'At school they never flogged him,
    At college, though not fast,
Yet his little-go and great-go
    He creditably passed,
And made his year's allowance
    For eighteen months to last.

'He never owed a shilling,
    Went never drunk to bed;
He has not two ideas
    Within his honest head;—
In all respects he differs
    From my second son, Prince Ned.

'When Tom has half his income
    Laid by at the year's end,
Poor Ned has ne'er a stiver
    That rightly he may spend;
But spunges on a tradesman,
    Or borrows from a friend.

'While Tom his legal studies
    Most soberly pursues,
Poor Ned must pass his mornings
    A-dawdling with the nurse;
While Tom frequents his banker,
    Young Ned frequents the Jews.

'Ned drives about in buggies,
    Tom sometimes takes a 'bus;
Ah! cruel Fate, why made you
    My children differ thus?
Why make of Tom a *dullard*,
    And Ned a *genius?*'

'You'll cut him with a shilling,'
   Exclaimed the man of writs ;—
'I'll leave my wealth,' said Brentford,
   'Sir Lawyer, as befits ;
And portion both their fortunes
   Unto their several wits.'

'Your Grace knows best,' the lawyer said,
   'On your commands I wait.'
'Be silent, sir,' says Brentford,
   'A plague upon your prate !
Come, take your pens and paper,
   And write as I dictate.'

The will as Brentford spoke it
   Was writ, and signed, and closed ;
He bade the lawyer leave him,
   And turned him round and dozed ;
And next week in the churchyard
   The good old king reposed.

Tom, dressed in crape and hat-band,
   Of mourners was the chief ;
In bitter self-upbraidings
   Poor Edward showed his grief ;
Tom hid his fat white countenance
   In his pocket-handkerchief.

Ned's eyes were full of weeping,
   He faltered in his walk ;
Tom never shed a tear,
   But onwards he did stalk,
As pompous, black, and solemn
   As any catafalque.

And when the bones of Brentford,
   That gentle king and just,
With bell, and book, and candle,
   Were duly laid in dust,
'Now, gentlemen,' says Thomas,
   'Let business be discussed.

' When late our sire beloved
    Was taken deadly ill,
Sir Lawyer, you attended him
    (I mean to tax your bill);
And as you signed and wrote it,
    I prythee read the will.'

The lawyer wiped his spectacles,
    And drew the parchment out;
And all the Brentford family
    Sate eager round about.
Poor Ned was somewhat anxious,
    But Tom had ne'er a doubt.

' My son, as I make ready
    To seek my last long home,
Some cares I feel for Neddy,
    But none for thee, my Tom;
Sobriety and order
    You ne'er departed from.

' Ned hath a brilliant genius,
    And thou a plodding brain;
On thee I think with pleasure,
    On him with doubt and pain.'
(' You see, good Ned,' says Thomas,
    ' What he thought about us twain.')

' Tho' small was your allowance,
    You saved a little store,
And those who save a little
    Shall get a plenty more '
(As the lawyer read this compliment,
    Tom's eyes were running o'er).

' The tortoise and the hare, Tom,
    Set out at each his pace;
The hare it was the fleeter,
    The tortoise won the race;
And since the world's beginning
    This ever was the case.

' Ned's genius, blithe and singing,
   Steps gaily o'er the ground ;
As steadily you trudge it,
   He clears it with a bound ;
But dulness has stout legs, Tom,
   And wind that's wondrous sound.

' O'er fruits and flowers alike, Tom,
   You pass with plodding feet ;
You heed not one nor t'other,
   But onwards go your beat :
While Genius stops to loiter
   With all that he may meet ;

'And ever as he wanders
   Will have a pretext fine
For sleeping in the morning,
   Or loitering to dine,
Or dozing in the shade,
   Or basking in the shine.

' Your little steady eyes, Tom,
   Though not so bright as those
That restless round about him
   Your flashing genius throws,
Are excellently suited
   To look before your nose.

' Thank heaven then for the blinkers
   It placed before your eyes ;
The stupidest are steadiest,
   The witty are not wise ;
O bless your good stupidity,
   It is your dearest prize !

' And though my lands are wide,
   And plenty is my gold,
Still better gifts from nature,
   My Thomas, do you hold—
A brain that's thick and heavy,
   A heart that's dull and cold—

'Too dull to feel depression,
    Too hard to heed distress,
Too cold to yield to passion
    Or silly tenderness.
March on ; your road is open
    To wealth, Tom, and success.

'Ned sinneth in extravagance,
    And you in greedy lust.'
('I' faith,' says Ned, 'our father
    Is less polite than just.')
'In you, son Tom, I've confidence,
    But Ned I cannot trust.

'Wherefore my lease and copyholds,
    My lands and tenements,
My parks, my farms, and orchards,
    My houses and my rents ;
My Dutch stock and my Spanish stock,
    My five and three per cents,

'I leave to you, my Thomas—'
    ('What, all ?' poor Edward said ;
'Well, well, I should have spent them,
    And Tom's a prudent head.')
'I leave to you, my Thomas—
    To you, IN TRUST for Ned.'

The wrath and consternation
    What poet e'er could trace,
That at this fatal passage
    Came o'er Prince Tom his face ;
The wonder of the company,
    And honest Ned's amaze !

''Tis surely some mistake,'
    Good-naturedly cries Ned.
The lawyer answered gravely,
    ''Tis even as I said ;
'Twas thus his gracious majesty
    Ordained on his death-bed.

'See here, the will is witnessed,
  And here's his autograph.'
'In truth our father's writing,'
  Says Edward with a laugh;
'But thou shalt not be a loser, Tom,
  We'll share it half-and-half.'

'Alas! my kind young gentleman,
  This sharing may not be;
'Tis written in the testament
  That Brentford spoke to me:
"I do forbid Prince Ned to give
  Prince Tom a halfpenny.

' " He hath a store of money,
  But ne'er was known to lend it;
He never helped his brother,
  The poor he ne'er befriended;
He hath no need of property
  Who knows not how to spend it.

' " Poor Edward knows but how to spend,
  And thrifty Tom to hoard;
Let Thomas be the steward, then,
  And Edward be the lord;
And as the honest labourer
  Is worthy his reward,

' " I pray Prince Ned, my second son,
  And my successor dear,
To pay to his intendant
  Five hundred pounds a-year;
And to think of his old father,
  And live and make good cheer." '

Such was old Brentford's honest testament.
  He did devise his moneys for the best,
  And lies in Brentford church in peaceful rest.
Prince Edward lived, and money made and spent;
  But his good sire was wrong, it is confessed,
To say his son, young Thomas, never lent.
  He did; young Thomas lent at interest,
And nobly took his twenty-five per cent.

Long time the famous reign of Ned endured
   O'er Chiswick, Fulham, Brentford, Putney, Kew ;
But of extravagance he ne'er was cured.
   And when both died, as mortal men will do,
'Twas commonly reported that the steward
   Was a deuced deal the richer of the two.

THE

CHRONICLE OF THE DRUM.[1]

PART I.

At Paris, hard by the Maine barriers,
  Whoever will choose to repair,
'Midst a dozen of wooden-legged warriors,
  May haply fall in with old Pierre.
On the sunshiny bench of a tavern,
  He sits and he prates of old wars;
And moistens his pipe of tobacco
  With a drink that is named after Mars.

The beer makes his tongue run the quicker,
  And as long as his tap never fails,
Thus over his favourite liquor
  Old Peter will tell his old tales.
Says he, 'In my life's ninety summers,
  Strange changes and chances I've seen,—
So here's to all gentlemen drummers
  That ever have thumped on a skin.

'Brought up in the art military
  For four generations we are;
My ancestors drummed for King Harry,
  The Huguenot lad of Navarre.
And as each man in life has his station
  According as Fortune may fix,
While Condé was waving the baton,
  My grandsire was trolling the sticks.

[1] [Issued in book-form, with *The Second Funeral of Napoleon*, in 1841.]

' Ah ! those were the days for commanders !
    What glories my grandfather won,
Ere bigots, and lackies, and panders
    The fortunes of France had undone.
In Germany, Flanders, and Holland,—
    What foeman resisted us then ?
No ; my grandsire was ever victorious,
    My grandsire and Monsieur Turenne.

' He died, and our noble battalions
    The jade, fickle Fortune, forsook ;
And at Blenheim, in spite of our valiance,
    The victory lay with Malbrook.
The news it was brought to King Louis ;
    Corbleu ! how his majesty swore
When he heard they had taken my grandsire :
    And twelve thousand gentlemen more !

' At Namur, Ramilies, and Malplaquet
    Were we posted, on plain or in trench,
Malbrook only need to attack it,
    And away from him scampered we French.
Cheer up ! 'tis no use to be glum, boys,—
    'Tis written, since fighting begun,
That sometimes we fight and we conquer,
    And sometimes we fight and we run.

' To fight and to run was our fate,
    Our fortune and fame had departed ;
And so perished Louis the Great,—
    Old, lonely, and half broken-hearted.
His coffin they pelted with mud,
    His body they tried to lay hands on ;
And so having buried King Louis
    They loyally served his great-grandson.

' God save the beloved King Louis !
    (For so he was nicknamed by some,)
And now came my father to do his
    King's orders and beat on the drum.
My grandsire was dead, but his bones
    Must have shaken, I'm certain, for joy,
To see Daddy drumming the English
    From the meadows of famed Fontenoy.

'So well did he drum in that battle
　　That the enemy showed us their backs;
Corbleu! it was pleasant to rattle
　　The sticks and to follow old Saxe!
We next had Soubin for a leader,
　　And as luck hath its changes and fits,
At Rosbach, in spite of Dad's drumming,
　　'Tis said we were beaten by Fritz.

'And now Daddy crossed the Atlantic,
　　To drum for Montcalm and his men;
Morbleu! but it makes a man frantic
　　To think we were beaten again!
My daddy he crossed the wide ocean,
　　My mother brought me on her neck,
And we came in the year fifty-seven
　　To guard the good town of Quebec.

'In the year fifty-nine came the Britons,—
　　Full well I remember the day,—
They knocked at our gates for admittance,
　　Their vessels were moored in our bay.
Says our general, "Drive me yon red-coats
　　Away to the sea whence they come!"
So we marched against Wolfe and his bull-dogs,
　　We marched at the sound of the drum.

'I think I can see my poor mammy
　　With me in her hand as she waits,
And our regiment, slowly retreating,
　　Pours back through the citadel gates.
Dear mammy! she looks in their faces,
　　And asks if her husband is come?
—He is lying all cold on the glacis,
　　And will never more beat on the drum.

'Come, drink, 'tis no use to be glum, boys,
　　He died like a soldier—in glory;
Here's a glass to the health of all drum-boys,
　　And now I'll commence my own story.
Once more did we cross the salt ocean,
　　We came in the year eighty-one;
And the wrongs of my father the drummer
　　Were avenged by the drummer his son.

'In Chesapeak-bay we were landed,
    In vain strove the British to pass;
Rochambeau our armies commanded,
    Our ships they were led by De Grasse.
Morbleu! how I rattled the drumsticks
    The day we marched into York town;
Ten thousand of beef-eating British
    Their weapons we caused to lay down.

'Then homewards returning victorious,
    In peace to our country we came,
And were thanked for our glorious actions
    By Louis Sixteenth of the name.
What drummer on earth could be prouder
    Than I, while I drummed at Versailles
To the lovely court ladies in powder
    And lappets, and long satin-tails?

'The Princes that day passed before us.
    Our countrymen's glory and hope;
Monsieur, who was learned in Horace,
    D'Artois, who could dance the tight-rope.
One night we kept guard for the Queen
    At her Majesty's opera-box,
While the King, their majestical monarch,
    Sat filing at home at his locks.

'Yes, I drummed for the fair Antoinette,
    And so smiling she looked and so tender,
That our officers, privates, and drummers
    All vowed they would die to defend her.
But she cared not for us honest fellows,
    Who fought and who bled in her wars,
She sneered at our gallant Rochambeau,
    And turned Lafayette out of doors.

'Ventrebleu! then I swore a great oath,
    No more to such tyrants to kneel,
And so just to keep up my drumming,
    One day I drummed down the Bastille!
Ho landlord! a stoup of fresh wine;
    Come, comrades, a bumper we'll try,
And drink to the year eighty-nine
    And the glorious fourth of July!

'Then bravely our cannon it thundered,
    As onwards our patriots bore ;
Our enemies were but a hundred,
    And we twenty thousand or more.
They carried the news to King Louis,
    He heard it as calm as you please,
And like a majestical monarch,
    Kept filing his locks and his keys.

'We showed our republican courage,
    We stormed and we broke the great gate in,
And we murdered the insolent governor
    For daring to keep us a-waiting.
Lambesc and his squadrons stood by,
    They never stirred finger or thumb,
The saucy aristocrats trembled
    As they heard the republican drum.

'Hurrah ! what a storm was a-brewing,
    The day of our vengeance was come,
Through scenes of what carnage and ruin
    Did I beat on the patriot drum.
Let's drink to the famed tenth of August,
    At midnight I beat the tattoo,
And woke up the pikemen of Paris
    To follow the bold Barbaroux.

''Twas here stood the altar of freedom,
    And though neither marble nor gilding
Were used in those days to adorn
    Our simple republican building,
Corbleu ! but the Mère Guillotine
    Cared little for splendour or show,
So you gave her an axe and a beam,
    And a plank and a basket or so.

'Awful, and proud, and erect,
    Here sat our republican goddess ;
Each morning her table we decked
    With dainty aristocrats' bodies.
The people each day flocked around
    As she sat at her meat and her wine ;
'Twas always the use of our nation
    To witness the sovereign dine.

'Young virgins with fair golden tresses,
    Old silver-haired prelates and priests,
Dukes, Marquises, Barons, Princesses,
    Were splendidly served at her feasts.
Ventrebleu! but we pampered our ogress
    With the best that our nation could bring,
And dainty she grew in her progress,
    And called for the head of a King!

'She called for the blood of our King,
    And straight from his prison we drew him;
And to her with shouting we led him,
    And took him, and bound him, and slew him.
"The monarchs of Europe against me
    Have plotted a godless alliance;
I'll fling them the head of King Louis,"
    She said, "as my gage of defiance."

'I see him as now, for a moment,
    Away from his gaolers he broke;
And stood at the foot of the scaffold,
    And lingered, and fain would have spoke.
"Ho, drummer! quick! silence yon Capet,"
    Says Santerre, "with a beat of your drum;"
Lustily then did I tap it,
    And the son of Saint Louis was dumb.'

Part II.

'The glorious days of September
    Saw many aristocrats fall;
'Twas then that our pikes drunk the blood
    In the beautiful breast of Lamballe.
Pardi, 'twas a beautiful lady!
    I seldom have looked on her like;
And I drummed for a gallant procession
    That marched with her head on a pike.

'Let's show the pale head to the Queen,
    We said—she'll remember it well;
She looked from the bars of her prison,
    And shrieked as she saw it, and fell.

We set up a shout at her screaming,
 We laughed at the fright she had shown
At the sight of the head of her minion ;
 How she'd tremble to part with her own !

'We had taken the head of King Capet,
 We called for the blood of his wife ;
Undaunted she came to the scaffold,
 And bared her fair neck to the knife.
As she felt the foul fingers that touched her,
 She shrunk, but she deigned not to speak,
She looked with a royal disdain,
 And died with a blush on her cheek !

' 'Twas thus that our country was saved ;
 So told us the safety committee !
But psha ! I've the heart of a Frenchman,
 All gentleness, mercy, and pity.
I loathed to assist at such deeds,
 And my drum beat its loudest of tunes
As we offered to justice offended
 The blood of the bloody tribunes.

' Away with such foul recollections !
 No more of the axe and the block ;
I saw the last fight of the sections
 As they fell 'neath our guns at Saint Rock.
Young BONAPARTE led us that day ;
 When he sought the Italian frontier,
I followed my gallant young captain,
 I followed him many a long year.

' We came to an army in rags,
 Our general was but a boy,
When we first saw the Austrian flags
 Flaunt proud in the fields of Savoy.
In the glorious year ninety-six
 We marched to the banks of the Po ;
I carried my drum and my sticks,
 And we laid the proud Austrian low.

' In triumph we entered Milan,
 We seized on the Mantuan keys ;
The troops of the Emperor ran,
 And the Pope he fell down on his knees.'—

Pierre's comrades here called a fresh bottle,
  And clubbing together their wealth,
They drank, the Army of Italy
  And General Bonaparte's health.

The drummer now bared his old breast
  And showed us a plenty of scars,
Rude presents that Fortune had made him
  In fifty victorious wars.
' This came when I followed bold Kleber—
  'Twas shot by a Mameluke gun ;
And this from an Austrian sabre
  When the field of Marengo was won !

' My forehead has many deep furrows,
  But this is the deepest of all ;
A Brunswicker made it at Jena,
  Beside the fair river of Saal.
This cross, 'twas the Emperor gave it ;
  (God bless him !) it covers a blow ;
I had it at Austerlitz fight,
  As I beat on my drum in the snow.

' 'Twas thus that we conquered and fought ;
  But wherefore continue the story ?
There's never a baby in France
  But has heard of our chief and our glory,—
But has heard of our chief and our fame,
  His sorrows and triumphs can tell,
How bravely Napoleon conquered,
  How bravely and sadly he fell.

' It makes my old heart to beat higher,
  To think of the deeds that I saw ;
I followed bold Ney through the fire,
  And charged at the side of Murat.'
And so did old Peter continue
  His history of twenty brave years ;
His audience followed with comments—
  Rude comments of curses and tears.

He told how the Prussians in vain
  Had died in defence of their land ;
His audience laughed at the story,
  And vowed that their captain was grand !

He had fought the red English, he said,
   In many a battle of Spain ;
They cursed the red English, and prayed
   To meet them and fight them again.

He told them how Russia was lost,
   Had winter not driven them back ;
And his company cursed the quick frost,
   And doubly they cursed the Cossack.
He told how the stranger arrived ;
   They wept at the tale of disgrace ;
And they longed but for one battle more,
   The stain of their shame to efface !

' Our country their hordes overran,
   We fled to the fields of Champagne,
And fought them, though twenty to one,
   And beat them again and again !
Our warrior was conquered at last ;
   They bade him his crown to resign ;
To fate and his country he yielded
   The rights of himself and his line.

' He came, and among us he stood,
   Around him we pressed in a throng,
We could not regard him for weeping,
   Who had led us and loved us so long.
" I have led you for twenty long years,"
   Napoleon said ere he went ;
" Wherever was honour I found you,
   And with you, my sons, am content.

' " Though Europe against me was armed,
   Your chiefs and my people are true ;
I still might have struggled with fortune,
   And baffled all Europe with you.

' " But France would have suffered the while,
   'Tis best that I suffer alone ;
I go to my place of exile
   To write of the deeds we have done.

' " Be true to the king that they give you.
   We may not embrace ere we part ;
But, General, reach me your hand,
   And press me, I pray, to your heart."

' He called for our old battle standard ;
    One kiss to the eagle he gave.
" Dear eagle," he said, " may this kiss
    Long sound in the hearts of the brave ! "
'Twas thus that Napoleon left us ;
    Our people were weeping and mute
As he passed through the lines of his guard,
    And our drums beat the notes of salute.

.   .   .   .

' I looked when the drumming was o'er,
    I looked, but our hero was gone ;
We were destined to see him once more
    When we fought on the Mount of St. John.
The Emperor rode through our files ;
    'Twas June, and a fair Sunday morn ;
The lines of our warriors for miles
    Stretched wide through the Waterloo corn.

' In thousands we stood on the plain,
    The red coats were crowning the height ;
" Go scatter yon English," he said ;
    We'll sup, lads, at Brussels to-night."
We answered his voice with a shout ;
    Our eagles were bright in the sun ;
Our drums and our cannon spoke out,
    And the thundering battle begun.

' One charge to another succeeds,
    Like waves that a hurricane bears ;
All day do our galloping steeds
    Dash fierce on the enemy's squares.
At noon we began the fell onset :
    We charged up the Englishman's hill ;
And madly we charged it at sunset—
    His banners were floating there still.

' — Go to !   I will tell you no more ;
    You know how the battle was lost.
Ho ! fetch me a beaker of wine,
    And, comrades, I'll give you a toast.
I'll give you a curse on all traitors
    Who plotted our Emperor's ruin ;
And a curse on those red-coated English,
    Whose bayonets helped our undoing.

' A curse on those British assassins
 Who ordered the slaughter of Ney ;
A curse on Sir Hudson, who tortured
 The life of our hero away.
A curse on all Russians—I hate them—
 On all Prussian and Austrian fry ;
And, O ! but I pray we may meet them,
 And fight them again ere I die.'

'Twas thus old Peter did conclude
 His chronicle with curses fit.
He spoke the tale in accents rude,
 In ruder verse I copied it.

Perhaps the tale a moral bears
 (All tales in time to this must come),
The story of two hundred years
 Writ on the parchment of a drum.

What Peter told with drum and stick
 Is endless theme for poet's pen :
Is found in endless quartos thick,
 Enormous books by learned men.

And ever since historian writ,
 And ever since a bard could sing,
Doth each exalt with all his wit
 The noble art of murdering.

We love to read the glorious page,
 How bold Achilles killed his foe ;
And Turnus, fell'd by Trojans' rage,
 Went howling to the shades below.

How Godfrey led his red-cross knights,
 How mad Orlando slashed and slew ;
There's not a single bard that writes,
 But doth the glorious theme renew.

And while in fashion picturesque
   The poet rhymes of blood and blows,
The grave historian, at his desk,
   Describes the same in classic prose.

Go read the works of Reverend Cox,
   You'll duly see recorded there
The history of the self-same knocks
   Here roughly sung by Drummer Pierre.

Of battles fierce and warriors big
   He writes in phrases dull and slow,
And waves his cauliflower wig,
   And shouts 'Saint George for Marlborow!'

Take Doctor Southey from the shelf,
   An LL.D.,—a peaceful man :
Good Lord, how doth he plume himself
   Because we beat the Corsican !

From first to last his page is filled
   With stirring tales how blows were struck.
He shows how we the Frenchmen killed,
   And praises God for our good luck.

Some hints, 'tis true, of politics
   The doctors give, and statesman's art :
Pierre only bangs his drum and sticks,
   And understands the bloody part.

He cares not what the cause may be,
   He is not·nice for wrong and right ;
But show him where's the enemy,
   He only asks to drum and fight.

They bid him fight,—perhaps he wins.
   And when he tells the story o'er,
The honest savage brags and grins,
   And only longs to fight once more.

But luck may change, and valour fail,
   Our drummer, Peter, meet reverse,
And with a moral points his tale—
   The end of all such tales—a curse.

Last year, my love, it was my hap
  Behind a grenadier to be,
And, but he wore a hairy cap,
  No taller man, methinks, than me.

Prince Albert and the Queen, God wot,
  (Be blessings on the glorious pair!)
Before us passed, I saw them not,
  I only saw a cap of hair.

Your orthodox historian puts
  In foremost rank the soldier thus,
The red-coat bully in his boots,
  That hides the march of men from us.

He puts him there in foremost rank,
  You wonder at his cap of hair;
You hear his sabre's cursed clank,
  His spurs a-jingling everywhere.

Go to! I hate him and his trade:
  Who bade us so to cringe and bend,
And all God's peaceful people made
  To such as him subservient!

Tell me what find we to admire
  In epaulets and scarlet coats,
In men, because they load and fire,
  And know the art of cutting throats?

Ah, gentle, tender lady mine,
  The winter wind blows cold and shrill,
Come, fill me one more glass of wine,
  And give the silly fools their will.

And what care we for war and wrack,
  How kings and heroes rise and fall;
Look yonder, in his coffin black,
  There lies the greatest of them all!

To pluck him down, and keep him up,
   Died many million human souls :
'Tis twelve o'clock, and time to sup,
   Bid Mary heap the fire with coals.

He captured many thousand guns,
   He wrote 'The Great' before his name ;
And dying, only left his sons
   The recollection of his shame.

Though more than half the world was his,
   He died without a rood his own ;
And borrowed from his enemies
   Six foot of ground to lie upon.

He fought a thousand glorious wars,
   And more than half the world was his,
And somewhere, now, in yonder stars,
   Can tell, mayhap, what greatness is.

Paris, 1st January.

THE MAHOGANY TREE.[1]

CHRISTMAS is here ;
Winds whistle shrill,
Icy and chill :
Little care we.
Little we fear
Weather without,
Sheltered about
The Mahogany Tree.

Commoner greens,
Ivy and Oaks,
Poets, in jokes,
Sing, do ye see :
Good fellows' shins
Here, boys, are found,
Twisting around
The Mahogany Tree.

Once on the boughs,
Birds of rare plume
Sang, in its bloom ;
Night-birds are we :
Here we carouse,
Singing, like them,
Perched round the stem
Of the jolly old tree.

Here let us sport,
Boys, as we sit ;
Laughter and wit
Flashing so free.
Life is but short—
When we are gone,
Let them sing on,
Round the old tree.

Evenings we knew,
Happy as this ;
Faces we miss,
Pleasant to see.
Kind hearts and true,
Gentle and just,
Peace to your dust !
We sing round the tree.

Care, like a dun,
Lurks at the gate :
Let the dog wait ;
Happy we'll be !
Drink, every one ;
Pile up the coals,
Fill the red bowls,
Round the old tree !

Drain we the cup.—
Friend, art afraid ?
Spirits are laid
In the Red Sea.
Mantle it up ;
Empty it yet ;
Let us forget,
Round the old tree.

Sorrows, begone !
Life and its ills,
Duns and their bills,
Bid we to flee.
Come with the dawn,
Blue-devil sprite,
Leave us to-night,
Round the old tree.

[1] [*Punch*, January 9, 1847.]

THE BALLAD OF BOUILLABAISSE.[1]

FROM THE CONTRIBUTOR AT PARIS.

A STREET there is in Paris famous
  For which no rhyme our language yields,
Rue Neuve des petits Champs its name is—
  The New Street of the Little Fields ;
And here's an inn, not rich and splendid,
  But still in comfortable case,
To which in youth I oft attended,
  To eat a bowl of Bouillabaisse.

This Bouillabaisse a noble dish is—
  A sort of soup, or broth, or brew,
Or hotchpotch of all sorts of fishes,
  That Greenwich never could outdo :
Green herbs, red peppers, mussels, saffron,
  Soles, onions, garlic, roach, and dace ;
All these you eat at TERRÉ's tavern,
  In that one dish of Bouillabaisse.

Indeed, a rich and savoury stew 'tis ;
  And true philosophers, methinks,
Who love all sorts of natural beauties,
  Should love good victuals and good drinks.
And Cordelier or Benedictine
  Might gladly, sure, his lot embrace,
Nor find a fast-day too afflicting,
  Which served him up a Bouillabaisse.

I wonder if the house still there is ?
  Yes, here the lamp is, as before ;
The smiling red-cheeked *écaillère* is
  Still opening oysters at the door.
Is TERRÉ still alive and able ?
  I recollect his droll grimace ;
He'd come and smile before your table,
  And hoped you liked your Bouillabaisse.

      [*Punch*, February, 17, 1849.]

We enter—nothing's changed or older.
   'How's Monsieur TERRÉ, Waiter, pray?'
The waiter stares and shrugs his shoulder—
   'Monsieur is dead this many a day.'
'It is the lot of saint and sinner.
   So honest TERRÉ's run his race?'
'What will Monsieur require for dinner?'
   'Say, do you still cook Bouillabaisse?'

'*Oh, oui, Monsieur,*' 's the waiter's answer;
   '*Quel vin Monsieur désire-t-il?*'
'Tell me a good one.'   'That I can, Sir:
   The Chambertin with yellow seal.'
'So TERRÉ's gone,' I say, and sink in
   My old accustomed corner place;
'He's done with feasting and with drinking,
   With Burgundy and Bouillabaisse.'

My old accustomed corner here is,
   The table still is in the nook;
Ah! vanished many a busy year is,
   This well-known chair since last I took.
When first I saw ye, *Cari luoghi*,
   I'd scarce a beard upon my face,
And now a grizzled, grim old fogy,
   I sit and wait for Bouillabaisse.

Where are you, old companions trusty,
   Of early days, here met to dine?
Come, Waiter! quick, a flagon crusty—
   I'll pledge them in the good old wine.
The kind old voices and old faces
   My memory can quick retrace;
Around the board they take their places,
   And share the wine and Bouillabaisse.

There's JACK has made a wondrous marriage;
   There's laughing TOM is laughing yet;
There's brave AUGUSTUS drives his carriage;
   There's poor old FRED in the Gazette;
On JAMES's head the grass is growing:
   Good Lord! the world has wagged apace
Since here we set the Claret flowing,
   And drank, and ate the Bouillabaisse.

Ah me ! how quick the days are flitting !
  I mind me of a time that's gone,
When here I'd sit, as now I'm sitting,
  In this same place—but not alone.
A fair young form was nestled near me,
  A dear, dear face looked fondly up,
And sweetly spoke and smiled to cheer me
  —There's no one now to share my cup.

.   .   .   .

I drink it as the Fates ordain it.
  Come, fill it, and have done with rhymes :
Fill up the lonely glass, and drain it
  In memory of dear old times.
Welcome the wine, whate'er the seal is ;
  And sit you down and say your grace
With thankful heart, whate'er the meal is.
  —Here comes the smoking Bouillabaisse !

MAY DAY ODE.[1]

But yesterday a naked sod,
  The dandies sneered from Rotten-row,
  And cantered o'er it to and fro ;
      And see, 'tis done !
As though 'twere by a wizard's rod
  A blazing arch of lucid glass
  Leaps like a fountain from the grass
      To meet the sun !

A quiet green but few days since,
  With cattle browsing in the shade :
  And lo ! long lines of bright arcade
      In order raised.
A palace as for fairy Prince,
  A rare pavilion, such as man
  Saw never, since mankind began
      And built and glazed !

[1] [*The Times*, April 30, 1851.]

E

A peaceful place it was but now,
 And lo ! within its shining streets
 A multitude of nations meets :
   A countless throng,
I see beneath the crystal bow,
 And Gaul and German, Russ and Turk,
 Each with his native handiwork
   And busy tongue.

I felt a thrill of love and awe
 To mark the different garb of each,
 The changing tongue, the various speech
   Together blent :
A thrill, methinks, like His who saw
 ' All people dwelling upon earth
 Praising our God with solemn mirth
   And one consent.'

High Sovereign in your Royal state !
 Captains and Chiefs and Councillors,
 Before the lofty palace doors
   Are open set,—
Hush ! ere you pass the shining gate ;
 Hush ! ere the heaving curtain draws,
 And let the Royal pageant pause
   A moment yet.

People and Prince a silence keep !
 Bow coronet and kingly crown,
 Helmet and plume bow lowly down ;
   The while the priest,
Before the splendid portal step,
 While still the wondrous banquet stays,
 From Heaven supreme a blessing prays
   Upon the feast !

Then onwards let the triumph march ;
 Then let the loud artillery roll,
 And trumpets ring and joy-bells toll,
   And pass the gate :
Pass underneath the shining arch,
 'Neath which the leafy elms are green—
 Ascend unto your throne, O Queen,
   And take your state !

Behold her in her Royal place :
  A gentle lady—and the hand
  That sways the sceptre of this land,
      How frail and weak !
Soft is the voice, and fair the face ;
  She breathes Amen to prayer and hymn ;
  No wonder that her eyes are dim,
      And pale her cheek.

This moment round her empire's shores
  The winds of Austral winter sweeps,
  And thousands lie in midnight sleep
      At rest to-day.
O ! awful is that crown of yours,
  Queen of innumerable realms,
  Sitting beneath the budding elms
      Of English May !

A wondrous sceptre 'tis to bear,
  Strange mystery of God which set
  Upon her brow yon coronet,—
      The foremost crown
Of all the world, on one so fair !
  That chose her to it from her birth,
  And bade the sons of all the earth
      To her bow down.

The representative of man
  Here from the far Antipodes
  And from the subject Indian seas
      In congress meet ;
From Afric and from Hindostan,
  From Western continent and isle,
  The envoys of her empire pile
      Gifts at her feet.

Our brethren cross the Atlantic tides,
  Loading the gallant decks which once
  Roared a defiance to our guns
      With peaceful store ;
Symbol of peace, their vessel rides ! [1]
  O'er English waves float Star and Stripe,
  And firm their friendly anchors gripe
      The father shore !

---

[1] The *St. Lawrence.*

From Rhine and Danube, Rhone and Seine,
  As rivers from their sources gush
  The swelling floods of nations rush,
        And seaward pour :
From coast to coast in friendly chain,
  With countless ships we bridge the straits,
  And angry Ocean separates
        Europe no more.

From Mississippi and from Nile—
  From Baltic, Ganges, Bosphorus,
  In England's Ark assembled thus
        Are friend and guest.
Look down the mighty sunlit aisle,
  And see the sumptuous banquet set,
  The brotherhood of nations met
        Around the feast !

Along the dazzling colonnade,
  Far as the straining eye can gaze,
  Gleam cross and fountain, bell and vase,
        In vistas bright ;
And statues fair of nymph and maid,
  And steeds and pards, and Amazons,
  Writhing and grappling in the bronze,
        In endless fight.

To deck the glorious roof and dome,
  To make the Queen a canopy,
  The peaceful hosts of industry
        Their standards bear.
Yon are the works of Brahmin loom ;
  On such a web of Persian thread
  The desert Arab bows his head,
        And cries his prayer.

Look yonder where the engines toil ;
  These England's arms of conquest are,
  The trophies of her bloodless war :
        Brave weapons these.
Victorious over wave and soil,
  With these she sails, she weaves, she tills,
  Pierces the everlasting hills,
        And spans the seas.

The engine roars upon its race,
  The shuttle whirrs along the woof,
  The people hum from floor to roof,
        With Babel tongue.
The fountain in the basin plays,
  The chanting organ echoes clear,
  An awful chorus 'tis to hear,
        A wondrous song!

Swell, organ, swell your trumpet blast,
  March, Queen and Royal pageants, march
  By splendid aisle and springing arch
        Of this fair Hall :
And see ! above the fabric vast,
  God's boundless Heaven is bending blue,
  God's peaceful Sun is beaming through
        And shining over all.[1]

THE PEN AND THE ALBUM.[2]

' I AM Miss Catherine's book ' (the Album speaks) ;
' I've lain among your tomes these many weeks ;
I'm tired of their old coats and yellow cheeks.

' Quick, Pen ! and write a line with a good grace ;
Come ! draw me off a funny little face ;
And, prithee, send me back to Chesham Place.'

PEN.

' I am my master's faithful old Gold Pen,
I've served him three long years, and drawn since then
Thousands of funny women and droll men.

' O Album ! could I tell you all his ways
And thoughts, since I am his these thousand days,
Lord, how your pretty pages I'd amaze !'

---

[1] In subsequent reprints the last line runs :
      ' And shines o'er all.'

[2] [*The Keepsake*, 1853.]

Album.

'His ways? his thoughts? just whisper me a few;
Tell me a curious anecdote or two,
And write 'em quickly off, good Mordan, do!'

Pen.

'Since he my faithful service did engage
To follow him through his queer pilgrimage,
I've drawn and written many a line and page.

'Caricatures I scribbled have and rhymes,
And dinner-cards, and picture-pantomimes,
And merry little children's books at times.

'I've writ the foolish fancy of his brain;
The aimless jest that, striking, hath caused pain;
The idle word that he'd wish back again.

.   .   .   .   .

'I've helped him to pen many a line for bread;
To joke, with sorrow aching in his head;
And make your laughter when his own heart bled.

'I've spoke with men of all degree and sort—
Peers of the land, and ladies of the Court;
Oh, but I've chronicled a deal of sport!

'Feasts that were ate a thousand days ago,
Biddings to wine that long hath ceased to flow,
Gay meetings with good fellows long laid low;

'Summons to bridal, banquet, burial, ball,
Tradesman's polite reminders of his small
Account due Christmas last—I've answered all.

'Poor Diddler's tenth petition for a half-
Guinea; Miss Bunyan's for an autograph;
So I refuse, accept, lament, or laugh,

'Condole, congratulate, invite, praise, scoff,
Day after day still dipping in my trough,
And scribbling pages after pages off.

'Day after day the labour's to be done,
And sure as comes the postman and the sun
The indefatigable ink must run.

'Go back, my pretty little gilded tome,
To a fair mistress and a pleasant home,
Where soft hearts greet us whensoe'er we come!

'Dear, friendly eyes, with constant kindness lit,
However rude my verse, or poor my wit,
Or sad or gay my mood, you welcome it.

'Kind lady! till my last of lines is penned,
My master's love, grief, laughter, at an end,
Whene'er I write your name, may I write friend!

'Not all are so that were so in past years;
Voices, familiar once, no more he hears!
Names, often writ, are blotted out in tears.

'So be it :—joys will end and tears will dry. . . .
Album! my master bids me wish good-bye,
He'll send you to your mistress presently.

'And thus with thankful heart he closes you;
Blessing the happy hour when a friend he knew
So gentle, and so generous, and so true.

'Nor pass the words as idle phrases by;
Stranger! I never writ a flattery,
Nor signed the page that registered a lie.'

VANITAS VANITATUM.[1]

How spake of old the Royal Seer?
    (His text is one I love to treat on.)
This life of ours, he said, is sheer
    Mataiotes Mataioteton.

O Student of this gilded Book,
    Declare, while musing on its pages,
If truer words were ever spoke
    By ancient or by modern sages?

[1] [*The Cornhill Magazine*, July 1860.]

The various authors' names but note,[1]
  French, Spanish, English, Russians, Germans :
And in the volume polyglot,
  Sure you may read a hundred sermons !

What histories of life are here,
  More wild than all romancer's stories ;
What wondrous transformations queer,
  What homilies on human glories !

What theme for sorrow or for scorn !
  What chronicle of Fate's surprises—
Of adverse Fortune nobly borne,
  Of chances, changes, ruins, rises !

Of thrones upset, and sceptres broke,
  How strange a record here is written !
Of honours, dealt as if in joke ;
  Of brave desert unkindly smitten.

How low men were, and how they rise !
  How high they were, and how they tumble !
O Vanity of Vanities !
  O laughable, pathetic jumble !

Here, between honest Janin's joke
  And his Turk Excellency's firman,
I write my name upon the book :
  I write my name—and end my sermon.

O Vanity of vanities !
  How wayward the decrees of Fate are ;
How very weak the very wise,
  How very small the very great are !

What mean these stale moralities,
  Sir Preacher, from your desk you mumble ?
Why rail against the great and wise,
  And tire us with your ceaseless grumble ?

[1] Between a page by Jules Janin and a poem by the Turkish Ambassador, in Madame de R———'s album, containing the autographs of kings, princes, poets, marshals, musicians, diplomatists, statesmen, artists, and men of letters of all nations.

Pray choose us out another text,
    O man morose and narrow-minded !
Come turn the page—I read the next,
    And then the next, and still I find it.

Read here how Wealth aside was thrust,
    And Folly set in place exalted ;
How Princes footed in the dust,
    While lacquey in the saddle vaulted.

Though thrice a thousand years are past
    Since David's son, the sad and splendid,
The weary King Ecclesiast,
    Upon his awful tablets penned it,—

Methinks the text is never stale,
    And life is every day renewing
Fresh comments on the old old tale
    Of Folly, Fortune, Glory, Ruin.

Hark to the Preacher, preaching still !
    He lifts his voice and cries his sermon,
Here at St. Peter's of Cornhill,
    As yonder on the Mount of Hermon :

For you and me to heart to take
    (O dear beloved brother readers)
To-day, as when the good King spake
    Beneath the solemn Syrian cedars.

II.

THE SICK CHILD.[1]

By the Honourable Wilhelmina Skeggs.

A WEAKNESS seizes on my mind—I would more pudding
　　take ;
But all in vain—I feel—I feel—my little head will ache.
Oh ! that I might alone be left, to rest where now I am,
And finish with a piece of bread that pot of currant-jam.

I gaze upon the cake with tears, and wildly I deplore
That I must take a powder if I touch a morsel more,
Or oil of castor, smoothly bland, will offer'd be to me,
In wave pellucid, floating on a cup of milkless tea.

It may be so—I cannot tell—I yet may do without ;
They need not know, when left alone, what I have been
　　about.
I long to cut that potted beef—to taste that apple-pie ;
I long—I long to eat some more, but have not strength
　　to try.

I gasp for breath, and now I know I've eaten far too much ;
Not one more crumb of all the feast before me can I touch.
Susan, oh ! Susan, ring the bell, and call for Mother, dear !
My brain swims round—I feel it all—mother, your child is
　　queer !

[1] [*Punch*, January 14, 1843.]

TITMARSH'S CARMEN LILLIENSE.[1]

Lille, September 2, 1843.

My heart is weary, my peace is gone,
    How shall I e'er my woes reveal?
I have no money, I lie in pawn,
    A stranger in the town of Lille.

I.

With twenty pounds but three weeks since
    From Paris forth did Titmarsh wheel,
I thought myself as rich a prince
    As beggar poor I'm now at Lille.

Confiding in my ample means—
    In troth, I was a happy chiel!—
I pass'd the gates of Valenciennes,
    I never thought to come by Lille.

I never thought my twenty pounds
    Some rascal knave would dare to steal;
I gaily pass'd the Belgic bounds
    At Quiévrain, twenty miles from Lille.

To Antwerp town I hasten'd post,
    And as I took my evening meal
I felt my pouch,—my purse was lost,—
    O Heaven! why came I not by Lille?

I straightway call'd for ink and pen,
    To grandmamma I made appeal;
Meanwhile, a loan of guineas ten
    I borrowed from a friend at Lille.

I got the cash from grandmamma
    (Her gentle heart my woes could feel);
But where I went, and what I saw,
    What matters? Here I am at Lille.

[1] [*Fraser's Magazine*, March 1844.]

My heart is weary, my peace is gone,
  How shall I e'er my woes reveal?
I have no cash, I lie in pawn,
  A stranger in the town of Lille.

II.

To stealing I can never come,
  To pawn my watch I'm too genteel.
Besides, I left my watch at home,—
  How could I pawn it, then, at Lille?

' *La note*,' sometimes the guests will say.
  I turn as white as cold boiled veal;
I turn and look another way,
  I dare not ask the bill at Lille.

I dare not to the landlord say,
  ' Good sir, I cannot pay your bill;'
He thinks I am a Lord Anglais,
  And is quite proud I stay at Lille.

He thinks I am a Lord Anglais,
  Like Rothschild or Sir Robert Peel,
And so he serves me every day
  The best of meat and drink in Lille.

Yet when he looks me in the face
  I blush as red as cochineal;
And think did he but know my case,
  How changed he'd be, my host of Lille!

My heart is weary, my peace is gone,
  How shall I e'er my woes reveal?
I have no money, I lie in pawn,
  A stranger in the town of Lille.

III.

The sun burns out in furious blaze,
  I perspirate from head to heel;
I'd like to hire a one-horse chaise,—
  How can I, without cash at Lille?

I pass in sunshine burning hot
    By *cafés* where in beer they deal;
I think how pleasant were a pot—
    A frothing pot of beer of Lille!

What is yon house with walls so thick,
    All girt around with guard and grille?
Oh! gracious gods, it makes me sick,
    It is the *prison-house* of Lille!

Oh! cursed prison strong and barred,
    It does my very blood congeal!
I tremble as I pass the guard,
    And quit that ugly part of Lille.

The church-door beggar whines and prays,
    All turn away at his appeal:
Ah, church-door beggar! go thy ways!
    You're not the poorest man in Lille.

My heart is weary, my peace is gone,
    How shall I e'er my woes reveal?
I have no money, I lie in pawn,
    A stranger in the town of Lille.

IV.

Say, shall I to yon Flemish church,
    And at a Popish altar kneel?
O do not leave me in the lurch,—
    I'll cry ye patron-saints of Lille!

Ye virgins dressed in satin hoops,
    Ye martyrs slain for mortal weal,
Look kindly down! before you stoops
    The miserablest man in Lille.

And lo! as I beheld with awe
    A pictured saint (I swear 'tis real)
It smiled, and turned to grandmamma!—
    It did!—and I had hope in Lille!

'Twas five o'clock, and I could eat,
    Although I could not pay, my meal:
I hasten back into the street
    Where lies my inn, the best in Lille.

What see I on my table stand,—
    A letter with a well-known seal?
'Tis grandmamma's!—I know her hand,—
    'To Mr. M. A. Titmarsh, Lille.'

I feel a choking in my throat,
    I pant and stagger, faint and reel!—
It is—it is—a ten-pound-note,
    And I'm no more in pawn at Lille!

He goes off by the diligence that evening, and is restored to
the bosom of his happy family.

GREAT NEWS! WONDERFUL NEWS![1]

SHAKSPEARE COMPRESSED.

Punch wondereth that Shakspeare hath at length appeared before ye Queene.

What wonderful news from the Court,
    Old Will's at the palace a guest,
The Queen and her Royal Consort
    Have received him 'a little compressed.'

He saith her Grace will heare no more Italians nor Almayne fiddlers but take the right Englishe waye.

Who'll venture to whisper henceforth
    Her Grace loves the Opera best?
Our Queen has acknowledged to the worth
    Of Shakspeare a little compress'd.

[1] [*Punch*, May 4, 1844.]

F

Neither will her
Grace see Amburgh
his beastes never no
mo.

Who'll talk of VAN AMBURGH again?
  No more are his beasts in request;
They're good but for poor Drury Lane,
  At home She has SHAKSPEARE compressed.

On ye little
Thumbe (a sillie vaine
fellowe).

Away with the tiny TOM THUMB,
  Like mighty NAPOLEON dress'd:
For SHAKSPEARE a courting has come,
  Like TOMMY 'a little compressed.'

Punch sees (in
imagynacion) the
courte assemble and
Master Kemble the
Player with his boke.

The Court in its splendour assembles
  (The Play gives its dulness a zest),
And the last of the Royal old KEMBLES
  Reads SHAKSPEARE a little compressed.

They forme round
Master Kemble a ring
royall and ting, ding,
ding! ye Playe be-
ginneth.

Behold them all diamonds and jewels,
  Our QUEEN and our PRINCE, and the rest;
As they sit upon gilded fauteuils,
  And listen to SHAKSPEARE compress'd.

ACT I.

Ye Firste Acte.
(After this ye ser-
vants hand muffinns
abowte.)

Great CYMBELINE's Court's in a gloom,
  Rash POSTHUMUS' flame is confess'd:
Poor IMOGEN's locked in her room,
  And her love is a little compressed.

ACT II.

Ye Seconde Acte.
After the which an
Interlude of Ginger-
Beere.

Fair IMOGEN sleeps in her bed,
  IACHIMO lurks in a chest;
What, locked in a drunk! the PRINCE said,
  I think *he's* a little gombress'd.

ACT III.

Ye Thirde Acte.
A strange incident
of Imogen.
  Flourish
of Trumpets.

Now IMOGEN, flying the Court,
  Appears in boys' trousers and vest;
O fie! MR. KEMBLE stops short
  And the act is a little compress'd.

ACT IV.

Ye Fourthe Acte.
Ye Queen's Grace
weepeth for Imogyn
poore mayde!

When the QUEEN heard how IMOGEN died
  (Poor child! like a dove in a nest),
She looked at the PRINCE at her side,
  And her tears were a little compress'd.

Act V.

Ye Queen's Grace rejoyceth that Imogyn is not dedde.

But O ! how HER MAJESTY laughed
  When she found 'twasn't dying she saw,
But fainting, brought on by a draught
  From IMOGEN's mother-in-law.

The Play draweth nigh to a close.
Virtue is rewarded.

And now come the Romans in force,
  And POSTHUMUS comes in their train ;
With their foot, and their chariots and horse,
  They come over England to reign.

Britannia ruleth ye waves.
Ye play endeth.

Impossible ! here says the QUEEN—
  Our lady, with pride in her breast :
O bring me the lovers again,
  And pray let the fight be compress'd.

Ye curtain falleth.

GRAND TABLEAU

Master Kemble boweth.

The lovers are happy as just ;
  The lecturer closes his book,
And bows from the presence august,
  Well paid with a smile and a look.

PUNCH MORALISETH.

Great lady ! the news of thy court
Poor *Punch* has oft read as a pest ;
But with this he inclines not to sport,
As he solemnly here does attest.
If it please you our bard to cut short
It doubtless is done for the best.
Be pleased, too, we pray to exhort
Sir Bob with your royal behest
To shorten his speeches and for't
Your Grace shall be heartily blest.
And fiercely I'll joke and retort
On all who your peace would infest.
And, though joking is known as my forte,
I never will jibe or will jest
If you'll list to our Poet immort-
al, and love him complete or compress'd.

JENNY WREN'S REMONSTRANCE.[1]

HAVING perused with wonder LORD MAIDSTONE'S poem, in the
Morning Post, JENNY WREN indites a humble remonstrance.
    JENNY does not consider it necessary to teach the genteel
reader that one of my Lord's respected names is Finch.

SHALL WE WHO CRUSHED THEIR FATHERS.[2]

Shall we who crushed their fathers at Cressy and *Poitiers*,
And bade their guard at Waterloo ' be off,' and ' clear the way,'
Sit tamely by and tremble when swords have left their sheath,
And Gallic threats are bandied in the British lion's teeth ?
     'Tis thus they prate of honour, and spit upon the hem
     Of Britannia's regal vesture, and shame her diadem.

No, by the soul of EDWARD, by the triumphs long ago
Of the strong Norman lance and gallant English bow,
We will not cower before them while yet a bosom stirs
At the tale of CRISPIN'S Morning or the Battle of the Spurs.
     And yet they, &c.

Their ships are rolling in our ports, their banners deck our walls,
The tri-colour is sighing in the breezes of St. Paul's.
For fear of us a hundred forts gird Paris with a chain.
And Jacobins and Anarchists look on, and daren't complain.
     And yet they, &c.

They begged of us a favour, and we yielded them their plea,
The ashes of NAPOLEON from the island in the sea.
We gave them all they asked for, but we could not give them back
The glory which departed when we thundered in the track.
     And yet they, &c.

The mark of England's heel is trampled on the neck
Of Paris and her citizens, of this they nothing reck ;
But though her youth may bluster, and swear they felt it not,
There are other youths in England can make the brand as hot.
     And yet they, &c.

---

[1] [*Punch*, August 24, 1844.]
[2] Vide *Morning Post*, August 14, 1844.

The DUPIN cease to prattle, and JOINVILLE cease to write ;
The ancients had a custom to hold their tongue—and fight.
Pray to the God of battles for a strong heart and hand,
And a better sword than HOCHE's to decimate our land.
    And cease to prate of honour, and spit upon the hem
    Of Britannia's regal vesture, and shame her diadem.

SILLY LITTLE FINCHES.[1]

SILLY little Finches have silly little ears,
Make Poi*tiay* to rhyme with way—little boy it is Poi*tiers*.
Why sit by and tremble ? when swords *have* left their sheath,
Then will British lions begin to show their teeth.
    Spitting is a nasty thing, which French people do,
    Little Lordling, don't begin expectorating too.

ROYAL EDWARD's in his grave—he and his long shanks—
Did he do our people good—butchering those Franks ?
HARRY FIFTH won Agincourt—won it at a pinch—
What became of HARRY SIXTH—silly little Finch ?
    With your wiggle-waggle, &c.

He's a silly fellow of rotten things who brags,
At church best look at your prayer-book not those bloody flags,
What ! the Paris forts were built all for fear of *you ?*
Silly little Finch, so to cockadoodledoo !
    With your wiggle-waggle, &c.

Was it then so generous, granting them their plea ?
BULL-FINCH ! are not islands *always* ' in the sea ' ?
Better read the story of the fight of Mount St. John,
He robs us half our glory who says the French had none.
    With your wiggle-waggle, &c.

---

[1] This poem was ordered from the young lady who writes the chief lyrical effusions for our establishment, and who received the strictest injunctions to inculcate peace. Hence the slaughter of LORD MAIDSTONE by JENNY WREN.

The bombardment of Tangiers has taken place since his Lordship was sacrificed. That event has much altered our opinions, and, indeed, our desire of maintaining terms of politeness with the chief of the French Government. And (though we laugh to scorn the pretensions of any man who would question our right to contradict ourselves as many times in a column as we please), yet we condescend to own that our opinions *are* considerably altered by the brutal onset on Tangiers.

LORD MAIDSTONE, then, has been untimely sacrificed. But his Lordship's mangled corpse will serve to show that we had a sincere desire to maintain the peace ; and, at the same time, it may be looked at as the first victim of what may be a long and fatal war.

The march of English Wellington-heels has trampled Frenchmen low,
Swaggering young poet, pray Heaven it be not so.
Trampled men will turn and hate, that full well we know
We should never trample on a fallen foe.
  O you wiggle-waggle, &c.

Then MAIDSTONE cease to rhyme, and JOINVILLE cease to write,
Better 'tis to hold your tongue in order *not* to fight.
Better 'tis that little boys remember the old rules,
Not cut their little fingers while playing with edge-tools.
  And cease to poke at Frenchmen with your wicked little pen ;
  So, to little FINCH, cries peaceful JENNY WREN.

A DOE IN THE CITY.[1]

Holborn Hill, Settling-day, October 30, 1845.

DEAR MR. PUNCH,—

As I was going down Stagg Alley yesterday, to sign the Great Didland deed, I saw the prettiest little brougham in the world pull up at Horn Street—and the sweetest little love of a figure you ever saw step out of the vehicle. Her appearance created quite a sensation among the stagging gents, and caused even *me* to pause and look round.

Greatly to my surprise, this lovely young lady tripped by me, walked into the Didland Office, where up comes all the clerks crowding and grinning about her, and signed the deed with the greatest coolness in the world ; I peeped over her shoulder, and saw her write :—

Name in Full.	Place of Residence.	Profession.	Place of Business, if any.	No. of Shares.	Sum.
KATHERINE LORIMER	Curzon St., Mayfair	Spinster.	...	100	£2000

O Sir, how my heart beat as she put her sweet little finger on the wafer, and said, in thrilling accents, ' *I deliver this as my act and deed !* '

I have not given her real name here, but if she took notice of a gent in a green coat and little blue satin stock, light auburn hair and whiskers, diamond pin and brown silk umbrella, and is

[1] [*Punch*, November 1, 1845.]

going to drive in the Park on Sunday next, she will see one at the ACHILLES statue whose intentions are strictly honourable.

If you would put this in your widely-extended journal (which I regularly subscribe to) I should be

Your most grateful Servant,
FREDERICK HALTAMONT DE MONTMORENCY.

P.S.—As some parties like poetry, and I have a pretty knack that way, I have put our *rencounter* into verse.

Little KITTY LORIMER,
    Fair, and young, and witty ;
What has brought your Ladyship
    Rambling to the City ?

All the Stags in Capel Court
    Saw her lightly trip it ;
All the lads of Stock Exchange
    Twigg'd her muff and tippet.

With a sweet perplexity,
    And a mystery pretty,
Threading through Threadneedle Street
    Trots the little KITTY.

What was my astonishment—
    What was my compunction,
When she reached the Offices
    Of the Didland Junction !

Up the Didland stairs she went,
    To the Didland door, Sir ;
Porters, lost in wonderment,
    Let her pass before, Sir.

' Madam,' says the old chief Clerk,
    ' Sure we can't admit ye.'
' Where's the Didland Junction deed ? '
    Dauntlessly says KITTY.

' If you doubt my honesty,
    Look at my receipt, Sir ; '
Up then jumps the old chief Clerk,
    Smiling as he meets her.

KITTY at the table sits
    (Whither the old Clerk leads her) ;
' *I deliver this,*' she says
    ' *As my act and deed, Sir.*'

When I heard these funny words
    Come from lips so pretty,
This, I thought, should surely be
    Subject for a ditty.

What ! are ladies stagging it ?
    Sure, the more's the pity ;
But I've lost my heart to her—
    Naughty little KITTY.

P.S.—2. If she reads this, I beg to add I am twenty-five years of age, unencumbered ; have a very good business in Holborn Hill ; and have myself done pretty well *in the Railway Line.*

KITCHEN MELODIES.—CURRY.[1]

THREE pounds of veal my darling girl prepares,
And chops it nicely into little squares :
Five onions next procures the little minx
(The biggest are the best, her SAMIWEL thinks),
And Epping butter nearly half-a-pound,
And stews them in a pan until they're brown'd.

What's next my dexterous little girl will do ?
She pops the meat into the savoury stew,
With curry-powder table-spoonfuls three,
And milk a pint (the richest that may be),
And, when the dish has stewed for half-an-hour,
A lemon's ready juice she'll o'er it pour ;
Then, bless her ! then she gives the luscious pot
A very gentle boil—and serves quite hot.

P.S.—Beef, mutton, rabbit, if you wish ;
Lobsters, or prawns, or any kind of fish
Are fit to make A CURRY. 'Tis, when done,
A dish for Emperors to feed upon.

[1] [*Punch*, November 28, 1846.]

MR. SMITH AND MOSES.[1]

A VETERAN gent, just stepped out of a boat,
In a tattered old hat and a ragged pea-coat,

Appeared at a shop whither many folks run,
And that was the palace of MOSES AND SON.

[1] [*Punch*, March 25, 1848.]

A respectable dame with the mariner went,
Most likely the wife of this veteran gent,
And the eyes of the pair were excited with won-
der on seeing the mansion of MOSES AND SON.

'I've looked upon many a palace before,
But splendour like this, love, I never yet sor!'
This party exclaimed. 'What a great sum of mon-
ey it sure must have cost MESSRS. MOSES AND SON!'

In the language of France his good lady replied,
'This house is well known through the universe wide;
And you, my dear PHILIP, to seed having run,
Had better refit with E. MOSES AND SON.'

E. MOSES stepped forth with a bow full of grace,
Inviting the couple to enter his place:
He thought they were poor—but the poor are not done,
And the rich are not fleeced by E. MOSES AND SON.

'What clothes can I serve you to-day, my good man?'
E. MOSES exclaimed: 'You shall pay what you can;
The peer or the peasant, we suit every one;
Republicans true are E. MOSES AND SON.'

The pea-coated gent at that word made a start,
And looked nervously round at the goods of our mart:
'A vest, coat, and trowsers, as soon as they're done,
I want, *s'il vous plaît*, MESSIEURS MOSES AND SON.

'I once was a king, like the monarch of Room,
But was forced from my throne and came off in a Br—m;
And in such a great hurry from P—r—s I run,
I forgot my portmanteau, dear MOSES AND SON.'

'Dear Sir,' we exclaimed, 'what a lucky escape!'
So one brought the patterns, another the tape;
And while with our patterns his 'peepers' we stun,
The gent is quick measured by MOSES AND SON.

The clothes when complete we direct in a hurry—
'— SMITH, Esquire, at PRINCE LEOPOLD's, Claremont, in Surrey.'
The cloth was first-rate, and the fit such a one
As only is furnished by MOSES AND SON.

As he paces the valley or roams in the grove,
All cry, ' What a very respectable cove ! '
How changed in appearance from him who late run
From Paris to refuge with MOSES AND SON.

Now who was this ' veteran gent,' Sirs, E. MOSES,
Although he may ' guess,' yet he never discloses.
Do you wish to know more, gents ? if you do, why then run
To Aldgate and ask of E. MOSES AND SON.

THE FRODDYLENT BUTLER.[1]

MR. PUNCH, SIR,

The abuv is the below ritten Pome, on a subjec of grate
delicasy, wich as a butler, I feel it a disgrase to the cloth that
any man calling hisself a butler, should go for to get wind on
false pretences, and such wind (as reported in the papers of
Tuesday last) from Richmond ; and in justice to self and feller
servants, have expressed my feelins in potry, wich as you 'ave
prevously admitted to your entertainin columns pomes by a futman
(and also a pleaceman), I think you 'ave a right to find a plaice
for a pome by a butler, wich I beg to subscribe myself your constant reder.   JOHN CORKS.

14 *Lushington Place, West Belgravy.*

It's all of one JOHN GEORGE MONTRESOR,
    And BRIGGS, Esquire, his master kind ;
This retch, all for his privat plesure,
    Did froddylently order wind.

To MISTER ELLIS, Richmond, Surrey,
    Were BRIGGS, Esquire, he did reside,
This wicked JOHN druv in an 'urry,
    On June the fust and tenth beside.

And then, this mene and shabby feller
    To MISTER ELLIS did remark,
BRIGGS 'ad gone out and took the cellar
    Kee away across the Park ;

And Cumpny comeng on a suddent,
    'Ad stayed to dine with MISSIS B.
Whereby in course the butler cooden't
    Get out the wind without the kee.

[1] [*Punch*, February 10, 1849.]

So MISSIS B. she would be werry
 Much obliged if e'd send in
'Arf a dozen best brown Sherry
 And single bottel 'Ollands gin.

But this was nothink but a story as
 This wicked butler went and told,
Whereby for nothink to get glorious
 Wich so he did, and grew more bold.

Until, at last grown more audashus,
 He goes and orders, wat d'ye think ?
He goes and orders, goodness grashus,
 Marsaly, wind no gent can drink.

It wasn't for his private drinkin—
 For that he'd BRIGGES wine enuff—
But, wen the Sherry bins was sinkin
 He filled 'em with this *nasty stough*.

And BRIGGS, Esquire, at 'is own tabel
 (To rite such things my 'art offends)
Might 'ave to drink, if he was abul,
 Marsaly wind, hisself and frends !

But praps JOHN ne'er to tabel brort it,
 And used it in the *negus* line ;
Or praps the raskal, when he bort it
 Knew BRIGGS was not a judge of wind.

At all ewents, all thro' the season
 This villin plaid these 'orrid games.
For butlers to commit such treson,
 I'm sure it is the wust of shames.

But masters, tho soft, has there senses,
 And roges, tho sharp, are cotcht at last ;
So BRIGGS, Esquire, at last commenses
 To find his wine goes werry fast.

Once when the famly gev a party,
 Shampain, in course, the bankwet crown'd
And BRIGGS, Esquire, so kind and 'arty,
 He ordered John to 'and it round.

No wind in general's drunk more quicker,
    But now his glass no gent would drane ;
When BRIGGS, on tastin, found the licker
    Was British 'arf-a-crown Shampain !

That they'd not drink it was no wunder,
    A dredful look did BRIGGS assoom,
And ordered, with a voice of thunder,
    The retched butler from the room.

Then, rushin edlong to the cellar,
    Regardless if he broke 'is shins,
He found wot tricks the wicked feller
    Had been a playin with the binns.

Of all his prime old Sherry, raelly
    There wasent none to speke of there,
And MR. ELLIS's Marsaly
    Was in the place the Sherry were.

Soon after that the wicked feller's
    Crimes was diskivered clear and clene,
By the small akount of MR. ELLIS
    For lickers, twenty pound fifteen.

And not content with thus embezzlin
    His master's wind, the skoundrel had
The Richmond tradesmen all been chizzlin,
    An' a doin' every think that's bad.

Whereby on Toosday, Janwry thirty,
    As is reported in *The Times*,
He wor 'ad up for his conduc dirty,
    And dooly punished for his crimes.

So masters, who from such base fellers,
    Would keep your wind upon your shelves,
This 'int accept—If you 'ave cellars,
    Always to mind the kee yourselves.

THE THREE SAILORS.[1]

(LITTLE BILLEE.)

THERE were three sailors in Bristol City,
Who took a boat and went to sea.

But first with beef and captains' biscuit,
And pickled pork they loaded she.

There was guzzling Jack and gorging Jimmy,
And the youngest he was little Bil-*ly*.

Now very soon they were so greedy,
They didn't leave not one split pea.

Says guzzling Jack to gorging Jimmy,
I am confounded hung-*ery*.

Says gorging Jim to guzzling Jacky,
We have no wittles, so we must eat *we*.

Says guzzling Jack to gorging Jimmy,
O gorging Jim, what a fool you be.

There's little Bill as is young and tender,
We're old and tough—so let's eat *he*.

O Bill, we're going to kill and eat you,
So undo the collar of your chemie.

When Bill he heard this information,
He used his pocket-handkerchee.

O let me say my Catechism,
As my poor mammy taught to me.

Make haste, make haste, says guzzling Jacky,
Whilst Jim pulled out his snicker-snee.

So Bill went up the main top-gallant mast,
When down he fell on his bended knee.

He scarce had said his Catechism,
When up he jumps : 'There's land I see !

[1] [From *Sand and Canvas*. By Samuel Bevan. 1849.]

'There's Jerusalem and Madagascar,
And North and South Ameri-*key*.

'There's the British fleet a-riding at anchor,
With Admiral Napier, K.C.B.'

So when they came to the Admiral's vessel,
He hanged fat Jack, and flogged Jim-*my*.

But as for little Bill, he made him
The Captain of a Seventy-three.

LUCY'S BIRTHDAY.[1]

SEVENTEEN rosebuds in a ring,[2]
Thick with sister-flowers beset,
In a fragrant coronet,
Lucy's servants this day bring.
Be it the birthday wreath she wears ;
Fresh and fair, and symbolling
The young number of her years,
The soft blushes of her Spring !

Types of Love, and Youth, and Hope,
Constant friends your mistress greet ;
Be you ever pure and sweet,
Growing lovelier as you ope !

[1] [*The Keepsake*, 1854.]

[2] *Lucy's Birthday* was rewritten before it appeared in *Miscellanies* (1855).
The following shows the changes :

.   .   .   .

The sweet blushes of her spring !

Types of youth and love and hope
Friendly hearts your mistress greet ;
Be you ever fair and sweet,
And grow lovelier as you ope !
Gentle nursling, fenced about
With fond care, and guarded,
Scare you've heard of storms without,
Frosts that bite, or winds that blow !

Kindly has your life begun,
And we pray that Heaven may send
To our floweret a warm sun,
A calm summer, a sweet end :
And, where'er shall be her home.

Cherished nursling, fenced about
By fond care, and tended so,
Scarce you've heard of storms without,
Thorns that bite, or winds that blow ;—

Kindly has your life begun,
And we pray that Heaven may send
To our flow'ret a bright sun,
A warm summer, a sweet end :
And, where'er her dwelling-place,
May she decorate her home ;
Still expanding into bloom,
And developing in grace.

PISCATOR AND PISCATRIX.[1]

LINES WRITTEN TO AN ALBUM PRINT.

As on this pictured page I look,
This pretty tale of line and hook
As though it were a novel-book
    Amuses and engages :
I know them both, the boy and girl ;
She is the daughter of the Earl,
The lad (that has his hair in curl),
    My lord the County's page is.

A pleasant place for such a pair !
The fields lie basking in the glare ;
No breath of wind the heavy air
    Of lazy summer quickens.
Hard by you see the castle tall ;
The village nestles round the wall,
As round about the hen its small
    Young progeny of chickens.

It is too hot to pace the keep ;
To climb the turret is too steep ;
My lord the Earl is dozing deep,
    His noonday dinner over ;

[1] [*Miscellanies*, 1855.]

The postern-warder is asleep
(Perhaps they've bribed him not to peep):
And so from out the gate they creep,
  And cross the fields of clover.

Their lines into the brook they launch ;
He lays his cloak upon a branch,
To guarantee his Lady Blanche
   's delicate complexion ;
He takes his rapier from his haunch,
That beardless doughty champion staunch ;
He'd drill it through the rival's paunch
  That question'd his affection !

O heedless pair of sportsmen slack !
You never mark, though trout or jack,
Or little foolish tickleback,
  Your baited snares may capture.
What care has *she* for line and hook ?
She turns her back upon the brook,
Upon her lover's eyes to look
  In sentimental rapture.

O loving pair ! as thus I gaze
Upon the girl who smiles always,
The little hand that ever plays
  Upon the lover's shoulder ;
In looking at your pretty shapes,
A short of envious wish escapes
(Such as the Fox had for the Grapes)
  The Poet your beholder.

To be brave, handsome, twenty-two ;
With nothing else on earth to do,
But all day long to bill and coo :
  It were a pleasant calling.
And had I such a partner sweet ;
A tender heart for mine to beat,
A gentle hand my clasp to meet ;—
I'd let the world flow at my feet,
  And never heed its brawling.

SORROWS OF WERTHER.[1]

WERTHER had a love for Charlotte
  Such as words could never utter ;
Would you know how first he met her ?
  She was cutting bread and butter.

Charlotte was a married lady,
  And a moral man was Werther,
And, for all the wealth of Indies,
  Would do nothing for to hurt her.

So he sighed and pined and ogled,
  And his passion boiled and bubbled,
Till he blew his silly brains out,
  And no more was by it troubled.

Charlotte, having seen his body
  Borne before her on a shutter,
Like a well-conducted person,
  Went on cutting bread and butter.

THE LAST OF MAY.[2]

(IN REPLY TO AN INVITATION DATED ON THE 1ST.)

By fate's benevolent award,
  Should I survive the day,
I'll drink a bumper with my lord
  Upon the last of May.

That I may reach that happy time
  The kindly gods I pray,
For are not ducks and peas in prime
  Upon the last of May ?

At thirty boards, 'twixt now and then,
  My knife and fork shall play,
But better wine and better men
  I shall not meet in May.

[1] [*Miscellanies*, 1855.]   [2] [*Miscellanies*, 1855.]

And though, good friend, with whom I dine,
   Your honest head is grey ;
And, like this grizzled head of mine,
   Has seen its last of May ;

Yet, with a heart that's ever kind,
   A gentle spirit gay,
You've spring perennial in your mind,
   And round you make a May !

THE IDLER [1]

WITH the London hubbub
   Overtired and pestered,
I sought out a subbub
   Where I lay sequestered,—
Where I lay for three days,
   From Saturday till Monday,
And (*per face aut neface*)
   Made the most of Sunday ;

Burning of a *chee*root
   When I'd had a skinful,
Squatting on a tree root,
   Doubting if 'twas sinful ;
As the bells of Kingston
   Made a pretty clangour,
I (forgiving heathen)
   Heard them not in anger ;—

Heard and rather fancied
   Their reverberations,
As I sat entrancèd
   With my meditations.
From my Maker's praises
   Easily I wandered
To pull up His daisies,
   As I sat and pondered.

As I pull'd His daisies
   Into little pieces,
Much I thought of life
   And how small its ease is ;

[1] [From *The Idler Magazine of Fiction*, March 1856.]

Much I blamed the world
    For its worldly vanity,
As my smoke up curl'd,
    Type of its inanity.

By world I meant the Town,
    Mayfair, and its high doings;
Or rather my own set,
    Its chatterings and cooings;
So I view'd the strife
    And the sport of London,
Doubting if its life
    Were overdone or undone.

Be it slow or rapid,
    If it wakes or slumbers,
Anyhow it's vapid;—
    Moonshine from cucumbers.
Man is useless too,
    Be he saint or satyr;
Nothing's new or true,
    And—it doesn't matter.

May not I and Jeames
    Be compared together,
I in inking reams,
    He in blacking leather?
Snob and swell are peers;
    Snuffer, chewer, whiffer,—
In a hundred years
    Wherein shall we differ?

Counting on to-morrow's
    'Oirish.'   Whither tendeth
He who simply borrows,
    He who simpler lendeth;
If we give or take,
    Where remains the profit?
Sold or wide awake
    All will go to Tophet.

To Tophet—shady club
    Where no one need propose ye,
Where Hamlet hints 'the rub,'
    Is not select or cosy.

In that mixed vulgar place,
    It doesn't matter who pays,
There's no more 'Bouillabaisse'
    And no more *petits soupers*.

Why then seek to vie
    With Solomons or Sidneys?
Why care for Strasbourg pie,
    For punch or devilled kidneys?
Why write 'Yellow Plush'?
    Why should we *not* wear it?
Wherefore should we blush?
    Rather grin and bear it.

These uprooted daisies
    Speak of useless trouble;
Cheroots that burn like blazes
    Show that life's a bubble.
Thus musing on our lot,
    A fogeyfied old sinner,
I'm glad to say I got—
    An appetite for dinner.

III.

'SOME LOVE THE MATIN-CHIMES.' [1]

(FRIAR'S SONG.)

SOME love the matin-chimes, which tell
    The hour of prayer to sinner :
But better far's the midday bell,
    Which speaks the hour of dinner ;
For when I see a smoking fish,
    Or capon drown'd in gravy,
Or noble haunch on silver dish,
    Full glad I sing mine ave.

My pulpit is an alehouse bench,
    Whereon I sit so jolly ;
A smiling rosy country wench
    My saint and patron holy.
I kiss her cheek so red and sleek,
    I press her ringlets wavy,
And in her willing ear I speak
    A most religious ave.

And if I'm blind, yet Heaven is kind,
    And holy saints forgiving ;
For sure he leads a right good life
    Who thus admires good living.
Above, they say, our flesh is air,
    Our blood celestial ichor :
Oh, grant ! 'mid all the changes there,
    They may not change our liquor !'

[1] [From *The Devil's Wager*.]

THE ALMACK'S ADIEU.[1]

YOUR Fanny was never false-hearted,
  And this she protests and she vows,
From the *triste moment* when we parted
  On the staircase at Devonshire House !
I blushed when you asked me to marry,
  I vowed I would never forget ;
And at parting I gave my dear Harry
  A beautiful vinegarette !

We spent *en province*, all December,
  And I ne'er condescended to look
At Sir Charles, or the rich county member,
  Or even at that darling old duke.
You were busy with dogs and with horses,
  Alone in my chamber I sat,
And made you the nicest of purses,
  And the smartest black satin cravat !

At night with that vile Lady Frances
  (*Je faisois moi tapisserie*)
You danced every one of the dances,
  And never once thought of poor me !
Mon pauvre petit cœur ! what a shiver
  I felt as she danced the last set,
And you gave, *oh, mon Dieu !* to revive her,
  My beautiful vinegarette !

Return, love ! away with coquetting ;
  This flirting disgraces a man !
And ah ! all the while you're forgetting
  The heart of your poor little Fan !
Reviens ! break away from these Circes,
  Reviens for a nice little chat ;
And I've made you the sweetest of purses,
  And a lovely black satin cravat !

[1] [From *Our Annual Execution.*]

THE BATTLE-AXE POLACCA.[1]

(THE KNIGHTLY GUERDON.)

UNTRUE to my Ulric I never could be,[2]
I vow by the saints and the blessed Marie.
Since the desolate hour when we stood by the shore,
And your dark galley waited to carry you o'er,
My faith then I plighted, my love I confessed,
As I gave you the BATTLE-AXE marked with your Crest!
      Eleleu! in the desolate hour![3]

When the bold barons met in my fathers old hall,
Was not Edith the flower of the banquet and ball?
In the festival hour, on the lips of your bride,
Was there ever a smile save with THEE at my side?
Alone in my turret I loved to sit best,
To blazon your BANNER and broider your crest.
      Eleleu! in the festival hour!

The knights were assembled, the tourney was gay!
Sir Ulric rode first in the warrior-*mêlée*.
In the dire battle-hour, when the tourney was done,
And you gave to another the wreath you had won!

[1] [From *A Shabby Genteel Story.*]

[2] This is a parody of—

WAPPING OLD STAIRS.

Your Molly has never been false she declares,
Since last time we parted at Wapping old stairs,
When I swore that I still would continue the same
And gave you the 'bacco-box mark'd with my name,
And gave you the 'bacco-box mark'd with my name.
When I pass'd a whole fortnight between decks with you,
Did I e'er give a kiss, Tom, to one of your crew?
To be useful and kind, with my Thomas I stay'd,
For his trowsers I wash'd, and his grog, too, I made.

Tho' you promis'd last Sunday to walk in the Mall,
With Susan from Deptford, and likewise with Sal,
In silence I stood, your unkindness to hear,
And only upbraided my Tom with a tear,
And only upbraided my Tom with a tear.
Why should Sal, or should Susan than me be more priz'd?
For the heart that is true, Tom, should ne'er be despis'd.
Then be constant and kind, nor your Molly forsake,
Still your trowsers I'll wash, and your grog, too, I'll make.

[3] [In later editions the last line of each verse has been deleted.]

Though I never reproached thee, cold, cold was my breast,
As I thought of that BATTLE-AXE, ah ! and that crest !
            Eleleu ! in the dire battle-hour !

But away with remembrance, no more will I pine
That others usurped for a time what was mine !
There's a FESTIVAL HOUR for my Ulric and me ;
Once more, as of old, shall he bend at my knee ;
Once more by the side of the knight I love best
Shall I blazon his BANNER and broider his CREST.
            Tralala ! for the festival hour !

SONG OF THE VIOLET.[1]

A HUMBLE flower long time I pined
    Upon the solitary plain,
And trembled at the angry wind,
    And shrank before the bitter rain.
And oh ! 'twas in a blessed hour
    A passing wanderer chanced to see,
And, pitying the lonely flower,
    To stoop and gather me.

I fear no more the tempest rude,
    On dreary heath no more I pine,
But left my cheerless solitude,
    To deck the breast of Caroline.
Alas ! our days are brief at best,
    Nor long, I fear, will mine endure,
Though sheltered here upon a breast
    So gentle and so pure.

It draws the fragrance from my leaves,
    It robs me of my sweetest breath,
And every time it falls and heaves,
    It warns me of my coming death.
But one I know would glad forego
    All joys of life to be as I :
An hour to rest on that sweet breast,
    And then, contented, die.

        [1] [From *A Shabby Genteel Story*.]

' ÆTHELFRED KONING MURNING POST REDINGE.' [1]

B. M. MSS. Claud. xxv.-xxvii.

A READING of the newspaper | in meditation lost,
Sate Æthelfred of England | and took his tea and toast ;
Sate Æthelfred of England | and read *The Morning Post*.

Among the new arrivals | the Journal did contain,
At Margate on the twentieth | his Majesty King Swayn,
Of Denmark with a retinue | of horseman and of Dane !

Loud laugh'd King Æthelfred, | and laid the paper down ;
' Margate is a proper place | for a Danish clown.'
' Take care,' said the Chancellor, | ' *he doesn't come to town*.'

' This King Swayn,' said Witfrid the fool, | laughing loud and free,
' Sea-king as he is | a boat-swain ought to be.'
' It is none of *our seeking*,' | says the Chancellor, says he.

' Let him come,' said the King (in his mouth | butter'd toast
    popping),
' At Wapping or at Redriff | this boatswain will be stopping.'
' Take care,' says Chancellor Wigfrid, | ' he don't give *you* a
    wapping.'

' I'm certain,' says wise Wigfrid, | ' the Sea-king means us evilly,
Herald, go to Margate, | and speak unto him civilly ;
And if he's not at Margate, | why then try Ramsgate and Tivoli.'

Herald, in obedience | to his master dear,
Goes by steam to Margate, | landing at the Pier ;
Says he, ' King Swayn of Denmark | I think is lodging here ? '

Swayn the bold Sea-king, | with his captains and skippers,
Walk'd on the sea-beach | looking at the dippers—
Walk'd on the sea-beach | in his yellow slippers.

' Nay, I cannot go,' said Swayn, | ' for my ships are leaking.'
' You shall have a fleet,' says the herald, | ' if that be what you're
    seeking.'
' Well, I *won't* go, and that's flat,' | answered Swayn the Sea-king.

[1] [From *Miss Tickletoby's Lectures on English History*.]

THE STORY OF KING CANUTE.[1]

KING CANUTE was weary-hearted, | he had reigned for years a score ;
Battling, struggling, pushing, fighting, | killing much, and robbing more ;
And he thought upon his actions | walking by the wild sea-shore.

'Twixt the Chancellor and Bishop | walk'd the King with step sedate ;
Chamberlains and Grooms came after, | Silver-sticks and Gold-sticks great ;
Chaplains, Aides-de Camp, and Pages, | all the officers of state.

Sliding after like his shadow, | pausing when he chose to pause,
If a frown his face contracted | straight the courtiers dropp'd their jaws ;
If to laughter he was minded | out they burst in loud hee-haws.

But that day a something vex'd him | that was clear to old and young ;
Thrice his Grace had yawn'd at table | when his favourite gleeman sung—
Once the Queen would have consoled him | and he bid her hold her tongue.

'Something ails my royal master,' | cried the Keeper of the Seal ;
'Sure, my Lord, it is the lampreys | served at dinner, or the veal.
Shall I call your Grace's doctor ?' | 'Psha, it is not *that* I feel.

''Tis the *heart* and not the stomach, | fool ! that doth my rest impair ;
Can a king be great as I am | prithee, and yet know no care ?
Oh ! I'm sick, and tired, and weary.' | Some one cried, 'The King's armchair !'

Then towards the lackeys turning, | quick my lord the Keeper nodded ;
Straight the king's great chair was brought him | by two footmen able-bodied ;
Languidly he sunk into it, | it was comfortably wadded.

[1] [From *Miss Tickletoby's Lectures on English History.*]

'Leading on my fierce companions,' | cried he, 'over storm and
    brine,
I have fought and I have conquer'd ; | where is glory like to mine?'
Loudly all the courtiers echoed, | 'Where is glory like to thine?'

'What avails me all my kingdoms? | I am weary now and old ;
Those fair sons I have begotten | long to see me dead and cold ;
Would I were, and quiet buried | underneath the silent mould.

'Oh, remorse ! the writhing serpent, | at my bosom tears and bites ;
Horrid, horrid things I look on | though I put out all the lights,—
Ghosts of ghastly recollections | troop about my bed of nights :

'Cities burning, convents blazing | red with sacrilegious fires ;
Mothers weeping, virgins screaming | vainly to their slaughtered
    sires.'—
'Such a tender conscience,' cries the | Bishop, 'every one admires.

'But for such unpleasant by-gones | cease, my gracious Lord, to
    search ;
They're forgotten and forgiven | by our holy mother Church.
Never, never doth she leave her | benefactors in the lurch.

'Look, the land is crown'd with ministers | whom your Grace's
    bounty raises ;
Abbeys fill'd with holy men, where | you and Heaven are daily
    praised ;—
You, my Lord, to think of dying ! | on my honour I'm amazed.'

'Nay, I feel,' replied King Canute, | 'that my end is drawing near.'
'Don't say so,' exclaimed the courtiers | (striving each to squeeze
    a tear) ;
'Sure your Grace is strong and lusty | and will live this fifty year!'

'Live these fifty years !' the Bishop | roar'd (with action made to
    suit) ;
'Are you mad, my good Lord Keeper | thus to speak of King
    Canute ?
Men have lived a thousand years, and | sure his Majesty will do't.

'Adam, Enoch, Lamech, Canan, | Mahaleel, Methusela,
Lived nine hundred years apiece ; and | is not he as good as they?'
'Fervently,' exclaimed the Keeper, | 'fervently I trust he may.'

'*He* to die !' resumed the Bishop ; | 'he, a mortal like to us ?
Death was not for him intended, | though *communis omnibus.*
Keeper, you are irreligious | for to talk and cavil thus.

'With his wondrous skill in healing | ne'er a doctor can compete ;
Loathsome lepers, if he touch them, | start up clean upon their
    feet ;
Surely he could raise the dead up | did his Highness think it meet.

'Did not once the Jewish Captain | stop the sun upon the hill,
And, the while he slew the foeman, | bid the silver moon stand
    still ?
So, no doubt, could gracious Canute | if it were his sacred will.'

'Might I stay the sun above us, | good Sir Bishop,' Canute cried,
'Could I bid the silver moon to | pause upon her heavenly ride ?
If the moon obeys my orders, | sure I can command the tide.

'Will the advancing waves obey me, | Bishop, if I make the sign ?'
Said the Bishop, bowing lowly, | 'Land and sea, my Lord, are
    thine.'
Canute look'd toward the ocean, | 'Back,' he said, 'thou foaming
    brine !

'From the sacred shore I stand on, | I command thee to retreat,
Venture not, thou stormy rebel, | to approach thy master's seat ;
Ocean, be thou still, I bid thee, | come not nearer to my feet.'

But the angry ocean answered | with a louder, deeper roar,
And the rapid waves drew nearer | falling sounding on the shore,—
Back the Keeper and the Bishop, | back the King and courtiers
    bore.

And he sternly bade them never | more to kneel to human clay,
But alone to praise and worship | that which earth and seas obey :
And his golden crown of empire | never wore he from that day.
King Canute is dead and gone ; | parasites exist alway.

THE WILLOW-TREE.[1]

Know ye the willow-tree
    Whose grey leaves quiver,
Whispering gloomily
    To yon pale river ?
Lady, at even-tide
    Wander not near it,
They say its branches hide
    A sad, lost spirit !

Once to the willow-tree
    A maid came fearful,
Pale seemed her cheek to be,
    Her blue eye tearful ;
Soon as she saw the tree,
    Her step moved fleeter.
No one was there—ah, me !
    No one to meet her !

Quick beat her heart to hear
    The far bell's chime
Toll from the chapel-tower
    The trysting time :
But the red sun went down
    In golden flame,
And though she looked round,
    Yet no one came ?

[1] [From *Ottilia*.]

H

Presently came the night,
    Sadly to greet her,—
Moon in her silver light,
    Stars in their glitter :
Then sank the moon away
    Under the billow,
Still wept the maid alone—
    There by the willow !

Through the long darkness,
    By the stream rolling,
Hour after hour went on
    Tolling and tolling.
Long was the darkness,
    Lonely and stilly ;
Shrill came the night-wind,
    Piercing and chilly.

Shrill blew the morning breeze,
    Biting and cold,
Bleak peers the grey dawn
    Over the world.
Bleak over moor and stream
    Looks the grey dawn,
Grey, with dishevelled hair,
Still stands the willow there—
    THE MAID IS GONE !

Domine, Domine !
    Sing we a litany,—
Sing for poor maiden-hearts broken and weary ;
Domine, Domine !
    Sing we a litany,
Wail we and weep we a wild Miserere !

ANOTHER VERSION.[1]

I.

LONG by the willow-trees
    Vainly they sought her,
Wild rang the mother's screams
    O'er the grey water :
' Where is my lovely one ?
    Where is my daughter ?

[1] [From *Ottilia*.]

II.

'Rouse thee, sir constable—
     Rouse thee and look ;
Fisherman, bring your net,
     Boatman, your hook.
Beat in the lily-beds,
     Dive in the brook!'

III.

Vainly the constable
     Shouted and called her ;
Vainly the fisherman
     Beat the green alder,
Vainly he flung the net,
     Never it hauled her !

IV.

Mother, beside the fire
     Sat, her nightcap in ;
Father, in easy-chair,
     Gloomily napping,
When at the window-sill
     Came a light tapping !

V.

And a pale countenance
     Looked through the casement.
Loud beat the mother's heart,
     Sick with amazement,
And at the vision, which
     Came to surprise her,
Shrieked in her agony,—
     'Lor'! it's Elizar!'

VI.

Yes, 'twas Elizabeth—
     Yes, 'twas their girl ;
Pale was her cheek, and her
     Hair out of curl.
'Mother!' the loving one,
     Blushing, exclaimed,
'Let not your innocent
     Lizzy be blamed.

VII.

'Yesterday, going to aunt
    Jones's to tea,
Mother, dear mother, I
    Forgot the door-key!
And as the night was cold,
    And the way steep,
Mrs. Jones kept me to
    Breakfast and sleep.'

VIII.

Whether her pa and ma
    Fully believed her
That we shall never know,
    Stern they received her;
And for the work of that
    Cruel, though short, night,
Sent her to bed without
    Tea for a fortnight.

IX.

MORAL.

Hey diddle diddlety,
    Cat and the Fiddlety!
Maidens of England, take caution by she!
    Let love and suicide
    Never tempt you aside,
And always remember to take the door-key!

THE MINARET BELLS.[1]

TINK-A-TINK, tink-a-tink ;
    By the light of the star,
On the blue river's brink,
    I heard a guitar.

I heard a guitar
    On the blue waters clear,
And knew by its mu-u-sic,
    That Selim was near !

Tink-a-tink, tink-a-tink,
    How the soft music swells,
And I hear the soft clink
    Of the minaret bells !

COME TO THE GREENWOOD TREE.[2]

COME to the greenwood tree,[3]
Come where the dark woods be,
Dearest, oh come with me !
Let us rove—oh my love—oh my love !
                    Oh my-y love !
(*Drunken cobbler without*)   Oh, my-y love !

Come—'tis the moonlight hour,
Dew is on leaf and flower,
Come to the linden bower,—
    Let us rove—oh my love—oh my love !
Let us ro-o-ove, lurlurliety ; yes, we'll rove, lurlurliety,
    Through the gro-o-ove, lurlurliety—lurlurli-e-i-e-i-e-i !
(*Cobbler as usual*)   Let us ro-o-ove, etc.

Dark is the wood, and wide,
Dangers, they say, betide ;
But, at my Albert's side,
Nought I fear, oh my love—oh my love !

Welcome the greenwood tree,
Welcome the forest free,
Dearest, with thee, with thee,
Nought I fear, oh my love—o-h ma-a-y love !

[1] [From *The Ravenswing*.]   [2] [From *The Ravenswing*.]
[3] The words of this song are copyright, nor will the copyright be sold for less than twopence-halfpenny.

PEG OF LIMAVADDY.[1]

RIDING from Coleraine
  (Famed for lovely Kitty),
Came a cockney bound
  Unto Derry city ;
Weary was his soul,
  Shivering and sad he
Bump'd along the road
  Leads to Limavaddy.

Mountains stretch'd around,
  Gloomy was their tinting,
And the horse's hoofs
  Made a dismal clinting ;
Wind upon the heath
  Howling was and piping,
On the heath and bog,
  Black with many a snipe in :
'Mid the bogs of black,
  Silver pools were flashing,
Crows upon their sides
  Picking were and splashing.
Cockney on the car
  Closer folds his plaidy,
Grumbling at the road
  Leads to Limavaddy.

Through the crashing woods
  Autumn brawl'd and bluster'd,
Tossing round about
  Leaves the hue of mustard ;
Yonder lay Lough Foyle,
  Which a storm was whipping,
Covering with mist
  Lake, and shores, and shipping.
Up and down the hill
  (Nothing could be bolder),
Horse went with a raw
  Bleeding on his shoulder.

[1] [From *The Irish Sketch Book.*]

'Where are horses changed?'
  Said I to the laddy
Driving on the box:
  'Sir, at Limavaddy.'

Limavaddy inn's
  But a humble bait-house,
Where you may procure
  Whisky and potatoes;
Landlord at the door
  Gives a smiling welcome
To the shivering wights
  Who to his hotel come.
Landlady within
  Sits and knits a stocking,
With a wary foot
  Baby's cradle rocking.

To the chimney nook
  Having found admittance,
There I watch a pup
  Playing with two kittens;
(Playing round the fire,
  Which of blazing turf is,
Roaring to the pot
  Which bubbles with the murphies);
And the cradled babe
  Fond the mother nursed it,
Singing it a song
  As she twists the worsted!

Up and down the stair
  Two more young ones patter
(Twins were never seen
  Dirtier nor fatter);
Both have mottled legs,
  Both have snubby noses,
Both have—Here the host
  Kindly interposes:
'Sure you must be froze
  With the sleet and hail, sir,
So will you have some punch,
  Or will you have some ale, sir?'

Presently a maid
   Enters with the liquor,
(Half a pint of ale
   Frothing in a beaker).
Gods! I didn't know
   What my beating heart meant,
Hebe's self I thought
   Enter'd the apartment.

As she came she smiled,
   And the smile bewitching,
On my word and honour,
   Lighted all the kitchen!

With a curtsey neat
   Greeting the new-comer,
Lovely, smiling Peg
   Offers me the rummer;

But my trembling hand
    Up the beaker tilted,
And the glass of ale
    Every drop I spilt it :
Spilt it every drop
    (Dames, who read my volumes,
Pardon such a word)
    On my whatd'yecall'ems !

Witnessing the sight
    Of that dire disaster,
Out began to laugh
    Missis, maid, and master ;
Such a merry peal,
    'Specially Miss Peg's was
(As the glass of ale
    Trickling down my legs was),
That the joyful sound
    Of that ringing laughter
Echoed in my ears
    Many a long day after.

Such a silver peal !
    In the meadows listening,
You who've heard the bells
    Ringing to a christening ;
You who ever heard
    Caradori pretty,
Smiling like an angel
    Singing ' Giovinetti,'
Fancy Peggy's laugh,
    Sweet, and clear, and cheerful,
At my pantaloons
    With half-a-pint of beer full !

When the laugh was done,
    Peg, the pretty hussy,
Moved about the room
    Wonderfully busy ;
Now she looks to see
    If the kettle keep hot,
Now she rubs the spoons,
    Now she cleans the teapot ;

Now she sets the cups
    Trimly and secure,
Now she scours a pot,
    And so it was I drew her.

Thus it was I drew her
    Scouring of a kettle,[1]
(Faith ! her blushing cheeks
    Redden'd on the metal !)
Ah ! but 'tis in vain
    That I try to sketch it ;
The pot perhaps is like,
    But Peggy's face is wretched
No : the best of lead,
    And of Indian rubber,
Never could depict
    That sweet kettle-scrubber !

See her as she moves !
    Scarce the ground she touches,
Airy as a fay,
    Graceful as a duchess ;
Bare her rounded arm,
    Bare her little leg is,
Vestris never show'd
    Ankles like to Peggy's ;
Braided is her hair,
    Soft her look and modest,
Slim her little waist
    Comfortably bodiced.

———

This I do declare,
    Happy is the laddy
Who the heart can share
    Of Peg of Limavaddy ;
Married if she were,
    Blest would be the daddy
Of the children fair
    Of Peg of Limavaddy ;

[1] The late Mr. Pope represents Camilla as '*scouring the plain*,' an absurd and useless task. Peggy's occupation with the kettle is much more simple and noble. The second line of this poem (whereof the author scorns to deny an obligation) is from the celebrated 'Frithiof' of Esaias Tigner. A maiden is serving warriors to drink, and is standing by a shield—' *Und die Runde des Schildes ward wie das Mägdelein roth*,'—perhaps the above is the best thing in both poems.

> Beauty is not rare
>   In the land of Paddy,
> Fair beyond compare
>   Is Peg of Limavaddy.
>
> Citizen or squire,
>   Tory, Whig, or Radi-
> cal would all desire
>   Peg of Limavaddy.
> Had I Homer's fire,
>   Or that of Sergeant Taddy,
> Meetly I'd admire
>   Peg of Limavaddy.
> And till I expire,
>   Or till I grow mad, I
> Will sing unto my lyre
>   Peg of Limavaddy!

JEAMES OF BUCKLEY SQUARE.[1]

A HELIGY.

COME all ye gents vot cleans the plate,
  Come all ye ladies'-maids so fair—
Vile I a story vil relate
  Of cruel JEAMES of Buckley Square.
A tighter lad, it is confest,
  Neer valked vith powder in his air,
Or vore a nosegay in his breast,
  Than andsum JEAMES of Buckley Square.

O Evns! it vas the best of sights,
  Behind his Master's coach and pair,
To see our JEAMES in red plush tights,
  A driving hoff from Buckley Square.
He vel became his·hagwiletts,
  He cocked his at with *such* a hair;
His calves and viskers *vas* such pets,
  That hall loved JEAMES of Buckley Square.

---

[1] [From *Jeames's Diary and Letters.*]

He pleased the hup-stairs folks as vell,
    And O ! I vithered vith despair,
Misses *vould* ring the parler bell,
    And call up JEAMES in Buckley Square.
Both beer and sperrits he abhord,
    (Sperrits and beer I can't a bear),
You would have thought he vas a lord
    Down in our All in Buckley Square.

Last year, he visper'd, 'MARY HANN,
    Ven I've an under'd pound to spare,
To take a public is my plan,
    And leave this hojous Buckley Square.'
O how my gentle heart did bound,
    To think that I his name should bear,
'Dear JEAMES,' says I, 'I've twenty pound,'
    And gev them him in Buckley Square.

Our master vas a City gent,
    His name's in railroads everywhere ;
And lord, vot lots of letters vent
    Betwigst his brokers and Buckley Square !
My JEAMES it was the letters took,
    And read 'em all (I think it's fair),
And took a leaf from Master's book,
    As *hothers* do in Buckley Square.

Encouraged with my twenty pound,
    Of which poor *I* was unaware,
He wrote the Companies all round,
    And signed hisself from Buckley Square.
And how JOHN PORTER used to grin,
    As day by day, share after share,
Came railvay letters pouring in,
    'J. PLUSH, Esquire, in Buckley Square.'

Our servants' All was in a rage—
    Scrip, stock, curves, gradients, bull and bear,
Vith butler, coachman, groom and page,
    Vas all the talk in Buckley Square.
But O ! imagine vat I felt
    Last Vensday veek as ever were ;
I gits a letter, which I spelt
    'MIS M. A. HOGGINS, Buckley Square.'

He sent me back my money true—
    He sent me back my lock of air,
And said, 'My dear, I bid ajew
    To MARY HANN and Buckley Square.
Think not to marry, foolish HANN,
    With people who your betters are ;
JAMES PLUSH is now a gentleman,
    And you—a cook in Buckley Square.

'I've thirty thousand guineas won,
    In six short months by genus rare ;
You little thought what JEAMES was on,
    Poor MARY HANN, in Buckley Square.
I've thirty thousand guineas net,
    Powder and plush I scorn to vear ;
And so, Miss MARY HANN, forget
    For hever JEAMES, of Buckley Square.'

The rest of the MS. is illegible, being literally washed away in a flood of tears.

SONNICK.[1]

SEJESTED BY PRINCE HALBERT GRATIOUSLY KILLING THE STAGGS AT SACKS-COBUG-GOTHY.

SOME forty Ed of sleak and hantlered dear
    In Cobug (where such hanimmles abound)
Were shot, as by the nusepapers I hear,
    By HALBERT Usband of the British Crownd.
BRITANNIA'S QUEEN let fall the purly tear ;
    Seeing them butcherd in their silvn prisns ;
Igspecially, when the keepers, standing round,
    Came up and cut their pretty hinnocent whizns.

Suppose, instead of this pore Germing sport,
    This Saxn wenison which he shoots and baggs,
Our Prins should take a turn in Capel Court
    And make a massyker of ENGLISH STAGGS.
Pore Staggs of Hengland ! were the Untsman at you,
    What avoc he would make & what a trimenjus battu !
                       JEAMS.

[1] [From *Jeames's Diary and Letters*.]

WHEN MOONLIKE ORE THE HAZURE SEAS.[1]

WHEN moonlike ore the hazure seas
   In soft effulgence swells,
When silver jews and balmy breaze
   Bend down the Lily's bells ;
When calm and deap, the rosy sleap
   Has lapt your soal in dreems,
R HANGELINE !   R lady mine !
   Dost thou remember JEAMES ?

I mark thee in the Marble All,
   Where England's loveliest shine—
I say the fairest of them hall
   Is LADY HANGELINE.
My soul, in desolate eclipse,
   With recollection teems—
And then I hask, with weeping lips,
   Dost thou remember JEAMES ?

Away ! I may not tell thee hall
   This soughring heart endures—
There is a lonely sperrit-call
   That Sorrow never cures ;
There is a little, little Star,
   That still above me beams ;
It is the Star of Hope—but ar !
   Dost thou remember JEAMES ?

[1] [From *Jeames's Diary and Letters.*]

LINES UPON MY SISTER'S PORTRAIT.[1]

By The Lord Southdown.

The castle towers of Bareacres are fair upon the lea,
Where the cliffs of bonny Diddlesex rise up from out the sea :
I stood upon the donjon keep and view'd the country o'er,
I saw the lands of Bareacres for fifty miles or more.
I stood upon the donjon keep—it is a sacred place,—
Where floated for eight hundred years the banner of my race ;
Argent, a dexter sinople, and gules an azure field,
There ne'er was nobler cognizance on knightly warrior's shield.

The first time England saw the shield 'twas round a Norman neck,
On board a ship from Valery, King William was on deck.
A Norman lance the colours wore, in Hastings' fatal fray—
St. Willibald for Bareacres ! 'twas double gules that day !
O Heaven and sweet St. Willibald ! in many a battle since
A loyal-hearted Bareacres has ridden by his Prince !
At Acre with Plantagenet, with Edward at Poitiers,
The pennon of the Bareacres was foremost on the spears !

'Twas pleasant in the battle-shock to hear our war-cry ringing :
O ! grant me, sweet Saint Willibald, to listen to such singing !
Three hundred steel-clad gentlemen, we drove the foe before us,
And thirty score of British bows kept twanging to the chorus !
O knights, my noble ancestors ! and shall I never hear
Saint Willibald for Bareacres through battle ringing clear ?
I'd cut me off this strong right hand a single hour to ride,
And strike a blow for Bareacres, my fathers, at your side !

Dash down, dash down, yon Mandolin, beloved sister mine !
Those blushing lips may never sing the glories of our line :
Our ancient castles echo to the clumsy feet of churls,
The spinning Jenny houses in the mansion of our Earls.
Sing not, sing not, my Angelina ! in days so base and vile,
'Twere sinful to be happy, 'twere sacrilege to smile.
I'll hie me to my lonely hall, and by its cheerless hob
I'll muse on other days, and wish—and wish I were—A Snob.

[1] [From *Jeames's Diary and Letters.*]

THE WHITE SQUALL.[1]

On deck, beneath the awning,
I dozing lay and yawning ;
It was the grey of dawning,
    Ere yet the sun arose ;
And above the funnel's roaring,
And the fitful wind's deploring,
I heard the cabin snoring
    With universal nose.
I could hear the passengers snorting,
I envied their disporting,
Vainly I was courting
    The pleasure of a doze.

So I lay, and wondered why light
Came not, and watched the twilight
And the glimmer of the skylight,
    That shot across the deck ;
And the binnacle pale and steady,
And the dull glimpse of the dead-eye,
And the sparks in fiery eddy,
    That whirled from the chimney neck :
In our jovial floating prison
There was sleep from fore to mizen,
And never a star had risen
    The hazy sky to speck.

Strange company we harboured :
We'd a hundred Jews to larboard,
Unwashed, uncombed, unbarbered,
    Jews black, and brown, and grey ;
With terror it would seize ye,
And make your souls uneasy,
To see those Rabbis greasy,
    Who did nought but scratch and pray :
Their dirty children puking,
Their dirty saucepans cooking,
Their dirty fingers hooking
    Their swarming fleas away.

[1] [From *A Journey from Cornhill to Grand Cairo.*]

To starboard Turks and Greeks were,
Whiskered, and brown their cheeks were,
Enormous wide their breeks were,
    Their pipes did puff alway ;
Each on his mat allotted,
In silence smoked and squatted,
Whilst round their children trotted,
    In pretty, pleasant play.
He can't but smile who traces
The smiles on those brown faces,
And the pretty prattling graces
    Of those small heathens gay.

And so the hours kept tolling,
And through the ocean rolling
Went the brave *Iberia* bowling
    Before the break of day——

When a SQUALL upon a sudden,
Came o'er the waters scudding ;
And the clouds began to gather,
And the sea was lashed to lather,
And the lowering thunder grumbled,
And the lightning jumped and tumbled,
And the ship, and all the ocean,
Woke up in wild commotion.
Then the wind set up a howling,
And the poodle-dog a yowling,
And the cocks began a crowing,
And the old cow raised a lowing,
As she heard the tempest blowing ;
And fowls and geese did cackle,
And the cordage and the tackle
Began to shriek and crackle ;
And the spray dashed o'er the funnels,
And down the deck in runnels ;
And the rushing water soaks all,
From the seamen in the fo'ksal,
To the stokers, whose black faces
Peer out of their bed-places ;
And the captain he was bawling,
And the sailors pulling, hauling ;
And the quarter-deck tarpauling
Was shivered in the squalling ;

I

And the passengers awaken,
Most pitifully shaken ;
And the steward jumps up, and hastens
For the necessary basins.

Then the Greeks they groaned and quivered,
And they knelt, and moaned, and shivered,
As the plunging waters met them,
And splashed and overset them ;
And they call in their emergence
Upon countless saints and virgins ;
And their marrowbones are bended,
And they think the world is ended.

And the Turkish women for'ard
Were frightened and behorror'd ;
And, shrieking and bewildering,
The mothers clutched their children ;
The men sung, ' Allah ! Illah !
Mashallah Bismillah ! '
As the warring waters doused them,
And splashed them and soused them ;
And they called upon the Prophet,
And thought but little of it.

Then all the fleas in Jewry
Jumped up and bit like fury ;
And the progeny of Jacob
Did on the main-deck wake up
(I wot those greasy Rabbins
Would never pay for cabins) ;
And each man moaned and jabbered in
His filthy Jewish gaberdine,
In woe and lamentation,
And howling consternation.
And the splashing water drenches
Their dirty brats and wenches ;
And they crawl from bales and benches,
In a hundred thousand stenches.

This was the White Squall famous,
Which latterly o'ercame us,
And which all will well remember
On the 28th September ;

When a Prussian captain of Lancers
(Those tight-laced, whiskered prancers)
Came on the deck astonished,
By that wild squall admonished,
And wondering cried, 'Potz tausend,
Wie ist der Stürm jetzt brausend?'
And looked at Captain Lewis,
Who calmly stood and blew his
Cigar in all the bustle,
And scorned the tempest's tussle.
And oft we've thought hereafter
How he beat the storm to laughter;

For well he knew his vessel
With that vain wind could wrestle;
And when a wreck we thought her,
And doomed ourselves to slaughter,
How gaily he fought her,
And through the hubbub brought her,
And, as the tempest caught her,
Cried, 'GEORGE! SOME BRANDY-AND-WATER!'

And when, its force expended,
The harmless storm was ended,
And as the sunrise splendid
    Came blushing o'er the sea;
I thought, as day was breaking,
My little girls were waking,
And smiling, and making
    A prayer at home for me.

AH! BLEAK AND BARREN WAS THE MOOR.[1]

Ah! bleak and barren was the moor,
　Ah! loud and piercing was the storm,
The cottage hearth was shelter'd sure,
　The cottage hearth was bright and warm—
An orphan boy the lattice pass'd,
　And, as he mark'd its cheerful glow,
Felt doubly keen the midnight blast,
　And doubly cold the fallen snow.

They mark'd him as he onward prest,
　With fainting heart and weary limb;
Kind voices bade him turn and rest,
　And gentle faces welcomed him.
The dawn is up—the guest is gone,
　The cottage hearth is blazing still;
Heaven pity all poor wanderers lone!
　Hark to the wind upon the hill!

THE ROSE UPON MY BALCONY.[2]

The rose upon my balcony, the morning air perfuming,
Was leafless all the winter-time and pining for the spring;
You ask me why her breath is sweet and why her cheek is
　blooming,
It is because the sun is out and birds begin to sing.

The nightingale, whose melody is through the greenwood ringing,
Was silent when the boughs were bare and winds were blowing
　keen:
And if, mamma, you ask of me the reason of his singing,
It is because the sun is out and all the leaves are green.

Thus each performs his part, mamma: the birds have found their
　voices,
The blowing rose a flush, mamma, her bonny cheek to dye;
And there's sunshine in my heart, mamma, which wakens and
　rejoices,
And so I sing and blush, mamma, and that's the reason why.

[1] [From *Vanity Fair.*]　　　　　　[2] [From *Vanity Fair.*]

DEAR JACK.[1]

DEAR JACK, this white mug that with GUINNESS I fill,
And drink to the health of sweet NAN of the Hill,
Was once TOMMY TOSSPOT'S, as jovial a sot,
As e'er drew a spiggot, or drained a full pot—
In drinking all round 'twas his joy to surpass,
And with all merry tipplers he drank off his glass.

One morning in summer, while seated so snug,
In the porch of his garden, discussing his jug,
Stern Death, on a sudden, to TOM did appear,
And said, 'Honest THOMAS, come take your last bier;'
We kneaded his clay in the shape of this can,
From which let us drink to the health of my NAN.

WHEN THE GLOOM IS ON THE GLEN.[2]

WHEN the moonlight's on the mountain
    And the gloom is on the glen,
At the cross beside the fountain
    There is one will meet thee then.
At the cross beside the fountain,
    Yes, the cross beside the fountain,
There is one will meet thee then!

I have braved, since first we met, love,
    Many a danger in my course;
But I never can forget, love,
    That dear fountain, that old cross,
Where, her mantle shrouded o'er her—
    For the winds were chilly then—
First I met my LEONORA,
    When the gloom was on the glen.
        Yes I met my, etc.

Many a clime I've ranged since then, love,
    Many a land I've wandered o'er;
But a valley like that glen, love,
    Half so dear I never sor!
Ne'er saw maiden fairer, coyer,
    Than wert thou, my true love, when
In the gloaming first I saw yer,
    In the gloaming of the glen!

[1] [From *Phil Fogarty*.]   [2] [From *A Night's Pleasure*.]

THE RED FLAG.[1]

WHERE the quivering lightning flings
    His arrows from out the clouds,
And the howling tempest sings,
    And whistles among the shrouds,
'Tis pleasant, 'tis pleasant to ride
    Along the foaming brine—
Wilt be the Rover's bride ?
    Wilt follow him, lady mine ?
                    Hurrah !
    For the bonny, bonny brine.

Amidst the storm and rack,
    You shall see our galley pass,
As a serpent, lithe and black,
    Glides through the waving grass ;
As the vulture, swift and dark,
    Down on the ring-dove flies,
You shall see the Rover's bark
    Swoop down upon his prize.
                    Hurrah !
    For the bonny, bonny prize.

Over her sides we dash,
    We gallop across her deck—
Ha ! there's a ghastly gash
    On the merchant-captain's neck !
Well shot, well shot, old NED !
    Well struck, well struck, black JAMES !
Our arms are red, and our foes are dead,
    And we leave a ship in flames !
                    Hurrah !
    For the bonny, bonny flames !

[1] [From *A Night's Pleasure.*]

THE CHURCH PORCH.[1]

(AT THE CHURCH GATE.)

ALTHOUGH I enter not,
Yet round about the spot
  Sometimes I hover,
And at the sacred gate,
With longing eyes I wait,
  Expectant of her.

The Minster bell tolls out
Above the city's rout
  And noise and humming:
They've stopp'd the chiming bell,
  I hear the organ's swell—
She's coming, she's coming!

My lady comes at last,
Timid and stepping fast,
  And hastening hither,
With modest eyes downcast.
She comes—she's here—she's past.
  May Heaven go with her!

Kneel undisturb'd, fair saint,
Pour out your praise or plaint
  Meekly and duly.
I will not enter there,
To sully your pure prayer
  With thoughts unruly.

But suffer me to pace
Round the forbidden place,
  Lingering a minute,
Like outcast spirits, who wait
And see through Heaven's gate
  Angels within it.

[1] [From *The History of Pendennis.*]

THE END OF THE PLAY.[1]

THE play is done; the curtain drops,
Slow falling, to the prompter's bell :
A moment yet the actor stops,
And looks around, to say farewell.
It is an irksome word and task ;
And when he's laughed and said his say,
He shows, as he removes the mask,
A face that's anything but gay.

One word, ere yet the evening ends,
Let's close it with a parting rhyme,
And pledge a hand to all young friends,
As fits the merry Christmas-time.
On life's wide scene you, too, have parts,
That Fate ere long shall bid you play ;
Good night ! with honest gentle hearts
A kindly greeting go away !

Good night !—I'd say, the griefs, the joys,
Just hinted in this mimic page,
The triumphs and defeats of boys,
Are but repeated in our age.
I'd say, your woes were not less keen,
Your hopes more vain, than those of men ;
Your pangs or pleasures of fifteen,
At forty-five played o'er again.

I'd say, we suffer and we strive
Not less nor more as men than boys ;
With grizzled beards at forty-five,
As erst at twelve, in corduroys ;
And if, in time of sacred youth,
We learned at home to love and pray,
Pray Heaven, that early Love and Truth
May never wholly pass away.

And in the world, as in the school,
I'd say, how fate may change and shift ;
The prize be sometimes with the fool,
The race not always to the swift.

[1] [From *Dr. Birch and His Young Friends.*]

The strong may yield, the good may fall,
The great man be a vulgar clown,
The knave be lifted over all,
The kind cast pitilessly down.

Who knows the inscrutable design?
Blessed be He who took and gave!
Why should your mother, Charles, not mine,
Be weeping at her darling's grave! [1]
We bow to Heaven that will'd it so,
That darkly rules the fate of all,
That sends the respite or the blow,
That's free to give or to recall.

This crowns his feast with wine and wit:
Who brought him to that mirth and state?
His betters, see, below him sit,
Or hunger hopeless at the gate.
Who bade the mud from Dives' wheel
To spurn the rags of Lazarus?
Come, brother, in that dust we'll kneel,
Confessing Heaven that ruled it thus.

So each shall mourn, in life's advance,
Dear hopes, dear friends, untimely killed;
Shall grieve for many a forfeit chance,
A longing passion unfulfilled.
Amen! whatever fate be sent,—
Pray God the heart may kindly glow,
Although the head with cares be bent,
And whitened with the winter snow.

Come wealth or want, come good or ill,
Let young and old accept their part,
And bow before the Awful Will,
And bear it with an honest heart.
Who misses, or who wins the prize?
Go, lose or conquer as you can:
But if you fail, or if you rise,
Be each, pray God, a gentleman.

[1] Charles Buller, ob. 29 Nov. 1848, æt. 42.

A gentleman, or old or young !
(Bear kindly with my humble lays) ;
The sacred chorus first was sung
Upon the first of Christmas days :
The shepherds heard it overhead—
The joyful angels raised it then :
Glory to Heaven on high, it said,
And peace on earth to gentle men.

My song, save this, is little worth ;
I lay the weary pen aside,
And wish you health, and love, and mirth,
As fits the solemn Christmas-tide.
As fits the holy Christmas birth,
Be this, good friends, our carol still—
Be peace on earth, be peace on earth,
To men of gentle will.

LOVE AT TWO SCORE.[1]

(THE AGE OF WISDOM.)

Ho ! pretty page, with dimpled chin,
    That never has known the barber's shear,
All your aim is woman to win.
This is the way that boys begin.
    Wait till you've come to forty year !

Curly gold locks cover foolish brains,
    Billing and cooing is all your cheer,
Sighing and singing of midnight strains
Under Bonnybells' window-panes.
    Wait till you've come to forty year !

Forty times over let Michaelmas pass,
    Grizzling hair the brain doth clear ;
Then you know a boy is an ass,
Then you know the worth of a lass,
    Once you have come to forty year.

[1] [From *Rebecca and Rowena.*]

Pledge me round, I bid ye declare,
    All good fellows whose beards are grey :
Did not the fairest of the fair
Common grow and wearisome, ere
    Ever a month was past away ?

The reddest lips that ever have kissed,
    The brightest eyes that ever have shone,
May pray and whisper and we not list,
Or look away and never be missed,
    Ere yet ever a month was gone.

Gillian's dead, Heaven rest her bier,
    How I loved her twenty years syne !
Marian's married, but I sit here,
Alive and merry at forty year,
    Dipping my nose in the Gascon wine.

ATRA CURA.[1]

BEFORE I lost my five poor wits,
I mind me of a Romish clerk,
Who sang how Care, the phantom dark,
Beside the belted horseman sits.
Methought I saw the griesly sprite
Jump up but now behind my knight.

And though he gallop as he may,
I mark that cursed monster black
Still sits behind his honour's back,
Tight squeezing of his heart alway.
Like two black Templars sit they there,
Beside one crupper, Knight and Care.

No knight am I with pennoned spear,
To prance upon a bold destrere :
I will not have black Care prevail
Upon my long-eared charger's tail,
For lo, I am a witless fool,
And laugh at Grief and ride a mule.

[1] {From *Rebecca and Rowena.*]

REQUIESCAT.[1]

UNDER the stone you behold,
Buried, and coffined, and cold,
Lieth Sir Wilfrid the Bold.

Always he marched in advance,
Warring in Flanders and France,
Doughty with sword and with lance.

Famous in Saracen fight,
Rode in his youth the good knight,
Scattering Paynims in flight.

Brian the Templar untrue,
Fairly in tourney he slew,
Saw Hierusalem too.

Now he is buried and gone,
Lying beneath the grey stone:
Where shall you find such a one?

Long time his widow deplored,
Weeping the fate of her lord,
Sadly cut off by the sword.

When she was eased of her pain,
Came the good Lord Athelstane,
When her ladyship married again.

COMMANDERS OF THE FAITHFUL.[2]

THE Pope he is a happy man,
His Palace is the Vatican:
And there he sits and drains his can;
The Pope he is a happy man.
I often say when I'm at home,
I'd like to be the Pope of Rome.

[1] [From *Rebecca and Rowena*.]   [2] [From *Rebecca and Rowena*.]

And then there's Sultan Saladin,
That Turkish Soldan full of sin ;
He has a hundred wives at least,
By which his pleasure is increased ;
I've often wished, I hope no sin,
That I were Sultan Saladin.

But no, the Pope no wife may choose,
And so I would not wear his shoes ;
No wine may drink the proud Paynim,
And so I'd rather not be him ;
My wife, my wine, I love I hope,
And would be neither Turk nor Pope.

POCAHONTAS.[1]

WEARIED arm and broken sword
    Wage in vain the desperate fight :
Round him press the countless horde,
    He is but a single knight.
Hark ! a cry of triumph shrill
    Through the wilderness resounds,
    As, with twenty bleeding wounds,
Sinks the warrior, fighting still.

Now they heap the fatal pyre,
    And the torch of death they light ;
Ah ! 'tis hard to die of fire !
    Who will shield the captive knight ?
Round the stake with fiendish cry
    Wheel and dance the savage crowd ;
    Cold the victim's mien and proud,
And his breast is bared to die.

Who will shield the fearless heart ?
    Who avert the murderous blade ?
From the throng, with sudden start,
    See, there springs an Indian maid.
Quick she stands before the knight,
    ' Loose the chain, unbind the ring,
    I am daughter of the king,
And I claim the Indian right ! '

[1] [From *The Virginians.*]

Dauntlessly aside she flings
    Lifted axe and thirsty knife ;
Fondly to his heart she clings,
    And her bosom guards his life !
In the woods of Powhattan,
    Still 'tis told, by Indian fires,
How a daughter of their sires
Saved the captive Englishman.

FROM POCAHONTAS.[1]

RETURNING from the cruel fight
How pale and faint appears my knight !
He sees me anxious at his side ;
'Why seek, my love, your wounds to hide ?
Or deem your English girl afraid
To emulate the Indian maid ? '

Be mine my husband's grief to cheer,
In peril to be ever near ;
Whate'er of ill or woe betide,
To bear it clinging at his side ;
The poisoned stroke of fate to ward,
His bosom with my own to guard ;
Ah ! could it spare a pang to his,
It could not know a purer bliss !
'Twould gladden as it felt the smart,
And thank the hand that flung the dart !

[1] [From *The Virginians.*]

FRENCH DITTIES.

IMITATIONS OF BÉRANGER.

LE ROI D'YVETOT.

Il était un roi d'Yvetot,
  Peu connu dans l'histoire ;
Se levant tard, se couchant tôt,
  Dormant fort bien sans gloire,
Et couronné par Jeanneton
D'un simple bonnet de coton,
        Dit-on.
    Oh ! oh ! oh ! oh ! ah ! ah ! ah ! ah !
    Quel bon petit roi c'était là !
        La, la.

Il fesait ses quatre repas
  Dans son palais de chaume,
Et sur un âne, pas à pas,
  Parcourait son royaume.
Joyeux, simple, et croyant le bien,
Pour toute garde il n'avait rien
        Qu'un chien.
    Oh ! oh ! oh ! oh ! ah ! ah ! ah ! ah !

Il n'avait de goût onéreux
  Qu'une soif un peu vive ;
Mais, en rendant son peuple heureux,
  Il faut bien qu'un roi vive.
Lui-même à table, et sans suppôt,
Sur chaque muid levait un pot
        D'impôt.
    Oh ! oh ! oh ! oh ! ah ! ah ! ah ! ah !

Aux filles de bonnes maisons
   Comme il avait su plaire,
Ses sujets avaient cent raisons
   De le nommer leur père :
D'ailleurs il ne levait de ban
Que pour tirer quatre fois l'an
     Au blanc.
      Oh ! oh ! oh ! oh ! ah ! ah ! ah ! ah !

Il n'agrandit point ses états,
   Fut un voisin commode,
Et, modèle des potentats,
   Prit le plaisir pour code.
Ce n'est que lorsqu'il expira,
Que le peuple qui l'enterra
     Pleura.
      Oh ! oh ! oh ! oh ! ah ! ah ! ah ! ah !

On conserve encor le portrait
   De ce digne et bon prince ;
C'est l'enseigne d'un cabaret
   Fameux dans la province.
Les jours de fête, bien souvent,
La foule s'écrie en buvant
     Devant :
      Oh ! oh ! oh ! oh ! ah ! ah ! ah ! ah !

THE KING OF BRENTFORD.[1]

THERE was a king in Brentford,
   Of whom no legends tell,
But who without his glory
   Could sleep and eat right well.
His Polly's cotton night-cap,
   It was his crown of state ;
He loved to sleep full early,
   And rise again full late.

---

[1] [*Fraser's Magazine*, May 1836.]

When the poem appeared in *Fraser's Magazine* it was introduced by the following passage, which is more likely to have been written by Dr. Maginn, the editor of the periodical, than by Thackeray :—

But we must leave off making *beaux yeux ;* and yet we need not quit French song-writing, for here's an imitation of Béranger's first song, the *Roi d'Yvetot.* A glorious chant it is, and, we presume, utterly untranslatable ; but 'the king of Brentford' is by no means to be despised. It is said that

All in a fine straw castle
    He ate his four good meals,
And for a guard of honour
    A dog ran at his heels :
Sometimes to view his kingdoms
    Rode forth this monarch good,
And then a prancing jackass
    He royally bestrode.

There were no evil habits
    With which this king was curst,
Except (and where's the harm on't ?)
    A somewhat lively thirst.
But subjects must have taxes,
    And monarchs must have sport ;
So out of every hogshead
    His grace he kept a quart.

He pleased the fine court ladies
    With manners soft and bland ;
They named him, with good reason,
    The Father of the Land.
Four times a-year his armies,
    To battle forth did go ;
But their enemies were targets,
    Their bullets they were tow.

He vexed no quiet neighbour,
    No bootless conquest made,
But by the laws of pleasure
    His peaceful realms he swayed ;
And in the years he reigned
    Through all his kingdom wide,
There was no cause for weeping,
    Save when the good man died.

Buonaparte, who was about to tumble when the *Roi d'Yvetot* made its appearance, did not like it by any means. He thought it too strongly impressed, very much to the disadvantage of himself, on the minds of the French people, then beginning to be getting tired of wars, no longer successful, and of harassing conscriptions every day becoming more and more galling, the picture of a quiet, easy, do-nothing sort of king, who would keep the peace of the world. Whatever else might be said of Napoleon, nobody could ever accuse him of being a Roi d'Yvetot. But we are detaining our readers from ' The King of Brentford.'

Long time the Brentford nation
  Their monarch did deplore—
His portrait yet is swinging
  Beside an ale-house door;
And topers, tender-hearted,
  Regard that honest phiz,
And envy times departed
  That knew a reign like his.

THE KING OF YVETOT.[1]

THERE was a king of Yvetot,
  Of whom renown hath little said,
Who let all thoughts of glory go,
  And dawdled half his days a-bed;
And every night, as night came round,
By Jenny, with a nightcap crowned,
          Slept very sound:
      Sing ho, ho, ho! and he, he, he!
      That's the kind of king for me.

And every day it came to pass,
  That four lusty meals made he;
And, step by step, upon an ass,
  Rode abroad, his realms to see;
And whenever he did stir,
What think you was his escort, sir?
          Why, an old cur.
      Sing ho, ho, ho! and he, he, he!
      That's the kind of king for me.

If e'er he went into excess,
  'Twas from a somewhat lively thirst;
But he who would his subjects bless,
  Odd's fish!—must wet his whistle first;
And so from every cask they got,
Our king did to himself allot,
          At least a pot.
      Sing ho, ho, ho! and he, he, he!
      That's the kind of king for me.

[1] [From *The Paris Sketch Book*, 1840.]

To all the ladies of the land,
    A courteous king, and kind, was he ;
The reason why you'll understand,
    They named him Pater Patriæ.
Each year he called his fighting men,
    And marched a league from home, and then
                Marched back again.
        Sing ho, ho, ho ! and he, he, he !
        That's the kind of king for me.

Neither by force nor false pretence,
    He sought to make his kingdom great,
And made (O princes, learn from hence)—
    ' Live and let live,' his rule of state.
'Twas only when he came to die,
That his people who stood by,
              Were known to cry.
        Sing ho, ho, ho ! and he, he, he !
        That's the kind of king for me.

The portrait of this best of kings
    Is extant still, upon a sign
That on a village tavern swings,
    Famed in the country for good wine.
The people in their Sunday trim,
Filling their glasses to the brim,
              Look up to him,
        Singing ha, ha, ha ! and he, he, he !
        That's the sort of king for me.

THE KING OF BRENTFORD.[1]

Another Version.

There was a king in Brentford—of whom no legends tell,
But who, without his glory,—could eat and sleep right well.
His Polly's cotton nightcap,—it was his crown of state,
He slept of evenings early,—and rose of mornings late.

All in a fine mud palace,—each day he took four meals,
And for a guard of honour,—a dog ran at his heels,
Sometimes, to view his kingdoms,—rode forth this monarch good,
And then a prancing jackass—he royally bestrode.

[1] [From *The Paris Sketch Book*, 1840.]

There were no costly habits—with which this king was curst,
Except (and where's the harm on't ?)—a somewhat lively thirst ;
But people must pay taxes,—and kings must have their sport,
So out of every gallon—His Grace he took a quart.

He pleased the ladies round him,—with manners soft and bland ;
With reason good, they named him,—the father of his land.
Each year his mighty armies—marched forth in gallant show ;
Their enemies were targets,—their bullets they were tow.

He vexed no quiet neighbour,—no useless conquest made,
But by the laws of pleasure,—his peaceful realm he swayed.
And in the years he reigned,—through all this country wide,
There was no cause for weeping,—save when the good man died.

The faithful men of Brentford—do still their king deplore,
His portrait yet is swinging—beside an alehouse door.
And topers, tender-hearted,—regard his honest phiz,
And envy times departed,—that knew a reign like his.

LE GRENIER.[1]

Je viens revoir l'asile où ma jeunesse
De la misère a subi les leçons.
J'avais vingt ans, une folle maîtresse,
De francs amis et l'amour des chansons.
Bravant le monde et les sots et les sages,
Sans avenir, riche de mon printemps,
Leste et joyeux je montais six étages,
Dans un grenier qu'on est bien à vingt ans !

C'est un grenier, point ne veux qu'on l'ignore.
Là fut mon lit, bien chétif et bien dur ;
Là fut ma table ; et je retrouve encore
Trois pieds d'un vers charbonnés sur le mur.
Apparaissez, plaisirs de mon bel âge,
Que d'un coup d'aile a fustigés le temps,
Vingt fois pour vous j'ai mis ma montre en gage
Dans un grenier qu'on est bien à vingt ans !

Lisette ici doit surtout apparaître,
Vive, jolie, avec un frais chapeau ;
Déjà sa main à l'étroite fenêtre
Suspend son schal, en guise de rideau.
Sa robe aussi va parer ma couchette ;
Respecte, Amour, ses plis longs et flottans.
J'ai su depuis qui payait sa toilette
Dans un grenier qu'on est bien à vingt ans !

A table un jour, jour de grande richesse,
De mes amis les voix brillaient en chœur,
Quand jusqu'ici monte un cri d'allégresse :
A Marengo Bonaparte est vainqueur.

[1] [From *The Paris Sketch Book*, 1840.]

Le canon gronde ; un autre chant commence ;
Nous célébrons tant de faits éclatans.
Les rois jamais n'envahiront la France.
Dans un grenier qu'on est bien à vingt ans !

Quittons ce toit où ma raison s'enivre.
Oh ! qu'ils sont loin ces jours si regrettés !
J'échangerais ce qu'il me reste à vivre
Contre un des mois qu'ici Dieu m'a comptés,
Pour rêver gloire, amour, plaisir, folie,
Pour dépenser sa vie en peu d'instans,
D'un long espoir pour la voir embellie,
Dans un grenier qu'on est bien à vingt ans !

THE GARRET.

With pensive eyes the little room I view,
    Where, in my youth, I weathered it so long ;
With a wild mistress, a staunch friend or two,
    And a light heart still breaking into song :
Making a mock of life, and all its cares,
    Rich in the glory of my rising sun,
Lightly I vaulted up four pair of stairs,
    In the brave days when I was twenty-one.

Yes ; 'tis a garret—let him know't who will—
    There was my bed—full hard it was and small ;
My table there—and I decipher still
    Half a lame couplet charcoaled on the wall.
Ye joys, that Time hath swept with him away,
    Come to mine eyes, ye dreams of love and fun ;
For you I pawned my watch how many a day,
    In the brave days when I was twenty-one.

And see my little Jessy, first of all ;
    She comes with pouting lips and sparkling eyes :
Behold, how roguishly she pins her shawl
    Across the narrow casement, curtain-wise ;
Now by the bed her petticoat glides down,
    And when did woman look the worse in none ?
I have heard since who paid for many a gown,
    In the brave days when I was twenty-one.

One jolly evening, when my friends and I
    Made happy music with our songs and cheers,
A shout of triumph mounted up thus high,
    And distant cannon opened on our ears:
We rise,—we join in the triumphant strain,—
    Napoleon conquers—Austerlitz is won—
Tyrants shall never tread us down again,
    In the brave days when I was twenty-one.

Let us begone—the place is sad and strange—
    How far, far off, these happy times appear;
All that I have to live I'd gladly change
    For one such month as I have wasted here—
To draw long dreams of beauty, love, and power,
    From founts of hope that never will outrun,
And drink all life's quintessence in an hour,
    Give me the days when I was twenty-one!

ROGER-BONTEMPS.[1]

Aux gens atrabilaires
Pour exemple donné,
En un temps de misères
Roger-Bontemps est né.
Vivre obscur à sa guise,
Narguer les mécontens ;
Eh gai ! c'est la devise
Du gros Roger-Bontemps.

Du chapeau de son père
Coiffé dans les grands jours,
De roses ou de lierre
Le rajeunir toujours ;
Mettre un manteau de bure,
Vieil ami de vingt ans ;
Eh gai ! c'est la parure
Du gros Roger-Bontemps.

Posséder dans sa hutte
Une table, un vieux lit,
Des cartes, une flûte,
Un broc que Dieu remplit ;
Un portrait de maîtresse,
Un coffre et rien dedans ;
Eh gai ! c'est la richesse
Du gros Roger-Bontemps.

Aux enfans de la ville
Montrer de petits jeux ;
Être fesseur habile
De contes graveleux ;
Ne parler que de danse
Et d'almanachs chantans :
Eh gai ! c'est la science
Du gros Roger-Bontemps.

[1] [From *The Paris Sketch Book*, 1840.]

Faute de vins d'élite,
Sabler ceux du canton :
Préférer Marguerite
Aux dames du grand ton :
De joie et de tendresse
Remplir tous ses instans :
Eh gai ! c'est la sagesse
Du gros Roger-Bontemps.

Dire au ciel : Je me fie,
Mon père, à ta bonté ;
De ma philosophie
Pardonne le gaîté :
Que ma saison dernière
Soit encore un printemps :
Eh gai ! c'est la prière
Du gros Roger-Bontemps.

Vous pauvres pleins d'envie,
Vous riches désireux,
Vous, dont le char dévie
Après un cours heureux ;
Vous, qui perdrez peut-être
Des titres éclatans,
Eh gai ! prenez pour maître
Le gros Roger-Bontemps.

JOLLY JACK.[1]

WHEN fierce political debate
   Throughout the isle was storming,
The Rads attacked the throne and state,
   And Tories the reforming,
To calm the furious rage of each,
   And right the land demented,
Heaven sent us Jolly Jack, to teach
   The way to be contented.

Jack's bed was straw, 'twas warm and soft,
   His chair, a three-legged stool;
His broken jug was emptied oft,
   Yet, somehow, always full.
His mistress' portrait decked the wall,
   His mirror had a crack;
Yet, gay and glad, though this was all
   His wealth, lived Jolly Jack.

To give advice to avarice,
   Teach pride its mean condition,
And preach good sense to dull pretence,
   Was honest Jack's high mission.
Our simple statesman found his rule
   Of moral in the flagon,
And held his philosophic school
   Beneath the 'George and Dragon.'

[1] [From *The Paris Sketch Book*, 1840.]

When village Solons cursed the Lords,
　　And called the malt-tax sinful,
Jack heeded not their angry words,
　　But smiled and drank his skinful.
And when men wasted health and life,
　　In search of rank and riches,
Jack marked aloof the paltry strife,
　　And wore his threadbare breeches.

'I enter not the church,' he said,
　　'But I'll not seek to rob it';
So worthy Jack Joe Miller read,
　　While others studied Cobbett.
His talk it was of feast and fun;
　　His guide the Almanack;
From youth to age thus gaily run
　　The life of Jolly Jack.

And when Jack prayed, as oft he would,
　　He humbly thanked his Maker;
'I am,' said he, 'O Father good!
　　Nor Catholic nor Quaker:
Give each his creed, let each proclaim
　　His catalogue of curses;
I trust in Thee, and not in them,
　　In Thee, and in Thy mercies!

'Forgive me if, midst all Thy works,
　　No hint I see of damning;
And think there's faith among the Turks,
　　And hope for e'en the Brahmin.
Harmless my mind is, and my mirth,
　　And kindly is my laughter;
I cannot see the smiling earth,
　　And think there's hell hereafter.'

Jack died; he left no legacy,
　　Save that his story teaches:—
Content to peevish poverty;
　　Humility to riches.
Ye scornful great, ye envious small,
　　Come follow in his track;
We all were happier, if we all
　　Would copy JOLLY JACK.

LE BON ANGE.[1]

Vierge, à qui le calice à la liqueur amère
    Fut si souvent offert,
Mère, que l'on nomma la douloureuse mère,
    Tant vous avez souffert !

Vous, dont les yeux divins, sur la terre des hommes,
    Ont versé plus de pleurs
Que vos pieds n'ont depuis, dans le ciel où nous sommes,
    Fait éclore de fleurs !

Vase d'élection, étoile matinale,
    Miroir de pureté,
Vous qui priez pour nous, d'une voix virginale,
    La suprême bonté ;

A mon tour, aujourd'hui, bienheureuse Marie,
    Je tombe à vos genoux ;
Daignez donc m'écouter, car c'est vous que je prie,
    Vous qui priez pour nous.

O VIRGIN BLEST !

O Virgin blest ! by whom the bitter draught
    So often has been quaffed,
That, for thy sorrow, thou art named by us
    The Mother Dolorous !

Thou, from whose eyes have fallen more tears of woe,
    Upon the earth below,
Than 'neath thy footsteps, in this heaven of ours,
    Have risen flowers !

O beaming morning star ! O chosen vase !
    O mirror of all grace !
Who, with thy virgin voice, dost ever pray
    Man's sins away ;

Bend down thine ear, and list, O blessed saint !
    Unto my sad complaint ;
Mother ! to thee I kneel, on thee I call,
    Who hearest all.

[1] [From *The Paris Sketch Book.*]

GERMAN DITTIES.

TRAGISCHE GESCHICHTE.

By Adelbert von Chamisso.

’s war einer, dem’s zu Herzen ging,
Dass ihm der Zopf so hinten hing,
    Er wollt’ es anders haben.

So denkt er denn : wie fang’ ich’s an ?
Ich dreh’ mich um, so ist’s getan—
    Der Zopf, der hängt ihm hinten.

Da hat er flink sich umgedreht,
Und wie es stund, es annoch steht—
    Der Zopf, der hängt ihm hinten.

Da dreht er schnell sich anders ’rum,
’s wird aber noch nicht besser drum—
    Der Zopf, der hängt ihm hinten.

Er dreht sich links, er dreht sich rechts,
Es tut nichts gut’s, es tut nichts schlecht’s—
    Der Zopf, der hängt ihm hinten.

Er dreht sich wie ein Kreisel fort,
Es hilft zu nichts, in einem Wort—
    Der Zopf, der hängt ihm hinten.

Und seht, er dreht sich immer noch,
Und denkt : es hilft am Ende doch—
    Der Zopf, der hängt ihm hinten.

     L

A TRAGIC STORY.[1]

THERE lived a sage in days of yore,
And he a handsome pigtail wore ;
But wondered much and sorrowed more
    Because it hung behind him.

He mused upon this curious case,
And swore he'd change the pigtail's place,
And have it hanging at his face,
    Not dangling there behind him.

Says he, ' The mystery I've found,—
I'll turn me round,'—he turned him round ;
    But still it hung behind him.

Then round, and round, and out and in,
All day the puzzled sage did spin ;
In vain—it mattered not a pin,—
    The pigtail hung behind him.

And right, and left, and round about,
And up, and down, and in, and out,
He turned ; but still the pigtail stout
    Hung steadily behind him.

And though his efforts never slack,
And though he twist, and twirl, and tack,
Alas ! still faithful to his back
    The pigtail hangs behind him.

       [1] [From *Ballads*, 1855.]

DER KRANZ.

LUDWIG UHLAND.

Es pflückte Blümlein mannigfalt
Ein Mägdlein auf der lichten Au ;
Da kam wohl aus dem grünen Wald
Ein wunderschöne Frau.

Sie trat zum Mägdlein freundlich hin,
Sie schlang ein Kränzlein ihm ins Haar :
"Noch blüht es nicht, doch wird es blühn ;
O trag es immerdar !"

Und als das Mägdlein grösser ward
Und sich erging im Monderglanz
Und Tränen weinte, süss und zart,
Da knospete der Kranz.

Und als ihr holder Bräutigam
Sie innig in die Arme schloss,
Da wanden Blümlein wonnesam
Sich aus den Knospen los.

Sie weigte bald ein süsses Kind
Auf ihrem Schosse mütterlich ;
Da zeigten an dem Laubgewind
Viel goldne Früchte sich.

Und als ihr Lieb gesunken war,
Ach, in des Grabes Nacht und Staub,
Da weht' um ihr zerstreutes Haar
Ein herzlich falbes Laub.

Bald lag auch sie erbleichet da,
Doch trug sie ihren werten Kranz ;
Da war's ein Wunder, denn man sah
So Frucht als Blütenglanz.

THE CHAPLET.[1]

A LITTLE girl through field and wood
   Went plucking flow'rets here and there,
When suddenly beside her stood
   A lady wondrous fair !

The lovely lady smiled, and laid
   A wreath upon the maiden's brow ;
' Wear it, 'twill blossom soon,' she said,
   ' Although 'tis leafless now.'

The little maiden older grew,
   And wandered forth of moonlight eves,
And sighed and loved as maids will do ;
   When, lo ! her wreath bore leaves.

Then was our maid a wife, and hung
   Upon a joyful bridegroom's bosom ;
When from the garland's leaves there sprung
   Fair store of blossom.

And presently a baby fair
   Upon her gentle breast she reared ;
When midst the wreath that bound her hair,
   Rich golden fruit appeared.

But when her love lay cold in death,
   Sunk in the black and silent tomb,
All sere and withered was the wreath
   That wont so bright to bloom.

Yet still the withered wreath she wore ;
   She wore it at her dying hour ;
When, lo ! the wondrous garland bore
   Both leaf, and fruit, and flower !

[1] [From *Ballads*, 1855.]

DER KÖNIG AUF DEM TURME.

Ludwig Uhland.

Da liegen sie alle, die grauen Höh'n,
Die dunkeln Thäler in milder Ruh ;
Der Schlummer waltet, die Lüfte wehn
Keinen Laut der Klage mir zu.

Für alle hab' ich gesorgt und gestrebt,
Mit Sorgen trank ich den funkelnden Wein ;
Die Nacht ist gekommen, der Himmel belebt,
Mein Seele will ich erfreun.

O du goldne Schrift durch den Sterneraum,
Zu dir ja schau' ich liebend empor ;
Ach Wunderklänge, vernommen Raum,
Wie besäuselt ihr sehnlich mein Ohr !

Mein Haar ist ergraut, mein Auge getrübt,
Die Siegeswaffen hängen im Saal,
Habe Recht gesprochen und Recht geübt ;
Wann darf ich rasten einmal ?

O selige Rast, wie verlang' ich dein !
O herrliche Nacht, wie saumst du so lang,
Da ich schaue der Sterne lichteren Schein
Und höre volleren Klang.

THE KING ON THE TOWER.[1]

The cold grey hills they bind me around,
    The darksome valleys lie sleeping below,
But the winds, as they pass o'er all this ground,
    Bring me never a sound of woe !

[1] [From *Ballads*, 1855.]

Oh ! for all I have suffered and striven,
  Care has embittered my cup and my feast ;
But here is the night and the dark blue heaven,
  And my soul shall be at rest.

O golden legends writ in the skies !
  I turn towards you with longing soul,
And list to the awful harmonies
  Of the spheres as on they roll.

My hair is grey and my sight nigh gone ;
  My sword it rusteth upon the wall ;
Right have I spoken, and right have I done :
  When shall I rest me once for all ?

O blessed rest ! O royal night !
  Wherefore seemeth the time so long
Till I see yon stars in their fullest light,
  And list to their loudest song ?

DIE GREISIN.

By Friedrich Baron de la Motte Fouqué.

Auch Du gingst einst, die Myrt' im Haare,
  An Braut'gams Arme zum Altare,
  Frischblühend wie der Mai;
Auch Du bist unter Blütenkränzen
Umhergeschwebt im muntern Tanzen,
  Von aller Sorge frei.

Ach nun, wie bleich Dir Deine Wangen,
  Die Deiner Augen Licht vergangen,
  So müde Seel' und Leib!
Ob Frühling blüh'; ob Herbstlaub gelbe,
Dein Sitz am Ofen stets derselbe,
  Schon halb entschlumbert Weib!

Und doch—ein Hauch! und Deine Mängel
  Sind abgefallen! Du ein Engel
  Vor Gottes lichtem Thron!—
Mühsam ist hier die Bahn zu wallen,
Schwer das Bestehen, leicht das Fallen,
  Doch überreich der Lohn.

TO A VERY OLD WOMAN.

And thou wert once a maiden fair,
  A blushing virgin warm and young,
With myrtles wreathed in golden hair,
And glossy brow that knew no care—
  Upon a bridegroom's arm you hung.

The golden locks are silvered now,
   The blushing cheek is pale and wan ;
The spring may bloom, the autumn glow,
All's one—in chimney corner thou
   Sitt'st shivering on.—

A moment—and then sink'st to rest !
To wake, perhaps an angel blest,
   In the bright presence of thy Lord.
Oh, weary is life's path to all !
Hard is the strife, and light the fall,
     But wondrous the reward !

DOCTOR LUTHER.[1]

(A CREDO.)

I.

FOR the souls' edification
Of this decent congregation,
Worthy people ! by your grant
I will sing a holy chant,
 I will sing a holy chant.
If the ditty sound but oddly,
'Twas a father, wise and godly,
Sang it so long ago.
 Then sing as Doctor Luther sang,
 As Doctor Luther sang,
 'Who loves not wine, woman, and song,
 He is a fool his whole life long.'

II.

He, by custom patriarchal,
Loved to see the beaker sparkle ;
And he thought the wine improved,
Tasted by the wife he loved,
 By the kindly lips he loved.
Friends ! I wish this custom pious
Duly were adopted by us,
To combine love, song, wine,
 And sing as Doctor Luther sang,
 As Doctor Luther sang :
 'Who loves not wine, woman, and song,
 He is a fool his whole life long.'

[1] [From *The Adventures of Philip.*]

153

III.

Who refuses this our credo,
And demurs to drink as we do,
Were he holy as John Knox,
I'd pronounce him heterodox !
  I'd pronounce him heterodox.
And from out this congregation,
With a solemn commination,
Banish quick the heretic,
    Who will not sing as Luther sang,
    As Doctor Luther sang :
    'Who loves not wine, woman, and song,
    He is a fool his whole life long.'

IMITATIONS OF HORACE.

TO HIS SERVING BOY.[1]

Persicos odi, puer, apparatus ;
Displicent nexae philyra coronae :
Mitte sectari rosa quo locorum
 Sera moretur.

Simplici myrto nihil allabores
Sedulus curae : neque te ministrum
Dedecet myrtus, neque me sub arcta
 Vite bibentem.

AD MINISTRAM.

DEAR Lucy, you know what my wish is,—
 I hate all your Frenchified fuss :
Your silly *entrées* and made dishes
 Were never intended for us.
No footman in lace and in ruffles
 Need dangle behind my arm-chair ;
And never mind seeking for truffles,
 Although they be ever so rare.

But a plain leg of mutton, my Lucy,
 I pr'ythee get ready at three :
Have it smoking, and tender, and juicy,
 And what better meat can there be ?
And when it has feasted the master,
 'Twill amply suffice for the maid :
Meanwhile I will smoke my canaster,
 And tipple my ale in the shade.

[1] [From *Memorials of Gormandising.*]

BE HAPPY AND THY COUNSEL KEEP.

' Est et fideli tuta silentio
Merces.   Vetabo qui Cereris sacrum
Vulgarit arcanae, sub iisdem
Sit trabibus, fragilemve mecum
Solvat phaselum.'

Be happy, and thy counsel keep,
  'Tis thus the bard adviseth thee ;
Remember that the silent lip
  In silence shall rewarded be.
And fly the wretch who dares to strip
  Love of its sacred mystery.
My loyal legs I would not stretch
  Beneath the same mahogany ;
Nor trust myself in Chelsea Reach,
  In punt or skiff, with such as he.
The villain who would kiss and peach,
  I hold him for mine enemy !

LOVE SONGS MADE EASY.

LOVE SONGS MADE EASY.[1]

OULD our readers ever forget the writings of our friend the Stout Contributor, there would be a necessity to remind them of that singular and erratic young poet's propensity to fall in love.

Few men, in fact, have gone through life without several attacks of that delightful fever. Some people (and they are not worth a fig) never feel it. Some fellows only have it once, like the small-pox, and very bad. Others are continually suffering under little attacks—and our friend was of the number. He never was *very* much hurt; but he always made a more prodigious noise and groaning when he was taken ill than a whole hospital of patients would do. Sometimes he was delirious—often violent. More than once he had the complicated form of the disease (that in which a man is heart-smitten by two or three women at once); once he was actually so ill that he couldn't eat any dinner, but it was in very early youth, and he owns that he made an uncommonly good supper at night. In fine, our Stout Friend was an inflammable and sentimental man.

When he went abroad last—to join GENERAL TAYLOR in Mexico—the F. C. left us a bundle of MSS. on various scraps of paper, and in different stages of his hand-writing. They were tied up with an old piece of pink ribbon, and entitled 'Passion Flowers'; they are signed FREDERICK CHUMLEIGH, FERDINAND CAVENDISH, FRANK CHESTERFIELD, FULKE CADOGAN, FITZROY CLARENCE (all names with the initials F. C., which in fact are his own, and which led us humorously to call him the Fat

[1] [*Punch*, March 6, 1847.]

Contributor).   His real name we are not at liberty to divulge
until his death, which he states is very near.

As these love verses are in all sorts of styles—and as the *Blind
God* (if we may be permitted the expression) is a favourite among
the younger readers of *Punch*, who may find every now and then
remarks suited to their *peculiar circumstances* in the lyrics of our
most sentimental friend—we shall from time to time print a few
of his verses.

Here are a set which may be considered a pretty fair specimen
of the Genteel or May Fair Love Song.

WHAT MAKES MY HEART TO THRILL AND GLOW?

Song by Fitzroy Clarence.

WINTER and summer, night and morn,
 I languish at this table dark ;
My office window has a corn-
 er looks into St. James's Park.
I hear the foot-guards' bugle horn,
 Their tramp upon parade I mark ;
I am a gentleman forlorn,
 I am a Foreign Office Clerk.

My toils, my pleasures, every one,
 I find are stale, and dull, and slow ;
And yesterday, when work was done,
 I felt myself so sad and low,
I could have seized a sentry's gun
 My wearied brains out out to blow.
What is it makes my blood to run ?
 What makes my heart to beat and glow ?

My notes of hand are burnt perhaps ?
 Some one has paid my tailor's bill ?
No ; every morn the tailor raps ;
 My I.O.U.'s are extant still.
I still am prey of debt and dun,
 My elder brother's stout and well.
What is it makes my blood to run,
 What makes my heart to glow and swell ?

I know my chief's distrust and hate;
    He says I'm lazy, and I shirk.
Ah! had I genius like the late
    Right Honourable Edmund Burke.
My chance of all promotion's gone,
    I know it is—he hates me so.
What is it makes my blood to run,
    And all my heart to swell and glow?

Why, why is all so bright and gay?
    There is no change, there is no cause;
My office-time I found to-day
    Disgusting as it ever was.
At three I went and tried the clubs,
    And yawned and sauntered to and fro;
And now my heart jumps up and throbs,
    And all my soul is in a glow.

At half-past four I had the cab;
    I drove as hard as I could do.
The London sky was dirty drab,
    And dirty brown the London snow.
And as I rattled in a cant-
    er down by dear, old Bolton Row,
A something made my heart to pant,
    And caused my cheek to flush and glow.

What could it be that made me find
    Old Jawkins pleasant at the club?
Why was it that I laughed and grinned
    At whist although I lost the rub?
What was it made me drink like mad
    Thirteen small glasses of Curaco?
That made my inmost heart so glad,
    And every fibre thrill and glow?

She's home again! she's home, she's home!
    Away all cares and griefs and pain;
I knew she would—she's back from Rome;
    She's home again! she's home again!
'The family's gone abroad,' they said,
    September last—they told me so;
Since then my lonely heart is dead,
    My blood I think's forgot to flow.

She's home again ! away all care !
  O, fairest form the world can show !
O, beaming eyes ! O, golden hair !
  O, tender voice, that breathes so low !
O, gentlest, softest, purest heart !
  O, joy, O, hope !—'My tiger, ho !'
Fitz-Clarence said ; we saw him start—
  He galloped down to Bolton Row.

Divested of the genteel, the circumstances of the above ballad
are as follow :—Our F. C. was not a 'Foreign-Office' Clerk, but
a Foreign Office-Clerk, in the service of Messrs. Todd and
Raddle, Turkey and Sponge Merchants, Tower Hill.   Hence
his military allusions, and his bitterness against his 'Chief,' Mr.
Raddle, acting partner, who, in fact, dismissed him for idleness
after three months.   The 'Clubs' he talks of were 'The Kidney'
held at the 'Cock and Woolpack,' Sweeting's Alley ; and 'The
Feast of Shells,' an Oyster Club at the Tobago Coffee House,
Monument Yard.   He *was* in debt a good deal at this time, and
has been, we believe, ever since.   The young lady in question did
not live in *Bolton* Row, but in *Bunhill* Row, commanding the
City Artillery Ground.   She was a Miss Crowder, and he wrote
these lines on her return from *Gravesend*, not Rome.   Hearing of
his irregularities, Miss C. refused him, and is at present the
respected lady of a sugar-baker, *not a hundred miles from White-
chapel*.   Thus it is that there is always a portion of truth in the
poet's fictions, and that he invests with romance and splendour
the circumstances of common life.

LOVE SONGS OF THE FAT CONTRIBUTOR.

THE DOMESTIC LOVE SONG.[1]

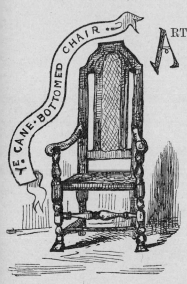

ARTICLES of furniture are deservedly favourite subjects with domestic poets; witness those celebrated verses, 'My uncle's old hat,' 'My grandmother's muff,' 'My ancestor's coal-scuttle,' etc., by MISS BUNION and other poetesses, which have taken such a strong hold on the affections of the public. Our stout friend evidently knew the value of furniture when he composed the following lyric. It is crammed full of goods, like a broker's shop, and has a touching and domestic pathos, which contrasts agreeably with the May Fair swagger of the poem we printed a fortnight since.

The circumstances of the poem are these — The Contributor, then lodging in Bidborough Street, Burton Crescent, had received a present of shrimps from a kind friend at Gravesend, and asked his landlady, MRS. RUNT, and her daughter to breakfast, when the young lady not only sate in the 'cane-bottomed chair,' but broke it. The little affair of the chair happened many years ago, and our friend has long quitted MRS. RUNT's apartments; he says it was despair in love that tore him thence, for he entertained a

[1] [*Punch*, March 27, 1847.]

165

violent passion for MISS R., as usual ; but her excellent mother persists that it was irregularity of rent-payments which caused the *serious* difference with her lodger.

Nor could a young man in impoverished circumstances, as the C. then was, expect much better treatment at the hands of MISS R. That young lady was virtuously attached to the first-floor, LIEUTENANT BONG of the Bombay Artillery, whom she married, and, as MRS. CAPTAIN BONG, is the happy mother of a very large family.

As for her spirit revisiting the Contributor's arm-chair, that is all bosh. People don't sit on it, but for the reason of breakage above stated ; and poems of later dates, 'To IANTHE,' 'To ZULEIKA,' 'To AURELIA,' etc., show that the rogue was not more inconsolable about other disappointments than about this one. Of course he makes the most of his feelings ; every poet does ; a true poet howls if he is pricked with a pin, as much as an ordinary man who got three dozen :—that is the beauty of poetic sensibility.

In tattered old slippers that toast at the bars,
And a ragged old jacket perfumed with cigars,
Away from the world and its toils and its cares,
I've a snug little kingdom up four pair of stairs.

To mount to this realm is a toil, to be sure,
But the fire there is bright and the air rather pure ;
And the view I behold on a sunshiny day
Is grand through the chimney-pots over the way.

This snug little chamber is crammed in all nooks,
With worthless old knicknacks and silly old books,
And foolish old odds and foolish old ends,
Cracked bargains from brokers, cheap keepsakes from friends.

Old armour, prints, pictures, pipes, china (all cracked),
Old rickety tables, and chairs broken-backed ;
A twopenny treasury, wondrous to see ;
What matter ? 'tis pleasant to you, friend, and me.

No better divan need the Sultan require
Than the creaking old sofa that basks by the fire ;
And 'tis wonderful, surely, what music you get
From the rickety, ramshackle, wheezy spinet.

That praying-rug came from a Turcoman's camp ;
By Tiber once twinkled that brazen old lamp ;
A Mameluke fierce yonder dagger has drawn :
'Tis a murderous knife to toast muffins upon.

Long long through the hours, and the night, and the chimes,
Here we talk of old books, and old friends, and old times ;
As we sit in a fog made of rich Latakie
This chamber is pleasant to you, friend, and me.

But of all the cheap treasures that garnish my nest,
There's one that I love and I cherish the best ;
For the finest of couches that's padded with hair
I never would change thee, my cane-bottomed chair.

'Tis a bandy-legged, high-shouldered, worm-eaten seat,
With a creaking old back, and twisted old feet ;
But since the fair morning when FANNY sat there,
I bless thee and love thee, old cane-bottomed chair.

If chairs have but feeling in holding such charms,
A thrill must have passed through your withered old arms !
I looked, and I longed, and I wished in despair ;
I wished myself turned to a cane-bottomed chair.

It was but a moment she sat in this place,
She'd a scarf on her neck, and a smile on her face !
A smile on her face, and a rose in her hair,
And she sate there, and bloomed in my cane-bottomed chair.

And so I have valued my chair ever since,
Like the shrine of a saint, or the throne of a prince ;
Saint FANNY, my patroness sweet I declare,
The queen of my heart and my cane-bottomed chair.

When the candles burn low, and the company's gone,
In the silence of night as I sit here alone—
I sit here alone, but we yet are a pair—
My FANNY I see in my cane-bottomed chair.

She comes from the past and revisits my room ;
She looks as she then did, all beauty and bloom,
So smiling and tender, so fresh and so fair,
And yonder she sits in my cane-bottomed chair.

THE GHAZUL, OR ORIENTAL LOVE-SONG.[1]

LYRICAL composition of almost every kind has been tried by our F. F., and it cannot be supposed that he should have practised so much without essaying the Oriental style of verse. Here are three specimens of his Eastern poems, from a large collection called by their gifted author, ' Draughts of Sherbet.'

His own account of the verses is as follows :—

1. THE ROCKS. This song is anterior to the times of Antar, and almost as popular among the tribes of the Lebanon as any chronicle of the indomitable lover of Ibla. I learned it in the

[1] [*Punch.* June 5, 1847.]

Seven Towers, Constantinople, from young BUKSHEESH BEY, a prisoner there along with his uncle, the ill-fated EMEER BESHEER. Sung to a guzla, and to a wild and plaintive air, the Antelope never failed to bring tears into the eyes of the Emeer's attendants. I regret not having noted the music.

2. THE MERRY BARD is the celebrated or rather notorious little KARA GUROO, the cobbler, philosopher, and bell-ringer at the mosque of SULTAN ACHMET. His *mots* are repeated all over Constantinople, and he is to be found at the Greek wine-houses, pretty regularly of an evening, with a dulcimer and a jar of wine beside him, tippling and singing verses of an epicurean and amatory tendency. 'The Little Brown Bulbul' is the name by which he is known in his quarter, where I was introduced to him by another delightful poet — I mean M. DE TITOFF, of the Russian Embassy.

3. THE CAICJKEE. This is a favourite song of His Highness ABD-UL-MEDJEED. I composed it (in the Turkish language, with which I am pretty familiar) on a melancholy occasion, of which I forbear to speak. The fate of the LEILAH of the song is well known. The REVEREND G——E BR——N, of the American Mission at Pera, has in his possession the sack in which the lovely and unfortunate Georgian girl was found floating in the Bosphorus. I have never been the same man since.

Such is our friend's explanation ; not one word of which, it gives us great pain to say, do we believe.

THE ROCKS.

> I was a timid little antelope ;
> My home was in the rocks, the lonely rocks.

> I saw the hunters scouring on the plain ;
> I lived among the rocks, the lonely rocks.

> I was a-thirsty in the summer-heat ;
> I ventured to the tents beneath the rocks.

> ZULEIKAH brought me water from the well ;
> Since then I have been faithless to the rocks.

> I saw her face reflected in the well ;
> Her camels since have marched into the rocks.

> I look to see her image in the well ;
> I only see my eyes, my own sad eyes.
> My mother is alone among the rocks.

The Merry Bard.

Zuleikah! The young Agas in the bazaar are slim-waisted and wear yellow slippers. I am old and hideous. One of my eyes is out, and the hairs of my beard are mostly grey. Praise be to Allah! I am a merry bard.

There is a bird upon the terrace of the Emir's chief wife. Praise be to Allah! He has emeralds on his neck, and a ruby tail. I am a merry bard. He deafens me with his diabolical screaming.

There is a little brown bird in the basket-maker's cage. Praise be to Allah! He ravishes my soul in the moonlight. I am a merry bard.

The peacock is an Aga, but the little bird is a Bulbul.

I am a little brown Bulbul. Come and listen in the moonlight. Praise be to Allah! I am a merry bard.

The Caïque.

Yonder to the kiosk, beside the creek,
Paddle the swift caïque.
Thou brawny oarsman with the sun-burnt cheek,
Quick! for it soothes my heart to hear the Bulbul speak.

Ferry me quickly to the Asian shores,
Swift bending to your oars.
Beneath the melancholy sycamores,
Hark! what a ravishing note the love-lorn Bulbul pours.

Behold, the boughs seem quivering with delight,
The stars themselves more bright,
As 'mid the waving branches out of sight
The Lover of the Rose sits singing through the night.

Under the boughs I sat and listened still,
I could not have my fill.
'How comes,' I said, 'such music to his bill?
Tell me for whom he sings so beautiful a trill.'

'Once I was dumb,' then did the Bird disclose,
'But looked upon the Rose;
And in the garden where the loved one grows,
I straightway did begin sweet music to compose.'

'O bird of song, there's one in this caïque
The Rose would also seek,
So he might learn like you to love and speak.'
Then answered me the bird of dusky beak,
'The Rose, the Rose of Love blushes on LEILAH'S cheek.

GHAZUL TO THE HOURI CHAI-REE-TOH.[1]

FAIR as the moon, when on tall cedar-trees brightly gleaming,
Houri, art thou, when upon mortals so gladly beaming.
When the seba[2] stirs thy locks, Houri, they are more fragrant
Than the young rose, or the musk, which with its sweets is
    teeming.
No ; not the rays by Zahrah[3] cast from the skies of evening
Are as the light from the black eyes of the Houri streaming.
And when she smiles, on her lips joys without end are dwelling ;
Joys which she sheds on the faithful, and the Giaour blaspheming.
Sunn'd by thy smile, Houri fair, oh ! I would live for ever,
For I should feel life was past, Paradise present seeming.
Sorrows and cares, haste away, quick, to the halls of Eblis ;
Haste where the Goule foully dwells, where evil Djins are
    screaming.
Here[4] would I bask, free from care, gazing upon the Houri,
And when I leave, still would I be of the Houri dreaming.

TO MARY.[5]

I SEEM, in the midst of the crowd,
    The lightest of all ;
My laughter rings cheery and loud,
    In banquet and ball.
My lip hath its smiles and its sneers,
    For all men to see ;
But my soul, and my truth, and my tears
    Are for thee, are for thee !

Around me they flatter and fawn—
    The young and the old,
The fairest are ready to pawn
    Their hearts for my gold.
They sue me—I laugh as I spurn
    The slaves at my knee,
But in faith, and in fondness, I turn
    Unto thee, unto thee !

[1] [From *A Second Turkish Letter concerning the Divertissement* ' *Les Houris*.']

[2] The Zephyr. Dragoman.   [3] The planet Venus. D.

[4] I presume by ' here ' he means his box or stall.

[5] [From *The Snobs of England*.]

Away ! for my heart knows no rest
   Since you taught it to feel ;
The secret must die in my breast
   I burn to reveal ;
The passion I may not . . .

NOW THE TOILS OF DAY ARE OVER.[1]

(Serenade.)

Now the toils of day are over,
   And the sun hath sunk to rest,
Seeking, like a fiery lover,
   The bosom of the blushing West—

The faithful night keeps watch and ward,
   Raising the moon, her silver shield,
And summoning the stars to guard
   The slumbers of my fair Mathilde !

The faithful night !   Now all things lie
   Hid by her mantle dark and dim,
In pious hope I hither hie,
   And humbly chaunt mine ev'ning hymn.

Thou art my prayer, my saint, my shrine !
   (For never holy pilgrim kneel'd
Or wept at feet more pure than thine)
   My virgin love, my sweet Mathilde !

RONSARD TO HIS MISTRESS.[2]

'*Quand vous serez bien vieille, au soir à la chandelle*
   Assise auprès du feu devisant et filant
   Direz, chantant mes vers en vous esmerveillant :
Ronsard me célébroit du temps que j'étois belle.'

Some winter night, shut snugly in,
   Beside the fagot in the hall,
I think I see you sit and spin,
   Surrounded by your maidens all.

---

[1] [From *The Devil's Wager*.]
[2] [*Fraser's Magazine*, January 1846.]

Old tales are told, old songs are sung,
   Old days come back to memory ;
You say, ' When I was fair and young,
   A poet sang of me ! '

There's not a maiden in your hall,
   Though tired and sleepy ever so,
But wakes as you my name recall,
   And longs the history to know.
And as the piteous tale is said,
   Of lady cold and lover true,
Each, musing, carries it to bed,
   And sighs and envies you !

' Our lady's old and feeble now,'
   They'll say ; ' she once was fresh and fair,
And yet she spurned her lover's vow,
   And heartless left him to despair ;
The lover lies in silent earth,
   No kindly mate the lady cheers ;
She sits beside a lonely hearth,
   With threescore and ten years ! '

Ah ! dreary thoughts and dreams are those,
   But wherefore yield me to despair,
While yet the poet's bosom glows,
   While yet the dame is peerless fair ?
Sweet lady mine ! while yet 'tis time,
   Requite my passion and my truth,
And gather in their blushing prime
   The roses of your youth !

ON THE LADY EMILY X——.[1]

*Who left dancing and came and talked to the poet at the déjeuner
at C—— Lodge.*

(MY NORA.)

BENEATH the gold acacia buds
My gentle Nora sits and broods,
Far, far away in Boston woods,
       My gentle Nora !

[1] [From *Fitz-Boodle's Professions.*]

I see the tear-drop in her e'e,
Her bosom's heaving tenderly ;
I know—I know she thinks of me,
   My darling Nora !

And where am I ? My love, whilst thou
Sitt'st sad beneath the acacia bough,
Where pearl's on neck and wreath on brow,
   I stand, my Nora !

'Mid carcanet and coronet,
Where joy-lamps shine and flowers are set—
Where England's chivalry are met,
   Behold me, Nora !

In this strange scene of revelry,
Amidst this gorgeous chivalry,
A form I saw, was like to thee,
   My love—my Nora !

She paused amidst her converse glad ;
The lady saw that I was sad,
She pitied the poor lonely lad,—
   Dost love her, Nora ?

In sooth, she is a lovely dame,
A lip of red, an eye of flame,
And clustering golden locks, the same !
   As thine, dear Nora !

Her glance is softer than the dawn's,
Her foot is lighter than the fawn's,
Her breast is whiter than the swan's,
   Or thine, my Nora !

Oh, gentle breast to pity me !
Oh, lovely Ladye Emily !
Till death—till death I'll think of thee—
   Of thee and Nora !

LYRA HYBERNICA.

THE PIMLICO PAVILION.[1]

BY THE MULLIGAN (OF KILBALLYMULLIGAN).

YE pathrons of janius, MINERVA, and VANIUS,
  Who sit on Parnassus, that mountain of snow,
Descind from your station and make observation
  Of the PRINCE'S Pavilion in sweet Pimlico.

This garden, by jakurs, is forty poor acres,
  (The garner he tould me, and sure ought to know ;)
And yet greatly bigger, in size and in figure,
  Than the Phanix itself, seems the Park Pimlico.

O 'tis there that the spoort is, when the QUEEN and the Coort is
  Walking magnanimous all of a rów,
Forgetful what state is among the pataties
  And the pine-apple gardens of sweet Pimlico.

There in blossoms odo'rous the birds sing a chorus,
  Of 'God save the QUEEN' as they hop to and fro ;
And you sit on the binches and hark to the finches,
  Singing melodious in sweet Pimlico.

There shuiting their phanthasies, they pluck polyanthuses
  That round in the gardens resplindently grow,
Wid roses and jessimins, and other sweet specimins,
  Would charm bould LINNAYUS in sweet Pimlico.

You see when you inther and stand in the cinther,
  Where the roses, and necturns, and collyflowers blow,
A hill so tremindous it tops the top-windows
  Of the elegant houses of famed Pimlico.

[1] [*Punch*, August 9, 1845.]

And when you've ascinded that precipice splindid
    You see on its summit a wondtherful show—
A lovely Swish building, all painting and gilding,
    The famous Pavilion of sweet Pimlico.

PRINCE ALBERT, of Flandthers, that Prince of Commandthers,
    (On whom my best blessings hereby I bestow,)
With goold and vermilion has decked that Pavilion,
    Where the QUEEN may take tay in her sweet Pimlico.

There's lines from JOHN MILTON the chamber all gilt on,
    And pictures beneath them that's shaped like a bow ;
I was greatly astounded to think that that Roundhead
    Should find an admission to famed Pimlico.

O lovely's each fresco, and most picturesque O,
    And while round the chamber astonished I go,
I think DAN MACLISE's it baits all the pieces,
    Surrounding the cottage of famed Pimlico.

EASTLAKE has the chimney (a good one to limn he),
    And a vargin he paints with a sarpent below ;
While bulls, pigs, and panthers, and other enchanthers,
    Is painted by LANDSEER in sweet Pimlico.

And nature smiles opposite, STANFIELD he copies it ;
    O'er CLAUDE or POUSSANG sure 'tis he that may crow :
But SIR ROSS's best faiture, is small mini-áture—
    He shouldn't paint frescoes in famed Pimlico.

There's LESLIE and UWINS has rather small doings ;
    There's DICE, as brave masther as England can show ;
And the flowers and the sthrawberries, sure he no dauber is,
    That painted the pannels of famed Pimlico !

In the pictures from WALTHER SCOTT, never a fault there's got,
    Sure the marble's as natural as thrue Scaglio ;
And the Chamber Pompayen is sweet to take tay in,
    And ait butther'd muffins in sweet Pimlico.

There's landscapes by GRUNER, both solar and lunar,
    Them two little DOYLES, too, deserve a bravo ;
Wid de piece by young TOWNSEND (for janius abounds in't) ;
    And that's why he's shuited to paint Pimlico.

That picture of SEVERN's is worthy of rever'nce,
 But some I won't mintion is rather so so;
For sweet philoso'phy, or crumpets and coffee,
 O where's a Pavilion like sweet Pimlico?

O to praise this Pavilion would puzzle QUINTILIAN,
 DAYMOSTHENES, BROUGHAM, or young CICERO;
So, heavenly Goddess, d'ye pardon my modesty,
 And silence my lyre! about sweet Pimlico.

THE BATTLE OF LIMERICK.[1]

YE Genii of the nation,
 Who look with veneration,
And Ireland's desolation onsaysingly deplore;
 Ye sons of GENERAL JACKSON,
 Who thrample on the Saxon,
Attend to the thransaction upon Shannon shore.

When WILLIAM, Duke of Schumbug,
 A tyrant and a humbug,
With cannon and with thunder on our city bore,
 Our fortitude and valiance
 Insthructed his battalions
To rispict the galliant Irish upon Shannon shore.

Since that capitulation,
 No city in this nation
So grand a reputation could boast before,
 As Limerick prodigious,
 That stands with quays and bridges,
And the ships up to the windies of the Shannon shore.

A chief of ancient line,
 'Tis WILLIAM SMITH O'BRINE,
Reprisints this darling Limerick, this ten years or more:
 O the Saxons can't endure
 To see him on the flure,
And thrimble at the CICERO from Shannon shore!

   [1] [*Punch*, May 13, 1848.]

This valiant son of MARS
Had been to visit Par's,
That land of Revolution, that grows the tricolor ;
And to welcome his return
From pilgrimages furren,
We invited him to tay on the Shannon shore.

Then we summoned to our board
Young MEAGHER of the sword :
'Tis he will sheathe that battle-axe in Saxon gore ;
And MITCHIL of Belfast,
We bade to our repast,
To dthrink a dish of coffee on the Shannon shore.

Convaniently to hould
These patriots so bould,
We tuck the opportunity of TIM DOOLAN's store ;
And with ornamints and banners
(As becomes gintale good manners)
We made the loveliest tay-room upon Shannon shore.

'Twould binifit your sowls,
To see the butthered rowls,
The sugar-tongs and sangwidges and craim galore,
And the muffins and the crumpets,
And the band of harps and thrumpets,
To celebrate the sworry upon Shannon shore.

Sure the Imperor of Bohay
Would be proud to dthrink the tay
That MISTHRESS BIDDY ROONEY for O'BRINE did pour :
And, since the days of STRONGBOW,
There never was such Congo—
MITCHIL dthrank six quarts of it—by Shannon shore.

But CLARNDON and CORRY
CONNELLANN beheld this sworry
With rage and imulation in their black hearts' core ;
And they hired a gang of ruffins
To interrupt the muffins,
And the fragrance of the Congo on the Shannon shore.

When full of tay and cake,
O'BRINE began to spake,

But juice a one could hear him, for a sudden roar
      Of a ragamuffin rout
      Began to yell and shout,
And frighten the propriety of Shannon shore.

      As SMITH O'BRINE harangued,
      They batthered and they banged :
TIM DOOLAN'S doors and windies, down they tore ;
      They smashed the lovely windies
      (Hung with muslin from the Indies),
Purshuing of their shindies upon Shannon shore.

      With throwing of brickbats,
      Drowned puppies, and dead rats,
These ruffin democrats themselves did lower ;
      Tin kettles, rotten eggs,
      Cabbage stalks, and wooden legs,
They flung among the patriots of Shannon shore.

      O the girls began to scrame,
      And upset the milk and crame ;
And the honourable gintlemin, they cursed and swore :
      And MITCHIL of Belfast,
      'Twas he that looked aghast,
When they roasted him in effigy by Shannon shore.

      O the lovely tay was spilt
      On that day of Ireland's guilt ;
Says JACK MITCHIL, 'I am kilt ! Boys, where's the back door ?
      'Tis a national disgrace ;
      Let me go and veil me face ' ;
And he boulted with quick pace from the Shannon shore.

      ' Cut down the bloody horde ! '
      Says MEAGHER of the sword,
' This conduct would disgrace any blackamoor ' ;
      But the best use TOMMY made
      Of his famous battle blade
Was to cut his own stick from the Shannon shore.

      Immortal SMITH O'BRINE
      Was raging like a line ;
'Twould have done your sowl good to have heard him roar ;
      In his glory he arose,
      And he rushed upon his foes,
But they hit him on the nose by the Shannon shore.

Then the Futt and the Dthragoons
In squadthrons and platoons,
With their music playing chunes, down upon us bore ;
And they bate the rattatoo,
But the Peelers came in view,
And ended the shaloo on the Shannon shore.

MR. FINIGAN'S LAMENT.[1]

(MOLONY'S LAMENT.)

THE following Poem, upon an event which at present
occupies much of the public attention in Ireland, has
been sent to us by a gentleman connected with the
Knife Board of Dublin Castle :—

O Tim, did you hear of thim Saxons,
    And read what the peepers repoort ?
They're goan to recal the Liftinant,
    And shut up the Castle and Coort !
Our desolate counthry of Oireland,
    They're bint, the blagyards, to desthroy,
And now having murdthered our counthry,
    They're goin to kill the Viceroy,
            Deay boy ;
        'Twas he was our proide and our joy !

And will we no longer behould him,
    Surrounding his carriage in throngs,
As he weaves his cocked-hat from the windies,
    And smiles to his bould aide-de-congs ?
I liked for to see the young haroes,
    All shoining with sthripes and with stars,
A horsing about in the Phaynix,
    And winking the girls in the cyars,
            Like Mars,
        A smokin' their poipes and cigyars.

Dear MITCHELL exoiled to Bermudies,
    Your beautiful oilids you'll ope,
And there'll be an abondance of croyin
    From O'BRINE at the Keep of Good Hope,

[1] [*Punch*, March 23, 1850.]
[The Earl of Clarendon was Lord Lieutenant.]

When they read of this news in the peepers,
    Acrass the Atlantical wave,
That the last of the Oirish Liftinints
    Of the oisland of Seents has tuck lave.
        God save
    The QUEEN—she should betther behave.

And what's to become of poor Dame Sthreet,
    And who'll ait the puffs and the tarts,
Whin the Coort of imparial splindor
    From Doblin's sad city departs ?
And who'll have the fiddlers and pipers,
    When the deuce of a Coort there remains ;
And where'll be the bucks and the ladies,
    To hire the Coort-shuits and the thrains ?
        In sthrains,
    It's thus that ould Erin complains !

There's COUNSELLOR FLANAGAN's leedy,
    'Twas she in the Coort didn't fail,
And she wanted a plinty of popplin,
    For her dthress, and her flounce, and her tail ;
She bought it of MISTHRESS O'GRADY,
    Eight shillings a yard tabinet,
But now that the Coort is concluded,
    The divvle a yard will she get ;
        I bet,
    Bedad, that she wears the old set.

There's SURGEON O'TOOLE and MISS LEARY,
    They'd daylings at MADAM O'RIGGS' ;
Each year at the dthrawing-room sayson,
    They mounted the neatest of wigs.
When Spring, with its buds and its daisies,
    Comes out in her beauty and bloom,
Thim tu'll never think of new jaisies,
    Because there is no dthrawing-room,
        For whom
    They'd choose the expence to ashume.

There's ALDERMAN TOAD and his lady,
    'Twas they gave the Clart and the Poort,
And the poine-apples, turbots, and lobsters,
    To feast the Lord Liftinint's Coort ;

But now that the quality's goin,
   I warnt that the aiting will stop,
And you'll get at the Alderman's teeble
   The devil a bite or a dthrop,
      Or chop,
   And the butcher may shut up his shop.

Yes, the grooms and the ushers are goin,
   And his Lordship, the dear honest man,
And the Duchess, his eemiable leedy,
   And CORRY, the bould Connellan,
And little LORD HYDE, and the childthren,
   And the Chewter and Governess tu ;
And the servants are packing their boxes,—
   Oh, murther, but what shall I due
      Without you ?
   O MEERY, with oi's of the blue !

MR. MOLONY'S ACCOUNT OF THE BALL GIVEN TO THE NEPAULESE AMBASSADOR BY THE PENINSULAR AND ORIENTAL COMPANY.[1]

O WILL ye choose to hear the news,
   Bedad I cannot pass it o'er :
I'll tell you all about the Ball
   To the Naypaulase Ambassador.
Begor ! this *fête* all balls does bate
   At which I wore a pump, and I
Must here relate the splendthor great
   Of th' Oriental Company.

These men of sinse dispoised expinse
   To fete these black ACHILLESES.
' We'll show the blacks,' says they, ' Almack's
   And take the rooms at Willis's.'
With flags and shawls for these Nepauls,
   They hung the rooms of Willis up,
And decked the walls, and stairs and halls,
   With roses and with lilies up.

[1] [*Punch*, August 3, 1850.]

And JULLIEN's band, it tuck its stand,
  So sweetly in the middle there,
And soft bassoons played heavenly chunes,
  And violins did fiddle there.
And when the Coort was tired of spoort,
  I'd lave you, boys, to think there was,
A nate buffet before them set,
  Where lashins of good dhrink there was!

At ten before the ball-room door,
  His moighty Excellency was,
He smoiled and bowed to all the crowd,
  So gorgeous and immense he was.
His dusky shuit, sublime and mute,
  Into the doorway followed him ;
And O the noise of the blackguard boys,
  As they hurrood and hollowed him!

The noble Chair [1] stud at the stair,
  And bade the dthrums to thump ; and he
Did thus evince, to that Black Prince,
  The welcome of his Cumpany.
O fair the girls and rich the curls,
  And bright the oys, you saw there was ;
And fixed each oye, ye there could spoi,
  On GINERAL JUNG BAHAWTHER was!

This Gineral great then tuck his sate
  With all the other ginerals,
(Bedad his troat, his belt, his coat,
  All bleezed with precious minerals) ;
And as he there, with princely air,
  Recloinin on his cushion was,
All round about his royal chair
  The squeezin and the pushin was.

O PAT, such girls, such Jukes, and Earls,
  Such fashion and nobilitee !
Just think of TIM and fancy him,
  Amidst the hoigh gentility !

[1] JAMES MATHESON, ESQUIRE, to whom, and the Board of Directors of the Peninsular and Oriental Company, I, TIMOTHEUS MALONY, late stoker on board the 'Iberia,' the 'Lady Mary Wood,' the 'Tagus,' and the Oriental steam ships, humbly dedicate this production of my grateful muse.

There was LORD DE L'HUYS, and the Portygeese
    Ministher and his lady there,
And I reckonised, with much surprise,
    Our messmate, BOB O'GRADY, there;

There was BARONESS BRUNOW, that looked like JUNO,
    And BARONESS REHAUSEN there,
And COUNTESS ROULLIER, that looked peculiar
    Well, in her robes of gauze in there.
There was LORD CROWHURST (I knew him first,
    When only MR. PIPS he was),
And MICK O'TOOLE, the great big fool,
    That after supper tipsy was.

There was LORD FINGALL, and his ladies all,
    And LORDS KILLEEN and DUFFERIN,
And PADDY FIFE, with his fat wife;
    I wondther how he could stuff her in.
There was LORD BELFAST, that by me past,
    And seemed to ask how should *I* go there?
And the WIDOW MACRAE, and LORD A. HAY,
    And the MARCHIONESS OF SLIGO there.

Yes, Jukes and Earls, and diamonds and pearls,
    And pretty girls, was spoorting there;
And some beside (the rogues!) I spied
    Behind the windies, coorting there.
O, there's one I know bedad would show
    As beautiful as any there,
And I'd like to hear the pipers blow,
    And shake a fut with FANNY there!

MR. MOLONY'S ACCOUNT OF THE CRYSTAL PALACE.[1]

WITH ganial foire
Thransfuse me loyre,
Ye sacred nymphs of Pindus,
The whoile I sing
That wondthrous thing,
The Palace made o' windows!

[1] [*Punch*, April 26, 1851.]

Say, PAXTON, truth,
Thou wondthrous youth,
What sthroke of art celistial,
What power was lint
You to invint
This combineetion cristial.

O would before
That THOMAS MOORE,
Likewise the late LORD BOYRON,
Thim aigles sthrong
Of godlike song,
Cast oi on that cast oiron !

And saw thim walls,
And glittering halls,
Thim rising slendther columns,
Which I, poor pote,
Could not denote,
No, not in twinty vollums.

My Muse's words
Is like the birds
That roosts beneath the panes there ;
Her wings she spolls
'Gainst them bright iles,
And cracks her silly brains there.

This Palace tall,
This Cristial Hall,
Which Imperors might covet,
Stands in High Park
Like Noah's Ark,
A rainbow bint above it.

The towers and fanes,
In other scaynes,
The fame of this will undo,
Saint Paul's big doom,
Saint Payther's Room,
And Dublin's proud Rotundo.

'Tis here that roams,
As well becomes

Her dignitee and stations,
    VICTORIA Great,
    And houlds in state
The Congress of the Nations.

    Her subjects pours
    From distant shores,
Her Injians and Canajians ;
    And also we,
    Her kingdoms three,
Attind with our allagiance.

    Here come likewise
    Her bould allies,
Both Asian and Europian ;
    From East and West
    They send their best
To fill her Coornucopean.

    I seen (thank Grace !)
    This wondthrous place
(His Noble Honour MISTHER
    H. COLE it was
    That gave the pass
And let me see what is there).

    With conscious proide
    I stud insoide
And looked the World's Great Fair in,
    Until me sight
    Was dazzled quite,
And couldn't see for staring.

    There's holy saints
    And window paints,
By Maydiayval Pugin ;
    Alhamborough JONES
    Did paint the tones
Of yellow and gambouge in.

    There's fountains there
    And crosses fair ;
There's water-gods with urrns ;
    There's organs three
    To play, d'ye see,
' God save the QUEEN,' by turrns.

There's Statues bright
Of marble white,
Of silver, and of copper ;
And some in zinc,
And some, I think,
That isn't over proper.

There's staym Ingynes,
That stands in lines,
Enormous and amazing,
That squeal and snort
Like whales in sport,
Or elephants a-grazing.

There's carts and gigs,
And pins for pigs ;
There's dibblers and there's harrows,
And ploughs like toys
For little boys,
And elegant wheel-barrows.

For them genteels
Who ride on wheels,
There's plenty to indulge 'em ;
There's Droskys snug
From Paytersbug
And vayhcles from Bulgium.

There's Cabs on Stands
And Shandthry-danns ;
There's Waggons from New York here ;
There's Lapland Sleighs
Have crossed the seas,
And Jaunting Cyars from Cork here.

Amazed I pass
From glass to glass
Deloigted I survey 'em ;
Fresh wondthers grows
Before me nose
In this sublime Musayum !

Look, here's a fan
From far Japan,

A sabre from Damasco ;
　　There's shawls ye get
　　From far Thibet,
And cotton prints from Glasgow.

　　There's German flutes,
　　Marocky boots,
And Naples Macaronies ;
　　Bohaymia
　　Has sent Bohay ;
Polonia her polonies.

　　There's granite flints
　　That's quite imminse,
There's sacks of coals and fuels,
　　There's swords and guns,
　　And soap in tuns,
And Ginger-bread and Jewels.

　　There's taypots there,
　　And cannons rare ;
There's coffins filled with roses ;
　　There's canvass tints,
　　Teeth insthrumints,
And shuits of clothes by MOSES.

　　There's lashins more
　　Of things in store,
But thim I don't remimber ;
　　Nor could disclose
　　Did I compose
From May time to Novimber !

　　Ah, JUDY thrue !
　　With eyes so blue,
That you were here to view it !—
　　And could I screw
　　But tu pound tu,
'Tis I would thrait you to it !

　　So let us raise
　　VICTORIA's praise,
And ALBERT's proud condition,
　　That takes his ayse
　　As he surveys
This Cristial Exhibition.

THE LAST IRISH GRIEVANCE.[1]

ON reading of the general indignation occasioned in Ireland by the appointment of a Scotch Professor to one of HER MAJESTY'S Godless Colleges, MASTER MOLLOY MOLONY, brother of THADDEUS MOLONY, ESQ., of the Temple, a youth only fifteen years of age, dashed off the following spirited lines :—

As I think of the insult that's
    done to this nation,
Red tears of rivinge from
    me faytures I wash,
And uphold in this pome,
    to the world's daytista-
    tion,
The sleeves that appointed PROFESSOR M'COSH.

I look round me counthree, renowned by exparience,
    And see, midst her childthren, the witty, the wise,—
Whole hayps of logicians, potes, schollars, grammarians,
    All ayger for pleeces, all panting to rise.

I gaze round the world in its utmost diminsion ;
    LARD JAHN and his minions in Council I ask,
Was there ever a Government-pleece (with a pinsion)
    But children of Erin were fit for that task ?

What, Erin beloved, is thy fetal condition ?
    What shame in aych boosom must rankle and burrun,
To think that our countree has ne'er a logician
    In the hour of her deenger will surrev her turrun !

On the logic of Saxons there's little reliance,
    And, rather from Saxons than gather its rules,
I'd stamp under feet the base book of his science,
    And spit on his chair as he taught in the schools !

[1] [*Punch*, November 22, 1851.]

O, False SIR JOHN KANE! is it thus that you praych me?
  I think all your Queen's Universitees Bosh;
And if you've no neetive Professor to taych me,
  I scawurn to be learned by the Saxon M'COSH.

There's WISEMAN, and CHUME, and His Grace the Lord Primate,
  That sinds round the box, and the world will subscribe;
'Tis they'll build a College that's fit for our climate,
  And taych me the saycrets I burn to imboibe!

'Tis there as a Student of Science I'll enther,
  Fair Fountain of Knowledge, of Joy, and Contint!
SAINT PATHRICK'S sweet Statue shall stand in the centher,
  And wink his dear oi every day during Lint.

And good DOCTOR NEWMAN, that praycher unwary,
  'Tis he shall preside the Academee School,
And quit the gay robe of ST. PHILIP of Neri,
  To wield the soft rod of ST. LAWRENCE O'TOOLE!

THE ROSE OF FLORA.[1]

*Sent by a Young Gentleman of Quality to Miss Br—dy, of
Castle Brady.*

ON Brady's tower there grows a flower,
  It is the loveliest flower that blows,—
At Castle Brady there lives a lady,
  (And how I love her no one knows);
Her name is Nora, and the goddess Flora
  Presents her with this blooming rose.

'O Lady Nora,' says the goddess Flora,
  'I've many a rich and bright parterre;
In Brady's towers there's seven more flowers,
  But you're the fairest lady there:
Not all the county, nor Ireland's bounty,
  Can projuice a treasure that's half so fair!'

What cheek is redder? sure roses fed her!
  Her hair is maregolds, and her eye of blew,

[1] [From *The Luck of Barry Lyndon.*]

Beneath her eyelid is like the vi'let,
  That darkly glistens with gentle jew !
The lily's nature is not surely whiter
  Than Nora's neck is,—and her arrums too.

'Come, gentle Nora,' says the goddess Flora,
  'My dearest creature, take my advice :
There is a poet, full well you know it,
  Who spends his lifetime in heavy sighs,—
Young Redmond Barry, 'tis him you'll marry,
  If rhyme and raisin you'd choose likewise.'

LARRY O'TOOLE.[1]

You've all heard of Larry O'Toole,
Of the beautiful town of Drumgoole ;
    He had but one eye,
    To ogle ye by—
O, murther, but that was a jew'l !
        A fool
He made of de girls, dis O'Toole.

'Twas he was the boy didn't fail,
That tuck down pataties and mail ;
    He never would shrink,
    From any sthrong drink,
Was it whisky or Drogheda ale ;
        I'm bail   ·
This Larry would swallow a pail.

O, many a night, at the bowl,
With Larry I've sot cheek by jowl ;
    He's gone to his rest,
    Where there's dthrink of the best,
And so let us give his old sowl
        A howl,
For 'twas he made the noggin to rowl.

[From *Phil Fogarty*.]

THE BALLADS OF POLICEMAN X.

A BOW STREET BALLAD.[1]

By a Gentleman of the Force.

(The Knight and the Lady.)

HERE'S in the Vest a city
    pleasant,
  To vich King Bladud
    gev his name,
And in that city there's a
    Crescent,
  Vere dwelt a noble knight
    of fame.

Although that galliant
    knight is oldish,
  Although Sir John as
    grey, grey air,
Hage has not made his
    busum coldish,
  His Art still beats
    tewodds the Fair!

'Twas two years sins, this knight so splendid,
  Peraps fateagued with Bath's routines,
To Paris towne his phootsteps bended
  In sutch of gayer folks and seans.

His and was free, his means was easy,
  A nobler, finer gent than he
Ne'er drove about the Shons-Eleesy,
  Or paced the Roo de Rivolee.

[1] [*Punch*, November 28, 1848.]
199

A brougham and pair SIR JOHN prowided,
    In which abroad he loved to ride ;
But ar ! he most of all enjyed it,
    Whon some one helse was sittin' inside !

That 'some one helse' a lovely dame was,
    Dear ladies, you will heasy tell—
COUNTESS GRABROWSKI her sweet name was,
    A noble title, ard to spell.

This faymus COUNTESS ad a daughter
    Of lovely form and tender art ;
A nobleman in marridge sought her,
    By name the BARON OF SAINT BART.

Their pashn touched the noble SIR JOHN,
    It was so pewer and profound ;
LADY GRABROWSKI he did urge on,
    With Hyming's wreeth their loves to crownd.

'O, come to Bath, to Lansdowne Crescent,'
    Says kind SIR JOHN ; 'and live with me ;
The living there's uncommon pleasant—
    I'm sure you'll find the hair agree.

'O, come to Bath, my fair GRABROWSKI,
    And bring your charming girl,' sezee ;
'The BARRING here shall have the ouse-key,
    Vith breakfast, dinner, lunch, and tea.

'And when they've passed an appy winter,
    Their opes and loves no more we'll bar ;
The marridge-vow they'll enter inter,
    And I at Church will be their Par.'

To Bath they went to Lansdowne Crescent,
    Where good SIR JOHN he did provide
No end of teas, and balls incessant,
    And hosses both to drive and ride.

He was so Ospitably busy,
    When Miss was late, he'd make so bold
Upstairs to call out, 'Missy, Missy,
    Come down, the coffy's getting cold !'

But O ! 'tis sadd to think such bounties
   Should meet with such return as this ;
O, BARRING OF SAINT BART, O COUNTESS
   GRABROWSKI, and O, cruel Miss !

He married you at Bath's fair Habby,
   SAINT BART he treated like a son—
And wasn't it uncommon shabby
   To do what you have went & done !

My trembling And amost refewses
   To write the charge which SIR JOHN swore,
Of which the COUNTESS he ecuses,
   Her daughter and her son in lore.

My Mews quite blushes as she sings of
   The fatle charge which now I quote :
He says Miss took his two best rings off,
   And pawned 'em for a tenpun note.

' Is this the child of honest parince,
   To make away with folk's best things ?
Is this, pray, like the wives of Barrins,
   To go and prig a gentleman's rings ? '

Thus thought SIR JOHN, by anger wrought on,
   And to rewenge his injured cause,
He brought them hup to MR. BROUGHTON,
   Last Vensday veek as ever waws.

If guiltless, how she have been slanderd !
   If guilty, wengeance will not fail ;
Meanwhile, the lady is remanderd
   And gev three hundred pounds in bail.

                    PLEACEMAN X 54.

BOW STREET BALLADS.—No. II.[1]

JACOB OMNIUM'S HOSS.—A NEW PALLICE COURT CHAUNT.

NE sees in Viteall Yard,
    Vere pleacemen do resort,
A wenerable hinstitute,
    'Tis called the Pallis Court.
A gent as got his i on it,
    I think it'll make some sport.

The natur of this Court
    My hindignation riles ;
A few fat legal spiders
    Here set & spin their viles ;
To rob the town theyr privlege is,
    In a hayrea of twelve miles.

The Judge of this year Court
    Is a mellitary beak,
He knows no more of Lor
    Than praps he does of Greek,
And prowides hisself a deputy
    Because he cannot speak.

Four counsel in this Court—
    Misnamed of Justice—sits ;
These lawyers owes their places to
    Their money, not their wits ;
And there's six attornies under them,
    As here their living gits.

These lawyers, six and four,
    Was a livin at their ease,
A sendin of their writs abowt,
    And droring in the fees,
When there erose a cirkimstance
    As is like to make a breeze.

It now is some monce since,
    A gent both good and trew

[1] [*Punch*, December 9, 1848.]

Possest an ansum oss vith vich
   He didn know what to do :
Peraps he did not like the oss,
   Peraps he was a scru.

This gentleman his oss
   At TATTERSALL's did lodge ;
There came a wulgar oss-dealer,
   This gentleman's name did fodge,
And took the oss from TATTERSALL's :
   Wasn't that a artful dodge ?

One day this gentleman's groom
   This willain did spy out,
A mounted on this oss
   A ridin him about :
' Get out of that there oss, you rogue,'
   Speaks up the groom so stout.

The thief was cruel whex'd
   To find hisself so pinn'd ;
The oss began to whinny,
   The honest groom he grinn'd ;
And the raskle thief got off the oss
   And cut avay like vind.

And phansy with what joy
   The master did regard
His dearly bluvd lost oss again
   Trot in the stable yard.

Who was this master good
   Of whomb I makes these rhymes?
His name is JACOB HOMNIUM, Exquire ; [1]
   And if I'd committed crimes,
Good Lord ! I wouldn't ave that mann
   Attack me in *The Times !*

Now shortly after, the groomb
   His master's oss did take up,
There came a livery-man
   This gentleman to wake up ;

[1] ['Jacob Omnium' was the pseudonym of Mr. M. J. Higgins, the well-known member of the staff of *The Times*, and an intimate friend of Thackeray.]

And he handed in a little bill,
 Which hangered MR. JACOB.

For two pound seventeen
 This livery-man replied
For the keep of MR. JACOB's oss,
 Which the thief had took to ride.
'Do you see anything green in me?'
 MR. JACOB HOMNIUM cried.

'Because a raskle chews
 My oss away to robb,
And goes tick at your Mews
 For seven-and-fifty bobb,
Shall I be called to pay?—It is
 A iniquitious Jobb.'

Thus MR. JACOB cut
 The conwasation short;
The livery-man went ome,
 Detummingd to ave sport,
And summingsd JACOB HOMINM, Exquire,
 Into the Pallis Court.

Pore JACOB went to Court
 A Counsel for to fix
And choose a barrister out of the four,
 An attorney of the six;
And there he sor these men of Lor,
 And watch'd 'em at their tricks.

The dreadful day of trile
 In the Pallis Court did come;
The lawyers said their say,
 The Judge looked very glum,
And then the British Jury cast
 Pore JACOB HOM—NI—UM.

O a weary day was that
 For JACOB to go through;
The debt was two seventeen,
 (Which he no more owed than you)
And then there was the plaintives costs,
 Eleven pound six and two.

And then there was his own,
  Which the lawyers they did fix
At the wery moderit figgar
  Of ten pound one and six.
Now Evins bless the Pallis Court,
  And all its bold ver-dicks!

I cannot settingly tell
  If JACOB swaw and cust,
At aving for to pay this sumb,
  But I should think he must,
And av drawn a cheque for £24 4s. 8d.
  With most igstreme disgust.

O Pallis Court, you move
  My pity most profound.
A most emusing sport
  You thought it, I'll be bound,
To saddle hup a three-pound debt
  With two-and-twenty pound.

Good sport it is to you,
  To grind the honest pore;
To pay their just or unjust debts
  With eight hundred per cent for Lor;
Make haste and git your costes in,
  They will not last much mor.

Come down from that tribewen,
  Thou Shameless and Unjust;
Thou Swindle, picking pockets in
  The name of Truth august;
Come down, thou hoary Blasphemy,
  For die thou shalt and must.

And go it, JACOB HOMNIUM,
  And ply your iron pen,
And rise up SIR JOHN JERVIS,
  And shut me up that den;
That sty for fattening lawyers in,
  On the bones of honest men.

                              PLEACEMAN X.

THE THREE CHRISTMAS WAITS.[1]

MY name is Pleaceman X ;
  Last night I was in bed,
A dream did me perplex,
  Which came into my Edd.
I dreamed I sor three Waits
  A playing of their tune,
At Pimlico Palace gates,
  All underneath the moon.
One puffed a hold French horn,
  And one a hold Banjo,
And one chap seedy and torn
  A Hirish pipe did blow.
They sadly piped and played,
  Dexcribing of their fates ;
And this was what they said,
  Those three pore Christmas Waits :—

'When this black year began,
  This Eighteen-forty-eight,
I was a great great man,
  And king both vise and great,
And MUNSEER GUIZOT by me did show
  As Minister of State.

'But Febuwerry came,
  And brought a rabble rout,
And me and my good dame
  And children did turn out,
And us, in spite of all our right,
  Sent to the right about.

'I left my native ground,
  I left my kin and kith,
I left my royal crownd,
  Vich I couldn't travel vith,
And without a pound came to English ground,
  In the name of MR. SMITH.

'Like any anchorite
  I've lived since I came here,
I've kep myself quite quite,
  I've drank the small small beer,

[1] [*Punch*, December 23, 1848.]

And the vater, you see, disagrees vith me
    And all my famly dear.

' O, Tweeleries so dear,
    O, darling Pally Royl,
Vas it to finish here
    That I did trouble and toyl ?
That all my plans should break in my ands,
    And should on me recoil ?

' My state I fenced about
    Vith baynicks and vith guns ;
My gals I portioned hout,
    Rich vives I got my sons ;
O, varn't it crule to lose my rule,
    My money and lands at once ?

' And so, vith arp and woice,
    Both troubled and shagreened,
I bid you to rejoice
    O glorious England's QUEEND !
And never ave to veep, like pore LOUIS-PHILEEP,
    Because you out are cleaned.

' O, Prins, so brave and stout,
    I stand before your gate ;
Pray send a trifle hout
    To me, your pore old Vait ;
For nothink could be vuss than its been along
      vith us,
    In this year Forty-eight.'

' Ven this bad year began,'
    The nex man said, saysee,
' I vas a Journeyman,
    A taylor black and free,
And my wife went out and chaired about,
    And my name's the bold CUFFEE.

' The QUEEN and HALBERT both,
    I swore I would confound,
I took a hawfle hoath
    To drag them to the ground ;
And sevral more with me they swore
    Against the British Crownd.

'Against her Pleaceman all,
    We said we'd try our strength ;
Her scarlick soldiers tall,
    We vow'd we'd lay full lenth :
And out we came, in Freedom's name,
    Last Aypril was the tenth.

'Three 'underd thousand snobs
    Came out to stop the vay,
Vith sticks vith iron knobs,
    Or else we'd gained the day.
The harmy kept quite out of sight,
    And so ve vent avay.

'Next day the Pleacemen came—
    Rewenge it was their plann—
And from my good old dame
    They took her tailor-mann :
And the hard hard beak did me bespeak
    To Newgit in the Wann.

'In that etrocious Cort
    The Jewry did agree ;
The Judge did me transport,
    To go beyond the sea :
And so for life, from his dear wife
    They took poor old CUFFEE.

'O HALBERT, Appy Prince !
    With children round your knees,
Ingraving ansum Prints,
    And takin hoff your hease ;
O think of me, the old CUFFEE,
    Beyond the solt solt seas !

'Although I'm hold and black,
    My hanguish is most great ;
Great Prince, O call me back,
    And I vill be your Vait !
And never no more vill break the Lor,
    As I did in 'Forty-eight.'

The tailer thus did close
    (A pore old blackymore rogue),
When a dismal gent uprose,
    And spoke with Hirish brogue ;

'I'm SMITH O'BRINE, of Royal Line,
  Descended from RORY OGUE.

'When great O'CONNLE died,
  That man whom all did trust,
That man whom Henglish pride
  Beheld with such disgust,
Then Erin free fixed eyes on me,
  And swore I should be fust.

'"The glorious Hirish Crown,"
  Says she, "it shall be thine:
Long time, its wery well known,
  You kep it in your line;
That diadem of hemerald gem
  Is yours, my SMITH O'BRINE.

'"Too long the Saxon churl
  Our land encumbered hath;
Arise, my Prince, my Earl,
  And brush them from thy path;
Rise, mighty SMITH, and sveep em vith
  The besom of your wrath."

'Then in my might I rose,
  My country I surveyed,
I saw it filled with foes,
  I viewed them undismayed;
"Ha, ha!" says I, "the harvest's high,"
  I'll reap it with my blade.

'My warriors I enrolled,
  They rallied round their lord;
And cheafs in council old
  I summoned to the board—
Wise DOHENY and DUFFY bold,
  And MEAGHER of the Sword.

'I stood on Slieveanamaun,
  They came with pikes and bills;
They gathered in the dawn,
  Like mist upon the hills,
And rushed adown the mountain side
  Like twenty thousand rills.

P

'Their fortress we assail ;
　　Hurroo ! my boys, hurroo !
The bloody Saxons quail
　　To hear the wild shaloo ;
Strike, and prevail, lovely Innisfail,
　　O'BRINE aboo, aboo !

' Our people they defied ;
　　They shot at 'em like savages,
Their bloody guns they plied
　　With sanguinary ravages ;
Hide, blushing Glory, hide
　　That day among the Cabbages !

' And so no more I'll say,
　　But ask your Mussy great,
And humbly sing and pray,
　　Your Majesty's poor Wait :
Your SMITH O'BRINE in " Forty-nine "
　　Will blush for " Forty-eight." '

THE BALLAD OF ELIZA DAVIS.[1]

ALLIANT gents and lovely ladies,
　　List a tail vich late befell,
Vich I heard it, bein on duty
　　At the Pleace Hoffice, Clerken-
　　　　well.

Praps you know the Fondling
　　Chapel,
　　Vere the little children sings ;
(Lor ! I likes to hear on Sundies
　　Them there pooty little things!)

In this street there lived a
　　housemaid,
　　If you particklarly ask
　　me where—
　　　Vy, it vas at four-and-
　　　　tventy,
Guilford Street by Brunsvick Square.

[1] [*Punch*, February 9, 1850.]

Vich her name was ELIZA DAVIS,
   And she went to fetch the beer ;
In the street she met a party
   As was quite surprised to see her.

Vich he vas a British Sailor,
   For to judge him by his look :
Tarry jacket, canvas trowsies,
   Ha-la MR. T. P. COOKE.

Presently this Mann accostes
   Of this hinnocent young gal—
'Pray,' saysee, 'excuse my freedom,
   You're so like my SISTER SAL !

'You're so like my SISTER SALLY,
   Both in valk and face and size ;
Miss, that—dang my old lee scuppers,
   It brings tears into my heyes !

'I'm a mate on board a wessel,
   I'm a sailor bold and true ;
Shiver up my poor old timbers,
   Let me be a mate for you !

'What's your name, my beauty, tell me ?'
   And she faintly hansers, 'Lore,
Sir, my name's ELIZA DAVIS,
   And I live at tventy-four.'

Hofttimes came this British seaman,
   This deluded gal to meet ;
And at tventy-four was welcome,
   Tventy-four in Guilford Street.

And ELIZA told her Master,
   (Kinder they than Missuses are),
How in marridge he had ast her,
   Like a galliant British Tar.

And he brought his landlady vith him,
   (Vich vas all his hartful plan),
And she told how CHARLEY THOMPSON
   Reely vas a good young man ;

And how she herself had lived in
    Many years of union sweet,
Vith a gent she met promiskous,
    Valkin in the public street.

And ELIZA listened to them,
    And she thought that soon their bands
Vould be published at the Fondlin,
    Hand the clergyman jine their 'ands.

And he ast about the lodgers,
    (Vich her master let some rooms),
Likevise vere they kep their things, and
    Vere her master kep his spoons.

Hand this vicked CHARLEY THOMPSON
    Came on Sundy veek to see her,
And he sent ELIZA DAVIS
    Hout to fetch a pint of beer.

Hand while pore ELIZA vent to
    Fetch the beer, dewoid of sin,
This etrocious CHARLEY THOMPSON
    Let his wile accomplish hin.

To the lodgers, their apartments,
    This abandinged female goes,
Prigs their shirts and umberellas ;
    Prigs their boots, and hats, and clothes.

Vile the scoundrel CHARLEY THOMPSON,
    Lest his wictim should escape,
Hocust her vith rum and vater,
    Like a fiend in huming shape.

But a hi was fixt upon 'em
    Vich these raskles little sore ;
Namely, MR. HIDE the landlord,
    Of the house at tventy-four.

He vas valkin in his garden,
    Just afore he vent to sup ;
And on looking up he sor the
    Lodgers' vinders lighted hup.

Hup the stairs the landlord tumbled ;
   ' Something's going wrong,' he said ;
And he caught the vicked voman
   Underneath the lodger's bed.

And he called a brother Pleaseman,
   Vich vas passing on his beat ;
Like a true and galliant feller,
   Hup and down in Guilford Street.

And that Pleaseman able-bodied
   Took this voman to the cell ;
To the cell vere she was quodded,
   In the Close of Clerkenwell.

And though vicked CHARLEY THOMPSON
   Boulted like a miscrant base,
Presently another Pleaseman
   Took him to the self-same place.

And this precious pair of raskles
   Tuesday last came up for doom ;
By the beak they was committed,
   Vich his name was MR. COMBE,

Has for poor ELIZA DAVIS,
   Simple gurl of tventy-four,
She, I ope, vill never listen
   In the streets to sailors moar.

But if she must 'ave a sweet-art,
   (Vich most every gurl expec),
Let her take a jolly pleaseman ;
   Vich 'is name peraps is—X.

THE LAMENTABLE BALLAD OF THE FOUNDLING
OF SHOREDITCH.[1]

FROM *THE TIMES* OF FEBRUARY 14.

OME, all ye Christian people,
   and listen to my tail,
It is all about a doctor was
   travelling by the rail,
By the Heastern Counties
   Railway (vich the shares
   I don't desire),
From Ixworth town in
   Suffolk, vich his name did
   not transpire.

A travelling from Bury
   this Doctor was em-
   ployed
With a gentleman, a friend
   of his, vich his name
   was CAPTAIN LOYD,
And on reaching Marks
   Tey Station, that is
   next beyond Colchest-
   er, a lady entered into them
   most elegantly dressed.

She entered into the Carriage all with a tottering step,
And a pooty little Baby upon her bussum slep;
The gentlemen received her with kindness and siwillaty,
Pitying this lady for her illness and debillaty.

She had a fust class ticket this lovely lady said,
Because it was so lonesome she took a secknd instead.
Better to travel by secknd class, than sit alone in the fust,
And the pooty little Baby upon her breast she nust.

[1] [*Punch*, February 23, 1850.]

A seein of her cryin, and shiverin and pail,
To her spoke this surging, the Ero of my tail ;
Saysee, 'You look unwell, Ma'am, I'll elp you if I can,
And you may tell your case to me, for I'm a meddicle man.'

'Thank you, Sir,' the lady said, 'I only look so pale,
Because I ain't accustom'd to travelling on the rale ;
I shall be better presnly when I've 'ad some rest :'
And that pooty little Baby she squeeged it to her breast.

So in conwersation the journey they beguiled,
CAPTING LOYD and the medical man, and the lady and the child,
Till the warious stations along the line was passed,
For even the Heastern Counties' trains must come in at last.

When at Shoreditch tumminus at lenth stopped the train,
This kind meddicle gentleman proposed his aid again.
'Thank you, Sir,' the lady said, 'for your kyindness dear ;
My carridge and my osses is probbibly come here.

'Will you 'old this baby, please, vilst I step out and see ?'
The Doctor was a famly man : 'That I will,' says he.
Then the little child she kist it very gently,
Vich was sucking his little fist, sleeping innocently.

With a sigh from her 'art, as though she would have bust it,
Then she gave the doctor the child—wery kind he nust it :
Hup then the lady jumped hoff the bench she sate from,
Tumbled down the carridge steps and ran along the platform.

Vile hall the other passengers vent upon their vays,
The Capting and the Doctor sate there in a maze ;
Some vent in a Homminibus, some vent in a Cabby,
The Capting and the Doctor vaited vith the babby.

There they sate looking queer, for an hour or more,
But their feller passinger neather on 'em sore :
Never, never, back again did that lady come
To that pooty sleeping Hinfnt a suckin of his Thum !

What could this pore Doctor do, bein treated thus,
When the darling Baby woke, cryin for its nuss ?
Off he drove to a female friend, vich she was both kind and mild,
And igsplained to her the circumstance of this year little child.

That kind lady took the child instantly in her lap,
And made it very comfortable by giving it some pap ;
And when she took its close off, what d'you think she found ?
A couple of ten pun notes sewn up in its little gownd !

Also in its little close was a note which did conwey,
That this little baby's parents lived in a handsome way :
And for its Headucation they reglarly would pay,
And sirtingly like gentlefolks would claim the child one day,
If the Christian people who'd charge of it would say,
Per advertisement in *The Times*, where the baby lay.

Pity of this bayby many people took,
It had such pooty ways and such a pooty look ;
And there came a lady forrard (I wish that I could see
Any kind lady as would do as much for me.

And I wish with all my 'art, some night in my night gownd,
I could find a note stitched for ten or twenty pound)—
There came a lady forrard, that most honorable did say,
She'd adopt this little baby which her parents cast away.

While the Doctor pondered on this hoffer fair,
Comes a letter from Devonshire, from a party there,
Hordering the Doctor, at its Mar's desire,
To send the little Infant back to Devonshire.

Lost in apoplexity, this pore meddicle man,
Like a sensable gentleman, to the Justice ran ;
Which his name was MR. HAMMILL, a honorable beak,
That takes his seat in Worship Street four times a week.

' O Justice ! ' says the Doctor, ' instrugt me what to do,
I've come up from the country to throw myself on you ;
My patients have no doctor to tend them in their ills,
(There they are in Suffolk without their draffts and pills !)

' I've come up from the country, to know how I'll dispose
Of this pore little baby, and the twenty pun note, and the clothes,
And I want to go back to Suffolk, dear Justice, if you please,
And my patients wants their Doctor, and their Doctor wants his
        feez.'

Up spoke MR. HAMMILL, sittin at his desk,
' This year application does me much perplesk ;
What I do adwise you, is to leave this babby
In the Parish where it was left by its mother shabby.'

The Doctor from his Worship sadly did depart—
He might have left the baby, but he hadn't got the heart,
To go for to leave that Hinnocent, has the laws allows,
To the tender mussies of the Union House.

Mother, who left this little one on a stranger's knee,
Think how cruel you have been, and how good was he!
Think if you've been guilty, innocent was she ;
And do not take unkindly this little word of me :
Heaven be merciful to us all, sinners as we be !

X.

LINES ON A LATE HOSPICIOUS EWENT.[1]

BY A GENTLEMAN OF THE FOOT-GUARDS (BLUE).

I PACED upon my beat
    With steady step and slow,
All huppandownd of Ranelagh Street ;
    Ranelagh St., Pimlico.

While marching huppandownd
    Upon that fair May morn,
Beold the booming cannings sound,
    A royal child is born !

The Ministers of State
    Then presnly I sor
They gallops to the Pallis gate,
    In carridges and for.

With anxious looks intent,
    Before the gate they stop,
There comes the good Lord President
    And there the Archbishopp.

LORD JOHN he next elights ;
    And who comes here in haste ?
'Tis the 'ero of one underd fights,
    The caudle for to taste.

[1] [*Punch*, May 11, 1850.]
[The birth of Prince Arthur, afterwards Duke of Connaught.]

Then MRS. LILY, the nuss,
   Towards them steps with joy ;
Says the brave old Duke, 'Come tell to us,
   Is it a gal or a boy ?'

Says MRS. L. to the Duke,
   'Your Grace, it *is a Prince.*'
And at that nuss's bold rebuke,
   He did both laugh and wince.

He vews with pleasant look
   This pooty flower of May,
Then says the wenerable Duke,
   'Egad it 's my buthday.'

By memory backards borne,
   Peraps his thoughts did stray
To that old place where he was born
   Upon the first of May.

Peraps he did recal
   The ancient powers of Trim ;
And County Meath and Dangan Hall
   They did rewisit him.

I phansy of him so
   His good old thoughts employin' ;
Fourscore years and one ago
   Beside the flowin' Boyne.

His father praps he sees,
   Most musicle of Lords,
A playing maddrigles and glees
   Upon the 'Arpsicords.

Jest phansy this old 'Ero
   Upon his mother's knee !
Did ever lady in this land
   'Ave greater sons than she ?

And I shouldn be surprize
   While this was in his mind,
If a drop there twinkled in his eyes.
   Of unfamiliar brind.

To Hapsly 'Ouse next day
    Drives up a Broosh and for,
A gracious prince sits in that Shay
    (I mention him with Hor !)

They ring upon the bell,
    The Porter shows his 'ed,
(He fought at Vaterloo as vell,
    And vears a Veskit red.)

To see that carriage come
    The people round it press :
' And is the galliant Duke at 'ome ? '
    ' Your Royal 'Ighness, yes.'

He stepps from out the Broosh
    And in the gate is gone,
And X, although the people push,
    Says wery kind, ' Move hon.'

The Royal Prince unto
    The gallant Duke did say,
' Dear Duke, my little son and you
    Was born the self same day.'

' The Lady of the Land,
    My wife and Sovring dear,
It is by her horgust command
    I wait upon you here.

' That lady is as well
    As can expected be ;
And to your Grace she bid me tell
    This gracious message free.

' That offspring of our race,
    Whom yesterday you see,
To show our honour for your Grace,
    PRINCE ARTHUR he shall be.

' That name it rhymes to fame ;
    All Europe knows the sound :
And I couldn't find a better name
    If you'd give me twenty pound.

'KING ARTHUR had his knights
   That girt his table round,
But you have won a hundred fights,
   Will match 'em I'll be bound.

'You fought with BONYPART,
   And likewise TIPPOO SAIB:
I name you then with all my heart
   The Godsire of this babe.'

That Prince his leave was took,
   His hinterview was done,
So let us give the good old Duke
   Good luck of his god-son,

And wish him years of joy
   In this our time of Schism,
And hope he'll hear the royal boy
   His little catechism.

And my pooty little Prince
   That's come our 'arts to cheer,
Let me my loyal powers ewince
   A welcomin of you 'ere.

And the Poit-Laureat's crownd,
   I think, in some respex,
Egstremely shootable might be found
   For honest PLEASEMAN X.

THE WOFLE NEW BALLAD OF JANE RONEY AND MARY BROWN.[1]

AN igstrawnary tail I vill tell yer this veek—
I stood in the Court of A'BECKETT the Beak,
Vere MRS. JANE RONEY, a vidow, I see,
Who charged MARY BROWN with a robbin of she.

[1] [*Punch*, May 25, 1850.]
[Gilbert Abbott à Beckett, of *Punch*, author of the *Comic History of England* and the *Comic History of Rome*, etc.]

This MARY was pore and in misery once,
And she came to MRS. RONEY it's more than twelve monce.
She 'adn't got no bed, nor no dinner, nor no tea,
And kind MRS. RONEY gave MARY all three.

MRS. RONEY kep MARY for ever so many veeks,
(Her conduct surprised the best of all Beax),
She kep her for nothink, as kind as could be,
Never thinkin that this MARY was a traitor to she.

'MRS. RONEY, O MRS. RONEY, I feel very ill;
Will you jest step to the Doctor's for to fetch me a pill?'
'That I will, my poor MARY,' MRS. RONEY says she;
And she goes off to the Doctor's as quickly as may be.

No sooner on this message MRS. RONEY was sped,
Than hup gits vicked MARY, and jumps out a bed;
She hopens all the trunks without never a key—
She bustes all the boxes, and vith them makes free.

MRS. RONEY's best linning gownds, petticoats, and close,
Her children's little coats and things, her boots and her hose,
She packed them, and she stole 'em, and avay vith them did flee.
MRS. RONEY's situation—you may think vat it vould be!

Of MARY, ungrateful, who had served her this vay,
MRS. RONEY heard nothink for a long year and a day.
Till last Thursday in Lambeth, ven whom should she see?
But this MARY as had acted so ungrateful to she.

She was leaning on the helbo of a worthy young man;
They were going to be married, and were walkin hand in hand,
And the Church bells was a ringing for Mary and he,
And the parson was ready, and a waitin for his fee.

When up comes MRS. RONEY, and faces MARY BROWN,
Who trembles and castes her eyes upon the ground.
She calls a jolly pleaseman, it happens to be me;
'I charge this young woman, Mr. Pleaseman,' says she.

'MRS. RONEY, O, MRS. RONEY, O, do let me go,
I acted most ungrateful I own, and I know,
But the marriage bell is a ringing, and the ring you may see,
And this young man is a waitin,' says MARY says she.

'I don't care three fardens for the parson and clark,
And the bell may keep ringing from noon day to dark ;
MARY BROWN, MARY BROWN, you must come along with me,
And I think this young man is lucky to be free.'

So, in spite of the tears which bejew'd MARY's cheek,
I took that young gurl to A'BECKETT the Beak ;
That exlent Justice demanded her plea —
But never a sullable said MARY said she.

On account of her conduck so base and so vile,
That wicked young gurl is committed for trile,
And if she's transpawted beyond the salt sea,
It's a proper reward for such willains as she.

Now you young gurls of Southwark for MARY who veep,
From pickin and stealin your 'ands you must keep,
Or it may be my dooty, as it was Thursday veek,
To pull you all hup to A'BECKETT the Beak.

DAMAGES, TWO HUNDRED POUNDS.[1]

SPECIAL Jurymen of England! who admire your country's laws,
And proclaim a British Jury worthy of the realm's applause ;
Gaily compliment each other at the issue of a cause
Which was tried at Guildford 'sizes, this day week as ever was.

Unto that august tribunal comes a gentleman in grief,
(Special was the British Jury, and the Judge, the Baron Chief,)
Comes a British man and husband—asking of the law relief,
For his wife was stolen from him—he'd have vengeance on the
thief.

Yes, his wife, the blessed treasure with the which his life was
crowned,
Wickedly was ravished from him by a hypocrite profound.
And he comes before twelve Britons, men for sense and truth
renowned,
To award him for his damage, twenty hundred sterling pound.

[1] [*Punch*, August 24, 1850.]

He by counsel and attorney there at Guildford does appear,
Asking damage of the villain who seduced his lady dear :
But I can't help asking, though the lady's guilt was all too clear,
And though guilty the defendant, wasn't the plaintiff rather
    queer?

First the lady's mother spoke, and said she'd seen her daughter cry
But a fortnight after marriage : early times for piping eye.
Six months after, things were worse, and the piping eye was black,
And this gallant British husband caned his wife upon the back.

Three months after they were married, husband pushed her to
    the door,
Told her to be off and leave him, for he wanted her no more.
As she would not go, why *he* went : thrice he left his lady dear ;
Left her, too, without a penny, for more than a quarter of a year.

Mrs. Frances Duncan knew the parties very well indeed,
She had seen him pull his lady's nose and make her lip to bleed ;
If he chanced to sit at home not a single word he said :
Once she saw him throw the cover of a dish at his lady's head.

Sarah Green, another witness, clear did to the jury note
How she saw this honest fellow seize his lady by the throat,
How he cursed her and abused her, beating her into a fit,
Till the pitying next-door neighbours crossed the wall and
    witnessed it.

Next door to this injured Briton Mr. Owers a butcher dwelt ;
Mrs. Owers's foolish heart towards this erring dame did melt ;
(Not that she had erred as yet, crime was not developed in her,) ⎫
But being left without a penny, Mrs Owers supplied her dinner— ⎬
God be merciful to Mrs. Owers, who was merciful to this sinner ! ⎭

Caroline Naylor was their servant, said they led a wretched life,
Saw this most distinguished Briton fling a teacup at his wife ;
He went out to balls and pleasures, and never once in ten months'
    space,
Sat with his wife or spoke her kindly.   This was the defendant's
    case.

Pollock, C.B., charged the Jury ; said the woman's guilt was clear :
That was not the point, however, which the Jury came to hear ;
But the damage to determine which, as it should true appear,
This most tender-hearted husband, who so used his lady dear—

Beat her, kicked her, caned her, cursed her, left her starving
     year by year,
Flung her from him, parted from her, wrung her neck, and boxed
     her ear—
What the reasonable damage this afflicted man could claim,
By the loss of the affections of this guilty graceless dame?

Then the honest British Twelve, to each other turning round,
Laid their clever heads together with a wisdom most profound :
And towards his lordship looking, spoke the foreman wise and
     sound :—
'My Lord, we find for this here plaintiff, damages two hundred
     pound.'

So, God bless the Special Jury ; pride and joy of English ground,
And the happy land of England, where true justice does abound !
British jurymen and husbands, let us hail this verdict proper :
If a British wife offends you, Britons, you've a right to whop her.

Though you promised to protect her, though you promised to
     defend her,
You are welcome to neglect her : to the devil you may send her :
You may strike her, curse, abuse her ; so declares our law
     renowned ;
And if after this you lose her,—why, you're paid two hundred
     pound.

A WOEFUL NEW BALLAD OF THE PROTESTANT CONSPIRACY [1] TO TAKE THE POPE'S LIFE. [2]

(By a Gentleman who has been on the Spot.)

Come, all ye Christian people, unto my tale give ear,
'Tis about a base consperacy, as quickly shall appear ;
'Twill make your hair to bristle up, and your eyes to start and
     glow,
When of this dread consperacy you honest folks shall know.

---

[1] See the account of this conspiracy in the Roman Correspondence of the
Daily News.
[2] [*Punch*, March 15, 1851.]

The news of this consperracy and villianous attempt,
I read it in a newspaper, from Italy it was sent :
It was sent from lovely Italy, where the olives they do grow,
And our Holy Father lives, yes, yes, while his name it is No no.

And 'tis there our English noblemen goes that is Puseyites no
    longer,
Because they finds the ancient faith both better is and stronger,
And 'tis there I knelt beside my lord when he kiss'd the Pope
    his toe,
And hung his neck with chains at Saint Peter's Vinculo.

And 'tis there the splendid churches is, and the fountains playing
    grand,
And the palace of Prince Torlonia, likewise the Vatican ;
And there's the stairs where the bagpipe-men and the piffrarys
    blow,
And it's there I drove my lady and lord in the Park of Pincio.

And 'tis there our splendid churches is in all their pride and
    glory,
Saint Peter's famous Basilisk and Saint Mary's Maggiory ;
And them benighted Protestants, on Sunday they must go
Outside the town to the preaching-shop by the gate of Popolo.

Now in this town of famous Room, as I dessay you have heard,
There is scarcely any gentleman as hasn't got a beard.
And ever since the world began it was ordained so,
That there should always barbers be wheresumever beards do
    grow.

And as it always has been so since the world it did begin,
The Pope, our Holy Potentate, has a beard upon his chin ;
And every morning regular when cocks begin to crow,
There comes a certing party to wait on Pope Pio.

There comes a certing gintleman with razier, soap, and lather,
A shaving most respectfully the Pope, our Holy Father.
And now the dread consperracy I'll quickly to you show,
Which them sanguinary Protestants did form against Nono.

Them sanguinary Prodestants, which I abore and hate,
Assembled in the preaching-shop by the Flaminian gate ;
And they took counsel with their selves to deal a deadly blow
Against our gentle Father, the holy Pope Pio.

Q

Exhibiting a wickedness which I never heerd or read off;
What do you think them Prodestants wish'd? to cut the good
    Pope's head off!
And to the kind POPE's 'Air-dresser the Prodestant Clark did go,
And proposed him to decapitate the innocent PIO!

'What hever can be easier,' said this Clerk—this Man of Sin,
'When you're call'd to hoperate on his Holiness's chin,
Than just to give the razier a little slip—just so?—
And there's an end, dear barber, of innocent PIO!'

This wicked conversation it chanced was overerd
By an Italian lady; she heard it every word;
Which by birth she was a Marchioness, in service forced to go
With the Parson of the preaching-shop at the gate of Popolo.

When the lady heard the news, as duty did obleege,
As fast as her legs could carry her she ran to the Polege.
'O, Polegia,' says she (for they pronounts it so),
'They're going for to massyker our Holy POPE PIO.

'The ebomminable Englishmen, the Parsing and his Clark,
His Holiness's 'Air-dresser devised it in the dark!
And I would recommend you in prison for to throw
These villians would essassinate the Holy POPE PIO!

'And for saving of his Holiness and his trebble crownd
I humbly hope your Worships will give me a few pound;
Because I was a Marchioness many years ago,
Before I came to service at the gate of Popolo.'

That sackreligious 'Air-dresser, the Parson and his man,
Wouldn't, though ask'd continyally, own their wicked plan—
And so the kind Authoraties let those villians go
That was plotting of the murder of the good PIO NONO.

Now isn't this safishnt proof, ye gentlemen at home,
How wicked is them Prodestans, and how good our Pope at
    Rome;
So let us drink confusion to LORD JOHN and LORD MINTO,
And a health unto his Eminence, and good PIO NONO.

THE ORGAN BOY'S APPEAL.[1]

' WESTMINSTER POLICE COURT,—POLICEMAN X brought a paper of doggrel verses to the MAGISTRATE, which had been thrust into his hands, X said, by an Italian boy, who ran away immediately afterwards.

' The MAGISTRATE, after perusing the lines, looked hard at X, and said he did not think they were written by an Italian.

' X, blushing, said, he thought the paper read in Court last week, and which frightened so the old gentleman to whom it was addressed, was also not of Italian origin.'

O SIGNOR BRODERIP, you are a wickid ole man,
You wexis us little horgan boys whenever you can,
How dare you talk of Justice, and go for to seek
To pussicute us horgin boys, you senguinary Beek ?

Though you set in Vestminster surrounded by your crushers
Harrogint and habsolute like the Hortacrat of hall the Rushers,
Yet there is a better vurld I'd have you for to know
Likewise a place vere the henimies of horgin boys will go.

O you vickid HEROD without any pity,
London vithout horgin boys vood be a dismal city !
Sweet SAINT CICILY who first taught horgin-pipes to blow
Soften the heart of this Magistrit that haggerywates us so !

Good Italian gentlemen, fatherly and kind,
Brings us over to London here our horgins for to grind ;
Sends us out vith little vite mice and guinea pigs also
A popping of the Veasel and a Jumpin of JIM CROW.

And as us young horgin boys is grateful in our turn
We gives to these kind gentlemen hall the money we earn,
Because that they vood vop us as wery wel we know
Unless we brought our hurnings back to them as loves us so.

O MR. BRODERIP ! wery much I'm surprise
Ven you take your valks abroad where can be your eyes ?
If a Beak had a heart then you'd compryend
Us pore little Horgin boys was the poor man's friend.

Don't you see the shildren in the droring rooms
Clapping of their little ands when they year our toons ?
On their mothers' bussums don't you see the babbies crow
And down to us dear horgin boys lots of apence throw ?

[*Punch*, October 1853.]

Don't you see the ousemaids (pooty POLLIES and MARIES),
Ven ve bring our urdigurdis, smilin from the hairies?
Then they come out vith a slice o' cole puddn or a bit o' bacon
    or so
And give it us young horgin boys for lunch afore we go.

Have you ever seen the Hirish children sport
When our velcome music-box brings sunshine in the Court?
To these little paupers who can never pay
Surely all good organ boys, for GOD's love, will play.

Has for those proud gentlemen, like a serting B—k
(Vich I von't be pussonal and therefore vil not speak),
That flings their parler-vinders hup ven ve begin to play
And cusses us and swears at us in such a wiolent way,

Instedd of their abewsing and calling hout Poleece
Let em send out JOHN to us vith sixpence or a shillin apiece.
Then like good young horgin boys avay from there we'll go
Blessing sweet SAINT-CICILY that taught our pipes to blow.

RAILROAD SPECULATORS.[1]

THE night was stormy and dark,   The town was shut up in sleep:
Only those were abroad who were out on a lark,   Or those who'd
no beds to keep.

    I pass'd through the lonely street,   The wind did sing and blow;
I could hear the policeman's feet,   Clapping to and fro.

    There stood a potato-man   In the midst of all the wet;   He
stood with his 'tato-can   In the lonely Haymarket.

    Two gents of dismal mien,   And dank and greasy rags,   Came
out of a shop for gin,   Swaggering over the flags:

    Swaggering over the stones,   These shabby bucks did walk:
And I went and followed those seedy ones,   And listened to
their talk.

    Was I sober or awake?   Could I believe my ears?   Those
dismal beggars spake   Of nothing but railroad shares.

               [1] [*Punch*, May 31, 1845.]

I wondered more and more :   Says one—'Good friend of mine
How many shares have you wrote for,   In the Diddlesex Junction
line ?'

'I wrote for twenty,' says Jim,   'But they wouldn't give me
one ;'   His comrade straight rebuked him   For the folly he had
done :

'HOW MANY HUNDRED SHARES HAVE YOU WROTE FOR?'

'O Jim, you are unawares   Of the ways of this bad town ;   I
always write for five hundred shares,   And *then* they put me
down.'

'And yet you got no shares,'   Says Jim, 'for all your boast ;'
'I *would* have wrote,' says Jack, 'but where   Was the penny to
pay the post ?'

'I lost, for I couldn't pay   That first instalment up ;   But
here's taters smoking hot—I say,   Let's stop, my boy, and sup.'

And at this simple feast   The while they did regale,   I drew each ragged capitalist   Down on my left thumb-nail.

Their talk did me perplex,   All night I tumbled and tost,   And thought of railroad specs.,   And how money was won and lost.

'Bless railroads everywhere,' I said, 'and the world's advance ; Bless every railroad share   In Italy, Ireland, France ;   For never a beggar need now despair,   And every rogue has a chance.'

POLITICAL AND TOPICAL VERSES.

DADDY, I'M HUNGRY.[1]

Daddy, I'm Hungry.

A SCENE IN AN IRISH COACHMAKER'S FAMILY, DESIGNED BY
LORD LOWTHER, JULY, 1843.

A SWEET little picture, that's fully desarving
    Your lordship's approval, we here riprisint—
A poor Irish coachmaker's family starving
    (More thanks to your lordship) is dhrawn in the print.

[1] [*The Nation* (Dublin), May 13, 1843.]

See the big lazy blackguard! although it is Monday,
  He sits at his ease with his hand to his cheek,
And doin' no more work nor a Quaker on Sunday,
  Nor your lordship's own self on most days of the week.

And thim's the two little ones, Rory and Mysie,
  Whom he'd dandle and jump every night on his knee—
Faith he gives the poor darlin's a welcome as icy
  As I'd give a bum-bailiff that came after me!

He turns from their prattle as angry as may be,
  ' O, daddy, I'm hungry,' says each little brat ;
And yonder sits mammy, and nurses the baby,
  Thinking how long there'll be dinner for that.

For daddy and children, for babby and mammy,
  No work and no hope, O! the prospect is fine ;
But I fancy I'm hearing your lordship cry—' Dammee,
  Suppose they *do* starve, it's no business of mine.'

Well, it's ' justice,' no doubt, that your lordship's obsarving,
  And that must our feelings of hunger console ;
We've five hundred families, wretched and starving,
  But what matters that, so there's *Justice for Croal ?*

A RARE NEW BALLAD OF MALBROOK.[1]

TO A NEW TUNE.

To be sung at Woodstock, at the Election Dinners there.

LAST evening I did sup at Joy's Hotel,
Where, to the merry clinking of the can,
Great EVANS (who can troll the chorus well)
Did sing " The Good Old English Gentleman."
A gallant song it is, of moral plan
And somehow always makes my bosom swell.

Strange visions in my sleep that evening ran :
I was again a boy of Oxenford,
And, all unheeding of the Proctor's ban,
To famous Woodstock town had driven my tan-

---

[1] [*Punch*, May 11, 1844.]

dem, and was strolling upon Blenheim sward :
Whom should I see approach but Blenheim's Lord.
He, too, the tune I heard at JOY's began,
And thus he sung—

THE

GOOD OLD ENGLISH GENTLEMAN.

I'll sing you a good old song, about England's days of splendour :
JOHN CHURCHILL was the famous Duke that did our race engender,
And as he beat the French, and was our country's best defender,
Why he took money from Queen Anne and likewise from the Pre-
    tender.
> Like a good old English nobleman,
> Of the good old honest time.

Lord, Lord, it is a dreadful thing to think what my sires got
    thro' in
A century or so of reckless life, and made extravagant doing ;
With building, racing, dicing, eating, drinking, courting, Jewing,
They emptied Great JOHN CHURCHILL'S bags and left poor me to
    ruin.
> Those brave old English noblemen, &c.

This nation was ungrateful, and so I plainly tell them,
Why give us CHURCHILL'S park of trees and then not let us fell
    them ?
Why give us gold and silver plates, and then not let us sell them ?
Plate we had, but mutton and beef we could very seldom smell
    them.
> We poor old English noblemen, &c.

As the people treated us so base, why, it is my maxim,
Whenever I get a poor man down, never to relax him ;
Whenever I have a tenant safe, how I squeeze and tax him ;
Whenever he will not pay his rent, I sells him up and racks him.
> Like a true old English nobleman, &c.

My ancestors an almshouse built ! (the greater asses they)
For a score of poor old women, as could eat but couldn't pay ;
And they used to come and crawl about, in my great park way ;
Hang their eyes ! like so many flies, all in the sunshine gay !
> What a sight for an English nobleman, &c.

Their rags and wrinkles made me sick, as sure as I wear ermine ;
To turn them out of Blenheim Park I graciously did determine ;
So I bricked the Almshouse gate up, and I read my keepers a
    sermon :
Says I, No more let into my door that poor old crawling vermin !
            For I'm a true old English nobleman, &c.

There was JOHN BARTLET, who picked up a half-eaten rabbit—
How dared JOHN BARTLET for to venture for to go for to grab it ?
I sent him to Oxford Gaol because he dared to nab it.
No more, I warrant you, he'll indulge in that there villanous habit,
            And steal from an English nobleman, &c.

Before he went to Oxford Gaol, this BARTLET had the cholera.
I promise you, when he came out, his cheeks looked paler and
    hollorer,
Fourteen days he lay in gaol, his conduct was intolera-
ble ; and such as practices vice will rue it if they foller her,
            Says a moral old English nobleman, &c.

There was JOHN HARRIS, too ; and, sir, what d'ye think,
He was a-riding on his old horse, and actually gave him drink—
Gave him drink in Woodstock Pond, at which I could not wink ;
For I am Lord of Woodstock Town, and will suffer no such *think*,
           As sure as I'm a nobleman, &c.

The parker might have let him off, but I was firm to hold out,
I committed and fined him myself, and so his goods were sold out,
Ruined he was and turned out of doors, with nought to keep the
    cold out,
And the knackers got his silly old horse, and so JOHN HARRIS was
    bowled out
           By a true old English nobleman, &c.

So now let's sing God save the king, and the house of bold Mal-
    brook,
Take this here example, rogues, of a gallant English Duke,
And voters all of Woodstock, let all grumbling be forsook,
And let my son, the Marquis, for your parliament-man be took.
           For he's a true young English nobleman,
           And loves the olden time.

THE DREAM OF JOINVILLE.[1]

CONTINENTAL gossip says, that the PRINCE DE JOINVILLE having had a row with his royal father, concerning his famous pamphlet, rushed away to Saint Cloud, where he slept at an inn, and dreamed the following dream :—

Stealthily we speed along,
   I and my black steamers,
None can see the colours three
   Painted on our streamers.
Not a star is in the sky,
   Black and dull and silent ;
Stealthily we creep along
   Towards the wicked Island !

Ne'er an English ship is out
   Somehow to defend it ;
So we reach the Thames's mouth—
   Swiftly we ascend it.
Then I give a lesson fit
   To Albion perfidious ;
Properly I punish it,
   For its treasons hideous.

Swiftly down the Thames we go,
   All pursuit outstripping,
Blowing every village up,
   Burning all the shipping.
Fancy Ramsgate in a blaze,
   Margate pier a-dropping,
Woolwich burnt and red-hot shot
   Plunging into Wapping !

London town's a jolly place,
   England's pride and wonder ;
Mortal eyes have never seen
   Such a place for plunder.
Lord ! it is a glorious night
   As my steamers pretty
Moor there, and my lads and I
   Pour into the City.

[1] [*Punch*, June 15, 1844.]

'Here's enough for each, says I,
    Whatsoe'er his rank, lads,
PIERRE shall rifle Lombard Street,
    And JEAN shall gut the Bank, lads;
Every seaman in my crews
    Shall take as much as suits his
Wish, and needs but pick and choose
    From JONES and LOYD'S to COUTTS'S.'

When my speech the seamen hear,
    Each man does salute his
Admiral with loyal cheer,
    And then begins his duties.
Some burn down the Monument,
    And some the Tower invest, sir;
Some bombard the Eastern end,
    And some attack the West, sir.

Gods! it is a royal sight,
    All the town in flames is,
Burning all the way from White-
    Chapel to Saint James's!
See the Mayor, in cotton cap,
    Asking what the blaze meant.
When we hang his worship up,
    Fancy his amazement!

Kill me every citizen,
    But spare their pretty spouses;
Hang me the policemen up
    At the station houses.
Beat St. Paul's with red-hot balls,
    Set Temple Bar a-blazing;
Burn me Paper Buildings down,
    And Lincoln's Inn and Gray's Inn.

List to no man's prayers and vows,
    Grant to none their pardons;
BLOMFIELD hang at London House,
    PEEL at Whitehall Gardens.
Apsley House is stormed and won,
    Seize the IRON DUKE, boys;
Have him out, and hang him up
    To the lantern-hook, boys!

Gods, it is a noble flame !
  Now my fellows thunder
At the gates of Buckingham—
  How the PRINCE does wonder.
Out he comes with sword and lance ;
  Boys, stand back impartial,
See an Admiral of France
  Pink an English Marshal !

Tell us who's the best at blows,
  The Army or the Navy ?
Carte and Tierce ! and down he goes ;
  Albert cries, ' Peccavi ! '
' Spare my precious husband's life : '
  The Queen upon her knees is,
The little Princes kneeling round
  In their night-chemises.

Just as I had raised my arm,
  To finish Albion's ruin,
Came a cock, and crow'd a cursed
  Cock-a-doodle-dooing.
It was morning,—and I lost
  That delightful vision—
Cruel morning, to dispel
  Such a dream Elysian !

THE PROBABLE EFFECTS OF GOOD LIVING AND NO EXERCISE

PUNCH TO DANIEL IN PRISON.[1]

IMMURED in Dublin's prison base,
    Great DANIEL, while thou smartest,
'Tis thus thy venerable face
    Appeared to Punch's artist.

[1] [*Punch*, July 20, 1844.]

He reads those weekly bulletins,
  Which of your health inform us,
And thus the prisoner paints, who grins
  Contented and enormous !

Perhaps the wicked limner shows,
  Inclined to laughter spiteful,
That certain patriots' vaunted woes
  Are not so *very* frightful.
Perhaps he would insinuate,
  By that stupendous figure,
That those who free are Truly Great,
  When wronged are Doubly Bigger !

I know not which ; but love to read
  Each speech of DAN the younger,
Which tells us how your people feed
  Their chief's imprisoned hunger.
How matrons cook you soups and broths,
  How cakes are baked by virgins,
How weavers weave your table-cloths,
  And fishers hook you sturgeons.[1]

Says DAN, 'My father's cheek's as red,
  His mood as blithe and merry,
As when at morn his dogs he led
  Along the hills of Kerry.
His mighty lungs more free to talk,
  His body stronger waxen,
Than when at Tara or Dundalk,
  He bullyragged the Saxon.'

Amen ! I hope the tale is true,
  Thus brought by Irish rumour ;
May each day's prison bring to you
  Good health, sir, and good humour !
Amen, cries Lord Chief-Justice PUNCH,
  Approving of your sentence,
It is, I swear it by my hunch,
  A jovial repentance !

---

[1] MR. DANIEL O'CONNELL, jun., thought the prisoners were looking right well and getting fat, they had just received an enormous cake weighing 45 lbs., a sturgeon from Limerick weighing 200 lbs., and table-cloth of Irish manufacture, etc., etc,

No chains shall in his prison clink,
    No ruthless jailor urge him,
With lashings of the best of drink
    I'd pitilessly scourge him.
'Tis thus that noble Justice PUNCH
    Would treat his Celtic neighbour,
And thus a dinner, supper, lunch,
    Condemn him to 'hard labour.'

Nor you alone, but good son JOHN,
    And RAY, and STEELE, and DUFFY ;
Ye dire Repealers every one,
    Remorselessly I'd stuff ye !
I'd have you all, from last to first,
    To grow such desperate gluttons,
That you should eat until ye burst
    Your new Repealers' Buttons ! '

A PAINTER'S WISH.[1]

I WISH that I could ETTY be,
A mighty man methinks is he ;
And strong enough to try a fall
With TITIAN or with PETER PAUL.
And yet, why deck a palace wall
As gorgeously as PETER PAUL ?
He'd love and honour from his Prince,
My gracious lord would blush and wince ;
And so I would not ETTY be,
To shock my Prince's modesty.

I would I were the great LANDSEER,
To paint the best of dogs and deer ;
I would not care for glory, since
I pleased my Queen and charmed my Prince.
And yet I must not wish for that ;
To paint my gracious Prince's hat,
To paint his cane, his gloves, his shoes,
To paint his dogs and cockatoos,
And nought beside, would weary me ;
And so I would not LANDSEER be.

[1] [*Punch*, April 5, 1845.]

Let famous EDWIN still be free
To paint his Queen's menagerie ;
Let ETTY toil for Queen and Crown,
And princely patrons spoon him down ; ·
I will not ask for courtly fame,
When veterans are brought to shame—
I will not pine for royal job,
Let my MAECENAS be a snob.

PAUL PINDAR.[1]

ODE TO SIBTHORP, BY THE POET LAUREATE.[2]

NOTICE.

IN the distant solitude of my mountains, the echoes of the great
world reach me faintly and seldom.   But as the storm sometimes
ruffles the placid bosom of my lakes, the political tempest breaks
over the Poet, too, occasionally, and blows into commotion the
placid depths of his soul.

It was on reading in my paper (*The St. James's Chronicle*,
which, with some friends, I have taken in for thirty-three years)
the announcement, by my admirable friend COLONEL SIBTHORP,
that he was about to sacrifice his life and his whiskers upon the
altar of his country, that I felt a tumultuous movement to me
very unusual.

I bathed twice in the lake, and, having ascended Mount

---

[1] ERRATUM.[3]

PAUL PINDAR, whose poem, called 'A Painter' Wish,' we
published in the last number, writes an indignant letter complaining of a misprint in his ballad.   Speaking of our admirable
painter ETTY, he wrote, 'and Princely patrons spurn him down,'
(which they did, and no mistake,) when we printed, '*spoon* him
down,' which we confess to be absurd.   'Spoon him down, indeed,'
says PAUL; 'spoon yourself, MR. PUNCH,' and adds further ribald
vituperation.   As we made the mistake, we are bound to correct
it, but as for the *spoon*, we thrust it contemptuously back down
PAUL'S own throat.

[2] [*Punch*, April 26, 1845.]   [3] [*Punch*, April 12, 1845.]

Rydal, I lay down upon the topmost peak there, and flung my feelings into the following lyrical shape. I chose the Anapæstic measure, as best suited to express the agitation of the subject of the sacrifice. The other metres employed in the ode are of a calmer tendency, as the reader will see.

The Genius of Britain is made to interpose between Our CURTIUS and the sacrifice he meditates. That she may be successful is the earnest hope of

W. W.

P.S.—I cannot but think the accompanying design of singular significance and beauty.

ODE.

ON MY FRIEND COLONEL SIBTHORP PROPOSING TO SACRIFICE HIS LIFE AND HIS WHISKERS.

'In the cause of my country, who says I'm afear'd—'
Says WALDO of Lincoln, 'to cut off my beard?
Her rights to maintain, and her honour to save,
Who questions how much or how little I'd shave?

A Protestant born, and a gentleman bred,
I'd cut my mustashes with pitiless gashes—
I'd shave off my whiskers, my tuft, my eyelashes—
    I'd shave off my beard, and I'd shave off my head.'

Pleased with the Colonel and his courage wild
The British Lion wagged his tail and smiled ;
And Britain thus addressed her wayward, whiskered child :—

'My bold Dragoon, my favourite son,
    With heart as bold and manly
As beats the ribs of WELLINGTON,
    Or warms the breast of STANLEY :

Thou art my boy, my pride and joy,
    Of chivalry the model ;
And yet the sense is not immense
    In that poor honest noddle.

What cause hath wrought thy rambling thought
    This martyrdom to think on ?
There's many here that I can spare,
    But not my man of Lincoln.

What would they in the Commons do,
    And in the strangers' gall'ry,
Were they by death deprived of you,
    My model of chivalry.

That head, now fixed on your body,
    Is wondrous small of profit ;
But smaller yet the good would be,
    My son, when shaven off it.

Retain your head, my son, and prize
    Your face above all money :
That face so vacuously wise,
    So dolorously funny.

Ah, never cause those meagre jaws
    To lose their tufted glories ;
And never shave that face so grave,
    My Champion of the Tories.

Keep on your beard, your head keep on,
  My orders are explicit ;
You might not know that it was gone—
  But *I*, my son, should miss it.'

Thus spoke Britannia's Genius excellent ;
  The British Lion wagged his tail intent ;
And SIBTHORP, *blushing deep, and loth to risk her*
  Displeasure, humbly at her footstool leant,
And swore he would maintain both head, and tuft, and whisker.

THE EXCELLENT NEW BALLAD OF MR. PEEL.
AT TOLEDO.[1]

SAYS BULWER to PEEL,
  'This note where my seal
And ambassador's [2] are displayed O,
  Is big with a freight
  Of secrets of weight
Concerning a town of Tolaydo.[3]
  'Tis a delicate job,
  And I've chosen you, BOB,
And beg you will hasten with speed O,
  And deliver the note,
  Where you see that I've wrote
The address—at the town of Toledo.[4]

'So quit your cigars
  And your twanging guitars,
And the beautiful dames on the Prado ; [5]

[1] [*Punch*, May 3, 1845.]
[2] MR. BULWER is only our minister at Madrid, but I have thought it more respectful to give him the ambassadorial title.
[3] *Toledo, Tolaydo.* As in our country the name of that famous city is always pronounced in the former manner, *Toleedo*, whilst in Spain it is invariably called *Tolaydo*, I have thought proper to make a compromise in my little poem, and to give each method of pronunciation a chance in the course of the stanza of twelve lines.
[4] I consider this mystery as very fine—you see the address is not specified —I only say *of the town of Toledo*—whereabouts in Toledo ? *that* remains a secret between his Excellency and his Attaché.
[5] The Prado, the Hyde Park of Madrid, where the nobility drive about in their tertulias, and the idlers pass their time in dancing the Muchacha, etc., and amusing themselves with 'cigars' and 'guitars' as above described.

And haste and fulfil
Your Ambassador's will,
By posting away to Tolaydo.'
    'Some pangs I may feel
    To part,' says young Peel,
'From music, and woman, and weed O!
    But to honour my Queen,
    I would run to Pekin,
And shall I not go to Toledo?'

So he uttered a roar [1]
For his carriage and four.
The order was straightway obey'd, O,
    And he bade his young man to
    Pack up his portmanteau,
And was off in a trice to Tolaydo.
    'My pistols I'll load
    (Says he) for the road,
And make the banditti to bleed, O;
    With powder and ball,
    I'll massacre all
The rogues between this and Toledo.'

Now galloping fast,
The journey is past
As quick as four animals may do;
    Till at length the postillions
    (Those faithful Sevillians) [2]
Drive up to the gates of Tolaydo.
    They pull up their mules,
    (For such do the fools
Employ, and not horses as we do),
    And say—'Monsignor,
    We are now at the door
Of the elegant town of Toledo.' [3]

Some carabineers
Kept guard, it appears,
At the gate, and imagine what they do!

[1] *A roar for his carriage and four.* As indicating impetuous youthful haste, I must be permitted to consider this expression very fine.

[2] Though Toledo is not in Seville, yet as the postillions *may* have been of that city, I conceive myself quite authorised in using the expression.

[3] And it *is* an elegant town, as may be seen by ROBERTS'S delightful sketches.

The rascals approach
To examine the coach
As it stops at the door of Tolaydo !
'Let go my barouche,'
With a scream and a push,
Says PEEL, as they ventur'd the deed, O.
And, inspired with disgust,
His pistols he thrust
In the face of the men of Toledo.

'Have a care, my signors,'
The gentleman roars,
As fierce as a Western tornado ;
'Approach my coach panes,
And I'll blow out the brains
Of each carabineer in Tolaydo.
I swear with an oath
To murder I'm loath,
But if ever you venture on me do,
With powder and ball
I'll murder you all,
As sure as you live at Toledo.'

The Carabineers,
They heard him with fears,
And stood, in their glory arrayed, O !
All formed in long lines,
With their big carabines,[1]
Across the main street of Tolaydo.
'Be hanged to his shot,'
Says the Captain. 'For what
'Gainst fifty can one such as he do ?'
His pistols PEEL cocks
(They were MANTON's or NOCKS'),
And prepares to encounter Toledo.

But what sudden alarms
Make the soldiers ground arms,
As if they were told on parade, O !
What angel of peace
Bids the hubbub to cease

[1] *As they form in long lines with their big carabines.* Surely this is a noble way of expressing the armament of the gallant fellows, and gives a fine picture to the imagination.

'Twixt PEEL and the guard of Tolaydo ?
Inform'd of the rout,
And what 'twas about,
As quickly as if he were fee'd, O,[1]
At double quick trot
There comes to the spot
The POLITICAL CHIEF OF TOLEDO.

He beseeches his sons
To fling down their guns,
With a voice like the canes of Barbado ; [2]
'Why seek, silly boy,'
He said, 'to destroy,
The peace of the town of Tolaydo.'
Young PEEL, at his frown,
Was fain to look down,
As mute as a fish or torpedo ;
And looking sheepish,[3]
Says, 'It wasn't my wish
To kick up a row in Toledo.'

It wasn't for quarrels
That these double-barrels
From out my coach-door were displayed, O ;
But to ask if a pistol
Was subject to fiscal
Or custom-house dues at Tolaydo ?
The Political Chief
Expressed his belief,
BOB grinned at the simpleton's credo ; [4]
The Carabineers
They uttered three cheers,
And bade the young hero proceed, O !
And the name of the youth
Is famous for truth
Henceforth, in Madrid and Toledo.

[1] Can haste be more dexterously described ?—as quickly as if he were *fee'd*.
[2] I mean *sweet*, like the well-known sugar-cane, which renders our tea
agreeable, and is so indispensable an adjunct to our puddings.
[3] I have made him look like a sheep, a fish, and a torpedo in two lines.
This is by way of giving an idea of doubt, perplexity, hesitation—all incidental
to the young gentleman's situation.
[4] I need not tell my accomplished friends that *credo* in Spanish means, 'I
believe,' and a great many monstrous fibs, humbugs, and absurd statements
those Spanish simpletons *do* believe, according to the authority of travellers.

MORAL.

My tale it is said,
And now it is read,
My jolly philosophers, say do,
    If BOBBY the old
    Isn't sometimes as bold
As BOBBY the young at Tolaydo.
    Yes, the sire and the colt,
    Both know how to bolt,
'Tis the chivalrous blood of the breed, O,
    And we see in the youth
    The Man of Maynooth,
And in Parliament House *his* Toledo.

PEEL AT TOLEDO.[1]

A roguy-pogy, who signs himself PEPPER BIRCH, has sent us the
following letter :—

' MISTER PUNCH,
    ' Is *Tertulia* a carriage ? if so, what kind of one ?   Is *Muchacha*
a dance ?   For shame, PUNCH, naughty Boy, refer to your dictionary ; *Tertulia* is an evening party in Spain, and *Muchacha* is a
girl ; let me see that your error is corrected in your next week's
number, and
                ' I remain,
                        ' Your loving School Master,
                                            ' PEPPER BIRCH.'

We have had other letters regarding that noble ballad which
appeared in our columns a fortnight since. One of the letters
purported to come from F.M. the DUKE OF VICTORY, who charged
us ' with wilful falsehood ' in calling a *tertulia* a carriage, and a
muchacha a dance.   Let F.M. the DUKE OF VICTORY mind his
own affairs—there is only one man in England who is to give the
lie with impunity, and that is F.M. the DUKE OF WELLINGTON.

As for PEPPER BIRCH, to show him our knowledge of Spanish,
we beg to say that *mangiuto* is the Spanish for a muff ; *euchara*
in the Castilian dialect means a spoon ; and in the Aragonese the
word *bomba* is universally used to signify a pump.

[May 17, 1845.]

THE ALLEGORY OF THE FOUNTAINS.[1]

'SINCE the Fountains of Trafalgar Square have begun to play, a well
which the Union Club sunk at a great expense is quite dry.'

THE Clubbists of the Union sunk a well
Deep, deep into the bowels of Pall Mall,
The rushing water gurgled in the shaft,
And all the footmen washed, and all the members quaffed.

Two wondrous fontanels arose to grace
LORD NELSON's column and Trafalgar Place ;
Deep in the bosom of the earth below,
The builder digg'd to make his fountains froth and flow.

Up, up to heaven Trafalgar's Fountains rose,
Their spray bedewed the DUKE OF BRONTE'S nose,
GEORGE's fat statue, and St. Martin's Rail,
And bathed in silver dew Northumbria's Lion Tail.

Down, deeper down, the Union's waters sank,
No more the footmen washed, the members drank ;
Ask ye the fatal reason of the drought ?
The Unions wells were sold and up Trafalgar's spout.

A moral from those Fountains twain I drew,
(Each thing in life a moral hath, or two,)
And thought St. Stephen's Chapel could compete
With those two aqueducts of Cockspur Street.

The Liberals sought and found the spring and sank it—
It was the cunning Tories came and drank it ;
'Twas RUSSELL bade the water rise and flow ;
Lo, from PEEL's brazen pipes it issues now !

Thus recognising Whig and Tory types
In voluble and brazen water-pipes—
I'm thankful that the stream at last is free ;
BOBBY or JOHNNY, what's the odds to me ?

[1] [*Punch*, May 31, 1845.]

'Tis hard for JOHN, no doubt, that Stealthy BOB
His stream of fame should thus divert and rob ;
And that for which he toiled through seasons hot,
Should fructify another's garden-plot.

Let us, not caring for the strife a dump,
Accommodate ourselves with PEEL for pump ;
And so the liberal waters to compel,
Pump, freemen, day and night! AND WORK THE HANDLE WELL!

PUNCH'S REGENCY.[1]

INTRODUCTION.

THE only man of any mark
    In all the town remaining,
I sauntered in St. James's Park,
    And watched the daylight waning.
' The SPEAKER'S lips,' I said, ' are sealed,
    They've shut up both the Houses ;
SIR ROBERT'S [2] gone to Turnabout field,
    SIR JAMES [3] to shoot the grouses.
The QUEEN and all the Court are out
    In Germany and Flanders,
And, happy midst his native *kraut*,
    My princely ALBERT wanders.
No more the dumpy Palace arch
    The Royal Standard graces ;
Alone, upon his lonely march,
    The yawning sentry paces.'
Beneath an elm-tree, on a bank,
    I mused, (for tired my hunch was,)
And there in slumber soft I sank,
    And this the dream of PUNCH was.

THE DREAM.

I dreamed it was a chair of gold,
    The grassy bank I sat on ;
I dreamed SAINT EDWARD'S sceptre old
    I wielded for a baton.

[1] [*Punch*, August 23, 1845.]
[2] [Sir Robert Peel.]   [3] [Sir James Graham.]

Men crowded to my throne, the elm,
    In reverend allegiance ;
And PUNCH was publish'd through the realm
    The jolliest of Regents.

Back came the ministerial rout
    From touring and carousing ;
Back came SIR BOB from Turnabout,
    And back SIR JAMES from grousing.
I turn'd upon a scornful heel,
    When GRAHAM ask'd my favour ;
I sternly banish'd BOBBY PEEL
    To Turnabout for ever.

To courtly ABERDEEN I sent
    A mission influential,
To serve the Yankee President
    As Flunky Confidential.
LORD BROUGHAM and VAUX in banishment
    I order'd to Old Reekie,
And STANLEY[1] to New Zealand went
    Ambassador to Heki.[2]

And KELLY,[3] whom the world assails,
    But whom the bar takes fame from,
I made Lord Viscount New South Wales,
    Where poor JOHN TAWELL[4] came from.
And then I asked His Grace, the Duke,[5]
    What ministers to go to,
On which he generously took
    The Cabinet *in toto*.

O then ! all other reigns which shine
    Upon our page domestic
Were mean and dim compared to mine,
    That Regency majestic ;
And ages hence the English realm
    Shall tell the wondrous legend
Of PUNCH, when at the nation's helm,
    HER MAJESTY'S High Regent.

---

[1] [Lord Stanley.]   [2] [A Maori chief.]
[3] [Sir Fitzroy Kelly.]   [4] [The murderer of Sarah Hart.]
                        [5] [The Duke of Wellington.]

Around my empire's wide frontier
  No greedy bully swaggered,
Nor swindling Yankee buccaneer,
  Nor savage Gallic braggart.
For threats and arms were flung aside,
  And war-ships turned to traders,
And all our ports were opened wide,
  To welcome the invaders.

At home the cottier coursed his hare,
  Beside the Duke his neighbour ;
The weaver got his living fair
  For his ten hours of labour.
And every man without employ
  Got beef—not bones—to feed on,
And every little working boy
  His page of *Punch* could read on.

And Irishmen learned common sense,
  And prudence brought them riches ;
Repeal ceased pilfering for pence
  In PADDY's mended breeches.
Old DAN [1] was grown too rich to beg,
  And in a Union jolly
I linked MacHALE [2] with TRESHAM GREGG, [3]
  And BERESFORD [4] with CROLLY. [5]

Then gentlemen might earn their bread,
  And think there was no shame in't ;
And at my court might hold their head
  Like any Duke or Dame in't.
A Duchess and her governess
  The same quadrille I clapt in ;
I asked old WELLINGTON to mess,
  And meet a half-pay Captain.

The Bar and Press I reconciled
  (They thanked me one and all for't),
Benignantly the Thunderer smiled
  On MR. SERJEANT TALFOURD . . .

[1] [Daniel O'Connell.]
[2] [Archbishop of Tuam.]
[3] [Chaplain of the Orangemen of Ireland.]
[4] [Lord John de la Poer Beresford, Primate of Ireland.]
[5] [Primate of the Irish Roman Catholic Church.]

I know not where my fancy strayed,
  My dream grew wilder—bolder—
When suddenly a hand was laid
  Full roughly on my shoulder.

It was the Guardian of the Park,—
  The sun was sunk in Heaven ;
'Git up,' says he, ' it's after dark,
  We shuts at half-past seven.'
And so I rose and shook myself,
  And, *satiatus ludi*,
Resigned the crown to ROYAL GUELPH,
  And went to tea to Judy.

SERENADE.[1]

WE have been (exclusively) favoured with a copy of the following graceful verses composed by DOCTOR PRÆTORIUS, and sung by him to the guitar before the windows of the Royal guests at Rosenau. They show considerable aptness in a German, and there is only one word, that of *Ritter* (knight), which is not idiomatic English. The Doctor has been appointed Knight of the George and Blue Boar of Coburg in consequence of the effusion.

Sleep, softly sleep, O royal pair ! and be your slumbers cosy now ;
Watch round their pillows, angels fair, and give their eyes repose enow ;
And summer flowers and summer air breathe soft around Schloss
    Rosenau !

No jealous gates are locked and barred around the Dame and Ritter here,
Nor sentinels keep watch and ward, save wakeful stars which glitter
    here,
Or larks, which come relieving guard at morn, and sing and twitter here.

Though England is an Empire grand, and but a humble Duchy's this ;
And though the realm which you command a thousand times as much
    as this ;
You cannot take, in all England, a pleasant slumber such as this.

As calm as in his infancy the royal ALBERT dozes here ;
Forgetting cares of royalty the Stranger QUEEN reposes here,
Though citizens and peasantry come walk amid the roses here.

---

[1] [*Punch*, September 6, 1845.]

In Pimlico there roses blow, if true the papers write of you,
But 'tis not thus in Pimlico your people take delight of you ;
Were ever English people so allowed to take a sight of you ?

Then softly sleep, O royal pair, and pleasantly repose ye now,
In England there is state and care, and weariness and woes enow ;
But summer wind and summer air breathe gently round Schloss
    Rosenau.

NEW VERSION OF GOD SAVE THE QUEEN.[1]

THE Coburg children sang our national melody in presence of
their Majesties with great sweetness and precision. It is not
generally known that DOCTOR PRÆTORIUS, who invariably
accompanies his Royal patrons, was present at the rehearsals of
the poem, and instructed the little darlings personally.

When the occasion came for singing it, *one* little rogue (son of
PROFESSOR VON MUFF) pipes out—

> Send her victorious,
> Happy and glorious,
> DOCTOR PRÆTORIUS.
>   God save the QUEEN.

At which the royal revellers laughed with much good humour.

THE CAMBRIDGE ADDRESS TO PRINCE ALBERT.[2]

WE have received a version of the above document,[3] freely rendered
into English by a gentleman of the name of GYP, of Trinity
College, Cambridge.

> Stern fate hath clipped, with cruel shear,
>   In spite of all physick,
> A worthy duke, a noble peer,
> To virtue and to Cambridge dear,
>   (Says REVEREND MR. CRICK.)[4]

[1] [*Punch*, September 6, 1845.]   [2] [*Punch*, March 13, 1847.]

[3] [When it was necessary to appoint a successor to the Duke of North-
umberland as Chancellor of Cambridge University, some courtly dignitaries
solicited Prince Albert to accept the office. The manner in which the Prince's
candidature had been manœuvred disgusted the University, and Lord Power
came forward in opposition. Prince Albert won by 112 votes, the number
polled being about 1800. He was installed in great state, the Queen being
present. See also *Mr. Jeames's Sentiments on the Cambridge Election*
(vol. xi. of this edition, p. 244.)]

[4] [The Rev. Mr. Crick was the Public Orator.]

He ruled us but for seven short year,
  His death was all too quick ;
We howl, and drop the briny tear
Upon his lamentable bier,
    (Says REVEREND MR. CRICK.)

About his venerated dust,
  Our tear-drops tumble thick ;
He was our champion kind and just,
In him was all our hope and trust
    (Says REVEREND MR. CRICK.)
But weep and blubber though we must,
  For this of dukes the pick,
We must not cry until we bust—
Such conduct would inspire disgust,
    (Says REVEREND MR. CRICK.)

My GRANTA ! wipe your weeping face,
  And be philosophick ;
Look round and see can we replace
In any way his poor dear Grace,
    (Says REVEREND MR. CRICK.)
Who is the man to meet our case ?
  Who enters in the nick,
To take Northumbria's vacant mace ?
There is a gent of royal race,
    (Says REVEREND MR. CRICK.)

There is a gent of royal breed,
  There is a princely brick,
Who doth on every virtue feed,
As wise in thought as great in deed ;
  To him we'll fly, (says CRICK.)
O Prince ! come succour at our need,
  This body politic ;
Heal up our wounds, which gape and bleed ;
Prevent us running quite to seed,
    (Cries REVEREND MR. CRICK.)

On thee our hopes and faith we pin ;
  Without thee, ruined slick ;
To thee we kneel with humble shin ;
Stand by us, guide us, hem us in,
    Great Prince ! (cries MR. CRICK.)

S

Thou bright exemplar of all Prin-
   ces, here your shoes we lick!
Kings first endowed us with their tin,
Why mayn't we hope for kings agin?
   (Says independent CRICK.)

CRICK Yᴇ PUBLICK ORATOR SPOWTS BEFORE Yᴇ PRINCE'S HIGHNESS.

Our tree is of an ancient root,
   And straightway perpendic-
ular to heaven its boughs will shoot,
If you but listen to our suit,
   (Says REVEREND MR. CRICK.)
We grovel at your royal boot
   Ah! don't in anger kick,
Great Prince! the suppliants at your foot,
See how our lips cling fondly to 't,
   (Cries that true Briton, CRICK.)

From faction's sacrilegious claws
  Keep Church and Bishopric ;
Support our academic cause ;
Uphold our rights ; defend our laws,
  (Ejaculated CRICK.)

The speech was done.   He made a pause
  For ALBERT and for VIC ;
Three most vociferous huzzaws
Then broke from mighty WHEWELL'S jaws,
  Who, as a proof of his applause,
Straight to the buttery goes and draws
  A pint of ale for CRICK.

THE YANKEE VOLUNTEERS.[1]

' A SURGEON of the United States Army says, that, on inquiring
of the Captain of his company, he found *that nine-tenths* of the
men had enlisted on account of some female difficulty.'—*Morning
Paper.*

Ye Yankee volunteers !
It makes my bosom bleed
When I your story read,
  Though oft 'tis told one.
So—in both hemispheres
The women are untrue,
And cruel in the New,
  As in the Old one !

What !—in this company
Of sixty sons of MARS,
Who march 'neath Stripes and Stars,
  With fife and horn,
Nine-tenths of all we see
Along the warlike line
Had but one cause to join
  This Hope Forlorn ?

Deserters from the Realm
Where tyrant VENUS reigns,
You slipped her wicked chains,
  Fled and outran her.

[1] [*Punch*, January 4, 1851.]

And now, with sword and helm,
Together banded are
Beneath the Stripe and Star-
      Embroidered banner !

And is it so with all
The warriors ranged in line,
With lace bedizened fine
      And swords gold-hilted—
You, lusty corporal,
You, Colour-man, who gripes
The flag of Stars and Stripes—
      Has each been jilted ?

Come, each man of this line,
The privates strong and tall,
'The pioneers and all,'
      The fifer nimble—
Lieutenant and Ensign,
Captain with epaulets,
And Blacky there, who beats
      The clanging cymbal—

O cymbal-beating black,
Tell us, as thou canst feel,
Was it some LUCY NEAL
      Who caused thy ruin ?
O nimble fifing JACK,
And drummer making din
So deftly on the skin,
      With thy rat-tattooing.

Confess, ye volunteers,
Lieutenant and Ensign,
And Captain of the line,
      As bold as Roman—
Confess, ye grenadiers,
However strong and tall,
The Conqueror of you all
      Is Woman, Woman !

No corselet is so proof
But through it from her bow
The shafts that she can throw
      Will pierce and rankle.

> No champion e'er so tough,
> But's in the struggle thrown,
> And tripped and trodden down
>   By her slim ankle.
>
> Thus, always it was ruled :
> And when a woman smiled,
> The strong man was a child,
>   The sage a noodle.
> ALCIDES was befooled,
> And silly SAMSON shorn,
> Long, long ere you were born,
>   Poor Yankee Doodle !

THE IRISH MARTYRS.[1]

'The martyrs wore the uniform of the '82 Club.'

WE have received, and hasten to publish, the enclosed favour from LADY MORGAN :—

> At Kilkenny King DAN and his Marthyrs
>   Sat down to their platthers and jorums,
> In lovely green-coats and goold garthers—
>   Och sure they are sweet uniforms !
> But there's martyrs besides those repailers
>   Who on the occasion displayed them—
> The martyrs I mean are the tailors,
>   The tailors at Dublin who made them.

THE '82 CLUB UNIFORM.[2]

SMITH O'BRIEN, swaggering about in the green and gold of the '82 Club, said that those who wore it were the natural leaders of the Irish people, (hear, hear !) ; that the uniform only wanted a sword to make it completely military, (loud cheers) ; and that they were ready to assume the sword when their country required such a weapon, (hurrah !).

This threat of the sword had its effect at once, and dreadfully frightened—MR. O'CONNELL.

[1] [*Punch*, April 12, 1845.]   [2] [*Punch*, April 5, 1845.]

FATHER MATHEW'S DEBTS.[1]

' MY circumstances have become known to friends in England, and with their aid, and some partial help from Ireland, a sum over £7000 has been raised, and my debts are liquidated.'

Who paid the good Father's debts?
I, said JOHN BULL ;
And I'd do it again :
For I honour honest men ;
So I paid his debts.

Who paid BIG DAN ?
I, says starving PADDY,
Though I'm a poor laddy,
But I'll do all I can
For that sootherin man,
Who discoorsis so gran',
Och DAN !

THE EUREKA.[2]

THAT notable invention, the Eureka, or Latin Verse-grinder, was tried yesterday before a committee of young gentlemen from the public schools, who are anxious to have their Latin exercises done with the least possible trouble.

The proprietor asked the young gentlemen to fix a subject upon which the instrument might perform, accordingly MR. SNOOKS, of Westminster, proposed the quarrel between ROEBUCK and SOMERS.

The machinery of the wondrous instrument was set in motion, and the following lines ground out to the music of a barrel organ :—

Sligonis membrum, BUCKI vult pellere nasum,
    Transfugit ARCTURUS Rhetoris in gremium.
Hunc pius ASHLEIUS laudat, decus Exeter Aulae,
    Pontificumque comes BOBBIUS INGLISIUS.
Hunc laudat Dominus PEELEIDES Turnabout agri,
    Laudat HUMUSQUE ferox ille tremendus aper.
Desine BUCKE Domum nostram examinare querelis
    Inque potatones, Padde, retro propera.

---

[1] [*Punch,* May 24, 1845.]   [2] [*Punch,* July 5, 1845.]

As some decidedly English expressions had crept into the lines, the inventor explained that he was educating his machine to grind English verses likewise ; hence, that for the present a little confusion might arise between the languages. A translation of the above verses was then called for by MASTER SPOON, of Charterhouse, when the following appeared, the organ playing ' Rule Britannia.'

> When Sligo's member aims at ROEBUCK'S nose,
> The frightened BUCK to Speaker's bosom goes.
> Him ASHLEY praises, piousest of lords,
> And INGLIS, known at missionary boards ;
> Him HUME the Caledonian boar so stout
> Admires, and PEEL, the Lord of Turnabout.
> BUCK, plague the House no more ! and, Paddy, clap
> A 'tato into thy potato trap.

Several double - barrelled Eurekas were ordered for Eton, Harrow, and Rugby, and we hear of a forthcoming *soirée*, where LORD W—m L—nn—x proposes to perform some choice fantasias on this extraordinary instrument.

A LITTLE DINNER AT TIMMINS'S.

I.

MR. AND MRS. FITZROY TIMMINS live in Lilliput Street, that neat little street which runs at right angles with the Park and Brobdingnag Gardens. It is a very genteel neighbourhood, and I need not say they are of a good family.

Especially MRS. TIMMINS, as her mamma is always telling MR. T. They are Suffolk people, and distantly related to the Right Honourable the EARL OF BUNGAY.

Besides his house in Lilliput Street, MR. TIMMINS has Chambers in Fig-tree Court, Temple, and goes the Northern Circuit.

The other day, when there was a slight difference about the payment of fees between the great Parliamentary Counsel and the Solicitors, STOKE and POGERS, of Great George Street, sent the papers of the Lough Foyle and Lough Corrib Junction Railway to MR. FITZROY TIMMINS, who was so elated that he instantly purchased a couple of looking-glasses for his drawing-rooms (the front room is 16 by 12, and the back a tight but elegant apartment, 10 ft. 6 by 8 ft. 4), a coral for the baby, two new dresses for MRS. TIMMINS, and a little rosewood desk, at the Pantechnicon, for which ROSA had long been sighing, with crumpled legs, emerald-green and gold morocco top, and drawers all over.

MRS. TIMMINS is a very pretty poetess (her ' Lines to a Faded Tulip,' and her ' Plaint of Plinlimmon,' appeared in one of last year's Keepsakes), and FITZROY, as he impressed a kiss on the snowy forehead of his bride, pointed out to her, in one of the innumerable pockets of the desk, an elegant ruby-tipped pen, and six charming little gilt blank books, marked ' My Books,' which MRS. FITZROY might fill, he said (he is an Oxford man, and very polite), ' with the delightful productions of her Muse.' Besides these books, there was pink paper, paper with crimson edges, lace paper, all stamped with R. F. T. (ROSA FITZROY TIMMINS), and the hand and battle-axe, the crest of the TIMMINSES (and borne at Ascalon by ROALDUS DE TIMMINS, a crusader, who is now buried in the Temple Church, next to SERJEANT SNOOKS), and yellow, pink, light-blue, and other scented sealing-waxes, at the service of ROSA when she chose to correspond with her friends.

ROSA, you may be sure, jumped with joy at the sight of this sweet present; called her CHARLES (his first name is SAMUEL, but they have sunk that) the best of men! embraced him a great number of times, to the edification of her buttony little page, who stood at the landing; and as soon as he was gone to Chambers, took the new pen and a sweet sheet of paper, and began to compose a poem.

'What shall it be about?' was naturally her first thought. 'What should be a young mother's first inspiration?' Her child lay on the sofa asleep, before her; and she began in her neatest hand—

LINES

ON MY SON, BUNGAY DE BRACY GASHLEIGH TYMMYNS, AGED TEN MONTHS.

Tuesday.

How beautiful! how beautiful thou seemest,
 My boy, my precious one, my rosy babe!
Kind angels hover round thee, as thou dreamest:
Soft lashes hide thy beauteous azure eye which gleamest.

'Gleamest? thine eye which gleamest? Is that grammar?' thought ROSA, who had puzzled her little brains for some time with this absurd question, when baby woke; then the cook came up to ask about dinner; then MRS. FUNDY slipped over from No. 27, (they are opposite neighbours, and made an acquaintance through MRS. FUNDY's macaw): and a thousand things happened. Finally, there was no rhyme to babe except TIPPOO SAIB (against whom MAJOR GASHLEIGH, ROSA's grandfather, had distinguished himself), and so she gave up the little poem about her DE BRACY.

Nevertheless, when FITZROY returned from Chambers to take a walk with his wife in the Park, as he peeped through the rich tapestry hanging which divided the two drawing-rooms, he found his dear girl still seated at the desk, and writing, writing away with her ruby pen as fast as it could scribble.

'What a genius that child has!' he said; 'why, she is a second MRS. NORTON!' and advanced smiling to peep over her shoulder and see what pretty thing ROSA was composing.

It was not poetry, though, that she was writing, and Fitz read as follows :—

'*Lilliput Street, Tuesday, 22nd May.*

'Mr. and Mrs. Fitzroy Tymmyns request the pleasure of Sir Thomas and Lady Kicklebury's company at dinner on Wednesday, at 7½ o'clock.'

'My dear!' exclaimed the barrister, pulling a long face.

'Law, Fitzroy!' cried the beloved of his bosom, 'how you do startle one!'

'Give a dinner party with our means!' said he.

'Ain't you making a fortune, you miser?' Rosa said. 'Fifteen guineas a day is four thousand five hundred a year; I've calculated it.' And, so saying, she rose, and, taking hold of his whiskers, (which are as fine as those of any man of his circuit,) she put her mouth close up against his and did something to his long face, which quite changed the expression of it : and which the little page heard outside the door.

'Our dining-room won't hold ten,' he said.

'We'll only ask twenty,' my love; 'ten are sure to refuse in this season, when everybody is giving parties. Look, here is the list.

'EARL and COUNTESS OF BUNGAY, and LADY BARBARA SAINT MARY'S.'

'You are dying to get a Lord into the house,' TIMMINS said (*he* has not altered his name in Fig-tree Court yet, and therefore I am not so affected as to call him *Tymmyns*).

'Law, my dear, they are our cousins, and must be asked,' ROSA said.

'Let us put down my sister and TOM CROWDER, then.'

'BLANCHE CROWDER is really so *very* fat, FITZROY,' his wife said, 'and our rooms are so *very* small.'

FITZ laughed. 'You little rogue,' he said, 'LADY BUNGAY weighs two of BLANCHE, even when she's not in the f——'

'Fiddlestick!' ROSA cried out. 'DOCTOR CROWDER really cannot be admitted; he makes such a noise eating his soup, that it is really quite disagreeable;' and she imitated the gurgling noise performed by the Doctor while inhausting his soup, in such a funny way, that FITZ saw inviting him was out of the question.

'Besides, we mustn't have too many relations,' ROSA went on. 'Mamma, of course, is coming. She doesn't like to be asked in the evening; and she'll bring her silver bread-basket, and her candlesticks, which are very rich and handsome.'

'And you complain of BLANCHE for being too stout!' groaned out TIMMINS.

'Well, well, don't be in a pet,' said little ROSA. 'The girls won't come to dinner; but will bring their music afterwards.' And she went on with the list.

'SIR THOMAS and LADY KICKLEBURY, 2. No saying no : we *must* ask them, CHARLES. They are rich people, and any room in their house in Brobdingnag Gardens would swallow up *our* humble cot. But to people in *our* position in *society*, they will

be glad enough to come. The City people are glad to mix with the old families.'

'Very good,' said FITZ, with a sad face of assent—and MRS. TIMMINS went on reading her list.

'MR. and MRS. TOPHAM SAWYER, Belgravine Place.'

'MRS. SAWYER hasn't asked you all the season. She gives herself the airs of an Empress ; and when——'

'One's Member, you know, my dear, one must have,' ROSA replied, with much dignity; as if the presence of the representative of her native place would be a protection to her dinner; and a note was written and transported by the page early next morning to the mansion of the SAWYERS, in Belgravine Place.

The TOPHAM SAWYERS had just come down to breakfast, MRS. T. in her large dust-coloured morning dress and Madonna front, (she looks rather scraggy of a morning, but I promise you her ringlets and figure will stun you of an evening); and having read the note, the following dialogue passed :—

Mrs. Topham Sawyer. 'Well, upon my word, I don't know where things will end.   MR. SAWYER, the TIMMINSES have asked us to dinner.'

Mr. Topham Sawyer. 'Ask us to dinner!   What d — impudence!'

Mrs. Topham Sawyer. 'The most dangerous and insolent revolutionary principles are abroad, MR. SAWYER; and I shall write and hint as much to these persons.'

Mr. Topham Sawyer. 'No, d— it, JOANNA, they are my constituents, and we must go.   Write a civil note, and say we will come to their party.'   (*He resumes the perusal of the 'Times,' and* MRS. TOPHAM SAWYER *writes*)—

'MY DEAR ROSA,

'We shall have *great pleasure* in joining your little party. I do not reply in the third person, as *we are old friends*, you know, and *country neighbours*.   I hope your mamma is well: present my *kindest remembrances* to her, and I hope we shall see much MORE of each other in the summer, when we go down to the Sawpits (for going abroad is out of the question in these *dreadful times*).   With a hundred kisses to your dear little *pet*,

'Believe me your attached

'J. T. S.'

She said *Pet*, because she did not know whether ROSA's child was a girl or a boy: and MRS. TIMMINS was very much pleased with the kind and gracious nature of the reply to her invitation.

II.

THE next persons whom little MRS. TIMMINS was bent upon asking were MR. and MRS. JOHN ROWDY, of the firm of STUMPY, ROWDY, AND Co., of Brobdingnag Gardens, of the Prairie, Putney, and of Lombard Street, City.

MRS. TIMMINS and MRS. ROWDY had been brought up at the same school together, and there was always a little rivalry between them, from the day when they contended for the French prize at school, to last week, when each had a stall at the Fancy Fair for the benefit of the Daughters of Decayed Muffin-men; and when MRS. TIMMINS danced against MRS. ROWDY in the Scythe Mazurka at the Polish Ball, headed by MRS. HUGH SLASHER. ROWDY took twenty-three pounds more than TIMMINS in the Muffin transaction (for she had possession of a kettle-holder worked by the hands of R—y—lty, which brought crowds to her stall); but in the Mazourk ROSA conquered; she has the prettiest little foot possible (which in a red boot and silver heel looked so lovely that even the Chinese Ambassador remarked it), whereas MRS. ROWDY's foot is no trifle, as LORD CORNBURY acknowledged when it came down on his Lordship's boot tip as they danced together amongst the Scythes.

'Those people are ruining themselves,' said MRS. JOHN ROWDY to her husband, on receiving the pink note. It was carried round by that rogue of a buttony page in the evening, and he walked to Brobdingnag Gardens and in the Park afterwards, with a young lady who is kitchen-maid at 27, and who is not more than fourteen years older than little Buttons.

'Those people are ruining themselves,' said MRS. JOHN to her husband. 'ROSA says she has asked the BUNGAYS.'

'BUNGAYS, indeed! TIMMINS was always a tuft-hunter,' said ROWDY, who had been at College with the barrister, and who, for his own part, has no more objection to a Lord than you or I have; and adding, 'Hang him, what business has *he* to be giving parties?' allowed MRS. ROWDY, nevertheless, to accept ROSA's invitation.

'When I go to business to-morrow, I will just have a look at MR. FITZ's account,' MR. ROWDY thought, 'and if it is overdrawn, as it usually is, why.' . . . The announcement of MRS. ROWDY's brougham here put an end to this agreeable train of thought, and the banker and his lady stepped into it to join a snug little family party of two-and-twenty, given by MR. and MRS. SECOND-CHOP, at their great house on the other side of the Park.

'ROWDYS 2, BUNGAYS 3, ourselves and mamma 3, 2 SAWYERS,' calculated little ROSA.

'GENERAL GULPIN,' ROSA continued, 'eats a great deal, and is very stupid, but he looks well at a table, with his star and ribbon; let us put *him* down!' and she noted down 'SIR THOMAS and LADY GULPIN, 2. LORD CASTLENOODLE, 1.'

'You will make your party abominably genteel and stupid,' groaned TIMMINS. 'Why don't you ask some of our old friends? Old MRS. PORTMAN has asked us twenty times, I am sure, within the last two years.'

'And the last time we went there, there was pea-soup for dinner!' MRS. TIMMINS said, with a look of ineffable scorn.

'Nobody can have been kinder than the HODGES have always been to us; and some sort of return we might make, I think.'

'Return, indeed! A pretty sound it is on the staircase to hear MR. and MRS. ODGE and the MISS ODGES, pronounced by BILLITER, who always leaves his h's out. No, no; see attornies at your Chambers, my dear—but what could the poor creatures do in *our* society?' And so, one by one, TIMMINS's old friends were tried and eliminated by MRS. TIMMINS, just as if she had

been an Irish Attorney-General, and they so many Catholics on
Mr. Mitchel's Jury.

Mrs. Fitzroy insisted that the party should be of her very
best company. Funnyman, the Great Wit, was asked, because
of his jokes; and Mrs. Butt, on whom he practises; and
Potter, who is asked because everybody else asks him ; and Mr.
Ranville Ranville of the Foreign Office, who might give some
news of the Spanish squabble ; and Botherby, who has suddenly
sprung up into note because he is intimate with the French
Revolution, and visits Ledru-Rollin and Lamartine. And
these, with a couple more who are *amis de la maison*, made up
the twenty, whom Mrs. Timmins thought she might safely invite
to her little dinner.

But the deuce of it was, that when the answers to the
invitations came back, everybody accepted ! Here was a pretty
quandary. How they were to get twenty into their dining-room
was a calculation which poor Timmins could not solve at all ;
and he paced up and down the little room in dismay.

'Pooh !' said Rosa with a laugh ; 'your sister Blanche
looked very well in one of my dresses, last year ; and you know
how stout she is. We will find some means to accommodate them
all, depend upon it.'

Mrs. John Rowdy's note to dear Rosa, accepting the latter's
invitation, was a very gracious and kind one : and Mrs. Fitz
showed it to her husband when he came back from Chambers.
But there was another note which had arrived for him by this
time from Mr. Rowdy—or rather from the firm : and to the
effect that Mr. F. Timmins had overdrawn his account £62 : 18 : 6,
and was requested to pay that sum to his obedient servants,
Stumpy, Rowdy, and Co.

And Timmins did not like to tell his wife that the contending
parties in the Lough Neagh and Lough Corrib Railroad had come
to a settlement, and that the fifteen guineas a day had consequently
determined. 'I have had seven days of it, though,' he thought ;
'and that will be enough to pay for the desk, the dinner, and the
glasses, and make all right with Stumpy and Rowdy.'

III.

THE cards for dinner having been issued, it became the duty of MRS. TIMMINS to make further arrangements respecting the invitations to the tea - party which was to follow the more substantial meal.

These arrangements are difficult, as any lady knows who is in the habit of entertaining her friends.   There are—

People who are offended if you ask them to tea whilst others have been asked to dinner—

People who are offended if you ask them to tea at all; and cry out furiously, 'Good Heavens! JANE, my love, why do these TIMMINSES suppose that I am to leave my dinner-table to attend their —— soirée ?' (the dear reader may fill up the —— to any strength, according to his liking)—or, 'Upon my word, WILLIAM, my dear, it is too much to ask us to pay twelve shillings for a Brougham, and to spend I don't know how much in gloves, just to make our curtsies in MRS. TIMMINS'S little drawing-room.' MRS. MOSER made the latter remark about the TIMMINS affair, while the former was uttered by MR. GRUMPLEY, Barrister-at-Law, to his lady, in Gloucester Place.

That there are people who are offended if you don't ask them at all, is a point which I suppose nobody will question.   TIMMINS'S earliest friend in life was SIMMINS, whose wife and family have taken a cottage at Mortlake for the season.

'We can't ask them to come out of the country,' ROSA said to her FITZROY—(between ourselves, she was delighted that MRS. SIMMINS was out of the way, and was as jealous of her as every well-regulated woman should be of her husband's female friends)— 'we can't ask them to come so far for the evening.'

'Why, no, certainly,' said FITZROY, who has himself no very great opinion of a tea-party ; and so the SIMMINSES were cut out of the list.

And what was the consequence ? The consequence was, that SIMMINS and TIMMINS cut when they meet at Westminster ; that MRS. SIMMINS sent back all the books which she had borrowed from ROSA, with a withering note of thanks ; that ROSA goes about saying that MRS. SIMMINS squints ; that MRS. S., on her side, declares that ROSA is crooked, and behaved shamefully to CAPTAIN HICKS, in marrying FITZROY over him, though she was forced to do it by her mother, and prefers the Captain to her husband to this day.   If, in a word, these two men could be made to fight, I believe their wives would not be displeased ; and the reason of all this misery, rage, and dissension lies in a poor little twopenny dinner-party in Lilliput Street.

Well, the guests, both for before and after meat, having been asked—old MRS. GASHLEIGH, ROSA's mother—(and, by consequence, FITZROY's *dear* mother-in-law, though I promise you that 'dear' is particularly sarcastic)—MRS. GASHLEIGH of course was sent for, and came with MISS ELIZA GASHLEIGH, who plays on the guitar, and EMILY, who limps a little, but plays sweetly on the concertina. They live close by—trust them for that. Your mother-in-law is always within hearing, thank our stars for the attentions of the dear woman. The GASHLEIGHS, I say, live close by, and came early on the morning after ROSA's notes had been issued for the dinner.

When FITZROY, who was in his little study, which opens into the little dining-room—one of those absurd little rooms that ought to be called a Gentleman's Pantry, and is scarcely bigger than a shower-bath, or a state cabin in a ship—when FITZROY heard his mother-in-law's knock, and her well-known scuffling and chattering in the passage, in which she squeezed up young BUTTONS, the page, while she put questions to him regarding baby, and the cook's health, and whether she had taken what MRS. GASHLEIGH had sent over night, and the housemaid's health, and whether MR. TIMMINS had gone to Chambers or not? and when, after this preliminary chatter, BUTTONS flung open the door, announcing, 'MRS. GASHLEIGH and the young ladies,' FITZROY laid down his *Times* newspaper with an expression that had best not be printed in a Journal which young people read, and took his hat and walked away.

MRS. GASHLEIGH has never liked him since he left off calling her Mamma, and kissing her. But he said he could not stand it any longer—he was hanged if he would. So he went away to Chambers, leaving the field clear to ROSA, Mamma, and the two dear girls.

—Or to one of them, rather; for, before leaving the house, he thought he would have a look at little FITZROY up-stairs in the Nursery, and he found the child in the hands of his maternal aunt ELIZA, who was holding him and pinching him as if he had been her guitar, I suppose; so that the little fellow bawled pitifully—and his father finally quitted the premises.

No sooner was he gone, and although the party was still a fortnight off, yet the women pounced upon his little Study, and began to put it in order. Some of his papers they pushed up over the bookcase, some they put behind the Encyclopædia, some they crammed into the drawers, where MRS. GASHLEIGH found

.three cigars, which she pocketed, and some letters, over which she cast her eye, and by FITZ's return they had the room as neat as possible, and the best glass and dessert-service mustered on the study-table.

It was a very neat and handsome service, as you may be sure MRS. GASHLEIGH thought, whose rich uncle had purchased it for the young couple, at SPODE AND COPELAND'S : but it was only for twelve persons.

It was agreed that it would be, in all respects, cheaper and better to purchase a dozen more dessert plates ; and with 'my silver basket in the centre,' MRS. G. said (she is always bragging about that confounded bread-basket), 'we need not have any extra china dishes, and the table will look very pretty.'

On making a roll-call of the glass, it was calculated that at least a dozen or so tumblers, four or five dozen wines, eight water-bottles, and a proper quantity of ice-plates were requisite ; and that, as they would always be useful, it would be best to purchase the articles immediately. FITZ tumbled over the basket containing them, which stood in the hall, as he came in from Chambers, and over the boy who had brought them—and the little bill.

The women had had a long debate, and something like a quarrel, it must be owned, over the bill of fare. MRS. GASHLEIGH, who had lived a great part of her life in Devonshire, and kept house in great state there, was famous for making some dishes, without which, she thought, no dinner could be perfect. When she proposed her mock-turtle, and stewed pigeons, and gooseberry-cream, ROSA turned up her nose—a pretty little nose it was, by the way, and with a natural turn in that direction.

'Mock-turtle in June, Mamma !' she said.

'It was good enough for your grandfather, ROSA,' the mamma replied ; 'it was good enough for the Lord High Admiral, when he was at Plymouth ; it was good enough for the first men in the county, and relished by LORD FORTYSKEWER and LORD ROLLS ; SIR LAWRENCE PORKER ate twice of it after Exeter races ; and I think it might be good enough for——'

'I will *not* have it, Mamma !' said ROSA, with a stamp of her foot—and MRS. GASHLEIGH knew what resolution there was in that ; once, when she had tried to physic the baby, there had been a similar fight between them.

So MRS. GASHLEIGH made out a *carte*, in which the soup was left with a dash—a melancholy vacuum ; and in which the pigeons were certainly thrust in amongst the *entrées;* but ROSA determined they never should make an *entrée* at all into *her* dinner-party, but that she would have the dinner her own way.

When FITZ returned, then, and after he had paid the little bill of £6 : 14 : 6 for the glass, ROSA flew to him with her sweetest smiles, and the baby in her arms. And after she had made him remark how the child grew every day more and more like him, and after she had treated him to a number of compliments and caresses, which it were positively fulsome to exhibit in public, and after she had soothed him into good humour by her artless tenderness, she began to speak to him about some little points which she had at heart.

She pointed out with a sigh how shabby the old curtains looked since the dear new glasses which her darling FITZ had given her had been put up in the drawing-room. Muslin curtains cost nothing, and she must and would have them.

The muslin curtains were accorded. She and FITZ went and bought them at SHOOLBRED'S, when you may be sure she treated herself likewise to a neat, sweet, pretty half-mourning (for the Court, you know, is in mourning)—a neat sweet *barège*, or calimanco, or bombazine, or tiffany, or some such thing; but MADAME CAMILLE of Regent Street made it up, and ROSA looked like an angel in it on the night of her little dinner.

'And my sweet,' she continued, after the curtains had been given in, 'Mamma and I have been talking about the dinner. She wants to make it very expensive, which I cannot allow. I have been thinking of a delightful and economical plan, and you, my sweetest FITZ, must put it into execution.'

'I have cooked a mutton-chop, when I was in Chambers,' FITZ said, with a laugh. 'Am I to put on a cap and an apron?'

'No; but you are to go to the Megatherium Club (where, you wretch, you are always going without my leave), and you are to beg MONSIEUR MIROBOLANT, your famous cook, to send you one of his best aides-de-camp, as I know he will, and with his aid we can dress the dinner and the confectionery at home for *almost nothing*, and we can show those purse-proud TOPHAM SAWYERS and ROWDYS that the *humble cottage* can furnish forth an elegant entertainment as well as the gilded halls of wealth.'

FITZ agreed to speak to MONSIEUR MIROBOLANT. If ROSA had had a fancy for the cook of the Prime Minister, I believe the deluded creature of a husband would have asked Lord John for the loan of him.

IV

FITZROY TIMMINS, whose taste for wine is remarkable for so young a man, is a member of the Committee of the Megatherium Club, and the great MIROBOLANT, good-natured as all great men are, was only too happy to oblige him. A young friend and *protégé* of his, of considerable merit, M. CAVALCADOUR, happened to be disengaged, through the lamented death of LORD HAUNCHER, with whom young CAVALCADOUR had made his *début* as an artist. He had nothing to refuse to his master, MIROBOLANT, and would impress himself to be useful to a *gourmet* so distinguished as MONSIEUR TIMMINS. FITZ went away as pleased as Punch with this encomium of the great MIROBOLANT, and was one of those who voted against the decreasing of MIROBOLANT's salary, when that measure was proposed by MR. PARINGS, COLONEL CLOSE, and the Screw party in the Committee of the Club.

Faithful to the promise of his great master, the youthful CAVALCADOUR called in Lilliput Street the next day. A rich crimson velvet waistcoat, with buttons of blue glass and gold, a variegated blue satin stock, over which a graceful mosaic chain hung in glittering folds, a white hat worn on one side of his long curling ringlets, redolent with the most delightful hair oil— one of those white hats which looks as if it had just been skinned —and a pair of gloves not exactly of the colour of *beurre frais* but of *beurre* that has been up the chimney, with a natty cane with a gilt knob, completed the upper part at any rate of the costume of the young fellow whom the page introduced to MRS. TIMMINS.

Her mamma and she had been just having a dispute about the gooseberry cream when CAVALCADOUR arrived. His presence silenced MRS. GASHLEIGH ; and ROSA, in carrying on a conversation with him in the French language, which she had acquired perfectly in an elegant finishing establishment in Kensington Square, had a great advantage over her mother, who could only pursue the dialogue with very much difficulty, eyeing one or other interlocutor with an alarmed and suspicious look, and gasping out 'We' whenever she thought a proper opportunity arose for the use of that affirmative.

'I have two leetl *menus* weez me,' said CAVALCADOUR to MRS. GASHLEIGH.

'*Minews*—yes, oh indeed,' answered the lady.

'Two little *cartes*.'

'Oh, two *carts !* Oh we,' she said—'coming, I suppose ;' and she looked out of window to see if they were there.

CAVALCADOUR smiled ; he produced from a pocket-book a pink paper and a blue paper, on which he had written two bills of fare, the last two which he had composed for the lamented HAUNCHER, and he handed these over to MRS. FITZROY.

The poor little woman was dreadfully puzzled with these documents (she has them in her possession still), and began to read from the pink one as follows :—

DINER POUR 16 *PERSONNES.*

Potage (clair) à la Rigodon.
Do. à la Prince de Tombouctou.

DEUX *POISSONS.*

Saumon de Severne   *Rougets Gratinés*
à la Boadicée.   *à la Cléopâtre.*

DEUX RELEVÉS.

Le Chapeau-à-trois-cornes farci à la Robespierre.
Le Tire-botte à l'Odalisque.

SIX ENTRÉES.

Sauté de Hannetons à l'Epinglière.
Côtelettes à la Mégathérium.
Bourrasque de Veau à la Palsambleu.
Laitances de Carpe en goguette à la Reine Pomaré.
Turban de Volaille à l'Archevêque de Cantorbery.

And so on with the *entremets,* and *hors-d'œuvre* and the *rôtis,* and *relevés.*

'Madame will see that the dinners are quite simple,' said M. CAVALCADOUR.

'Oh quite !' said ROSA, dreadfully puzzled.

'Which would Madame like ?'

'Which would we like, Mamma?' ROSA asked; adding, as if after a little thought, 'I think, Sir, we should prefer the blue one.' At which MRS. GASHLEIGH nodded as knowingly as she could; though, pink or blue, I defy anybody to know what these cooks mean by their jargon.

'If you please, Madame, we will go down below and examine the scene of operation,' MONSIEUR CAVALCADOUR said; and so he was marshalled down the stairs to the kitchen, which he didn't like to name, and appeared before the cook in all his splendour.

He cast a rapid glance round the premises, and a smile of something like contempt lighted up his features. 'Will you bring pen and ink, if you please, and I will write down a few of the articles which will be necessary for us? We shall require, if you please, eight more stew-pans, a couple of braising-pans, eight *sauté* - pans, six *bain-marie* pans, a freezing-pot with accessories, and a few more articles of which I will inscribe the names;' and MR. CAVALCADOUR did so, dashing down, with the rapidity of genius, a tremendous list of ironmongery goods, which he handed over to MRS. TIMMINS. She and her mamma were quite frightened by the awful catalogue.

'I will call three days hence and superintend the progress of matters; and we will make the stock for the soup the day before dinner.'

'Don't you think, Sir,' here interposed MRS. GASHLEIGH, 'that one soup—a fine rich mock-turtle, such as I have seen in the best houses in the west of England and such as the late LORD FORTYSKEWER——'

'You will get what is wanted for the soups, if you please,' MR. CAVALCADOUR continued, not heeding this interruption, and as bold as a captain on his own quarter-deck; 'for the stock of clear soup, you will get a leg of beef, a leg of veal, and a ham.'

'We, Munseer,' said the cook, dropping a terrified curtsey. 'A leg of beef, a leg of veal, and a ham.'

'You can't serve a leg of veal at a party,' said MRS. GASH-LEIGH; 'and a leg of beef is not a company dish.'

'Madame, they are to make the stock of the clear soup, MR. CAVALCADOUR said.

'*What?*' cried MRS. GASHLEIGH; and the cook repeated his former expression.

'Never, whilst I am in this house, cried out MRS. GASH-LEIGH indignantly; 'never in a Christian *English* household; never shall such sinful waste be permitted by *me*. If you wish me to dine, ROSA, you must get a dinner less *expensive*. The

RIGHT HONOURABLE LORD FORTYSKEWER could dine, Sir, without these wicked luxuries, and I presume my daughter's guests can.'

'Madame is perfectly at liberty to decide,' said M. CAVALCADOUR, 'I came to oblige Madame, and my good friend MIROBOLANT, not myself.'

'Thank you, Sir, I think it *will* be too expensive,' ROSA stammered in a great flutter. 'But I am very much obliged to you.'

'*Il n'y a point d'obligation, Madame,*' said MONSIEUR ALCIDE CAMILLE CAVALCADOUR in his most superb manner; and, making a splendid bow to the lady of the house, was respectfully conducted to the upper regions by little BUTTONS, leaving ROSA frightened, the cook amazed and silent, and MRS. GASHLEIGH boiling with indignation against the dresser.

Up to that moment MRS. BLOWSER, the cook who had come out of Devonshire with MRS. GASHLEIGH (of course that lady garrisoned her daughter's house with servants, and expected them to give her information of everything which took place there)—up to that moment, I say, the cook had been quite contented with that subterraneous station which she occupied in life, and had a pride in keeping her kitchen neat, bright, and clean. It was, in her opinion, the comfortablest room in the house (we all thought so when we came down of a night to smoke there) and the handsomest kitchen in Lilliput Street.

But after the visit of CAVALCADOUR the cook became quite discontented and uneasy in her mind. She talked in a melancholy manner over the area railings to the cooks at twenty-three and twenty-five. She stepped over the way and conferred with the cook there. She made inquiries at the baker's and at other places about the kitchens in the great houses in Brobdingnag Gardens, and how many spits, *bangmarry* pans, and stoo-pans they had. She thought she could not do with an occasional help, but must have a kitchen-maid. And she was often discovered by a gentleman of the police force, who was, I believe, her cousin, and occasionally visited her when MRS. GASHLEIGH was not in the house or spying it;—she was discovered seated with MRS. RUNDELL in her lap, its leaves bespattered with her tears. 'My Pease be gone, Pelisse,' she said, 'zins I zaw that ther Franchman;' and it was all the faithful fellow could do to console her.

'—— the dinner,' said TIMMINS, in a rage at last; 'having it cooked in the house is out of the question; the bother of it, and the row your mother makes, are enough to drive one mad.

It won't happen again, I can promise you, Rosa—order it at Fusby's at once. You can have everything from Fusby's—from footmen to saltspoons. Let's go and order it from Fusby's.'

'Darling, if you don't mind the expense, and it will be any relief to you, let us do as you wish,' Rosa said ; and she put on her bonnet, and they went off to the grand cook and confectioner of the Brobdingnag quarter..

V.

On the arm of her Fitzroy, Rosa went off to Fusby's, that magnificent shop at the corner of Parliament Place and Alcompayne Square—a shop into which the rogue had often cast a glance of approbation as he passed ; for there are not only the most wonderful and delicious cakes and confections in the window, but at the counter there are almost sure to be three or four of the prettiest women in the whole of this world, with little darling caps of the last French make, with beautiful wavy hair, and the neatest possible waists and aprons.

Yes, there they sit ; and others, perhaps, besides Fitz have cast a sheep's eye through those enormous plate-glass window panes. I suppose it is the fact of perpetually living amongst such a quantity of good things that makes those young ladies so beautiful. They come into the place, let us say, like ordinary people, and gradually grow handsomer and handsomer, until they blow out into the perfect angels you see. It can't be otherwise ; if you and I, my dear fellow, were to have a course of that place, we should become beautiful too. They live in an atmosphere of the most delicious pine-apples, blancmanges, creams (some whipt, and some so good that of course they don't want whipping), jellies, tipsy-cakes, cherry-brandy—one hundred thousand sweet and lovely things. Look at the preserved fruits, look at the golden ginger, the outspreading ananas, the darling little rogues of China oranges, ranged in the gleaming crystal cylinders. Mon Dieu ! Look at the strawberries in the leaves. Each of them is as large nearly as a lady's reticule, and looks as if it had been brought up in a nursery to itself. One of those strawberries is a meal for those young ladies behind the counter ; they nibble off a little from the side ; and if they are very hungry, which can scarcely ever happen, they are allowed to go to the crystal canisters and take out a routcake or macaroon. In the evening they sit and tell each other little riddles out of the bon-bons; and when they wish to amuse themselves, they read the most delightful remarks, in the French language, about Love, and CUPID, and Beauty, before they place them inside the crackers. They always are writing down good things into MR. FUSBY's ledgers. It must be a perfect feast to read them. Talk of the Garden of Eden! I believe it was nothing to MR. FUSBY's house; and I have no doubt that after those young ladies have been there a certain time, they get to such a pitch of loveliness at last, that they become complete angels, with wings sprouting out of their lovely shoulders, when (after giving just a preparatory balance or two) they fly up to the counter and perch there for a minute, hop down again, and affectionately kiss the other young ladies, and say 'Good-bye, dears, we shall meet again *là haut*,' and then with a whirr of their deliciously scented wings, away they fly for good, whisking over the trees of Brobdingnag Square, and up into the sky, as the policeman touches his hat.

It is up there that they invent the legends for the crackers, and the wonderful riddles and remarks on the bon-bons. No mortal, I am sure, could write them.

I never saw a man in such a state as FITZROY TIMMINS in the presence of those ravishing houris. MRS. FITZ having explained that they required a dinner for twenty persons, the young ladies asked what MR. and MRS. FITZ would like, and named a thousand things, each better than the other, to all of which FITZ instantly said yes. The wretch was in such a state of infatuation that I believe if that lady had proposed to him a fricasseed elephant, or a boa-constrictor in jelly, he would have said, 'Oh yes, certainly, put it down.'

That Peri wrote down in her album a list of things which it would make your mouth water to listen to. But she took it all quite calmly. Heaven bless you! They don't care about things that are no delicacies to them! But whatever she chose to write down, FITZROY let her.

After the dinner and dessert were ordered (at FUSBY's they furnish everything; dinner and dessert, plate and china, servants in your own livery, and, if you please, guests of title too), the married couple retreated from that shop of wonders; ROSA delighted that the trouble of the dinner was all off their hands, but she was afraid it would be rather expensive.

'Nothing can be too expensive which pleases *you*, dear,' FITZ said.

'By the way, one of those young women was rather good-looking,' ROSA remarked: 'the one in the cap with the blue ribbons.' (And she cast about the shape of the cap in her mind, and determined to have exactly such another.)

'Think so ? I didn't observe,' said the miserable hypocrite by her side ; and when he had seen Rosa home, he went back, like an infamous fiend, to order something else which he had forgotten, he said, at Fusby's. Get out of that Paradise, you cowardly, creeping, vile serpent, you !

Until the day of the dinner, the infatuated fop was *always* going to Fusby's. He *was remarked there.* He used to go before he went to Chambers in the morning, and sometimes on his return from the Temple ; but the morning was the time which he preferred ; and one day, when he went on one of his eternal pretexts, and was chattering and flirting at the counter, a lady who had been reading yesterday's paper and eating a halfpenny bun for an hour in the back shop (if that paradise may be called a shop)—a lady stepped forward, laid down *The Morning Herald*, and confronted him.

That lady was Mrs. Gashleigh. From that day the miserable Fitzroy was in her power ; and she resumed a sway over his house, to shake off which had been the object of his life, and the result of many battles. And for a mere freak—(for on going into Fusby's a week afterwards he found the Peris drinking tea out of blue cups, and eating stale bread and butter, when his absurd passion instantly vanished)—I say, for a mere freak the most intolerable burden of his life was put on his shoulders again—his mother-in-law.

On the day before the Little Dinner took place—and I promise you we shall come to it in the very next chapter—a tall and elegant middle-aged gentleman, who might have passed for an Earl, but that there was a slight incompleteness about his hands and feet, the former being uncommonly red, and the latter large and irregular, was introduced to Mrs. Timmins by the page, who announced him as Mr. Truncheon.

'I'm Truncheon, Ma'am,' he said, with a low bow.

'Indeed ! ' said Rosa.

'About the dinner, M'm, from Fusby's, M'm. As you have no butler, M'm, I presume you will wish me to act as sich. I shall bring two persons as haids to-morrow ; both answers to the name of John. I'd best, if you please, inspect the primisis, and will think you to allow your young man to show me the pantry and kitching.'

Truncheon spoke in a low voice, and with the deepest and most respectful melancholy. There is not much expression in his eyes, but from what there is you would fancy that he was oppressed by a secret sorrow. ROSA trembled as she surveyed this gentleman's size, his splendid appearance, and gravity. 'I am sure,' she said, 'I never shall dare to ask him to hand a glass of water.' Even MRS. GASHLEIGH, when she came on the morning of the actual dinner-party, to superintend matters, was cowed, and retreated from the kitchen before the calm majesty of TRUNCHEON.

And yet that great man was, like all the truly great—affable. He put aside his coat and waistcoat (both of evening cut, and

looking prematurely splendid as he walked the streets in noon-day) and did not disdain to rub the glasses, and polish the decanters, and to show young BUTTONS the proper mode of preparing these articles for a dinner. And while he operated, the maids, and BUTTONS, and Cook, when she could—and what had she but the vegetables to boil?—crowded round him, and listened with wonder as he talked of the great families as he had lived with. That man, as they saw him there before them, had been cab-boy to LORD TANTALLAN, Valet to the EARL OF BAREACRES,

and Groom of the Chambers to the DUCHESS DOWAGER OF FITZ-
BATTLEAXE. Oh, it was delightful to hear MR. TRUNCHEON !

VI.

N the great, momentous,
stupendous day of the
dinner, my beloved female
reader may imagine that
FITZROY TIMMINS was
sent about his business
at an early hour in the
morning, while the women
began to make prepara-
tions to receive their
guests. 'There will be
no need of your going to
FUSBY'S,' MRS. GASH-
LEIGH said to him, with
a look that drove him
out of doors. 'Every-
thing that we require
has been ordered there !
You will please to be
back here at six o'clock, and not sooner ; and I presume you will
acquiesce in my arrangements about the *wine*.'

'Oh yes, Mamma,' said the prostrate son-in-law.

'In so large a party—a party beyond some folk's *means*—
expensive *wines* are *absurd*. The light Sherry at 26s., the
Champagne at 42s., and you are not to go beyond 36s. for the
Claret and Port after dinner. Mind, coffee will be served, and
you come upstairs after two rounds of the Claret.'

'Of course, of course,' acquiesced the wretch ; and hurried out
of the house to his Chambers, and to discharge the commissions
with which the womankind had entrusted him.

As for MRS. GASHLEIGH, you might have heard her bawling
over the house the whole day long. That admirable woman was
everywhere ; in the kitchen, until the arrival of TRUNCHEON,
before whom she would not retreat without a battle ; on the

stairs; in FITZROY's dressing-room; and in FITZROY minor's nursery, to whom she gave a dose of her own composition while the nurse was sent out on a pretext to make purchases of garnish for the dishes to be served for the Little Dinner. Garnish for the dishes! As if the folks at FUSBY's could not garnish dishes better than GASHLEIGH, with her stupid old-world devices of laurel leaves, parsley, and cut turnips! Why, there was not a dish served that day that was not covered over with skewers, on which troufles, crayfish, mushrooms, and forced meat were impaled. When old GASHLEIGH went down with her barbarian bunches of holly and greens to stick about the meats, even the cook saw their incongruity, and, at TRUNCHEON's orders, flung the whole shrubbery into the dust-house, where, while poking about the premises, you may be sure MRS. G. saw it.

Every candle which was to be burned that night (including the tallow candle, which she said was a good enough bed-light for FITZROY) she stuck into the candlesticks with her own hands, giving her own high-shouldered plated candlesticks of the year 1798 the place of honour. She upset all poor ROSA's floral arrangements, turning the nosegays from one vase into the other without any pity, and was never tired of beating, and pushing, and patting, and *wapping* the curtain and sofa draperies into shape in the little drawing-room.

In FITZ's own apartments she revelled with peculiar pleasure. It has been described how she had sacked his Study and pushed away his papers, some of which, including three cigars, and the commencement of an article for the *Law Magazine*, 'Lives of the Sheriff's Officers,' he has never been able to find to this day. Mamma now went into the little room in the back regions, which is FITZ's dressing-room (and was destined to be a cloakroom), and here she rummaged to her heart's delight.

In an incredibly short space of time she examined all his out-lying pockets, drawers, and letters; she inspected his socks and handkerchiefs in the top drawers, and on the dressing-table, his razors, shaving-strop, and hair-oil. She carried off his silver-topped scent-bottle out of his dressing-case, and a half-dozen of his favourite pills (which FITZ possesses in common with every well-regulated man), and probably administered them to her own family. His boots, glossy pumps, and slippers she pushed into the shower-bath, where the poor fellow stepped into them the next morning, in the midst of a pool in which they were lying. The baby was found sucking his boot-hooks the next day in the nursery; and as for the bottle of varnish for his shoes (which he generally paints upon the trees himself, having a pretty taste in

U

that way), it could never be found to the present hour; but it was remarked that the young MASTER GASHLEIGHS when they came home for the holidays always wore lacquered highlows; and the reader may draw his conclusions from *that* fact.

In the course of the day all the servants gave MRS. TIMMINS warning.

The cook said she coodn't abear it no longer, aving MRS. G. always about her kitching, with her fingers in all the saucepans. MRS. G. had got her the place, but she preferred one as MRS. G. didn't get for her.

The nurse said she was come to nuss MASTER FITZROY, and knew her duty; his grandmamma wasn't his nuss, and was always aggrawating her.—Missus must shoot herself elsewhere.

The housemaid gave utterance to the same sentiments in language more violent.

Little BUTTONS bounced up to his mistress, said he was butler of the family, MRS. G. was always poking about his pantry and dam if he'd stand it.

At every moment ROSA grew more and more bewildered. The baby howled a great deal during the day. His large china Christening-bowl was cracked by MRS. GASHLEIGH altering the flowers in it, and pretending to be very cool, whilst her hands shook with rage.

'Pray go on, Mamma,' ROSA said, with tears in her eyes. 'Should you like to break the chandelier?'

'Ungrateful, unnatural child!' bellowed the other; 'only that I know you couldn't do without me, I'd leave the house this minute.'

'As you wish,' said ROSA. But MRS. G. didn't wish; and in this juncture TRUNCHEON arrived.

That officer surveyed the dining-room, laid the cloth there with admirable precision and neatness; ranged the plate on the sideboard with graceful accuracy, but objected to that old thing in the centre, as he called MRS. GASHLEIGH's silver basket, as cumbrous and useless for the table, where they would want all the room they could get.

Order was not restored to the house, nor, indeed, any decent progress made, until this great man came; but where there was a revolt before, and a general disposition to strike work and to yell out defiance against MRS. GASHLEIGH, who was sitting bewildered and furious in the drawing-room—where there was before commotion, at the appearance of the master-spirit all was peace and unanimity: the cook went back to her pans, the housemaid busied herself with the china and glass, cleaning some articles and

breaking others, BUTTONS sprang up and down the stairs, obedient
to the orders of his chief, and all things went awell, and in their
season.

At six the man with the wine came from BINNEY AND
LATHAM'S. At a quarter-past six TIMMINS himself arrived.

At half-past six he might have been heard shouting out for
his varnished boots—but we know where *those* had been hidden
—and for his dressing things; but MRS. GASHLEIGH had put
them away.

As in his vain inquiries for these articles he stood shouting,
'Nurse! BUTTONS! ROSA, my dear!' and the most fearful
execrations up and down the stairs, MR. TRUNCHEON came out
on him.

'Igscuse me, Sir,' says he, 'but it's impawsable. We can't
dine twenty at that table—not if you set 'em out awinder, we
can't.'

'What's to be done?' asked FITZROY in an agony, 'they've
all said they'd come.'

'Can't do it,' said the other, 'with two top and bottom—and
your table is as narrow as a bench—we can't hold more than
heighteen, and then each person's helbows will be into his
neighbour's cheer.'

'ROSA! MRS. GASHLEIGH!' cried out TIMMINS, 'come down
and speak to this gentl—this——'

'TRUNCHEON, Sir,' said the man.

The women descended from the drawing-room. 'Look and
see, ladies,' he said, inducting them into the dining-room;
'there's the room, there's the table laid for heighteen, and I defy
you to squeege in more.'

'One person in a party always fails,' said MRS. GASHLEIGH,
getting alarmed.

'That's nineteen,' MR. TRUNCHEON remarked; 'we must
knock another hoff, m'am;' and he looked her hard in the face.

MRS. GASHLEIGH was very red and nervous, and paced, or
rather squeezed, round the table (it was as much as she could do)
—the chairs could not be put any closer than they were. It was
impossible, unless the *convive* sat as a centre-piece in the middle,
to put another guest at that table.

'Look at that lady movin' round, Sir. You see now the
difficklty; if my men wasn't thinner, they couldn't hoperate at
all,' MR. TRUNCHEON observed, who seemed to have a spite to
MRS. GASHLEIGH.

'What is to be done?' she said, with purple accents.

'My dearest Mamma,' ROSA cried out, 'you must stop at home

—how sorry I am !' And she shot one glance at FITZROY, who shot another at the great TRUNCHEON, who held down his eyes. 'We could manage with heighteen,' he said mildly.

MRS. GASHLEIGH gave a hideous laugh.

.   .   .   .   .   .

She went away. At eight o'clock she was pacing at the corner of the street, and actually saw the company arrive. First came the TOPHAM SAWYERS in their light-blue carriage, with the white hammer-cloth, and blue and white ribbons—their footmen drove the house down with the knocking.

Then followed the ponderous and snuff-coloured vehicle, with faded gilded wheels and brass Earl's coronets all over it, the conveyance of the House of BUNGAY. The COUNTESS OF BUNGAY and daughter stepped out of the carriage. The fourteenth EARL OF BUNGAY couldn't come.

SIR THOMAS and LADY GULPIN'S fly made its appearance, from which issued the General with his star, and LADY GULPIN in yellow satin. The ROWDY'S Brougham followed next ; after which MRS. BUTT'S handsome equipage drove up.

The two friends of the house, young gentlemen from the Temple, now arrived in cab No. 9996. We tossed up, in fact, which should pay the fare.

MR. RANVILLE RANVILLE walked, and was dusting his boots as the Templars drove up. LORD CASTLENODDY came out of a twopenny omnibus. FUNNYMAN, the wag, came last, whirling up rapidly in a Hansom, just as MRS. GASHLEIGH, with rage in her heart, was counting that two people had failed, and that there were only seventeen after all.

MR. TRUNCHEON passed our names to MR. BILLITER, who bawled them out on the stairs. ROSA was smiling in a pink dress, and looking as fresh as an angel, and received her company with that grace which has always characterised her.

The moment of THE DINNER arrived, old LADY BUNGAY scuffled off on the arm of FITZROY, while the rear was brought up by ROSA and LORD CASTLEMOULDY, of Ballyshanvanvoght Castle, Co. Tipperary. Some fellows who had the luck took down ladies to dinner. I was not sorry to be out of the way of MRS. ROWDY, with her dandified airs, or of that high and mighty County Princess, MRS. TOPHAM SAWYER.

VII.

F course, it does not become the present writer, who has partaken of the best entertainment which his friends could supply, to make fun of their (somewhat ostentatious, as it must be confessed) hospitality. If they gave a dinner beyond their means, it is no business of mine. I hate a man who goes and eats a friend's meat, and then blabs the secrets of the mahogany. Such a man deserves never to be asked to dinner again; and though at the close of a London season that seems no great loss, and you sicken of a white-bait as you would of a whale—yet we must always remember that there's another season coming, and hold our tongues for the present.

As for describing, then, the mere victuals on TIMMINS's table, that would be absurd. Everybody—(I mean of the genteel world, of course, of which I make no doubt the reader is a polite ornament)—everybody has the same everything in London. You see the same coats, the same dinners, the same boiled fowls and mutton, the same cutlets, fish, and cucumbers, the same lumps of Wenham Lake ice, etc. The waiters, with white neckcloths, are as like each other everywhere as the peas which they hand round with the ducks of the second course. Can't any one invent anything new?

The only difference between TIMMINS's dinner and his neighbour's was, that he had hired, as we have said, the greater part of the plate, and that his cowardly conscience magnified faults and disasters of which no one else probably took heed.

But ROSA thought, from the supercilious air with which MRS. TOPHAM SAWYER was eyeing the plate and other arrangements, that she was remarking the difference of the ciphers on the forks and spoons—(which had, in fact, been borrowed from every one of FITZROY's friends—I know, for instance, that he had my six, among others, and only returned five, along with a battered old black-pronged, plated abomination, which I have no doubt belongs to MRS. GASHLEIGH, whom I hereby request to send back mine in exchange)—their guilty consciences, I say, made them fancy that every one was spying out their domestic deficiencies, whereas it is probable that nobody present thought of their failings at all. People never do ; they never see holes in their neighbours' coats — they are too indolent, simple, and charitable.

Some things, however, one could not help remarking ; for instance, though FITZ is my closest friend, yet, could I avoid seeing and being amused by his perplexity and his dismal efforts to be facetious ? His eye wandered all round the little room with quick uneasy glances, very different from those frank and jovial looks with which he is accustomed to welcome you to a leg of mutton ; and ROSA, from the other end of the table, and over the flowers, *entrée* dishes, and wine-coolers, telegraphed him with signals of corresponding alarm. Poor devils ! why did they ever go beyond that leg of mutton ?

FUNNYMAN was not brilliant in conversation, scarcely opening his mouth, except for the purposes of feasting. The fact is, our friend TOM DAWSON was at table, who knew all his stories, and in his presence the great wag is always silent and uneasy.

FITZ has a very pretty wit of his own, and a good reputation on Circuit ; but he is timid before great people. And, indeed, the presence of that awful LADY BUNGAY on his right hand was enough to damp him. She was in Court-mourning (for the late PRINCE OF SCHLIPPENSCHLOPPEN). She had on a large black funereal turban, and appurtenances, and a vast breastplate of twinkling, twiddling, black bugles. No wonder a man could not be gay in talking to *her*.

MRS. ROWDY and MRS. TOPHAM SAWYER love each other as women do who have the same receiving nights, and ask the same society ; they were only separated by RANVILLE RANVILLE, who tries to be well with both ; and they talked at each other across him.

TOPHAM and ROWDY growled out a conversation about Rum, Ireland, and the Navigation Laws, quite unfit for print. SAWYER never speaks three words without mentioning the House and the Speaker.

The Irish Peer said nothing (which was a comfort) ; but he

ate and drank of everything which came in his way; and cut his usual absurd figure in dyed whiskers and a yellow under-waist-coat.

GENERAL GULPIN sported his star, and looked fat and florid, but melancholy. His wife ordered away his dinner, just like honest SANCHO'S physician at Barataria.

BOTHERBY'S stories about LAMARTINE are as old as the hills since the barricades of last month; and he could not get in a word or cut the slightest figure. And as for TOM DAWSON, he was carrying on an undertoned small talk with LADY BARBARA ST. MARY'S, so that there was not much conversation worth record going on *within* the dining-room.

Outside, it was different. Those houses in Lilliput Street are so uncommonly compact that you can hear everything which takes place all over the tenement; and so,

In the awful pauses of the banquet, and the hall-door being furthermore open, we had the benefit of hearing

The cook and the occasional cook, below stairs, exchanging rapid phrases regarding the dinner.

The smash of the soup-tureen, and swift descent of the kitchen-maid and soup-ladle down the stairs to the lower regions. This accident created a laugh, and rather amused FITZROY and the company, and caused FUNNYMAN to say, bowing to ROSA, that she was mistress of herself, though China fall. But she did not heed him, for at that moment another noise commenced, namely, that of

The baby in the upper rooms, who commenced a series of piercing yells which, though stopped by the sudden clapping to of the nursery door, were only more dreadful to the mother when suppressed. She would have given a guinea to go upstairs and have done with the whole entertainment.

A thundering knock came at the door very early after the dessert, and the poor soul took a speedy opportunity of summoning the ladies to depart, though you may be sure it was only old MRS. GASHLEIGH, who had come with her daughters—of course, the first person to come. I saw her red gown whisking up the stairs, which were covered with plates and dishes, over which she trampled.

Instead of having any quiet after the retreat of the ladies, the house was kept in a rattle, and the glasses jingled on the table, as the flymen and coachmen plied the knocker and the *soirée* came in. From my place I could see everything; the guests as they arrived (I remarked very few carriages, mostly cabs and flies), and a little crowd of blackguard boys and children, who were formed round the door, and gave ironical cheers to the folks as they stepped out of their vehicles.

As for the evening party, if a crowd in the dog-days is pleasant, poor MRS. TIMMINS certainly had a successful *soirée*. You could hardly move on the stair. MRS. STERNHOLD broke in the banisters and nearly fell through. There was such a noise and chatter you could not hear the singing of the MISS GASHLEIGHS, which was no great loss. LADY BUNGAY could hardly get to her carriage, being entangled with COLONEL WEDGEWOOD in the passage. An absurd attempt was made to get up a dance of some kind, but before MRS. CROWDER had got round the room, the hanging-lamp in the dining-room below was stove in and fell with a crash on the table, now prepared for refreshment.

Why, in fact, did the TIMMINSES give that party at all? It was quite beyond their means. They have offended a score of their old friends, and pleased none of their acquaintances. So angry were many who were not asked, that poor ROSA says she must now give a couple more parties and take in those not previously invited. And I know for a fact that FUSBY's bill is not yet paid; nor BINNEY AND LARHAM'S, the wine-merchants; that the breakage and hire of glass and china cost ever so much money; that every true friend of TIMMINS has cried out against his absurd extravagance, and that now, when every one is going out of town, FITZ has hardly money to pay his Circuit, much more to take ROSA to a watering-place as he wished and promised.

As for MRS. GASHLEIGH, the only feasible plan of economy which she can suggest is that she should come and live with her daughter and son-in-law, and that they should keep house together. If he agrees to this, she has a little sum at the banker's, with which she would not mind easing his present difficulties; and the poor wretch is so utterly bewildered and crestfallen that it is very likely he will become her victim.

The TOPHAM SAWYERS, when they go down into the country, will represent FITZ as a ruined man and reckless prodigal; his uncle, the attorney, from whom he has expectations, will most likely withdraw his business, and adopt some other member of his family—BLANCH CROWDER for instance, whose husband, the doctor, has had high words with poor FITZROY already, of course at the women's instigation;—and all these accumulated miseries fall upon the unfortunate wretch because he was good-natured and his wife would have a Little Dinner.

MISCELLANEOUS CONTRIBUTIONS
TO PUNCH.

WHY CAN'T THEY LEAVE US ALONE IN THE HOLYDAYS?[1]

From Home, as yet. 10th January.

ESPECTED MR. PUNCH,

I am a young gentleman of good family, and exceedingly gentle disposition, and at present at home for the Christmas holydays with my dear Papa and Mamma. I believe I am not considered clever at school, being always last in my class ; and the Doctor, the Usher, the French Master, and all the boys, except TIBBS MINIMUS (who is only six, and in the last form with me), beat me and ill use me a great deal. And it's a great shame that I for my part am not allowed to whop TIBBS MINIMUS, which I could, being 14 myself last birthday ; but that *nasty brute* TIBBS MINOR says he'll *thrash me* if I do—and it's very *unkind of him ;* for, when he was a child in petticoats, and I was ten, and he was in the last class with me, I never beat him, as I easily could have done, and now the *unkind boy* is always attacking and woориting me.

I cannot do *lessons and that*, MR. PUNCH ; for when the Dr. calls me up my tongue cleaves to the roof of *my mouf*, I'm so fritned ; and same way *in French*, and same in Arythmetic ; and I can't fight like some boys, because I'm a nervous boy ; but the big boys keep me awake telling stories to 'em *all night ;* and I know *ever so many*, and am always making stories *in my head ;* and somehow I feel that I'm better than *many of the chaps*—only

I *can't do anything.* And they chaff me and laugh at me because I'm afraid of *being in the dark and seeing ghosts,* and that, *which I can't help it.* My mamma had a fright *before* I was born, and *that's what it is,* I suppose.

Sir, I am very miserable at school with everybody licking me ; *and hate the place ;* and the going back to it—and the *idear* of it altogether. Why was schools ever invented ? When I'm at my dear home, with dear Ma and sisters, and in bed as long as I choose, and wish twice to meat, or three times, if I like ; and I walk in the Park, and go to see a *lovely Pantamime ;* and so I lose the horrid thought of school ; and it's only in my dreams, sometimes, I see that *abommanable* old Doctor.

What I want you to do in the interest of all School Boys, is to stop the *Times* in holy time from publishing those *advertisements about schools.* On this day, Wednesday, jest against the leading article, there's no less than 2 columns of schools ; and Papa, who's always jokin' and chaffin' me, reads 'em out and says, 'TOM, how'd you like this ?—Education of a superior kind, Birchwood Briars. No extras, no holydays.' Or, 'Tom, here's a chance for you :—To LAUNDRESSES.—A schoolmaster wishes to receive into his establishment the SON of a respectable LAUNDRESS, on reciprocal terms. Address,' etc. 'My dear,' Pa says to dear Ma, 'what a pity you wasn't a washerwoman, and we could get this stupid boy educated for nothing.' I'm sure I've been *mangled* enough by that bully, BOB CUFF, if I hav'n't been ironed and hung up to dry ! Or, 'To Booksellers, Grocers, Butchers, and Bakers.—In a well-appreciated seminary, within five miles of London, the children of the above tradesmen will be received. The whole of the school account will be taken in goods.' And Pa wonders if he were to send back our calf with me in our cart, and one of our sheep, whether the Doctor would take them in payment of the quarter's account ? And then he says that one .calf ought to pay for another, and laughs and makes me miserable for the whole day.

And next week my pleasures, I know, will be dampt by reading the Christmas Vacation of the Chipping-Rodbury Grammar School will conclude on the 24th inst., when the boys are expected. to reassemble ; the young gentlemen of DR. BLOXAM'S Academy will meet on the 25th ; or, MR. BROOMBACK'S young friends will reassemble after the Christmas recess ; or so and so. Why are these horrid thoughts always to be brought before us ? I'm sure at Christmas time managers of newspapers might be *kind* and keep these horrid advertisements out of sight. And if our uncles, and people who come to our house, when we're at

home for the holydays, would but be *so obliging* as never to
mention school, or make jokes about flogging, or going back, or
what we have *for dinner*, or *that*, I'm sure we should be very
much the happier, and you won't have heard in vain from

Your wretched reader,

UNDER PETTY.

NO NEWS FROM PARIS.[1]

BY A CYNICAL CORRESPONDENT.

Café des Aveugles, Feb. 1.

CERTAINLY it is as well for people who wish to lead an easy life
in the world that the inventions actually produced and perfected
by men of genius are by no means so numerous as their plans;
and that the Patent-office contains such a number of specifications
of discoveries, the knowledge of which is not carried beyond the
proprietor and transcriber of the sheets of stamped paper out of
which the Government takes its profit. If every man's discoveries
were practicable, and put in execution, what a restless, feverish,
and uncomfortable world ours would be, and how odious to those
who are lazy, or fond of old practices and customs, or desire to be
quiet! Suppose, for instance, CAPTAIN WARNER's long range
were to come into play next week; suppose the week after the
steam-carriage for London streets were to drive up and smoke the
cabs and omnibuses out of the town; suppose, ten days after, that
the new system for warming and lighting London simultaneously
with gas made from egg-shells or potato-peelings, or what not,
should be brought into use; and then suppose that the aerial
machines were completed, and every man had his balloon and
steam-engine in his back-yard ready to take him to business every
morning after his breakfast. Could we live with any comfort, or
keep pace with a world where the progress of discovery was so
abominably rapid? WARNER's machine being brought into action,
it is evident that the standing army, and our 'wooden walls,'
England's pride, the dock-yards, barracks, and Woolwich arsenals,
the Guards' Club, in Pall Mall, the Duke of Wellington, the
sentries, and the valuable clock at the Horse Guards, would all be
blown to annihilation;—there would be no use in Woolwich without artillery, no use for a Guards' Club without any guards, no

[1] [February 8, 1851.]

heroes in jack-boots to put into the sentry-boxes at Whitehall; nobody to wind up the clock there, and so forth. Then the steam-carriages would knock up the omnibus and horse-dealers; then the aerial locomotives would drive the steam-carriages proprietors into the gazette; then the gas companies would be extinguished, and go out in bankruptcy and darkness; then the coal proprietors would have no sale for their black diamonds; the wharf owners would not get their rents; the bargees would drown themselves from their useless vessels; and the great parties at Wallsend House would be given up; then the coal-whippers would drink no more beer—so that the aristocracy and the commonalty, the milliners, the lightermen, MESSRS. BARCLAY AND PERKINS, and the penny-liners who describe the magnificent entertainments at Wallsend House aforesaid, would all suffer by the new invention, and have their present means of livelihood cut off. I am of a timid, or, if you please, conservative turn: I like the pace of improvement to be so slow as scarcely to be felt; I am not sure that I don't admire LORD JOHN RUSSELL. At any rate, who would live in a country which gasps from one revolution into another, and in its progress perpetually tumbles down, has a fit, has the doctor fetched and is bled, and then rises up and staggers on to the next convulsion?

My dear MR. PUNCH, it has been my fortune to live in Paris for the last few weeks. I have seen M. THIERS walking in the Tuilleries Gardens; the President of the Republic made me (and a hundred others) a very polite bow in the Champs Élysées on Monday; I dined in the very next cabinet to M. CARLIER, the Prefect of Police, and a party at PHILIPPIS, in the Rue Montorgueil, on Wednesday last; and the conclusion to which I have come, after thus mixing with the highest French society, is, that I thank my fate I am an Englishman, and not born under the baleful star of the Legion of Honour. Who knows what explosive machines are getting ready to sweep down institutions here? Who knows what new method for firing Paris streets may be put into practice any day? what flying wonders are in the air? HENRI V., or the COMTE DE PARIS, may drop out of a balloon some morning, or the PRESIDENT go off in one! The changes in this country are so rapid; the lulls and tempests so surprising and sudden; the fierce quarrels so easily healed; the firm friendships so soon broken; the alliances so quickly made and dissolved; the illustrious reputation of yesterday so entirely forgotten to-day, to reappear and resplend to-morrow, perhaps, and without any assignable reason—that I say we may thank our stars that we live in a grave country, where the people have not such prodigious powers of inventing and destroying, and where demolition and edification do not recur so restlessly.

A fortnight ago—or is it a month?—or is it ten years?—or was it before the Empire or the Revolution?—the illustrious CHANGARNIER, his dismissal, his wrath, and the woes unnumbered of which it was to be the direful spring to France, was the subject of every newspaper discussion and drawing-room conversation. What will the Illustrious do? Will the President dare to do without him? Will the Chamber not rally round the Illustrious Sword? Will the Chamber and the Illustrious Sword together not turn the President out of doors, and send him to Vincennes or the frontier? Sir, we trembled at the withdrawal of the Illustrious Sword : that removed, people said the whole body politic which hung round it would collapse and fall to the ground. This is but a fortnight ago—a week since the majority of the Chamber, which had taken such offence at the dismissal of their cashiered champion, did not even mention his name in the debate in which they stormed the Government—and to-day he is no more talked about than GENERAL KLEBER OR MARSHAL TURENNE. He is illustrious —*c'est bien ;* France has such a number of illustrious Captains : you may see portraits of three thousand of them in the Museum at Versailles.

CHANGARNIER, THIERS, Burgraves, coalition of parties, attack on the Government, determined stand against the Empire—these sounds, so familiar at every café table, talked of by every woman in every drawing-room, heard in every group of Champs Elysées promenaders, or in the pit or the balcon at the play—are as if they had never been. If CHANGARNIER sulks in his tents, who cares? If the Burgraves wag their venerable heads together and prophesy too, who minds? The Titans of the coalition stormed and carried Olympus—and, then!—and then they marched out again, leaving Jove in possession, and unruffled. Coalition, and combat, and victory, and failure are nine days old, and the public does not care for them one jot. Sir, MR. PUNCH, I am an old Paris man, and I tell you that the excitement produced in the country by *Monte Christo* or the fight between the ' Chourineur ' and Rodolphe, in the *Mystères de Paris*, was infinitely more great and durable than the sparring-match between M. THIERS and M. BAROCHE the other day. *Parlez-moi de suffrage universel !* The nation has elected the Chamber, and having elected it, cares about its proceedings no more than about a theatrical *feuilleton* in the *Journal des Débats*. The representatives talk, and vote, and shout, and drink *eau sucrée*, and they have lively interpellations, agitations, and so forth—but nobody goes to their *Théâtre*

Historique. THIERS comes out in the spectacles, CHANGARNIER waves the grim sword and brandishes his moustachios, DUPIN rings the bell—but the audience doesn't care.   *La France possède sa Chambre*—and what happens after possession?—after courtship, and enthusiasm, and marriage before the Mayor of the arrondissement? The *Femme légitime* sits at home, keeps her chamber, and Monsieur goes out and walks on the Boulevard, and ogles the little *coupés* in the Bois.

Now, suppose a man, remarkable for coolness, simplicity, courage, a clear head, whom chance or luck has placed at the head of a Government like this;—and to this opinion of the Presiding Officer of the French Republic, you, MR. PUNCH, and almost all persons of sense in England, have come:—suppose a man endowed with all these qualities; and what great desire can such a one have to be called Emperor, or to be crowned at Rheims or Notre Dame? Would he be the better off, or the more secure, if anointed ever so much; or if the POPE consecrated him; or if the Chamber voted or the whole nation elected him Emperor for ever and ever? Every prince and his heirs for ever has been elected and received with cries of joy, and rallied round, and turned out; and from the Throne Room of the Tuilleries, to the back door, and the hackney-coach in the yard, seems to be the certain course of all French dynasties. It is *Arrivée du Roi—Sacre de sa Majesté—Fuite du Roi—Arrivée de M. le Lieutenant-Général du Royaume*, etc.,—over and over again. If it had been his Majesty NAPOLEON the Second or Third (which is it?)—meditating an assault upon the privileges of Parliament and the liberties of the country, whom the coalition attacked the other day—his Majesty's hackney-coach would have been ordered out, and he would have arrived in England as MR. JONES—leaving the field to the allies, white, red, and tricolor; and it was because there was no emperor that the President was safe, and that those balked conspirators took nothing by their victory.

And so, sir, as I look from this place at the course of events, and listen to the conversation of the people round me, I feel myself to be as incredulous as any man of the company, the highest and the lowest; I fancy the old Burgraves grinning to each other; the President yawning with a languid smile; and the porters at the gates of the *Ministères* eyeing cynically out of their holes the passing folks who take possession of the ministerial portfolio for to-day, and are gone to-morrow, after playing their little part in the comedy—the comedy to which nobody listens, or for which nobody cares any more.

A DELICATE CASE.[1]

In a Letter from MR. MUFF *to* MR. PUNCH.

DEAR P.,

In the midst of the agitation occasioned by the resignation of Ministers, the affairs of the *heart* can find little interest, perhaps ; and yet, dear P., what does a Cabinet Minister matter to me in comparison to domestic bliss ; and how would an Income-tax more or less, or a Popish aggression or so, aggravate me, and *terranize* over me, equal to a wife ? I have been for some weeks an *ingayged* mann. I am of age, *and an Aberdasher in a quiet line of business*, in Lambeth, left to self, Ma, and sisters, by Pa. I met MISS EMILY P–TTS at a *dancing acaddamy*, which I danced with her several times ; and had the honour of excorting her and her sister home to their Ma's apartments in the neighbourhood of K–nn–ngton Ov–l.

Me and SAM TH–MPS–N, a friend of mine, used *gennly* to be the partners of MISS A. and MISS E. P–TTS at the acaddamy, and walk home with them after the ball. MISS A. fell to TH–MPS–N, MISS E. fell to me. In our many walks and conversations, poetry and scentiment, LALLA ROOK, BYROM, ELIZA COOK—every think refined and *intalectial*, in a word, came from MISS EMILY P–TTS, which her Christian name there is no need to disguise, it being the same as that of the victim of the fascinating *Steerforth* (which she always called me STEERFORTH) in MR. DICKENS'S *most admirable novel*.

At that dancing Astabblishment, in those moonlike walks, no being could appear more charming than EMILY P–TTS. Her form is that of the Nymth ; her air dark auburn, and curling naturally ; her woice like the cooing of the ring-dove, which SAM TH–MPS–N (he is an air-dresser, and has a great phansy for pidgings and things) keeps in his shop. In fact, ' I *wandered by my* EMILY's *side, and wooed her for my blushing bride !* '—as I told her in the Valentine which I sent the 14th of this very month, Febyouary, having courted her for fourteen days.

My Ma and sisters keep house for me, I am jest 21 years of age, managing the business for the family ; and, after I had pledged myself to MISS P—, which she had it in my hand-writing, and no mistake—I did not like, for a few days, to break the news to Ma, whose temper is what I should call *uppish*, and who won't like to have a person put over her at a table where she have sate

[1] [March 1, 1851.]

X

and precided so long in my pore Pa's time.   At last, however,
last Friday, I told her, and there arose an *exceeding unpleasant
row*.   Ma and sisters all cried.   Ma asked how I could go for
and engage myself, being quite a boy (though I am of age these
six months, and SAM says, with the use of his Mycasser my
whiskers will very soon grow quite large)—how I could engage myself with a girl whom I'd met at a sixpenny Op, and whom I knew
nothink of?   I told her that Love is Love ; that ever since the
wurld begann, mann was the slave of woman ; that if I didn't
marry my EMILY, I felt I should *peridge in an untimely grave ;*
and that she was just as bad about me.   So being the Head of
the family, Mar had nothink for it but to conscent to my whishes,
which was for *immediate marridge*.   She kist my sisters all
round—said what must be must ; and, putting on her bonnet,
said she would go with me and see her daughter.

    This was not exactly to my liking.   I have forgot to tell you
that I didn't much like MRS. P–TTS, EMILY's Mamma, nor her big
brother (which he is an horse-rider at a sircus and a bullying
feller, always borroring money of me, and gettin' tipsy and
swearing, and thretnin' he'd have my life if he thought my
intentions towards EMILY was not honorable), and MRS. P–TTS'
lodgings was not kep as neat as they might be ; and she's a bigg
large woman with a black wigg and *very odd ways*, and I can't
help thinking that she is fond of drink too.

    Well, Ma and me goes to see MRS. P., and I couldn't help
seeing by Ma's face that she didn't like my EMILY's family at all.
They'd jest been having their dinner at 1 o'clock.   There was a
pewter pot, and a bottle of sperrits on the table, and the cloth
wasn't very nice—neither was MRS. Ps'. gownd, which she looked
as if she wore it in bed ; whereas pore Ma is always as neat as a
pinn, and they'd been having Hirish Stew, and Ma don't like that
neither—and EMILY scolded me for bringing MRS. MUFF (which
is our name) without giving warning beforehand.

    'O, Bob,' says Mar, going away and crying her eyes out, 'how
can you expect that young woman can make you happy ?   Her
horrid mother was, I'm afraid, tipsy ; she herself is ten years
older than you.'

    'Law, Ma,' I said, 'she's only twenty-two ;' but Ma said
EMILY was 30 if she was a day.   'Your sisters can never live
with her and that dreadful brother of hers.'   And Ma took on
and wouldn't be consoled, do the best I could : and again and
again asked how after six walks home (which I had but six, and
that is true) with MISS P——, I could give up my Mar and sisters
for sush a *creature*, Mar called her.

Then when I went back to EMILY *she* gave it me too. Her voice ain't so sweet when she scolds, as it is when she's walking by moonlight, nor she don't look so well by daylight as she do at the acaddemy in her musling dress, and I see she *is* a good bit older than me ; but she has my promise ; and there's that big brother (the beast) and the other brother, who is in the Attorney's office, which I hate him, almost worse than I do the big one— and I've given my word, and what can I do ?

Now, dear MR. P., I read in the paper to-day, that a party who was engaged to another party for a fortnight, and who have broke off his engagement, have been judged to pay the party *eight hundred pound*. I don't mean that our cases is in the least like ; but what am I to do in *my* case, and how much should I have to pay, suppose I broke off with EMILY P–TTS ? I *did* pop the question on rather a short acquaintance. I *do* think none of us will be happy if we marry. I do think, if I feel this, and say so honestly to a gal, it ought to be a reason, and a good reason, why we shouldn't be tied together for hever. I do think that the lor, which makes a matter of barging and money of this, has somethink immodest in it, somehow. I do think that a jury, sitting on a girl's feelings, and assessing the walue of them (where there has been no harm done, and nothing but honorable court-ship), ain't right ; and that the Law which forses a party to marry a party the other party don't like, is stoopid and wrong—and— and—I know I wish I hadn't been at that Dancing Academy : and am your obedient servant,

ROBERT MUFF.

P.S.—SAM THOMPSON has just come in, and told me that he has had it in confidence from a professional friend, that EMILY's Hair is *died*.

FROM 'THE OWN CORRESPONDENT OF THE *MONITEUR DES BOULEVARDS.*' [1]

London, 28th February.

MONSIEUR THE EDITOR,

I have not yet delivered my letters of introduction, or done more than arrive in the brumous capital of Albion, after a brief though stormy passage across the Channel. My sufferings were severe. They are over. I am now lodged in my hotel in the neighbourhood of L—st—r Square, the centre of the fogs, the fashion, the commerce of this city.

The proprietor of this hotel (an intelligent compatriot) informs me that little interest has been felt in the late ministerial perplexities and changes. This I shall see quickly for myself. For the present I have but the day's journal before me—reflex of daily opinion—and I read therein matters sufficient, indeed, for many a day's thought. Intimately acquainted with the English language and history, the contents of these journals is not a mystery to me —I give my views and shall transmit you other letters of time in time.

A singular process, illustrative of English manners and life, appears before me in the journal which is laid upon my table. You may not, perhaps, have heard of an English writer of merit, M. DISRAELI. In his first novel, called the *Curiosities of Literature,* he made proofs of esprit ; his *Letters of Junius,* published subsequently, were sufficiently picquantes, and caused their publisher, WOODFALL, more than one prosecution ; his *Life of Vivian Grey* was a bleeding satire upon the celebrated Whig

[1] [March 8, 1851.]

Earl, head of the powerful family the members of which have, for 20 years, governed this country.

The Whigs, since that satire, have vowed to him an undying detestation. Lay your heel upon one member of the English aristocracy, and the whole body writhes and turns, encircles you with its enormous folds, and crushes its poisoned victims.

Having quarrelled with the Whigs and PEEL, that transfuge to their camp, DISRAELI, the literrator, suddenly appears as the man politic. He enters the Chamber of Commons. He attaches himself to the party opposed to the Whigs. He defies the huge aristocratic dragon, lancing at the sweltering and venomous monster the shafts of his sarcasm, and piercing his scales with the brilliant glaive of his wit. PEEL, the champion of the oligarchy, falls under his blows—DISRAELI, like PEEL a man of the people, like PEEL rises to the command of a great aristocratical party in the state; he is unanimously elected as member for the Bucks, and leads them in their battle against their Whig enemy.

What arrives ? The aristocracy of England never pardons—it resorts to assassination rather than forgets. The death of DISRAELI was resolved upon, and very nearly put into execution but a few days past.

Would you know how ? By a stratagem brutal yet deadly. An infernal machine was invented by English treachery to destroy the first Consul; an omnibus is employed to crush DISRAELI.

Being in his brougham traversing the streets of London, an omnibus, waiting its opportunity, dashed into the vehicle of the illustrious author, burst the armoriated panels of his light carriage, and cast him to the ground.

The name of the proprietor of this omnibus was NELSON. Does not this explain the attack and the mystery ?

A NELSON does not retreat before armed force, brutal violence, and murderous stratagem.

It was a NELSON who bombarded the peaceful city of Copenhagen.

It was a NELSON who struck, like an assassin and incendiary, amidst the midnight flotilla of Boulogne; whence he was flung back by the strong arm of our braves. It was a NELSON who would have destroyed the member for the Bucks.

SIR DISRAELI, escaping by a miracle, carried his plaint before the tribunals of the first instance. And in this country of England, where everything judges itself by money, where the chastity of the spouse, the purity of the daughter, pays itself at so much; what do you think, what does France think, was the fine imposed upon the agent of NELSON, the bravo of the box, who, in fault of a dagger, would have driven the pole of an omnibus and two horses into the dauntless bosom of the Member for the Bucks.

SIR BINGHAM, the magistrate at the Court of Marlborough (remark, Marlborough!—another name full of fatal recollections to France, another name suggesting blood, retribution, vengeance!), sate under the Statue of outraged Themis, and delivered the astonishing verdict.

SIR BINGHAM fined SIR STANTON, the driver of the omnibus, SIXPENCE.

For the attempted murder of a poet, SIXPENCE!

For the assault on a statesman, SIXPENCE!

For the assassination of genius, SIXPENCE!

Do you know what it is, sixpence in this City of London? The drive in an omnibus (without correspondences) is sixpence. The waiter at the taverne where you eat the bleeding beef, grumbles at the gratuity of sixpence. The maid at the hotel, who makes your chamber, scornfully flings you back sixpence—it is not enough for her service; it is not enough for the smoothing of a bed, for the passing of a *bassinoire*, for the jug of hot water. The very pint of *hafanaf* costs sixpence; the beggar in the street expects sixpence; and the life of the greatest man in England is rated at the value of a chopine of ale, of a drive in an omnibus, of a waiter's fee, or a beggar's gratuity! Note, that this is true; that this is patent; that I read this in the public journals in the nineteenth century, in superb England, that builds palaces of crystal, and pretends to dominate the civilisation of the world!

SIR DISRAELI's menaced life is valued at sixpence, then; but his broken coach panel is rated at—how much think you—£8:10s. —at 212 francs 50 centimes!

A life, 65 centimes!—a coach panel, 212 francs 50 centimes! —Oh, Albion!

Yes, but the coach panel is armoriated; the coach panel has a blazon. It is an insult to attack a blazon in England; it costs 65 centimes to attempt a murder.

To attempt to assassinate an unpopular statesman is the same cost to you as a cigar.

Enough for the present regarding MONSIEUR DISRAELI. I grieve to find that another leader of the Chamber of Commons, LORD JOHN RUSSELL, has met with a still more melancholy fate, and has succumbed.

Flying from the odium which his administration had caused in this country, it appears that SIR RUSSELL took shelter in Ireland, which, as you know, is now joined to England by the vast Menai

Tunnel. The journals of to-day, the 28th, received from Ireland, announce his fate.

A Limerick paper states, that, 'On Monday last immense crowds paraded the streets of the town of Ennis, with blazing tar-barrels borne on rafts, and bearing in the centre LORD JOHN RUSSELL, wearing a hideous mask. The yells and shouts of the crowd were terrific, and after traversing the town—*not forgetting to visit Bindon Street, where the Judges of Assize were lodging*—the crowd returned opposite the Old Court House, and there committed LORD JOHN to the flames, amidst vociferous execrations, and repeated cheers for CARDINAL WISEMAN. No *stones were thrown or disrespect offered to the Protestant Church, which they passed twice.'

The EX-PREMIER seems to have escaped, however, from the roasting at Ennis; and probably fled in disguise from that beautiful city: for we find, by the *Tipperary Free Press*, that he was at Clonmel the next day, '*most ludicrously attired*, carried on the back of a brawny fellow, a number of men following and belabouring him with huge wattles. They conveyed him through several streets, and, at length, having suspended him from a lamp-post, it was set on fire, amidst the groans of those assembled.'

Is not this an awful picture—a haughty nobleman ludicrously attired—carried before the courts where the judges of the land were sitting, belaboured with wattles and hanged, and burned à la lanterne? O LEDRU ROLLIN! you said well that this country was hastening to dissolution, and was to pay a speedy penalty for historic crimes! The indignant people rise in their wrath upon the minister who has designated their beloved rites as super-stitious, carry him to the doors of the Protestant temple which they respect, dress him in ludicrous disguises, and slay him in the public place!

Were these facts not narrated in a newspaper, I should hesitate to believe them. But they are in print, and cause neither denial, nor surprise, nor indignation. The shops are not closed; the tocsin is not sounding; the phlegmatic people are not in arms, but move with restless egoism on the affairs of their commerce. I feel that I am about to gaze on awful convulsions in the midst of a great, a doomed, a terrible people!

Agree the assurances of my highest consideration,

GOBEMOUCHE.

JOHN BULL BEATEN.[1]

In a Letter from a CONTRIBUTOR *to* MR. PUNCH.

UNCH, MY DEAR AND ESTEEMED CHIEF,—At the meeting of your Privy Council, which you assembled upon the appearance of CARDINAL WISEMAN'S first letter, dated from the Flaminian Gate, the course which MR. PUNCH was to pursue, under the circumstances of the Papal aggression, was debated eagerly at your Board.[2] What was to be done? Would we stand it? Would we allow a foreign-eering Prince to appoint officers, and confer titles, in England? It was too bad—too insolent,—we would not have it at any price, and so forth. The Council was very stormy. I see our friend the Professor of Theology [3] battling with clenched fists, and thumping and defying the POPE and all his crew.

Our friend, the Professor of Belles Lettres,[4] sat by; sneered at the agitation; said it was absurd, and that we could do nothing; and was the only one of the conclave who seemed to be undisturbed by the general commotion. And our dear friend, the Professor of Mediæval Design, whose faith and whose affections were with the party which we were met to oppose, quitted us to join the banner displayed now for the first time these 300 years, and under which the Cardinal was marching upon our country. For this is amongst the consequences of religious debate: it separates brethren; estranges parent and child; parts dear friends; angers and embitters honest hearts. By JUPITER AMMON, sir, rather than have lost our friend the Professor of Mediæval Design,[5] I would have forgone a bench of Bishops and a whole conclave of Cardinals—the POPE can make those any day.

[1] [March 22, 1851.]   [2] [*Punch's* weekly dinner.]
[3] [Douglas Jerrold.]   [4] [Percival Leigh.]
[5] [Richard Doyle, who left *Punch* on account of the attacks on the Catholics which appeared in that periodical.]

To continue : amidst parties assembled at your table there was one Right Honourable Gentleman, the learned Professor of Gastronomy—your humble servant, indeed [1]—whose opinion with respect to the present crisis was, he believes, as follows :—'The insult,' said that gentleman, 'that we Englishmen, we lords of the world, have received from an Italian bishop, reviving pretensions as absurd and antiquated as those of the priests of Jupiter, or the Druids, is clear. How can we be otherwise than indignant? The indifference of the Right Honourable Gentleman, Professor of Belles Lettres, shocks me. With all our might, and with all our hearts, we must show that we are English citizens ; and, since these Roman priests *will* have a procession among us, we must greet them with a jeer and a growl. For toleration has its limits, if gentlemen choose to wear pigtails, or beards, or hats as broad as washing-tubs, against the custom of my country. I'll laugh at them—and have a right to laugh ; if they bring a winking statue into the Strand, I'll sneer, and say "Stuff—away with your rubbish of winking pictures and miraculous dolls!" If LORD SMOLLETT (let us call him) were to walk down Pall Mall, with a jack chain round his neck, his footman after him, I would join the mob that hooted him. Carry on these rites, friends, at home. Dress, undress, kneel, chant, shave, or not, as you like ; but don't bring your vagaries into our streets—we don't believe in them, we flout them utterly to scorn. My poor winking statue !—you may wink for a week, and what do I care? Narrate that legend to the marines—go and wink at Rimini, not here, *sub Jove* in Fleet Street, in the year 1851. And, as in Rome, when a procession passes, or the POPE blessed the city and the world, every man of good feeling would take off his hat and bow his head with the crowd ; so do you, of your part, respect our manners and religion—take off your hat to it decently, and don't keep on that absurd Cardinal's broad-brim in public.

'What then was our duty,' asked the Professor of Gastronomy, 'when His Eminence marched on us from the Flaminian Gate? To fling stones on the procession? No. To subject any single person who was carrying a banner, or tossing an incense pot, or twanging a chant, to imprisonment or violence? No. To laugh at the whole business, to meet it with denial, with scorn, with every imaginable PROTEST. Yes. To that public assertion of the Catholic party it was assuredly the duty of the Protestant party to shout a denial—and if *Punch*, and LORD JOHN, and all England did not bellow, Heaven help our lungs.'

'But why protest when you can do nothing more?' says the

[1] [Thackeray.]

Professor of Belles Lettres. I say, if we do nothing more than protest, that protest is good and wholesome. You do not knock down a man who insults you in the street, but you have a right to feel angry—or, suppose a lady boxes your ears, you do not, in reply, hit her on the nose; but it is quite consistent with good morality, that you should feel indignant at the outrage, and say, 'Madam, I protest that your behaviour is monstrous, and your aggression an impertinence.' And so we have protested, and done right to protest. It is a sentimental satisfaction, a record entered—a medal struck as it were—as when POPE-WHAT-DO-YOU-CALL-'EM struck a medal in commemoration of the murder of the Huguenots, he did not cause thereby the slaughter of any single Calvinist more, but simply recorded his ghostly satisfaction at that victorious assertion of his principles, and at that event so triumphant for his faith.

My counsel then to you, sir, was to protest once or twice as loudly as possible, and there's an end on't—to chalk up 'No Popery' in as large letters as you could, and so to leave the business. We can't persecute. We can deny. We can say ' pooh! psha! bosh! stuff and nonsense!' protesting, by various ways and arguments, but no more. And to some Right Honourable Professors at your table, who inclined to repressive measures, I had to offer a respectful opposition.

We can't use repressive measures—has not the agitation of the last three months proved it? *Lord Punch,* LORD JOHN, LORD ASHLEY, *The Times,* the whole country are in wrath; and we find we can do nothing but protest. We can't go back to religious any more than to any other kind of Protection; and having once announced free religion, and taken the duties off faith, we have not the means of setting them on again. We can't fight Roman Catholicism by enactments—Oh, me! and our enormous Establishment of Custom House officers is still on foot!

But that is a question (painfully interesting to the Bench of Bishops perhaps, and the rest of the ecclesiastical *douane*), but not at present in debate. The case at present seems to stand —so.

We are insulted; we are angry; we are beat. That is to say, if we want to retaliate for an insult committed upon us, we can't—and LORD JOHN, menaced by foe ecclesiastic, *has* stepped back, *has* lifted his mighty arm to defend himself (or rather to hit out), and has dropped that muscular weapon—not of defence, but offence. We can't strike. And thank heaven, we can't. Thank heaven, I say, that a great nation, stung, outraged as it has been by a monstrous insult and perfidy of priestly aggression, has in its imperial armoury no weapon of offence upon which it can lay a hasty hand to punish the outrage, and can't persecute though ever so angry. A few scores of years hence, when *haec certamina* come to be described; when that struggle is over, whereof we are but now at the beginning; when that battle is fought, for which we are taking our sides, and the ground seems to be getting cleared every day—when it shall be decided whether free thought, free speech, and free commerce among men are to exist—and we are to have railroads and Ross's Telescopes, and books for all—or a *régime* of Russian grenadiers, *Index Expurgatorius*, and LORD WISEMAN's hat,—I say, on that day, when this present one comes to be chronicled, I wonder how the history will go?

It will say perhaps :—

At the commencement of the second half of the nineteenth century the ancient faith was suddenly revived in England by the pious energy of SAINT NICHOLAS of Seville. Landing in the country, amidst the almost frantic hostility of the islanders, the most powerful in arts, arms, and commerce, although the most benighted of the inhabitants of Europe, SAINT NICHOLAS was assailed on his first arrival by the Sovereign (styled Head of the Sect calling itself a Church, and dominant in that part of Britain); by the Prime Minister, a deplorable fanatic of Calvinistic opinions; by the Legislature, and a vast majority of the nation. The country rose against him; persecutions were threatened; tortures were in preparation; chains, fines, and imprisonment were devised for SAINT NICHOLAS and his clergy. But aid was at hand, and the arm which the powerful Minister raised to smite the meek cheek of the Cardinal was stayed by an influence which we must, etc. etc. The clergy of the neighbouring Island of Ireland (since removed by the application of scientific means a thousand miles into the Atlantic), headed by the profound CULLEN and the gentle MACHALE, the Hibernian members of the Britannic Legislature, men remarkable for the polish of their manners and the fervid piety of their lives—above all, the dissensions among the English themselves—caused the uplifted arm to fall powerless, which was about to descend upon SAINT NICHOLAS, and averted the glaive which would have found a willing and joyful martyr. SAINT NICHOLAS and his clergy were suffered to live unmolested, and continued, in and about London, making many converts, until the invasion of the great Austro-French Force, under the two Emperors, accompanied by the POPE in person, when religion was established finally in this country to be disturbed no more. The unmarried Bishops of the late establishment were generously admitted *ad eundem*, etc. etc. etc.

Will this be the tale, or will it be one of a different tendency and moral, which the reader of future times will peruse—Mr. Macaulay's New Zealand Traveller, let us say—looking at the remains of Westminster and surveying the ruins of St. Paul's ?

NO BUSINESS OF OURS.[1]

EAR MR. PUNCH,

I hope that the little anecdotes connected with the Roman Catholic Church, which have of late been occupying a good deal of public attention, and which have had the effect of making some folks angry, will not tend to disturb your own serene judgment and temper.

What has happened ? A young lady, twenty years of age, a ward of Chancery, with eighty thousand pounds for her fortune, has been for education to a convent at Taunton, and, in the course of her residence there, has been so charmed and edified by the conventual life, that it is said she feels inclined to adopt it altogether ; and, taking the Church for her bridegroom, will possibly endow her mystic spouse with her eighty thousand pounds.[2]

Has she not a perfect right to do as she likes with her own ? If she were poor, would there be any great outcry made ? Has she not a right to her opinions and convictions ? Suppose that she likes better to get up to chapel at 3 o'clock in the morning than to dance polkas at that hour in Belgrave Square ? Suppose she is of opinion that that retreat at Taunton is far nearer heaven than any residence in London could be, and prefers a spiritual

[1] [March 29, 1851.]
[2] [Much excitement was occasioned by this case. Miss Talbot's stepfather, the Rev. Grantley Berkeley, interfered in time to prevent the lady taking the veil, when her fortune would have become the property of the convent. Miss Talbot subsequently married Lord Edward Howard.]

to a stepfather, how are you to prevent her from having her way?

You have no more right to force her to eat beef on a Friday than to compel me to dine on a slice of bread and a carrot. It is a question of tastes which ought surely to be left open in a free country.

And where there is liberty of opinion there must, of course, be expression of it. Everybody, who speaks, proselytises more or less. You engage to make converts just as much as His Eminence or dear FATHER HOLDSTOCK—and as his reverence excites by hope or terror, and says to his faithful, My beloved son or daughter, if you do so and so, you will be assured of so and so; and if you don't do so and so, you will be pretty certain to go to, etc.,—so, you on your side, flout and scout, and scorn, and fling ridicule on HOLDSTOCK and NICHOLAS, and all black friars and white, blue friars and grey,—their preternatural pretensions, the miracles which the poor creatures are compelled to swallow, the very morality which they inculcate, as odious, foolish, debasing, unmanly. I have been in a convent myself—perhaps in that very one of Taunton. I believe on my word and conscience that if that system is virtuous, Sutteeism in India is virtuous; I believe if those twenty-four ladies were married to twenty-four railway navvies, they would be better employed than they are in their present business. I believe that many of the duties which occupy them, and in which the poor souls are taught to take a pride, are meaner and more frivolous than waltzing with the dullest dandies in Mayfair—that the scheme of life held up to them as the highest and most virtuous of which human creatures are capable, is neither more nor less than despicable and shameful, and scorn the doctrine and the doctors inasmuch as they preach it. We laugh at the Doctors then: and they pity us and send us—you know where. They can't do otherwise, and we are perfectly content. Sir, they are all alike. Disagree with FATHER ATHANASIUS or JACK THE COBBLER, who is bawling on the common, and he can do nothing but consign you to the deuce. As far as he stands there, and to the best of his belief, he is the administrator of your ultimate happiness or perdition. Bawl on, JACK THE COBBLER; curse away, FATHER ATHANASIUS! Curse us and each other. You believe yourselves right; and if you are right, we are done for. Show us that you are right, one or the other of you, and the rest follows as a matter of course. But, holding your premises to be as absurd and monstrous as their consequences would be, I, for my part, take leave utterly to deny one and the other.

But give clerical gentlemen fair play. If I don't believe that FATHER ATHANASIUS can absolve me, or the contrary ; or decline to adopt the views of JACK THE COBBLER, who has pretty much the same pretensions, at least those divines have as good a right to be heard as we : and conclusions and consequences must come out of their opinions as out of all others.

If, for instance, a young lady is of opinion that FATHER ATHANASIUS is invested with powers to curse or bless her into eternity ; is the holder of an absolute truth of which he is the authorised and heaven-transmitted expounder ; and if the Father says, ' My dear, for the good of your soul, and the benefit of the Church, you had much better take the habit of a nun, and pay over that matter of eighty thousand pounds, which can be of no use to you ; ' of course, she has a right to follow the dictates of her conscience, and the keeper of her conscience ; and you and I have no right to object to the disposal of her money.

Take the other case again, about which there has been such a brawl and talk in the VICE-CHANCELLOR's Court.[1] An old French refugee and miser, who has scraped together ten thousand pounds, is on his death-bed in Somers Town. Shivering and starving, on the brink of the grave, and without the heart to spend a shilling for a pint of wine to warm his wretched carcase —his landlord finds the Roman Catholic clergyman of the district, and, of course, brings him to administer consolation to the dying old wretch.

Enemies may say that the old man, drivelling and trembling in the grasp of death, might fall an easy victim to an interested person disposed to exaggerate the terrors which already were agitating him, and take advantage of the weakness which had stretched him on his miserable couch. What does the REVEREND MR. HOLDSTOCK do, on the contrary ? He exhorts CARRÉ to good works—for what better work than charity ? What cause more sacred than that of education ? Those dear little girls of Saint Aloys' School want spelling-books and samplers ; and if the old miser, by screwing, by French lessons, by whatever means, has amassed a sum of money, which he can't take away with him to the place whither he is going, let him give seven thousand to the school, and he will be no worse for the donation.

The Catholics like pictures, and admit them as incitements of devotion. Here's a nice subject for a pious artist ! Let it hang up in the school amongst the little children—the miser dying

[1] [Mathurin Carré left seven thousand pounds to the church and schools of St. Aloysius, Somers Town. The will was disputed under the Law of Mortmain ; and compromise was made.]

on his miserable pallet—his wretched life flickering out—prostrate by ghastly terrors, by accumulated remorse, by mental and bodily weakness and imbecility—and the priest and the priest's friend, the barrister, hanging over him, and getting the donation from the almost corpse—look up at that, little girls! Count your little beads; sing your little song in chorus for the repose of the soul of the late MONSIEUR CARRÉ!

It is true that CARRÉ, for this pious purpose, gives his money away from his family, but what does this prove? Does this not prove how good an Englishman FATHER HOLDSTOCK is, in reply to those wicked assertions that the Roman Catholic Ecclesiastics are subjects of a foreign power? CARRÉ's relations are Frenchmen. He made his money in this country. Why should it go out of this country? He lived in Somers Town; let his piety enrich the suburb in which he practised the virtues of economy. If he had not lived so avariciously as he did, he could not have saved at his trade more than three thousand pounds. Let his family have that. A soul is saved; a school is built and improved, by which thousands of souls more are probably succoured. And I, for my part, say that FATHER HOLDSTOCK performed a GOOD MORNING'S WORK.

And this testimony which I give is at least impartial. I no more believe that the POPE of ROME or any officer of his has power to save (or the contrary) my soul than that the beadle of St. James's can do so; I have a right to my opinion, and to publish it too; and so repeat that the REVEREND MR. HOLDSTOCK did a good morning's business. A *coup* of seven thousand pounds in the course of a forenoon's conversation is very seldom made; and many a clergyman has passed six hours in taking a confession not worth twopence-halfpenny. MR. HOLDSTOCK would, no doubt, and has done; and would give his ear to the fetid breath of a beggar dying of typhus, as readily as listen to the last quivering directions of a perishing miser.

And if clergymen of his persuasion have a persuasion of their own so marvellous that they can alienate young girls from the world, sisters from sisters, dying old men yearning for their relatives from their natural affections, and the ordinary proofs of them—if they can get MISS TALBOT's money to build a cathedral, or CARRÉ's to found a school—if they can enter families, close doors and hold secret councils, remit, confirm, soothe, terrify, divide, govern,—what call have *we* to complain? If Catholic families choose to submit to this, how can we help it, or how interfere?

There is a pile of buildings at Taunton, say—there is a door.

Who is to forbid you to enter and mount the steps? And as a young English lady all but a minor, imaginative, beautiful, tender in years, and intellect, attended by the devout and influential friends of her family, by pious relatives, by a crowd of priests, with shaven polls, singing round about her, and pointing out the joys of heaven to her, has a perfect right to mount those steps, and disappear from the world—why is a lady in Bengal to be prevented from joining her spouse, whom her relations, the practice of the country, and the advice of the most eminent fakeers and Brahmins of her church, concur to press upon her?

An Oppressed Hindoo.

IF NOT: WHY NOT?[1]

ACCORDING to the *Guide Book*, Banbridge, in the County Down, is one of the most agreeable and flourishing places in Ireland. 'Banbridge is situated on the river Bann, which rises in the Moudne Mountains, and falls into Lough Neagh. Within these few years the place has risen into considerable importance, wholly from commercial enterprise, and if it was necessary to point out what can be accomplished by individual exertion, Banbridge might be cited as an example. Trees adorn the wavy country and the villas on the banks of the Bann. Bleaching greens chequer the surface: mills and factories, with their appurtenances of ponderous wheels and tall chimneys, are scattered along the river sides, mingled with the houses and gardens of the proprietors, the comfortable cottages of the workmen, and their small and minutely mixed tillage and pasture fields.' What more peaceful and beautiful sight can be conceived: and isn't it cruel

[1] [April 5, 1851.]

to think that the comfortable inhabitants of such a sweet district should be driven, by the ferocity of our law, into armed rebellion?

Such is the case—a case only too common in our dear sister country of Ireland. A man lives in this country : peacefully occupies a farm and premises there : tills and garners, sows and reaps, and naturally does not like to pay rent. Who does? What generous man, surrounded by his children, would like to give away money, and deprive his darlings of their bread—in order to fatten an already bloated landlord? What man, after four years' quiet possession, would like to give up his own—to see the Bailiff at his door—to see his cattle and sheep driven away—the lamb, that his pretty children loved and tended, led off, bleating, to alien shambles—and the armchair, in which his old mother very likely sate, occupied by the heartless carcase of the man in possession? The desecrated home, the insulted household gods, the desolated cupboard, the rifled poultry yard, the empty duck-pond and stable—it is hard to think of images like these without feeling sympathy for him who loses such treasures, or hate for the ruthless tyrant who ravishes them. There ought to be no rent ; no landlords ; no bum-bailiffs. What man—what body of men—what cursed Saxon law has a right to trample out the fire upon your hearthstone ?—to make a ruin of your paradise ? —to pluck the steed from your stall, the watch from your fob, the shawl from your wife's shoulders—and send her and your little ones shivering into the world? The men of Banbridge, who arose, in their might, to rescue one of their comrades from the grasp of the Law and the Landlord, deserve well of their country.

The above melancholy, but natural remarks, are inspired in my bosom (and, as I trust, in that of every honest man) by reading a report which appears in the Irish papers, that a gentleman, having a tenant at Banbridge, who owed, and refused to pay, four years' rent, took with him the sub-sheriff and a bailiff, and proceeded to distrain.

The bloodhounds of the law, the sub-sheriff and his attendant, armed with a writ ; the landlord with the rascal rapacity of his race, and urged with a fiendish lust to get his four years' tribute, were met, close to Banbridge, by two hundred gallant men, armed with guns ; and, so just and universal was the indignation of the people against them, that the whole of the two hundred opened a fire upon the landlord and the myrmidons of the bloody law. Nothing can be more simple or fair than this :—A dastardly attack, upon the part of the law, is met by an honourable and manly resistance on the part of the finest peasantry in the world. One of the law bloodhounds, at whom a gallant peasant fired, taking a coward advantage of the honest fellow, *when his gun was gone off*, sprang at him and tried to collar him ; but the brave Paddy slipt out of the ruffian clutches of the bailiff, and escaped with agility ; and finally, bailiff and sub-sheriff, and landlord were obliged to retire before an indignant population.

Let English landlords, who are grumbling about their rents, just look at this example, and take warning.   Here is a tyrant in Ireland, who does not get a shilling of rent for four years, and when he asks for it, the whole country turns out to shoot at him. How would the DUKE OF RICHMOND like to let his land upon such leases—and get (from behind one of his own hedges) such a pepper-corn rent ?   It is manifest that land held upon this tenure ought to fetch a good price, for tenants must be so eager to have it.

The Irish legislators are worthy of the legislation.   One of them gets up in the House of Commons and puts a series of questions to the Irish Secretary.   He wants to know—First, Whether the report is true ?   Secondly, Whether there is an official report ?   Thirdly, Whether the Secretary will lay that official report before the House ?

Fourthly, *Whether he considered it fair towards the misguided people of that country* on the one side, or the Lord Lieutenant on the other, that process of the kind in question should be issued by the sub-sheriff, without apparently taking the slightest trouble to ascertain whether the process would be opposed by the people ; and, if so, whether he had taken a sufficient force to overawe the misguided people ?

What would poor old Ireland do if she hadn't her real friends and representatives to stand by her ?   Here's the real state of the case.   The Government is in fault, of course, and acting unfairly towards the people of Down.   If a man wants his rent, after four years, he ought to ascertain whether the process for obtaining it will be opposed by the people.   If it will be opposed by the people, as of course it will, the landlord ought to get a sufficient force to overawe the people.   A bailiff should march with a couple of companies at his back, and, if convenient, say a field-piece.   The sharp-shooters of the peasantry line the outlying hedges, of course, in advance of the main body, and open a fire at the Regulars.   Regular skirmishers dislodge (with a considerable loss among the Redcoats and Peelers) Peasantry's advanced men, who fall back on the principal column : the action becomes general.   Having the advantage of artillery, the Peelers and Redcoats finally get the uppermost ; the gallant Peasantry retires in good order, after severely punishing the invading force. The firing from the stables and outhouses ceases ; the garrison is withdrawn ; the hall-door is burst open ; the wounded officers are brought in and laid on the drawing-room sofas, and the men are amputated on the billiard table ; and the sheriff (if not picked off) enters, and puts in his execution. This would clearly be the 'fair' way of doing things. It is savage, cruel, and unmanly for a sheriff and his officer to advance unarmed upon two hundred brave men, and ask for rent ; it is a sheer premium upon murder. What honest and ardent Patriot, knowing the wrongs of his country, and maddened by centuries of oppression, could resist the opportunity of shooting a bailiff ? A fellow who comes out on such an errand is no better than an amateur bull's eye ; and a government that employs him is merely provoking an honest people to revolt.

In England I own the case would be different. In England a landlord would most probably want his rent at the half-year, and if he waited for four years, and then distrained for it, it is probable that his officer would not be fired upon by two hundred of the tenant's friends, assembled upon a rising ground, with their picquets in advance. Nor would an English member for a Devonshire borough, let us say, hearing that such a disturbance had taken place in Yorkshire, rise up and ask the Home Secretary whether the conduct of the sheriff's officer was 'fair' towards those misguided Yorkshire folks—as a Munster gentleman spoke about the Ulster men the other day. Here, as yet, rent is considered to be fair, and it is not thought altogether unfair that a man should have to pay it. If my landlord were not to get his quarter and to put a distress into my house (both of which may Fate forbid !) the rest of the inhabitants of the street would not turn out with double-barrelled guns to shoot Mr. Levi or Mr. Sloman. If Levi and Sloman came unarmed, save by their writ, and were fired upon by two hundred men, no English member would inquire in Parliament why a regiment was not sent with Messrs. L. and S. and ask if the sending them unaccompanied was 'fair' upon my two hundred friends, armed with pike and gun. If Levi and Sloman were shot by my two hundred friends, people would use a stronger term than 'misguided' to describe the ten score champions. If even one score of armed ruffians were to attack a lawyer's clerk in his lawful and peaceful calling, fire at him from behind hedges, and deliberately attempt his murder, the sympathy of the public would, to say the least, be with the single and unprotected man ; but this is not Ireland, this is the sister country—our sister's morals, her religion, her virtues, her vices, her views of right and wrong, of black and white, are quite different from ours.

Oh, MR. PUNCH! when our sister's children wanted a Parliament of their own, why, why did we balk our eloquent cousins? Why shouldn't they have their own Commons, their own Lords, their own Bench of Bishops, and settle their own disputes their own way? Will you please to agitate for a Repeal party here? If you do, I suspect you will find many an Englishman ready to join it, and, in the matter of Repeal at least, like

Your very humble servant,

HIBERNIS HIBERNIOR.

THE FRENCH CONSPIRATION.[1]

From GOBEMOUCHE, *Man of Letters, to* SIR WORTLEY, *Member of Parliament.*

MILORD,

I have read in the journal the allocution which you have addressed to the Government, and in which you state that you have a proofs of a great conspiracy existing in this country, and of which this city is the threshold.

Milord. I am a Frenchman. I am a conspirator. I am proud of one and other title. Yes: we conspire: yes, we wish to conquer the old England. But it is in the full street that we conspire. It is by intelligence, by genius, by civilisation, and no more by sabres and bayonets, that we would vanquish. Yes, we will invade you by thousands; and our flotillas, unimpeded, shall discharge legions of our compatriots, from Boulogne, upon the Cliffs of Albion. But those invaders come with flowers in their fusils and your blondes country-women need fear no terrors of war from those who trust to overcome them. Yes, perhaps, I myself may hope to lead away some Britannic Briseis, the captive of my bow; but it is the bow of CUPID which I wield—it is with love and not war that we would be irresistible!

My lord—there is a conspiracy, but it is patent—a foreign envasion, but it is here. Our banners are planted amongst you, and yet your Kremlin on the Thames does not burn. Our legions are encamped in Regent's Quadrant and Leicester Square; and yet we do not fear poison in the houses where we are billeted, or dread ambuscades as we parade your city. Oh, vanquished! you

[1] [April 12, 1851.]

have nothing to fear from Frenchmen ! We smoke under NELSON'S column, and Trafalgar is ours. We promenade in Waterloo Place, and revenge Waterloo !

Already a letter from the important journal of which I was correspondent has appeared in these columns. Although the *Moniteur de Boulevardes* has ceased to exist, I am a man of letters still, and not idle. I study. I observe. I reflect. Educated with care, I write English with native purity.

I am not of those Frenchmen, light and frivolous, who think to approfound the institutions of a country in a visit of eight days : and having walked through London, attended by their guide of office, and spoken and smoked with their compatriots at the *cafés* of Leicester Square and Regent's Quadrant, believe themselves authorised to speak with confidence of the manners and the politics of a great nation. No ! Since my arrival I have deeply studied, carefully inspected, intimately meditated this City, this Carthage, superb rival of our Rome. I have marked all classes of Insularies, from the superb LORD MAYOR in his palace of the City, to the humble artisan taking his refreshment under the tents of the Crystal Exhibition. I have formed profound conclusions, I interview enormous changements for this country.

The insular habits are rapidly passing away. The Parisian civilisation has invaded and conquered the white cliffs, at which NAPOLEON pointed in vain his eyeglass and his flotillas. The male beard and costume of France no longer excites ridicule in the old England—on the contrary, the Insularies adopt our dress, and let to grow their moustachios. I saw of late, in the Chamber of Commons, the son of the greatest of English Statesmen. His discovered chest, his waving locks curled above his forehead in a BRUTUS, his rich imperial, his gallant air, are those of the Continent of our France—not of England, traditional country of the blue frock with buttons of copper, the culotte of skin, the boots to reverse. The young SIR P—L might be a Sportsman of our Jockey Club ; a lion of our Boulevard of Glove. And not he only, as I have said—not the young dandies of the clubs and brilliant militaries on leave—but the youth in general, the artists, the students of the schools of medicine, the advocates of the Temple, and the clerks of notary, the young officers of scheriffs in Chancery Lane, let grow the hair and carry the beard. Where our arms have not conquered, our arts have vanquished. The old England Frenchifies itself all the days.

I see on most of the shops the announcement that French here is spoken—an imperfect jargon it is true, but yet a great and remarkable advance and sign of civilisation ; and it is with no small feelings of delight and pride I remark that almost all the literature of the people is translation of the profound views of our own superior authors ; the seizing narratives of our incomparable ALEXANDRE — the large morality of SUE and SAND ; even the lively tales of the good old PAUL DE KOCK here find interpreters and admirers. In the English Theatre no pieces but of French origin are tolerated by the public. An accomplished country-woman of ours, speaking, it is true, in the English language, but with an accent which renders her adopted tongue a thousand times more melodious and charming than it is in native mouths, is the chief actress at the people's theatre in the Strand. At that of the Princess, where presides the Son of the KEAN, whom our ALEXANDRE DUMAS has rendered immortal, I found him and his wife performing a drama from our Boulevard. At Drury Lane, Azael the Prodigal, surrounded by the Bayadères of Memphis, has borrowed the decorations and voluptuous dances, if not the music, of our Academy. Tartuffe is acting upon the Haymarket scene, and those shafts which the immortal MOLIÈRE launched against the priests and bigots of his time are found still to be sharp and to have poison after two hundred years, when directed against Anglican Church zealots, and aimed at Britannic hypocrites.

Thus I say that we have conspired and that we have con-quered.

Is not the man of all England the most admired and beloved a Frenchman ? Whose name, whose good things are in so many peoples' mouths as the name, as the good things of ALEXIS SOYER ? Yes, ALEXIS is a great pacific conqueror. If merit is to be rewarded by public gratitude, his eminent services ought to be acknowledged by the two countries—the two countries which he has united, as were the twins of Siam, by the bond of the stomach. If there were a cordon (*bleu*) of the Legion of Honour, it should be sent to SOYER with the title of Grand Commander. This nation has paid him just and repeated honours. *Chef* of the Club of Reform, that once powerful party has been disorganised ever since he ceased to be its chief. It dwindles. One is dissatisfied with its leaders : LORD JOHN is scarcely esteemed ; SIR WOOD is little tasted since SOYER the Frenchman resigned his *bâton* of commandment, and threw himself upon a single party no more, but on the whole country.

Albion has responded to his appeal. In our days of college it was our habit to call her perfidious ; but where shall we find a country more faithful ; more grateful ? With us everything uses itself ; every man makes himself to forget. A week after February there was no more question of the House of Orleans

than of the House of Valois ; a month after LAMARTINE had been
the hero of a revolution, the saviour of a Republic, he was the
forgotten writer of books forgotten. Here it is different. We
(for almost I feel that this is France and that I am an Englishman)
honour and remember our public men. Honour to the country,
and to those to whom she is grateful !

An exploding proof of this worthy appreciation has lately been
conferred upon ALEXIS SOYER. The magistrates of the county of
Middlesex have summoned before them ALEXIS. He appeared
with the courage of his nation, of his genius, before the grave
administrators of the Britannic Themis. But it was not tortures,
it was not imposts, it was not Botanibay which they offered to
him ; it was to confer upon him the rights of citizenship, and to
present him, in the name of QUEEN VICTORIA, of the LORD
MAYOR, of England entire, with a splendid testimony of the
national gratitude.

In the neighbourhood of London—by the gigantesque Palace
of Crystal,[1] the fresh meadows of the Hyde Park, and the sombre
avenues of Kinsington's Gardens—little removed from the *Octroi*
(turnspikes)—there stands, amidst parks and prairies of its own,
a *château* called the *Château* of Gor.[2] The *Château* of Gor has
been purchased with the money of the municipality by this grateful nation, by these grave magistrates, and has been conferred,
with the patent of baronnet, upon ALEXIS SOYER, Frenchman.
SIR SOYER, in a warm allocution, responded to the LORD MAYOR
when this title, this domain, were conferred upon him—and asked
all the magistrates to dine in the palace of which he has become
master.

A palace of fairies is he making of it—truly a Symposium of
all nations, as SIR SOYER (faithful to his Bacchanalian tradition,
and proud of his religion of the apron) has styled it. Halls are
here filled in the manners of all nations, accommodated by the
presiding taste of SIR ALEXIS. The Saloon of Italy, the Saloon
of Turkey, the Saloon of Spain ; the Hall of France, the Hall of
Old England. You may consume here the cockaliquet of the
mountains of Scotland, the garbanzos of Castille, the shamrocks
of Ireland, the maccaroni of Vesuvius, the kari of the Ganges, and
the cabob of the Bosphorus ; you may call here for the golden
juice of the Rhine and the purple draught of the Garonne, as for
the whiski of the Liffi and the Afandaf (liquor which I adore) of
the Thames. SIR SOYER will soon be prepared to furnish you
with all these. Already his pavillions glow with the rich colours

[1] [The Crystal Palace in Hyde Park, erected for the Great Exhibition of 1851.]
[2] [Gore House, once the residence of Lady Blessington.]

of the lavish pencil : already banquet halls and feudal towers rise among his parterres : already quiet alcoves and particular cabinets twinkle from among the bosquets, where they will be covered by the discreet and beautiful foliage of Spring and Summer :—yet a few weeks and the palace of SOYER will be opened. This, Milord, is the Conspiracy by which France hopes to conquer you—this is the representative whom the Republic sends to Albion !

Agree the hommages of profound consideration with which
I have the honor to be, Milord,

GOBEMOUCHE,
Man of letters, man of progress.

LEICESTER SQUARE, 10th April.

A STRANGE MAN JUST DISCOVERED IN GERMANY.[1]

T has been mentioned in the German journals that a Foreigner from some unknown country, and speaking a jargon scarcely intelligible by the most profound German philologists, has lately made his appearance at Frankfort on the Oder, where, of course, he was handed over to the care of the police.

This individual was brought before us, JOHANN HUMPFFEN-STRUMPFFEN, Burgomaster of Frankfort, on Tuesday the 8th of April, and examined in our presence and that of our Clerk and Town Council.

The raiment and appearance of this individual, landed, no one knows how, in a remote and extremely quiet German city, are described by all persons as most singular. In height he is about five feet six inches, his hair is white, his face sallow, his beard red—that on his upper lip not so much grown as that on

[1] [April 19, 1851.]

his cheeks; his hands are large and dirty; his teeth useful, his appetite great, and his thirst constant.

His dress is most extraordinary and barbarous. On his head he wears a covering of a snuff-brown colour in shape something like a wash-basin—which it would be very advisable that he should use for his face and hands. Round his neck, which is exceedingly ugly and bare, he wears a strip of a shining stuff, spun out of worms, he says, in his own country, and called an Alberti; it is puffed in two bows round his cheeks and gives him a highly absurd appearance.

His outer garment was a loose, shaggy vest, made out of the skins of bears, most likely, and tainted strongly with a stale and exceedingly rancorous odour of what he calls 'backy-backy.' This outer dress—when asked its name, by BURGERMEISTER VON HUMPFFENSTRUMPFFEN—the nondescript called a 'Minorimosy,' and holding up his outstretched hand three times, cried out the syllable 'Bob' and wagged his head; from which the Burgomaster concluded that 'bob' is the name of a coin of the country.

His next garment, one without sleeves, was decorated with buttons of glass; and in the pockets were found bits of paper, which the nondescript tried to explain—by the words 'Uncle,' 'ticker,' 'spowt,' etc.—and showed by his gestures that the papers were to him of considerable value. They are greasy, and, to all appearances, worthless, coarsely printed, and marked with rude manuscript numerals. It is conjectured that they may form part of the paper-money of his country.

Beyond these tokens, no coin of any kind was found on the nondescript's person.

Under the glass-buttoned garment, from which he struggled violently not to be divested, the stranger had on two other very singular articles of costume. One was very ragged, and evidently old, and covered with printed figures in pink, representing Baya-deres dancing. Over this was a small piece of stuff worked with the needle, and once white—the name of which, after repeated and severe interrogatories, he said was 'Dicki.' It has been carried to the Museum, and placed between the breastplate of a Turkish vizier and the corslet of a knight of the Middle Ages.

His lower dress was of a broad check pattern, something resembling the stuff which is worn by the Scottish Highlanders, who, however, it is known, do not use braccæ, whence it is evident that the stranger cannot be one of these. When the Burgomaster pointed to these, the nondescript wagged his head, pleased seemingly, and said the word 'Stunnin,' which the clerk took down.

On his feet were a sort of short boot with large iron heels, in which he began to execute a queer dance before the Court, clinking the heels together and turning the toes fantastically in and out— pointing to this boot with the cane which he carries in his mouth, he winked to the clerk, and said 'Hylo,' but then presently looking round the room, and seeing a portrait of the late Field-Marshal PRINCE OF WALLSTADT, he ran up to it, and said— 'BLOOKER! BLOOKER!' and danced once more.

What relation can there be between the nondescript's boot and the late gallant and venerated MARSHAL FORWARDS, who destroyed BONAPARTE, after the latter had defeated and taken the HERZOG V. WELLINGTON prisoner at the battle of Mount St. John?

At this stage of the examination, and having been allowed to resume all his clothes, the stranger pointed to his mouth and laid his hand on his stomach crying out the monosyllable 'Grub,' which DR. BLINKHORN thinks must mean food in his language. Accordingly a sausage, some bread, and a can of beer were brought, of the first of which he partook greedily, devouring the whole bread and sausage. It was observed that he ate with his fork, not with his knife, as we Germans do.

Having tasted the drink, he, however, laid it down, making very wry faces, and calling out the word, 'Swipey, Swipey,' twice, which was taken down. And then, by more faces and contortions, he made us to understand as if the beer had disagreed with him, upon which the excellent Burgermeister, having a bottle of Rhum in the cupboard, gave the savage a glass, who smacked it off at once, crying out the word 'Jollybyjingo.'

'Jollybyjingo, was ist Jollybyjingo?' asked his worship, conjecturing with his usual acuteness that this was the savage's phrase for Rhum of Jamaica. 'Wilt thou have yet a glass Jollibijingo?' And his Honour poured out a second glass, which the nondescript seized, and tossed off this time, exclaiming—

'Aybaleaveyermibawawawy!'

Which expression being accurately taken down, his worship the Burgermeister considered the examination sufficient, and sent off the Foreigner under the guard of Gendarmes BLITZ and WETTER to Berlin.

A true copy. (Signed) HUMPFFENSTRUMPFF, *Burgomaster.*
BLINKHORN, *Clerk of the Court.*

From the Berlin 'Tagblatt.'

'The named SNOOKS, Bartholomæus, Student, out of Smithfield, London, was brought hither in custody, from Frankfort on

the Oder ; where, being tipsy, he had lost himself, allowing the
train to go away without him. SNOOKS was handed over to the
British Minister here, and will return to London as soon as any
one will lend or give him funds for that purpose.'

WHAT I REMARKED AT THE EXHIBITION.[1]

I REMARKED that the scene I witnessed was the grandest and
most cheerful, the brightest and most splendid show that eyes
had ever looked on since the creation of the world—but as everybody remarked the same thing, this remark is not of much value.

I remarked, and with a feeling of shame, that I had long
hesitated about paying three guineas—pooh-poohed—said I had
seen the QUEEN and PRINCE before, and so forth, and felt now
that to behold this spectacle, three guineas, or five guineas, or
any sum of money (for I am a man of enormous wealth) would
have been cheap ; and I remarked how few of us know really
what is good for us—have the courage of our situations, and
what a number of chances in life we throw away. I would not
part with the mere recollection of this scene for a small annuity ;
and calculate that after paying my three guineas, I have the
Exhibition before me, besides being largely and actually in
pocket.

I remarked that a heavy packet of sandwiches which JONES
begged me to carry, and which I pocketed in rather a supercilious
and grumbling manner, became most pleasant friends and useful
companions after we had been in our places two or three hours ;
and I thought to myself, that were I a lyric poet with a moral
turn, I would remark how often in the hour of our need our
humble friends are welcome and useful to us, like those dear
sandwiches, which we pooh-poohed when we did not need them.

I remarked that when the QUEEN bowed and courtesied, all
the women about began to cry.

I remarked how eagerly the young Prince talked with his
sister—how charmed everybody was to see those pretty young
persons walking hand in hand with their father and mother, and
how, in the midst of any magnificence you will, what touches us
most is nature and human kindness, and what we love to witness
most is love.

I remarked three Roman Catholic clergymen in the midst of
the crowd amusing themselves with an opera-glass.

[1] [May 10, 1851.]

I remarked to myself that it was remarkable that a priest should have an opera-glass.

I remarked that when the ARCHBISHOP OF CANTERBURY was saying his prayer, the Roman Catholic clergymen seemed no more to care than I should if MR. LONGEARS was speaking in the House of Commons—and that they looked, stared, peered over people's shoulders, and used the opera-glass during the prayer.

I remarked that it would have been more decorous if, during *that* part of the day's proceedings, the reverend gentlemen had not used the opera-glass.

I remarked that I couldn't be paying much attention myself, else how should I have seen the reverend gentlemen?

I remarked my LORD IVORYSTICK and my LORD EBONYSTICK backing all the way round the immense building before the QUEEN; and I wondered to myself how long is *that* sort of business going to last? how long will free-born men forsake the natural manner of walking, with which God endowed them, and continue to execute this strange and barbarous *pas*? I remarked that a royal Chamberlain was no more made to walk backwards than a royal coachman to sit on the box and drive backwards. And having just been laughing at the kotoos of honest LORD CHOPSTICK (the Chinese ambassador with the pantomime face), most of us in our gallery remarked that the performance of LORD IVORYSTICK and LORD EBONYSTICK was not more reasonable than that of his Excellency CHOPSTICK, and wished that part of the ceremony had been left out.

I remarked in the gold cage, to which the ladies would go the first thing, and in which the Koh-i-noor reposes, a shining thing like a lambent oyster, which I admired greatly, and took to be the famous jewel. But on a second visit I was told that this was not the jewel, that was only the case, and the real stone was that above, which I had taken to be an imitation in crystal.

I remarked on this, that there are many sham diamonds in this life which pass for real, and *vice versâ*, many real diamonds which go unvalued. This accounts for the non-success of those real mountains of light, my *Sonnets on Various Occasions*.

I remarked that, if I were QUEEN of England, I would have a piece of this crystal set into my crown, and wear it as the most splendid jewel of the whole diadem—that I would.

And in fact I remarked altogether—GOD SAVE THE QUEEN.

M. GOBEMOUCHE'S AUTHENTIC ACCOUNT OF THE GRAND EXHIBITION.[1]

In the good town of London, in the Squars, in the Coffees, in the Parks, in the society, at the billiards, there is but one conversation—it is of the Palace of Industry ; it is of the QUEEN and PRINCE ALBERT ; it is of the union of all nations. 'Have you been there, my friend ?' every one says to every one.

Yes, I have been there. Yes, I am one of the myriads who visited the Palace of Industry on the first of May, and witnessed the triumph of France.

Early in the day, following in the track of the myriads who were rushing towards the romantic village of Kinsington, and through the Bridge of Chevaliers, I engaged a cabriolet of place, and bidding the driver conduct me to the Palace of all Nations at Kinsington, sate in profound reverie smoking my cigar and thinking of France until my driver paused ; and the agglomeration of the multitude, and the appearance of the inevitable poliseman of London, sufficiently informed us that we were at the entrance of the Industrial Palace.

Polisemen flank the left pillar of the gate surmounted by a vase, emblem of plenty ; polisemen flank the right pillar decorated by a lion (this eternal Britannic lion, how his roars fatigue me ; his tail does not frighten me ; his eternal fanfaronades regarding his courage make me puff of to laugh)—and as nothing is to be seen in England without undoing purse, a man at a wicket stops the influx of the curious, and the tide cannot pass the barrier except through the filter of a schilling.

O cursed schilling ! He haunts me, that schilling. He pursues me everywhere. If a Frenchman has to produce his passport, there is no moment of the day when an Englishman must not produce his schilling. I paid that sum, and was with others admitted into the barrier, and to pass the outer wall of the Great Exhibition.

When one enters, the sight that at first presents itself has nothing of remarkable—a court, two pavilions on either side, a château, to the door of which you approach by steps of no particular height or grandeur, these were the simple arrangements which it appears that the Britannic genius has invented for the reception of all people of the globe.

I knock in the English fashion—the simple baronnet gives

[1] [May 10, 1851.]

but one knock, the postman, officer of the government, many and rapid strokes, the LORD MAYOR knocks and rings. I am but the simple baronnet, and SIR GOBEMOUCHE wishes to be thought no more singular than SIR BROWN or SIR SMITH.

Two pages—blond children of Albion—their little coats, it being springtime, covered with a multiplicity of buds—fling open the two beatings of the door, and I enter the little ante-hall.

I look up—above me is an azure dome like the vault ethereal, silver stars twinkle in its abysses, a left-hand lancing thunderbolt is above us—I read above, in characters resembling the lightning —*Fille de l'orage* in our own language, and 'Symbolium of all Nations' in English.

Is the daughter of the tempest then the symbol of all nations? Is the day's quiet the lull after yesterday's storm? Profound moralist, yes—it is so—we enter into repose through the initiation of the hurricane—we pass over the breakers and are in the haven!

This pretty moral conveyed in the French language, the world's language, as a prelude to the entertainment—this solemn antechamber to the palace of the world struck me as appropriate as sublime. With a beating heart I ascend further steps—I am in the world's vestibule.

What do I see around me? Another magnificent allegory. The cities of the world are giving each other the hand—the Tower of Pisa nods friendly to the Wall of China—the Pont Neuf and the Bridge of Sighs meet and mingle arches—Saint Paul, of London, is of accord with his brother Saint Peter, of Rome—and the Parthenon is united with the Luqsor Obelisk, joining its civilisation to the Egyptian mysteries, as the Greek philosophers travelled to Egypt of old; a great idea this— greatly worked out, in an art purposely naïve, in a design expressly confused.

From this vestibule I see a staircase ascending, emblazoned with the magic hieroglyphics and strange allegoric images. In everything that the Briton does lurks a deep meaning—the vices of his nobility, the quarrels of his priests, the peculiarities of his authors, are here dramatised—a Pope, a Cardinal appear among fantastic devils—the romancers of the day figure with their attributes—the statesmen of the three kingdoms with their various systems—fiends, dragons, monsters, curl and writhe through the multitudinous hieroglyphic, and typify the fate that perhaps menaces the venomous enemies that empoison the country.

The chambers of this marvellous palace are decorated in

various styles, each dedicated to a nation. One room flames in crimson and yellow, surmounted by a vast golden sun, which you see in regarding it must be the chamber of the East. Another, decorated with stalactites and piled with looking-glass and eternal snow, at once suggests Kamschatka or the North Pole. In a third apartment, the Chinese dragons and lanterns display their fantastic blazons; while in a fourth, under a canopy of midnight stars, surrounded by waving palm-trees, we feel ourselves at once to be in a primeval forest of Brazil, or else in a scene of fairy— I know not which—the eye is dazzled, the brain is feverous, in beholding so much of wonders.

Faithful to their national economy, of what, think you, are the decorations of the Palace? Of calico! Calico in the emblematic halls, calico in the pompadour boudoirs, calico in the chamber of the sun—calico everywhere. Indeed, whither have not the English pushed their cottons? their commerce! Calico has been the baleful cause of their foreign wars, their interior commotions. Calico has been the source of their wealth, of their present triumphant condition, perhaps of their future downfall! Well and deeply the decorators of the Palace meditated when they decorated its walls with this British manufacture.

Descending, as from a vessel's deck, we approach a fairy park, in which the works of art bud and bloom beside the lovely trees of spring. What green pelouses are here! what waving poplars! what alleys shaded by the buds and blossoms of spring! Here are *parterres* blooming with polyanthuses and coloured lamps; a fountain there where NUMA might have wooed EGERIA. Statues rise gleaming from the meadow; APOLLO bends his bow; DORO-THEA washes her fair feet; ESMERALDA sports with her kid. What know I? How select a beauty where all are beautiful? How specify a wonder where all is miraclè?

In yon long and unadorned arbour, it has been arranged by the English (who never do anything without rosbif and half an half) that the nations of the world are to feast. And that vast building situated on the eastern side of the pelouse, with battle-mented walls and transparent roof, is the much-vaunted Palace of Crystal? Yes; the roof is of crystal, the dimensions are vast—only the articles to be exhibited have not been unpacked yet; the walls of the Palace of Crystal are bare.

'That is the Baronial Hall of all Nations,' says a gentleman to me—a gentleman in a flowing robe and a singular cap, whom I had mistaken for a Chinese or an enchanter. 'The hall is not open yet, but it will be inaugurated by the grand sanitary dinner. There will be half-crown dinners for the commonalty, five-shilling dinners for those of mediocre fortune, ten-shilling dinners for gentlemen of fashion like monsieur. Monsieur, I have the honour to salute you.' And he passes on to greet another group.

I muse, I pause, I meditate. Where have I seen that face? where noted that mien, that cap? Ah, I have it!—in the books devoted to gastronomic regeneration, on the flasks of sauce called relish. This is not the Crystal Palace that I see—this is the rival wonder—yes, this is the Symposium of all Nations, and yonder man is ALEXIS SOYER!   GOBEMOUCHE.

THE CHARLES THE SECOND BALL.[1]

INCE the announcement of the Costume Ball a good deal of excitement has been prevalent about the Court regarding it. It is known that CHARLES THE SECOND used to feed ducks in St. James's Park, and it is thought that this amusement of the Merry Monarch is harmless, and may be repeated on the present festive occasion. Rewards have been offered at the Lord Chamberlain's Office for a means of keeping the ducks awake till twelve o'clock at night.

We hear that some Duchesses decline altogether to assume the characters of their namesakes in the time of CHARLES THE SECOND; and that the Dukes, their husbands, perfectly agree in this spirited decision.

For the same reason as their Graces', the parts of Maids of Honour are not in much request. But for the character of CATHERINE HYDE, who married the heir to the throne, there are numberless proposals among the young ladies of the polite world.

For the character of the DUKE OF BUCKINGHAM (of CHARLES

[1] [May 24, 1851.]

THE SECOND'S time), who kicked down a grand fortune without being able to account for it, we hear a great number of noblemen named ; among others, LORD ADDLESTONE, LORD MUDDLEHEAD, and the LORD VISCOUNT WILDGOOSE.

The young gentlemen about Downing Street are reading the *Biographie Universelle*, and acquiring a surprising fund of historical knowledge. Young TAPELY, old TAPELY's son, who is eighteen, and has just entered the Foreign Office, proposes to appear as COLBERT, whom GUTTLETON admires, not as a minister, but as inventor of Colbert-soles. VANDER SOUCHEY, of the Dutch legation, announced at the Club that he would go as the PENSIONARY DE WITT. 'Behold de miracle instead of de witt,' said FLICFLAC ; and added, that COUNT NARCISSI (the envoy from Pumpernickel) had best assume this character, because the women are always tearing him to pieces.

GENERAL THE EARL OF SLOWGO (who does his best to be an F.M.) has just been credibly informed that a work exists—a remarkable work—although a light work he may almost say a biographical work—relative to the times of CHARLES THE SECOND, called PEPYS's *Diary*, and purporting to be edited by a member of their Lordships' House, the LORD VISCOUNT BRAYBROOKE.

GENERAL SLOWGO has, therefore, presented his compliments to LORD VISCOUNT BRAYBROOKE and requests to know if the Viscount has edited the work in question ? Should his lordship's reply be in the affirmative, GENERAL LORD SLOWGO will write to the Librarian of the British Museum to know : 1st. Whether the work, entitled PEPYS's *Memoirs*, be in the Library of the British Museum ? 2nd. Whether that work contains an authentic account of the reign of his late Majesty, KING CHARLES THE SECOND ? 3rd. Whether the Librarian of the British Museum can bring the volume, if a rare one, to Slowgo House ? and, 4th, If not, whether, and at what time, GENERAL THE EARL OF SLOWGO can consult the work in question at the British Museum ?

The two little MISS BUDDS (who go about with LADY CRABB) have had another contemporary work lent to them by their cousin ROWLEY, and are busy reading GRAMMONT's *Memoirs*. When LADY CRABB heard that her wards were reading history, she was highly pleased, and observed that she has no doubt the volume is instructive, as the family of GRAMMONT is one of the highest in France. The MISS BUDDS say the book is—very instructive.

MISS GRIGG, who is exceedingly curious in books and antiquarianism, has come upon some surprising illustrative passages in her papa's library, in the works of WYCHERLEY, and SIR C. SEDLEY, and in SUCKLING's poems.

COLONEL SIR NIGEL M'ASSER, who has the largest and blackest whiskers not only in the Horse Guards Green, but (with the exception of one sapper, now at the Cape of Good Hope) in the British Army, when he heard that whiskers were not worn in the time of CHARLES THE SECOND, and that gentlemen would be expected to shave, instantly applied for leave of absence; and, if that is refused, he will send in his papers.

LADY ROSA TWENTYSTONE and her daughters have been to Hampton Court, and taken careful note of the LELYS there. But when they came down to dinner in the dresses which they had prepared and rehearsed the part before MR. TWENTYSTONE, he ordered the whole family up to their rooms, and the dinner to be covered until they were.

'LADY ROSA is so delightful,' VARGES says that he thinks 'one can't see too much of her.'

LORD VISCOUNT METHUSELAH has put himself into the hands of new artists, and will appear with the cheeks, hair, and teeth of twenty. He has selected the character of LORD ROCHESTER, and has sent a request to the Lord Chamberlain that he may be allowed to make his *entrée* into the ball through a window and up a rope-ladder.

LORD HULKINGTON hopes to be able to get into a page's dress, which he wore once in private theatricals, at the PRINCESS OF WALES'S Court at Naples in 1814; and the ladies of his family are busy (for his lordship, since he came into his fortune, is become very economical) in trying to enlarge it.

LADY HOWLBURY expects to make a great sensation, and not at large expense; having attired herself and daughters, each in a curtain of the state bed at Ivybush, under which CHARLES THE SECOND passed three days after the battle of Worcester.

If the LORD MAYOR is invited with his suite, the City Marshal, of course, will go as MARSHAL TUREEN.

LORD TOM NODDINGTON was much surprised when he heard that CHARLES THE SECOND had been up a tree, and always thought that he ran for the Oaks. His opinion was that CHARLES THE SECOND had had his head cut off just before his son, JAMES THE FIRST, came into this country from Scotland—where LORD TOM goes shooting every year. MR. BLAND VARGES, who is the most notorious wag at SPRATT'S, said that as TOM NODDING-TON had no head himself, he had better go as the MARQUIS OF MONTROSE—after his decapitation. TOM NODDINGTON said he would be hanged if he went as MONTROSE, which Varges said was more and more in character. LORD TOM said he didn't know. He knew that he had shot THE DUKE'S country, and hoped to shoot there again ; and he thought 'it was devilish dangerous, begad, in those confounded levelling times, by Jove, for fellas to go about saying that other fellas had their heads cut off ; and that sort of thing, begad, might put bad ideas into other fellas' heads, and radical fellas and dam republican fellas.' MR. VARGES said that LORD TOM needn't be afraid about *his* head, and that if he lost it he wouldn't miss it ; on which TOM NODDY said that VARGES was always chaffing him.

LORD ADDLESTONE——when his librarian informed him he had heard that LOUIS THE FOURTEENTH as a young man wore a periwig powdered with gold-dust——has hit upon a brilliant thought of his own, and ordered that his wig shall not only be powdered with gold, but that he will have a papillote of bank-notes.

If these are scarce, as his steward informs him, his Lordship's man is directed to use promissory notes bearing his Lordship's valuable signature.

The young officers of the Eclectic Regiments, horse and foot, Cornets and Lieutenant-Captains with ten shillings per diem of pay, are greatly gratified at the idea of having to pay £40 a piece for their wigs at the Ball.

It is said that a venerable Prelate of a Western Diocese is going to represent all the seven recusant Bishops of JAMES's time at once ; and CARDINAL DE RETZ, who had a genius for conspiracies, fights, rows, and hot water in general, has a representative in Golden Square with a hat and costume ready bought and paid for.

ENSIGN and LIEUTENANT TIPTON of the Coolstreams says that he intends to take MARLBOROUGH's part as a young man, for he is very good-looking, is as poor as a rat, and ready to borrow money of any woman who will lend it.

PANORAMA OF THE INGLESE——AN INGLESE FAMILY.[1]

(From ' The Beyrout Banner, Joppa Intelligencer and Jerusalem Journal.')

THE renowned and learned Sage and Doctor of Beyrout, the excellent HADJEE ABOO BOSH, has just returned to his beloved country from his wonderful travels in distant lands, having visited

[1] [September 27, 1851.]

most of the cities and people of Franghistan. He is familiar
with all languages, and has deeply studied the customs and
manners of the Infidels. He has caused skilful limners amongst
them, at the expense of many millions of piastres, to paint
pictures representing the chief towns of the Franks ; which works
are so wonderful, life-like, and resembling nature, that true
Believers, without leaving the cushion of repose, or the pipe of
meditation, may behold the towns of Europe presented before
them, and have the mountains to come to them, which would not
advance in former ages, no, not even to meet the Prophet.

The famous and skilful HADJEE has arranged, near the Bazaar,
by the Rope-makers' quarter, in the large vacant hall formerly
occupied by the baths of EL THAWER, a vast chamber, in which
he exhibits the wonders which he has brought from foreign
countries. Having paid money to a negro at the door, you are
introduced through obscure passages into a chamber as dark as
Gehenna, and into a place which they call a pit, where you sit in
expectant terror, before an awful curtain, lighted but by a few
faint lamps.

Many of the stoutest Agas and Effendis in Beyrout entered
this gloomy apartment not without awe. The women of the
hareem of PAPOOSH PASHA were placed in a box, guarded by a
gilt cage ; as were the ladies of the establishment of BLUEBEARD
BEY, and the three wives of the GRAND MOLLAH. Women's
curiosity, indeed, will go anywhere. As the poet has sung—

There is no secret so dark, but the eye of ZUTULBE will penetrate it.
There is no tangled skein, but the finger of LEILA will unravel it.
There is no lock so cunning, but the crooked nose of the hag, FATIMA,
    will pick it.

Indeed, a vast audience of the officers, lords, and topping merchants
of Beyrout were present to behold the ABOO BOSH'S wonderful
pictures.

Before the curtain drew aside, and our eyes were dazzled, our
ears were diverted by a dexterous slave, who executes the barbarous
music of Europe, and the favourite songs of the unbelievers, by
merely turning the handle of a small chest, called a Hurridee
Gurridee. The handle operates upon a number of bulbuls who
are confined within the box, each of whom at his signal comes
forward and pipes in his turn. One sings the hymn of the
French Feringhees ; he is called the Parees Yenn : when he is
tired, another warbles the war-song of the English ; he is called
the Roolbretawnia. This over, a third nightingale begins to pipe
the delicious love-song of the Yangkees, who are a kind of

Ingleez, and the name of this song-bird is Yangkeedoodool. The sweetest of all the songs is this, and fills the heart with delight.

When the birds are tired, he who turns the handle of the box stops turning, and the music ceases with a melancholy wail. And then, as in a blaze of splendour, the pictures begin to pass before the astonished beholders.

The city represented yesterday was the City of Lundoon, which lies upon a river called the Tameez; over which are twenty thousand bridges, each twenty hundred parasangs in length, and to which there come daily a hundred thousand ships.

In one quarter of Lundoon, during the winter months, it is always night. It is illuminated, however, with fire, which gushes out of the bowels of the earth, and affords a preternatural brilliancy. This quarter is called Stee; twenty thousand carriages rush thither every minute, each carriage holding forty persons: the drivers and grooms crying out Stee, Stee! In this quarter the Shroffs and principal merchants reside. The palace of the Lord Cadi is here, and each ward of the City has an Elderman: who becomes Cadi in his turn. They are all fat in this district, drinking much of an intoxicating liquor made of citrons and rakee, called Panj, or Poonj, and eating of a stew of tortoises, of which they take many platesfull. Aboo Bosh owned to having tasted and liked the stew, but about the liquor he was silent.

After seeing the Merchants' quarter, the view changed, and exhibited to us the great Mosque of Paul, whereof the dome is almost as high as Mount Lebanon. The faithful pay two paras to enter this Mosque; which sum goes to the support of the dervishes. Within, it is surrounded by white images of captains, colonels, and effendis; whose figures show that the Ingleez were but an ill-favoured people. In the court is an image of a beloved Queen: the people say "Queen Anne is dead," and tear their beards to this day, so much do they love her memory.

The next view was that of the building in which the Councillors and men of law of the kingdom meet for their affairs. In all Stambool there is not such a palace. It is carved without, and gilt within. The Chambers of Council are endless; the chair of the Queen is a treasure of splendour; and Aboo Bosh says, that when she comes in state, and surrounded by her vizeers, this intrepid Sovereign of an island race, that governs provinces more vast and distant than Serendib and Hind, always carries in her arms three lions. But the Hadjee did not see the Queen of the Ingleez, and I doubt of this story.

Besides the Mosque of Paul, there is the Mosque of Peter,

whereof we likewise saw a view. All religions are free in this country, but only one is paid. Some dervishes shave the top of their heads, some tighten a piece of white cloth round their necks, all are dressed in black—we saw pictures of these, as also of the common people, the carriages, the QUEEN's janissaries in scarlet, with silver caps on their heads, and cuirasses made of a single diamond. These giants are all ten feet high, their officers fifteen. It is said that each consumes a sheep and drinks a barrel of wine in the day.

ABOO then showed us the triumphal arch, near to the house of WELLINGTON PASHA, who has but to look from his window and see his own image on horseback. Ten thousand images of WELLINGTON are placed about the town, besides : the English being so proud of him, because he conquered the French JENERAL BOONAPOORT. But lovers of poetry know the opinion of the bard :—

The victory is not always with the bravest : nor the robe of honour given
    to him who deserves most.
An eagle is shot down, and a leopard runs away with the spoil.

Near this is the Maidaun, where the young lords and agas ride, with nymphs as beautiful as those of Paradise, arrayed in tight-fitting robes, and smiling from prancing chargers.

And now came a buzz of wonder in the crowd, and outcries of delight from the women's boxes, which made the eunuchs move about briskly with their rattans, when the wonderful picture dawned upon us, representing the prodigious Castle of Crystal, and pavilion of light.

It is many miles long, and in height several furlongs. It is built of rock crystal and steel, without putty, wood, bricks, or nails. On the walls are flags, in number one hundred and seventy-eight thousand. We said ' Praise to Allah ! ' when we saw the scarlet standard, with the crescent and star of our august master, ABDUL MEDJID.

This palace was built in a single night by an enchanter named PAXTOON. This wonderful man possesses all the secrets of nature ; he can make a melon in ten minutes grow as big as a camel, a rose spread out before your eyes to the size of an umbrella. Lately, in a convent of dervishes, he caused in one evening a cabbage to grow so big, that after hearing a sermon from one of their Mollahs, who got up into the boughs, axes were brought, the plant was felled, and the whole community dined off it ; several bursting with repletion, so delicious was the food. This was told ABOO BOSH by a Mollah of Birmingham, a twisting dervish, who had seen many wonders.

Having seen the exterior of this Hall of Light, ABOO BOSH now showed to us the wondrous interior. All the treasures of the world are there, surely. Ten hundred and ten thousand persons come thither daily, and they all go first to see the saddles and embroidery, from Beyroot. What arcades of splendour! what fountains! what images! The tallest trees grow in this palace. The birds cannot fly to the roof; it is so high. At one end is a place where travellers are served with cakes and sherbet by ravishing houris with moon faces. O ABOO! O HADJEE! I suspect that FATIMA, your one-eyed wife, has not heard the end of those tales! What says the poet?—

The best part of the tale is often that which is not told.
A woman's truth is like the cloth which the Armenian sells you in the
    bazaar: he always cribs a portion of it.

And now, having spent several hours in examining this picture, the bulbul box was again set in motion, and the greatest curiosity of all was represented to us. This is an Ingleez family of distinction, whom ABOO BOSH has brought with him, and who will be exhibited every day at three hours before, and three hours after sunset. But the account of their strange behaviour shall be reserved for the next Intelligence.

AN INGLEEZ FAMILY.[1]

LL along the Exhibition was explained to us by a Frank Interpreter, who understands perfectly our language.

Among the Ingleez, he said, men are allowed but one wife : a hard case, O Agas ! for these poor women ; for as the bard has remarked—

'When I am in a queer temper in my hareem, I may beat ZULEIKA with my slipper, but I smile upon LEILA and ZUTULBE.

'When LEILA's fatness becomes disagreeable, then ZUTULBE's leanness commences to be pleasing.

'When both annoy me, then little ZULEIKA resumes her reign ; for strawberries ripen at one season of the year, at another time figs, at another time water-melons. But always strawberries would be wearisome : as to hear bulbuls all day would cause one to yawn.

'Man takes delight in variety, as the bee sips of a thousand flowers.'

So, for any poor creature to be subject always to the caprices of one man is cruel on her ; as to compel one man to have but one wife, as amongst the Ingleez, is a tyranny unheard of amongst civilised nations like our own ; and we may thank our stars that we do not live in Lundoon, but Beyroot.

If all the old women among the Ingleez are no better-looking than the one whom ABOO BOSH showed to us, I do not envy the elderly gentlemen of that nation, and can quite understand their habitual ill-humour.

In the first part of the play appeared this old woman, the Khanum of the house, or 'Misseez,' as the Interpreter says she is

[1] [October 4, 1851.]

called ; her two daughters, LOLA and LOTA ; her son, the young Aga ; and the Father of the family, called BROWN EFFENDI.

BROWN EFFENDI is fifty-five or six years old. He is tall, and of a portly shape, and, like all the elderly Ingleez, is bald ; nor has he the decency to cover his baldness with a couple of caps, as we do, but appears with his shining pate without any shame.

His wife is two or three years younger ; they must have been married these thirty years : no wonder that they quarrel together, and that the Effendi is tired of such an old hag !

The Interpreter explains that it is the beginning of the day. A table is set out, covered with a snowy damask cloth, with urns and vases of silver for tea, cups of porcelain, one for each of the family, bits of roasted bread, hot cakes, meat, honey, and butter. This meal the Ingleez of distinction take in common. And Effendi often does not behold his family (always excepting the old hag of a wife) except at that hour.

'Before the girls come down, and you go away to the Stee, MR. BROWN,' says the Misseez, 'will you have the goodness to give me some money ? Look at these bills.'

'Jehannum take the bills !' roars out BROWN, rising up and stamping. 'Can't you let a man read his newspaper in quiet ? '

O Allah ! read his newspaper in quiet ! It is an immense sheet, as big as the Captain Pasha's mainsail. I should think it has as many letters and lines as the Koran itself. The Interpreter says, every Ingleez reads a paper every morning—it is called in their language *El Tims*—from beginning to end, every day, before going out. Praise be to Heaven that we live in Beyroot !

'Well, don't swear at a woman, MR. B.' she says ; 'don't swear when the children and servants are coming in. How can I help it if the house is expensive ? I lived in a better before I came to yours. My mamma——'

'Confound your mamma ! How much is it ? ' says BROWN EFFENDI ; and drawing a paper from his pocket-book, he writes an order to his Shroff to pay so much money.

The daughters now came in—there was a great sensation among us, especially in that rogue who sate by me, POOF ALLEE, who is always on the look-out for almond eyes. These virgins were young and fair, of fine shapes seemingly, wearing a sort of loose gowns buttoned up to the neck, with little collars, and little caps, with little ribbons ; their cheeks pale, their eyes heavy— nevertheless, comely damsels, that would fetch a round sum of piastres in the market.

'Why don't you come sooner ? ' growls the Father.

They were at LADY POLK'S, at MRS. WALLS'S, and were not home till four : the girls must have sleep, MR. B.'

'Why do they go to those confounded balls?' asks BROWN EFFENDI. The Interpreter explains that a ball is a dance where many hundred women assemble.

'They ought to be in bed at ten,' growls the House-father.

'We *do* go to bed at ten, when there is nothing at night, papa,' says the eldest. 'We couldn't live if we didn't go to sleep on the off nights.'

'You don't wish them not to go into the world, I suppose, MR. B.? You don't wish them not to get establishments? You don't suppose it is for *my* pleasure that I go about night after night with these poor things, whilst you are drinking with your male friends, or at your clubs?' (The Interpreter explains that a Club is the Coffee-house of the Ingleez : they sit there smoking until late hours.) 'You don't suppose that *I* go to dances?'

BROWN EFFENDI bursts into a laugh. '*You* dance, POLLY!' says he. 'Do I suppose the cow jumped over the moon?'

'I wish papa wouldn't use those expressions,' says MISS LOLA to MISS LOTA.

Papa now sits with his face buried in *El Tims*, and when he has read it (only in this Exhibition, or play, of course, the actor did not read the whole of the immense sheet, or we should have sat till night)—this labour over, and his breakfast done, he goes away to Stee.

'That is the commencement of the day with thousands of English EFFENDIS in Lundoon,' the Interpreter explains. 'He rises at eight. He shaves. He meets his family : kisses them, but rarely speaks, except to swear a little, and find fault. He reads through *El Tims*. He gives money to the Khanum. He goes to the Stee : where his counting-house or office of business is, and which is often a long way from his house. He goes on foot, while his wife has a chariot.'

'That I can understand,' says POOF ALLEE. 'A man will not allow his womankind to go out except in an Aroba, guarded by the slaves. Even an unbeliever is not such a fool as *that*.'

'You are in error, O Effendi,' said the Interpreter. 'The women are free to go whithersoever they please. They wear no veils. They go about the City unprotected, save by a male servant, and even he is not necessary. They frequent the shops, and bazaars, and public gardens. I have seen ten thousand in the Spring time basking in the gardens of Kensington.'

'O my eyes! I will go there,' said POOF ALLEE, stroking his beard, that sly rogue.

'They are to be seen everywhere,' continues the Interpreter, 'and at home, too, receive men into their houses.'

'This, I suppose, is one,' remarked a looker-on. 'He is splendid ; he is tall ; he has richly-carved buttons on his coat. He takes up the silver urn. Is this an officer of the Sultaun ?'

'That ? That is a servant,' said the Dragoman. 'He is bringing breakfast for the young Effendi, who comes down later than the rest of the family.'

'That,' cried POOR ALLEE, 'a servant ? Why, he is a pearl of beauty. He is a Roostum. He is strong, tall, young, and lovely. Does an old Ingleez allow such an Antar as that to walk about in his Hareem ? Psha ! friend Interpreter, you are joking.'

'It is even so, Sir,' said the Dragoman. 'So strange is the pride of certain classes of the Ingleez, and so barbarous—blasphemous, I had almost said—their notions with regard to rank, that the aristocracy among the Ingleez take no more account of the persons below them than your honour does of the black slave-boy who fills your pipe. And of late, one of the lootees—or buffoons among the Ingleez—acquired no small share of popularity, and received from his bookseller ten thousand pieces of gold, for a book of jests, in which a servant was made the principal hero, and brought to live among Lords and Agas—the point of the jest being, that the servant was made to feel like a man.' [1]

Here came in the young actor who, the Interpreter said, represented the Son of the house. He drawled into the apartment, nodded languidly to his sisters, kissed his mother's forehead, and sank into the vacant chair by his sisters.

He called to the servant. 'JOHN !' he said, 'pale ale.'

'My love !' said the Mamma.

'Tell the cook to devil some dam thing,' continued the youth.

'My darling !' said the old lady.

'Hot coppers, Ma'am !' said the young man, pulling a little tuft of hair on his chin. 'Keep sad hours—know I do. Out on the crawl till five o'clock this morning. Last thing I weckolect, shandy-gaff.'

'You'll kill yourself, child !' cried Mamma.

'So much the better for brother DICK. Youth is the season of enjoyment. O dam ! what a headache I've got ! "Gather ye roses while ye may." Youth is the season of pleasure.'

'What sort of pleasure ?' asked one of the sisters.

'Well—I think it was with two cabmen off the stand, at BOB CWOFT's,' said the young man. 'It's not very good fun, but

[1] [This is, presumably, a reference to *Jeames's Diary*.]

it's better than those dam balls that you go to every night. Here comes the breakfast.'

And the curtain-bell ringing, the first part of the entertainment was over.

During the interval, the Interpreter continued to explain to us the manners and customs of this queer people : and the curtain again rising, showed us a view of the Queen's Palace (before which there is a figure of a Lion and Unicorn, which makes one die of laughing) ; the Courts of Justice ; the Castle of Windsor, which seems, indeed, a pavilion of splendour in a rose-garden of delight ; and an immense hole bored under the sea, the dark appearance of which made POOF ALLEE shudder. And now, having seen the Ingleez in the morning, and heard how the men pass the day in their offices and counting-houses, the women in the shops buying, in their carriages, in the gardens, visiting one another, and receiving company at home,—the Dragoman said, ' We shall show them as they are dressed of an evening, expecting visitors for the evening.'

The curtain drew up. BROWN EFFENDI was now dressed with a white band round his neck, that made his eyeballs start out of his head, and his red face blaze like the standard of the Sultan. MRS. BROWN appeared so changed since the morning, that you would not know her, and POOF ALLEE (that rogue) said, ' O my eyes ! the old woman to-night looks quite young, and I always liked a stout woman.' They stood one on each side of the fireplace—the Interpreter said, in the attitude of receiving dinner-company.

SCHAUN, the servant, came in with a note on a silver salver.

' It's from WAGG,' said BROWN EFFENDI—' d—n him ! he says he's ill ; but he's asked by a lord, and has thrown us over. Take away one cover, JOHN.'

How splendidly attired now is this SCHAUN ! His costume of the morning is nothing to that which he now wears. A white coat barred with gold lace ; a waistcoat of red and gold ; shulwars of plush, the colour of buttercups—and has he grown grey since the morning ? No, he has put powder into his hair. He is beautiful to behold ; a peacock is not finer.

And now, who enter ? Who are these two houris ? Who are these moon-faced ones, with the lustrous ringlets, the round arms, the shining shoulders ? The heart beats to behold them. POOF ALLEE's eyes brighten with rapture. They are the damsels of the morning, LOLA and LOTA.

' This is the habit of Ingleez damsels,' says the Interpreter, with rather a sly look. ' All day they cover themselves up, but at night, because it is cold, they go with very little clothes. They are now going to dinner; they will then go to a concert; they will then drive to a ball or dance.'

'But a ball, of course, only amongst women,' said his Excellency PAPOOSH PASHA, Governor of Beyroot, who was smoking his kaboon in a box near the stage.

'Among women, excellent Sir! There are men, too. If there were no men, the women would stay at home. This is the way that the Ingleez——'

'Silence, shameless!' roared out his. Excellency. 'KISLAR BEG! Carry my women home this moment. Stop the Exhibition! All the principles of morality are violated. Women in that dress show themselves to men! Never! or if they do, it can only be amongst barbarians, and such a fact must not be known in a civilised country. HADJEE ABOO BOSH! this part of the Exhibition must be no more represented, under pain of the bastinado.' And his Excellency flung out of the room in a passion, and the Exhibition ended abruptly.

As for POOF ALLEE—that rogue—he has gone off to England by the last Peninsular and Oriental steamer.

POOR PUGGY.[1]

THOSE who know TOPHAM SAWYER, the accomplished young EARL OF SWELLMORE, are aware that, under a mask of languor and levity, he hides considerable powers of acuteness and observation. His letters are much prized, not only amongst the friends of his own rank, but by his Bohemian acquaintances in the *Coulisses*. Of a sarcastic turn, he is yet not without a natural benevolence; has cultivated his talents and his good qualities in secret, and as if he was ashamed of them ; and not blameless, alas ! in his life, he is correct, even to fastidiousness, in his spelling—in this affording an example to many of the younger nobility ; and may be pardoned some of his bitterness, which may be set to the account of his well-known disappointment, two years since (when he was, as yet, but the penniless and HONOURABLE TOPHAM SAWYER), when the lovely LADY BARBARA PENDRAGON, daughter, we need scarcely state, of the MARQUESS OF M—NGELW—RZELSHIRE, threw him over, and married the Roman PRINCE CORPODIBACCO, nephew of the Cardinal of that name. Trifles from the pens of the great are always acceptable in certain circles ; and the following extract of a letter from LORD SWELLMORE to his intimate and noble friend the MARQUESS OF MACASSAR, though on a trifling subject, will be read not without interest by those who admire our country's institutions. The noble Earl, whilst waiting at his Club to see MESSRS. AMINADAB and NEBUCHADNEZZAR, on pecuniary business, having promised to write to the MARQUESS OF MACASSAR at Paris (indeed, concerning Bills of Exchange, on which both the Noble Lords are liable), dashed off a letter, partly on private affairs, and concluding with the following lively passages :—

[1] [October 18, 1851.]

'I sit here, my dear MACASS, and see the people go by to the Exhibition. It's better than going there. *Suave mari magno :* you see the ocean devilish well from the shore. You're only sick if you go to sea. I wish they'd give us a smoking-room fronting Piccadilly. Why don't the new men who have been building have smoking-rooms to the street? I like those fellows at Brighton who sit on the cliff, in a ground-floor room, smoking —after dinner—having nuts and port-wine at three o'clock on Sundays. I saw a fellow there lately—his stout old wife went out to church—and there he sat, with his legs on the second chair, unbuttoned, and looking out of window with a jolly red face. I felt inclined to put my hand in and take a glass, and say, "Your health, old boy!" His cigars smelt offensively, but I envied him rather—not that I envy anybody much, or pity anybody, or despise anybody, or admire anybody. I've nothing what you call to live for—now you have, MACASS. You're very fond of your whiskers, and anxious about overcoming your waist. You have an aim, my boy, and a purpose in your existence ; coax your whiskers, and struggle manfully with your corporation, my poor old MACASS, and thank your stars that you have these to interest you.

'Here's a fellow who has had an object in life, too, it appears. I cut his advertisement out of *The Times*. It's a devilish deal better than the leading article.

DUTCH PUG FOR SALE.—A very fine specimen of this almost extinct breed. He is one year and a half old, and very gay and lively, and is the *bonâ fide* property of a gentleman, who, from continued ill-health, is unable to keep him. Lowest price 30 guineas. No dealer need apply, either directly or indirectly. May be seen at Mr. Harridge's Forge, Pitt Street Mews, Park Lane.

'Now, I say, here's something to excite your sympathy. An announcement more affecting than this can't well be imagined— a dog of an almost extinct breed, and the owner of that rare animal obliged, from continued ill-health, to part with him. Think, my dear MACASS, of a tender and benevolent-minded man, his fine faculties overclouded by disease, fondly attached to his darling pug, yet seeing that between him and that beloved being a separation must come! The last interviews are now taking place between them : the last breakfasts : the last *fricassée* of chickens : the last saucers of cream : the little darling is now lapping them up, and licking the hand which shall soon pat its black nose no more. He is "gay and lively" now, the poor little beggar—quite unconscious of his coming fate—but eighteen months old—it's heart-rending. Ain't it?

'What degree of ill-health is it, or what species of malady can it be, which obliges a gentleman to part from such a *bonâ fide* darling? This invalid's ill-health is "continuous," the advertisement says. Do the caresses of the pug increase his master's complaint? does continued anxiety for the pretty favourite prevent the owner's return to strength, and must he wean himself from the little black-nosed, cock-tailed, cream-coloured innocent, as delicate mammas do from their babies? What a separation, *mon Dieu!* Poor Puggy! poor, poor Master!

'Of course, he won't part with him to a dealer, directly or indirectly; no, no. Fancy a man's feelings, the separation over, at seeing Puggy some day in the Quadrant, in the red-waistcoat pocket of a dirty-looking blackguard, with six other dogs, and a wide-awake hat! An invalid, as this gentleman is, couldn't stand such a sudden shock. He would be carried off to a chemist's; and we should hear of an inquest on a gentleman at the White Bear. Puggy in the Quadrant—Puggy in the company of all sorts of low dogs, brought up in the worst habits, and barking in the vulgarest manner! Puggy, the once beautiful and innocent, in the Quadrant!—Oh don't—I can't bear the 'orrid thought!

'But must a man be in high health to keep a Dutch pug? Does the care and anxiety incident on Dutch pug-keeping make a man of naturally robust habit ill and delicate? If so, it's most generous of the owner of the little Dutchman to warn the public. You pay thirty guineas—the very lowest price—you incur responsibility, infinite care, unrest, disease: you lose your peace of mind, and break your heart in cherishing this darling; and then you part with him. You recollect what happened to the heroes in HOMER, how they were made to dogs a prey—here is a modern torn in pieces by a little pug.

'A little Dutch pug, with a little turned-up black nose. And is there no other pretty possessor of a *nez-retroussé*, which man coaxes and dandles, and feeds with cream and chicken, and which he parts with after a struggle? Ah, my good fellow! Ah, my dear MACASSAR! We are sad dogs! we are cynical! You take my allusion, and your knowledge of the world will enable you to understand the allegory of

'Your affectionate

'SWELLMORE.

'*The Marquess of Macassar.*'

PORTRAITS FROM THE LATE EXHIBITION.[1]

As a popular contemporary has given a number of highly interesting portraits and biographies of gentlemen connected with
the Exhibition, whose families and friends will naturally provide
themselves with copies of their relatives' lives and countenances,
MR. PUNCH, ever anxious to benefit self and public, has it in con-
templation to ornament his journal with

LIVES AND PORTRAITS OF THE EXHIBITORS

Who have not gained Prizes at the Exposition of 1851.

And to this highly interesting class he strongly recommends his
publication, of which if but six copies weekly be taken by every
Exhibitor, a decent remuneration cannot fail to attend the labours
of MR. P.

As specimens taken at hazard merely, MR. PUNCH offers for the
present week, pictures and biographies of—SAMUEL PODGERS,
ESQ., Exhibitor in the Agricultural Department: an improved
spud, not in the least noticed by the Committee.

MR. PODGERS is the eldest son, though the *third child*, of
MAJOR PODGERS, of the Horse Marines, which he commanded on
the death of their Colonel, in the flotilla action in the Bay of
Fundy. The Major married BELLA, seventh daughter of SIR
MUFFTON WROGGLES, of Wrogglesby, Northamptonshire, in which
county the old Saxon family of WROGGLES, or WOROGLES, has
been located since the days of ALFRED. The PODGERS family,
though ancient, is not of such antiquity. MR. PODGERS received
his elementary education under the care of the REVEREND DR.
GRIG, at Northampton, whence he was removed to Harrow-on-the-
Hill, where he would have been a contemporary of DR. PARR,
SIR WILLIAM JONES, LORD BYRON, and SIR ROBERT PEEL, had
he been placed at this famous school while those eminent individuals were studying there. It does not appear that MASTER
PODGERS took any prizes at Harrow, any more than at the
Exhibition of 1851; his genius, though useful, not being brilliant,
and his powers of application being only trifling.

MR. PODGERS was removed from Harrow to Coppernose
College, Oxford, in the year 18—, and here, though not distin-

[1] [November 1, 1851.]

guished for classical attainments, he was very near gaining the prize of valour in a single combat with a gigantic bargeman at Iffley Lock ; but the *mariner* proved the better man, and an injury to Mr. Podgers's nose was the only permanent consequence of the *rencontre*.

It was not till 1823 that he inherited, by the demise of the gallant Major, his father, his estate of Hodgers-Podgers, Hants, where he now resides, occupying himself with agricultural pur-

SAMUEL PODGERS, ESQ., EXHIBITOR IN THE AGRICULTURAL DEPART-
MENT : AN IMPROVED SPUD, NOT IN THE LEAST NOTICED BY THE
COMMITTEE.

suits, and with hunting, although increasing years and weight have rather wearied him of that occupation. Mr. Podgers is a magistrate and a married man ; the father (by Emily, daughter of the Reverend Felix Rabbits) of thirteen children.

His spud was invented towards the close of the year 1850, and it is unnecessary to particularise this invention, which has

not been found to answer better than, or indeed to differ greatly
from, implements of a like simple nature.

MR. PODGERS's opinions as a politician are well known.   Not
noisy, he is consistent ; and has often been heard to say, that if
all England were like him, we should get Protection back again.
England being of the contrary opinion, no such result is expected.
He is threescore years old, and weighs, we should think, a good
fourteen stone ten.

MRS. FREDERICA GLINDERS, AUTHOR OF A COUNTERPANE.

MRS. GLINDERS retained, by marrying her cousin, her own
maiden and respectable name.   MR. GLINDERS, her father, has

MRS. FREDERICA GLINDERS, AUTHOR OF A COUNTERPANE.

long been known as a distinguished medical practitioner at Bath.
MR. FITZROY GLINDERS, her husband, is a solicitor in that city.

In Bath, or its charming neighbourhood, the chief part of the
existence of MRS. GLINDERS has been passed.   It was here that
she contracted, in the year 1836, that matrimonial engagement
with the REVEREND MR. FIDDLEBURY, which was so scandalously
broken off by the Reverend Gentleman, who married MISS BLUFF.
The jury of an offended country awarded MISS GLINDERS £500

for the damage thus done to her affections, which sum she brought as dowry to her cousin, the (then) young FITZROY GLINDERS, who conducted her case. Their union has been blessed with a considerable family : and indeed MR. GLINDERS's *quiver* is so full of them, that he has been obliged to take another pew at church.

The washerwoman of Bath has ever had a constant friend in MRS. GLINDERS. The thoughtless chimney-sweep, the ignorant dog's-meat man of her own city, have always been plentifully supplied by her with means for bettering their spiritual condition. The Caffres and Mandingoes have found her eager in their behalf.

The counterpane sent for *previous* exhibition to the national Exposition is intended finally as a present for the King of Quacco. It is woollen, striped blue and pink, with a rich fringe of yellow and pea-green. It occupied MRS. GLINDERS two hundred and seventy-four evenings, and the prime cost of the wool was £17 : 14 : 6. For a web which was to pass under the eyes of her own Sovereign, over the feet of another, though a benighted, monarch, MRS. GLINDERS thought justly that expense was not to be regarded. She had fits on not finding her name in the prize list, and had even entertained an idea that MR. GLINDERS would receive a public honour. But time and her own strong spirit will console MRS. GLINDERS under these disappointments : and for the sake of her family and friends, it is to be hoped that she will be, in the words (slightly altered) of our immortal bard, 'herself again.'

PROFESSOR SLAMCOE :—' A KALONATURÆ,' OR ' SLAMCOE'S GENT'S OWN HEAD OF HAIR.'

HORATIO NELSON SLAMCOE was born in the New Cut, Lambeth, in the year when England lost her greatest naval hero. His mother, having witnessed the funeral procession of Trafalgar's conqueror, determined to bestow on her child, if a son, the glorious names of the departed ; hence, in due time, the two Christian names of the subject of this memoir. The parents of MR. SLAMCOE were in humble life ; and for the eminence which he has subsequently acquired, he has to thank his genius rather than his education, which was neglected for the labours necessary to one whose own hands must work his own livelihood.

Well and skilfully, through five-and-thirty years, have the hands of HORATIO SLAMCOE toiled. Early taken under the roof of a tonsorial practitioner in the Waterloo Road, MR. SLAMCOE

learned the rudiments of a trade which by him has been elevated
to an art ; for if to imitate beautiful Nature be Art, what man
deserves the proud name of artist better than the elegant perru-
quier ? At twenty-one years of age, Mr. Slamcoe had the
honour of attending at L–mb–th Palace, with a wig made by his
young hands, and offered to a late reverend Prelate of our Church.
Professor S. augured ill for Episcopacy when those ornaments
of our dignified divines fell into desuetude.

As Napoleon crowned himself King and Emperor, so it was,
we believe, that Horatio Slamcoe dubbed himself Professor.

PROFESSOR SLAMCOE :—' A KALONATURÆ,' OR ' SLAMCOE'S
GENT'S OWN HEAD OF HAIR.'

His inventions are known to the world, and their beneficent
influence is exemplified in his own person. Before he ever attempted continental travel, his 'Balsam of Bohemia' was discovered ; just as America was discovered by Columbus before
that philosophic Genoese put foot on shipboard. His Tuscan
Dentifrice ; his Carthaginian Hair-dye ; his Fountain of Hebe,
are world-celebrated cosmetics, without which (he says) no toilet
is complete. They are to be procured at his establishment, 'The
College of Beauty,' with the usual liberal allowance to the trade,
who should beware of unprincipled imitators, only too eager to
adopt the discoveries of the Professor.

That the Kalonaturæ, or Gent's own Head of Hair, should have been unrewarded by a Medal, is one of those instances which cries shame on the awards of the Committee. Let us hope it was not a conspiracy on the part of *rival wig-makers* (enemies of MR. SLAMCOE through life) which defeated the object of his ambition. But if there be any individuals blighted like himself, whose hair turned white in a single night, as some men's have through disappointment, the Professor recommends to such his Carthaginian dye, which will prevent the world, at least, from *guessing* what ravages grief has caused, and manly pride would hide ; though it will *scarcely* be credited, the Professor's *own* hair is indebted for its rich jelly colour *solely* to the Carthaginian discovery.

IMPORTANT FROM THE SEAT OF WAR![1]

LETTERS FROM THE EAST.

BY OUR OWN BASHI-BOZOUK.

I.

Camp before Redout Kale, 28th May,
(13th Shiboob, Turkish Calendar.)

Y DEAR SIR,
Though your periodical is jocular in its nature and title, and occasionally trifling in its details, I am told that a good deal of truth lurks in its satire ; indeed that much more of the commodity is to be found in your columns than in the broadsides of your gigantic contemporaries, who profess to supply only authentic information.

I am not myself a man of the least humour : I do not make jokes nor value them, nor understand them for the most part : so yours may be very good, though I for my part cannot

[1] [June 24 ; July 1, 8, 14, 1854.]

comprehend what sets your readers a-laughing. The same is the case with tunes. The other day at the review at Scutari, I mistook Abdul Medjeed's March for Rule Britannia ; some of my brother poets I am told (I am considered one of the first in the world) labour under a similar obtuseness of ear.

But this is parenthetic ; let us return to the subject in hand. I select you as the organ of my communications from the seat of WAR : 1st, because the Press, though often misled, is free in your country ; and I desire the liberty of saying EVERY-THING, which I could not do in the *Journal des Débats* or the *Allgemeine Zeitung :* 2nd, because I know you exercise a great influence in Europe ; and have seen personally the three Emperors, my friend the KING OF NAPLES, and HIS HOLINESS THE POPE, and CARDINAL ANTONELLI frantic at your satire : 3rd, because, strange to say, you appear to have engaged no correspondent : and 4th, because I am the best correspondent in the world.

'I took, but half an hour since, from the shako of a poor Russian friend, whom I have just killed in action, two or three copies of *The Times* newspaper, in which the editors seemed greatly to vaunt the skill of their correspondents in this quarter. Before I ever thought of putting pen to paper myself, I met this young man at Malta, and Gallipoli afterwards ; gave him every information in my power, and supplied him with many of the facts, which I need not say he ludicrously distorted and exaggerated in his journal. He was put out of an English ship of war (he says, at his own desire) on board of a Greek schooner, the *Hagid Alethea*, off Gallipoli, and would have been murdered by the crew and the master (a pirate, and a very old friend of mine), for the sake of his portmanteaus, which appeared to be pretty well plenished, had I not happened to be drinking in the cabin with my friend the piratical skipper. At my entreaties, nay, threats (for I had to produce my revolvers), the young man was saved : and I landed him at Gallipoli stairs with his bag and baggage, without receiving from him even the present of a single cigar. Nor, as I see by his printed letters, has he made the least subsequent mention of his preserver : it will be well for him for the future not to come into the neighbourhood of *the* 14*th Bashi-Bozouks, or their Colonel.* I shall not give *him* any information any more. What I have I shall send to you, and through you to the world ; and thus my indignation at the ingratitude of a newspaper writer is possibly the cause of enlightening and instructing all Europe.

Hitherto, all Europe has been wofully misled. Any one,

for instance, who will take the trouble to tot up the number of dead Russians, who are slaughtered in every newspaper bulletin that we get from the seat of war in the East, will find that they drop off at the rate of two or three thousand a day, and that a quarter of a million of them by this time must have gone to visit Hades. My good friend Mr. Punch, these murderous histories are all bosh! Newspaper correspondents I fully agree with my noble friends Lord Smotherem and Lord Botherem, in the House of Peers, are not to be relied upon, and ought to be put down. As for the Turks, they are notorious long-bow pullers. My poor friends the Russians, with and against whom I have served a good deal in the Caucasus, are greater liars than the unbelievers. What the nation wants is Truth. Truth pure, Truth unadulterated, Truth gushing from the original tap, such as perhaps no other man in Europe but myself is in a condition to supply.

I choose to sign myself Verax, though that of course is not my family name, which is the noblest in the three kingdoms; but have such a regard for truth in all things, that even of this little deviation from it I think fit to warn the reader. I never told a lie in my life (except, of course, a few to ladies, whom, I presume, no gentleman thinks of treating with the unadulterated article). I have lost fortunes, undergone imprisonment, braved and suffered the most frightful tortures for truth's sake. Every word of my letters may be relied upon; and I should like to know of what hireling scribe and camp follower, of what ancient or modern writer—in a word, except myself—as much can be said? Take a page of Macaulay—pooh! Ask the Quakers, or the old Tories, what they think of his accounts of the two Williams—William of Orange and William of Drab? Read Dean Milman's *History of the Latin Church;* learned and wise it is undoubtedly,—but if it were true, would Dr. Wiseman be wearing crimson silk gloves (with a crowd of boys laughing at him in the streets), and Father Newman be cutting jokes against the Establishment? Take Sir Archibald Alison's History, and if you can read *that*—but it is absurd that I should put so monstrous a proposition.

I speak about these gentlemen from memory of course (mine is the finest and most accurate in the world), but a colonel of Bashi-Bozouk's sitting, as I am, with my wild scoundrels round about me, warming my toes at a camp-fire over which my kabobjee is roasting a lamb, with the mountains of Anaon before me, the hoarse roar of the Black Sea discernible to my ear, the sun gilding the battered old minarets of Redout Kale, from which we have just driven out the Russians, and where I have hanged a rascally Greek spy (after addressing him a most beautiful speech in his native language, with which and twenty-three other European dialects I am perfectly familiar) ; and where, in the affair of the morning, it was my painful duty to send a ball from my revolver through the eye of my poor old friend, MAJOR TIMKOWSKI, at the head of his regiment—a man with whom I have drunk many a bottle in happier times ;—I say, were a man in my present position to pretend that he carried books about with him, and like FREDERIC or NAPOLEON had a campaign library, he would be humbugging the public. No, honest SELIM AGA, cooking the lamb yonder under my nose (By the laws, it smells very savoury, and a man who has not eaten for forty-nine hours, ridden two hundred and ten parasangs, had two horses and a mule shot under him, routed three regiments and fourteen squadrons of the enemy, taking nine of his guns, four of them with his own hand, shot a lamented old friend through the eye, and hung a Greek spy, has a right to feel a little hungry)—SELIM, the cook, I say, might as well expect to turn out a regular dinner of three courses, soup, fish, *entrées* and confectionery, from the carcase of yonder lamb, as I to produce a regular, careful, philosophical, ornate history, such as some of my other works have been, and such as I should turn out if I were seated at ease in one of my splendid libraries, either in my town house, or in my castles in the country.

Though we have quarrelled, I cannot but always remember that the EMPEROR OF RUSSIA was long my most particular friend. When I used to drive over to take tea with the family at Czwrkoe Seloe (for at Petersburg we stood of course much more upon etiquette) he was affable, even playful in his conversation, and would often say to me, ' MICK, my boy ' (I bear the name of the Archangel, I am descended from kings, and my ancestors, whose lineal heir I am, ruled magnificently over a fair green island of the west long ere the Saxon came to enslave it), ' MICK, my boy, we are all equals here. I am not the EMPEROR, but plain NICHOLAS ROMANOFF : ' and he would carry familiarity so far as to insist on my calling the EMPRESS by her name of FEODOROWNA. This I refused to do ; but the young princes and princesses I give you my honour I have never addressed by other than their Christian names, and should have been godfather to the CESAREWITCH's last (a sweet little archduchess) had I been of the orthodox persuasion.

I may say now that the war never would have happened had the EMPEROR listened to the advice of an old friend, who knows

men and the world as well as many a man who wears a star
upon his breast, and writes Privy Councillor before his name.
I never could get the EMPEROR OF RUSSIA to believe in the
possibility of an alliance between us and the French. 'Look at
these newspapers,' he used to say to me, rapping with his knuckles
on the table, a daily London journal of great circulation, the
T——, and a weekly comic periodical called *P*——,[1] under the
satire of which he writhes ;—' The head of the French nation
never can pardon these attacks upon him. He must declare war
against England. England must enter into an alliance with me ;
and, as the price of that alliance, I intend to have Turkey in
Europe, and my second capital at Constantinople. *Voilà tout,
mon cher, voilà tout.*

'*Parbleu ! C'est tout simple,*' said a great dignitary, whom
I need not name for fear of getting him into trouble, shrugging
his shoulders, and pulling out his eternal snuff-box.

I took a pinch myself, and tried to show them what the real
state of our press and our country was. I told the EMPEROR
NICHOLAS that I had long and intimately known HIS MAJESTY THE
EMPEROR OF THE FRENCH, as indeed I had in Switzerland, where
I put his first musket into his hands ; in the United States have
I saved his life ; at Ham, where I saw him and the poor dear
DUCHESSE DE BERRI before him, and in King Street, St. James's
and about town, where I promise you we have had some rare
doings together. I told the EMPEROR OF RUSSIA that HIS
MAJESTY THE EMPEROR OF THE FRENCH knew England well, and
narrated to him in confidence, but *in extenso,* a conversation
which I had had with PRINCE LOUIS NAPOLEON, when we were
special constables together in Eaton Place, on the 10th of April
'48. As for our papers abusing him, I told the Russian Autocrat
that was nothing ; that was our way ; that every man of mark
was abused ; that I myself had been satirised both in *P*—— and
in the *T*——.

What I said seemed to strike the EMPEROR a good deal.
Would that my advice had had more effect on him ; but——

'I am interrupted by OMAR PACHA'S Tatar, who has his foot
in the stirrup ready to take my despatches, and also by SELIM'S
announcement that the roast lamb is cooked. I shall continue

---

[1] His Majesty, between ourselves, is not so thin in the legs and so large in
the waist as the designers represent him. He is stouter, certainly, than when
he came over incog. to England in the year 1837, and I gave COLONEL ROFF
a dinner at the Megatherium Club ; but he is still a fine man, WILL ! What
of that ? are there not other fine men ? A blushing echo replies in the
affirmative. VERAX is a fine man, and I think some of the other sex will
not gainsay me.

my narrative (which I need not say is of thrilling interest), and forward it presently along with a pair of earrings for MRS. PUNCH which my poor friend TIMKOWSKI wore, by one of my own men.

So no more at present from your

BASHI-BOZOUK.

II.

Camp under Redout Kale,
13th Shiboob, 1271.

MY DEAR SIR,

The sudden departure of my Tatar yesterday prevented me from making a statement which would have been as well at the commencement of my correspondence, and explaining at full my reasons for joining the Turkish army, and the peculiar means of information which I possess now I am here. O'LOONEY, my second in command, is also here (the honest fellow, late an officer in the Nizam's service, is snoring on his sheepskins within a couple of yards of me), but what means of information does *he* possess ! He can judge the best taps in the various taverns of Scutari and Pera, is a connoisseur in horseflesh and a great consumer of raki ; but he knows no more about the war than my two black slaves which the SULTANA VALIDE gave me when I took leave of her three weeks since at Constantinople.

To resume my Petersburg narrative, then, and the causes of my quitting that capital and taking arms against its sovereign, with whom I have always been on terms of the most friendly and affectionate intercourse. The Imperial treatment of me, and the scoundrelly behaviour of a certain lieutenant of police— behaviour of which I have reason to think the highest personages in the Russian empire were not ignorant—are the causes why I transferred my services, my great strategical knowledge, and my exterminating projectiles (of which the war and the world will hear terrific news ere long) to HIS HIGHNESS ABDUL MEDJEED. I do not conceal that my sympathies are not with the Turks. They must ere long be swept out of Europe. Why should there not be an emperor in Byzantium as well as in Petersburg ? Say he were a Russian Prince. Why not ? The ROMANOFF of Turkey and the ROMANOFF of Russia would presently and infallibly quarrel, as the French and Spanish BOURBONS did. I am not particularly angry with NICHOLAS for meditating and attempting his great *coup ;* but his conduct towards myself, the traitorous behaviour of his subordinates, the indignities offered to a person of royal lineage—thirteen dozen with the knout, administered at midnight in my rooms at the Hôtel d'Angleterre, and a treacherous banishment into Siberia afterwards ; conduct such as this, I say, was enough to put any man in a rage, and to justify the defiance which hereby, and in the face of all Europe, I hurl at the Autocrat of Russia.

Knowing that England had set a price on my head after that wretched affair of Ballingarry, which, but for SMITH O'BRIEN'S foolish quarrel about the succession to the throne with me, might have had a very different issue,[1] and that my return home was impossible, the EMPEROR had made me advantageous proposals for entering into his service—proposals which I do not scruple to say I had entertained. The Grand Cross of the Russian St. George might have figured advantageously on a bosom which beats with only a chivalrous enmity against the Cappadocian warrior, who is England's patron. The rank of General and Marshal (on old PASKIEWITCH'S retirement) might gratify an honest ambition, and the title of Mulliganoff-Innisfailsky, of which the patent was actually made out, might be worn without shame, by one whose loftier claims and regal rights have been reft from him by the evil chance of war.

But when war was declared between the EMPEROR and the three kingdoms, there was *one* of them, as I told his Majesty, against which I never would fight. Unaccustomed for the last thirty years to contradiction from any quarter, you never saw a man in a greater rage than the EMPEROR NICHOLAS when I conveyed to him my firm but respectful resignation of his proposals. His usage of his GRAND CHAMBERLAIN, who happened to be in the room, was *absolutely humiliating.* The entreaties of the poor dear EMPRESS and the Imperial children and grand-children (who, I believe, love me like one of the family) were difficult to withstand ; harder still to bear were the wretched appealing looks, the tears welling in the beautiful azure eyes, the lips quivering with emotion, the soft little hands clasped in unavailing supplication, of the lovely MATILDA SCHOUZOFF, one of the Imperial Maids of Honour, and daughter of the second Mistress of Robes to her Majesty. I, for my part, have always preferred to face a thousand guns in battery than the tears of a loving woman. Every gentleman will understand the agonies

---

[1] As if the O'BRIEN, forsooth, could compete in ancestral merit or in personal right with the . . . but I had nearly divulged my name, which in the neighbourhood of LORD RAGLAN, HIS ROYAL HIGHNESS THE DUKE OF CAMBRIDGE, and 20,000 soldiers bearing the uniform of the QUEEN OF ENGLAND (I bear her Majesty no sort of enmity), might be inconvenient.

I felt in my battle with one who had been so victorious over my heart.

My dispute with his Majesty, and my rejection of his proposals, took place on the very day, I think it was the 18th of January last, when that poor deputation of Quakers, as you remember,

had their final interview with the despotic ruler over sixty millions of men. That the EMPEROR is a master of dissimulation is clear, not only from certain documents which have come to light subsequently, but from his behaviour towards those honest, broad-brimmed gentlemen whom he most imperially bamboozled. They and I lodged at the same hotel, the Hôtel d'Angleterre, on the Nepomuk Platz ; and with one of the junior members of the peaceful party, an agreeable, lively, young fellow, young DOBKINS of Godmanchester, I became rather intimate. I introduced him to the Guards' barracks, took him about the town to the public places, and presented him in some of the most fashionable houses, where '*le beau quakre,*' as he was called, was a considerable favourite. Out of his ridiculous costume, which he only wore on parade, he was an exceedingly handsome young fellow, not a little like myself, as the dear MATILDA insisted, though I am some nine inches broader between the shoulders, and twelve inches less in the waist, than my young broad-brimmed acquaintance.

We passed several merry evenings, and had rather a pleasant *table d'hôte* at the Hôtel d'Anglaise, where, however, there was one guest who, for private reasons, as well as for his own disgusting behaviour, was specially odious to me ; this was no other than the notorious COUNT TUFFSKIN, who is known at every gambling-house in Europe, who is at present commandant at Tamboff, and had come to the capital to solicit promotion ; and what is more, to dispute with me the hand of the lovely MATILDA SCHOUZOFF. He slept in the apartment No. 7, contiguous to my rooms, No. 8, on the second floor : many a time have I heard the fellow snoring, whilst I myself was pacing my chamber (haply turning verses in honour of MATILDA), and longed to go in and strangle my rival. MATILDA's mother was on my side, whilst her father, from old family connection, inclined towards TUFF- SKIN.

HIS EXCELLENCY PRINCE SCHOUZOFF is President of the Secret Correctional Police of St. Petersburg, an institution which everybody knows and fears in that capital, and nobody talks about. As I have broken off with the Romanoff Court, there is no reason why I should keep the secret or hesitate to divulge the scandal. Some years since in your own paper I remember there was a jocular account of a Russian dignitary in London being awakened in his apartments at LONG'S or MIVART'S, or it may have been GRILLION'S, but the hotel does not matter, by four drummers of the Preobajenski regiment, who entered his room disguised as waiters, and then and there gave him three dozen each, taking his receipt for the same. Every word of that narrative is true ; there's scarcely a man in Petersburg but for some offence to the Court he has had a visit from the Secret Correctional Police. What was the meaning at the commence- ment of the present season of CHAMBERLAIN X. keeping his bed, and PRINCE Y.'s lumbago ? This discipline is so common, so sharp, and decisive, that nobody dare speak of it above his breath, and it is dreadful to think how many of this proud nobility have had a taste of the rattan.

I have spoken before of this degrading punishment having been conferred upon me—upon me the descendant of kings, the inheritor and representative of centuries of honour!—not actually, for had I received a blow, the Chief of the House of ROMANOFF, or that of M., would now be no more; but in intent, the insult remains to be terribly avenged, though the degrading knout descended upon the shoulders of another.

The thing was the talk of Petersburg, as Petersburg talks—under its breath—and what really happened was briefly this. COUNT TUFFSKIN, like too many of the Russian nobility, indulges in the habit of frequent inebriation, and on the night after that painful morning and interview in which I had resigned the EMPEROR's service, TUFFSKIN, myself, one or two of the younger Quakers, and a few more *habitués* of the hotel, partook of a farewell supper. It was Wednesday, and our Quaker friends were to go on Friday, and gave us the last evening which was free.

During the supper I received a little note—blessings be on the hand!—which I read, kissed, and put in my pocket, not heeding the vulgar jokes of TUFFSKIN, and despising his low satire.

He had already drunk several bottles of Clicquot. I now pressed him with brandy; the wretch drank until he was perfectly intoxicated, when I took him, reeling and senseless, and conducted him to bed.

I put him into my room, No. 7 (it has a beautiful prospect over the Neva, the four bridges, the Naval Arsenal, the Pauloff Palace, and the Neuskoi Prospekt). The house is dear, but perhaps the best in Petersburg. I put TUFFSKIN into my room, No. 7, and into my bed; and I went into *his* room, No. 8.

At two o'clock in the morning, when the house was hushed, I heard the tramp of men on the corridor; *it was the Secret Correctional Police.*

At five minutes past two, No. 9, young DOBKINS, the Quaker before mentioned, put his head out of his bed-chamber door, but was thrust back by a sentinel posted there, and told to mind his own business.

. . . He had heard piercing shrieks from No. 7.

They were administering the knout to TUFFSKIN, *mistaking him for your*

BASHI-BOZOUK.

III.

My dear Sir,

The Police silently retired about three in the morning, leaving Tuffskin flayed alive, and myself burning with indignation, at an insult which, though it had fallen on Count Tuffskin's shoulders, had been intended for me. Matilda Schouzoff—beautiful, beloved, faithless Matilda—had rescued me from that peril; she had got an inkling, on the previous evening, from the Police Minister, her father, of the fate that was destined for me.

It was pretended that I was a Russian subject. I had indeed accepted service with the Emperor—and of what country am I a subject since that day when, a fugitive and an exile, I shook off my country and my allegiance with the bootless clods of Ballingarry?—nevertheless, writhing at the notion of the insult, I rushed away immediately after breakfast, and sent up a note to our—I mean the English minister, Sir H–m–lt–n S–m–r, intimating that the M— of B–m– desired to see him; his Excellency knew me as a gentleman before I was an exile; we have danced together at Almack's and the Tuileries many times, and always lived on terms of the greatest cordiality.

Sir H–m–lt–n said very fairly, 'My good fellow, what can I do for you? you are no longer a Chieftain and gentleman of the United Kingdom; or if you are, I must claim you. I must claim you as a rebel, send you back to Ireland for trial, when you will be transported to Van Diemen's Land, where probably you will not act as certain friends of yours have done.'

I said, if his Excellency meant Messrs. M. and N., though I might not possibly approve of their proceedings, yet I was prepared to blow out the brains of any man who questioned their strict honour, and so I tell Mr. Duffy to his face here as I write—thousands of miles away from home under the battlemented walls of Redout Kale!

When his Excellency heard of Tuffskin's misadventure, he burst out laughing as if the deuce was in him, and so did that queer fellow his Secretary, who was in the room when our interview took place. I can see for my part nothing comic in the transaction; however, as the bastinado had been administered in private, as all these things are kept dark in Petersburg, as Tuffskin to this day believes he got the rattan on his private account, I agreed with my friends the English diplomatists that it was best for me to make no noise about the business, and to walk the streets as if nothing had happened.

That afternoon, about two o'clock, I was standing before

JACOBS the printseller's shop, talking and joking with young ALEXIS MIROLADOWAX : who should pass us in his brown Droschki, in which the etiquette is never to recognise him, but the EMPEROR himself ! I happened to be cracking with laughter at one of ALEXIS's stories (a very queer one about my friend COUNT CANCRIM) when his Majesty passed.

A man who had been flayed alive at two o'clock in the morning shaking his sides with laughter on the Alexander Platz, at two in the afternoon—here was a strange occurrence ! The EMPEROR looked at me as if I had been a ghost ; he turned quite livid when he saw me. I appeared to take no notice, laughed and chatted on with ALEXIS, and pretended to be looking at the brass statue of ST. GREGORIUS NAZIANZENUS which stands in the Place.

Gallant men never kiss and tell, so I leave such to imagine the rapturous meeting which took place that evening in the blue saloon of the Winter Palace between me and my lovely rescuer— the pressure of the hand, which, though but momentary, causes the frame to thrill with happiness—the rapid glance of the eye, more eloquent than a thousand speeches. Oh ! MATILDA ! Can it be that you have forgotten me so soon, and for a Qu— ; but I am advancing matters—no woman could be fonder or truer than MATILDA was then.

It was, I have said, a Thursday evening, the night of the EMPRESS's weekly reception. Our Quaker friends had come to take leave ; they were to depart indeed before it was light the next morning ; and I recollect MATILDA asking me why young MR. DOBKINS was not present, whom I had introduced to her family, from which he had received great and constant attention. The young Quaker is a man of enormous wealth, and I recollect MATILDA and myself counting up, in roubles, the amount of the income which he receives in pounds sterling for his share of the business.

I laughed. I supposed DOBKINS wanted to keep his moustaches, and did not care to face his uncle, old JEDEDIAH DOBKINS, who, with some of the old members of the deputation, lived with an old friend, a serious tallow merchant on the English Quay.

I went into the Imperial presence with the rest, and made my bow to their Majesties. The dear EMPRESS, I thought, turned away her head from me with a very mournful expression, whereas the Autocrat looked as black as thunder. I did not mind his black looks ; made my obeisance, and retired presently into the pink and silver drawing-room, where FALCONNET's silver bust of the EMPRESS CATHERINE stands, and where the Maids-of-Honour commonly sit and have tea ; it is exceedingly good at St. Petersburg, as everybody knows, and I drank two or three and twenty cups whilst chattering with these charming girls.

Presently I saw MATILDA coming, with a look of great anxiety in her face ; she beckoned me to speak to her, and I followed her into the embrasure of the window, in which the CUPID and PSYCHE stands looking out on the Tolstoi Square.

'Oh, my MULLIGANOVITCH,' she said, 'my Nijni, my Moujik, my Caviare, my M—, my beautiful, my brave, my best beloved, I have dreadful news for you.'

'Speak, *cushla ma chree na boclish*,' says I (the Celtic and the Sclavonic dialects are very similar), seizing her lovely hand, and pressing it to my beating waistcoat ; 'speak, light of my eyes, and tell me what is the matter.'

'You asked for passports for Prussia this morning at the Police Office, and they were promised to you.'

'They were, adored creature ; will you fly with me ?'

'Oh, MULLIGANOVITCH' (such a heavenly expression of the eyes here), 'you will never be allowed to depart to Prussia : to-morrow at ten o'clock, somebody who tells me everything—get away, you jealous creature, and don't be jealous of him, or doubt your poor little MATILDA—informs me that you will be seized and sent to Siberia ; you are considered as a naturalised Russian subject. The EMPEROR laughed for a moment when he heard of poor COUNT TUFFSKIN being mistaken for you. Oh, dear, dear MULLIGANOVITCH, I could not sleep all night for thinking of what might befall you ; but after his laugh, he grew more angry than ever, and had it not been for the EMPRESS going on her knees to him this very evening, the horrid operation would have been performed on you.'

I ground my teeth, crunching between them the execration which otherwise had issued from my lips.   To be sent to Siberia —the thought was madness !

'Ladies are not allowed to go there,' sobbed out MATILDA, divining the causes of my emotion ; 'they will separate me from my MULLIGANOVITCH ; they will marry me to that horrid tipsy TUFFSKIN.'

I don't know what I should have done in that moment of grief and joy had not MATILDA'S mamma called her at this very juncture, and left me to contemplate my fate, and (to quote the beautiful words of GENERAL WOLFE) bitterly think of the morrow. Go to Siberia !   I swore I would die first.

BASHI-BOZOUK.

IV.

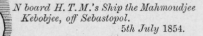

N board H. T. M.'s Ship the Mahmoudjee Kebobjee, off Sebastopol.

5th July 1854.

MY DEAR SIR,

I returned to the Hôtel d'Angleterre, immersed in disagreeable thought, for it is never pleasant to look on friends for the last time, more especially if you are going away from a pleasant place on a confoundedly disagreeable journey as a trip in a chain-gang to Siberia undoubtedly is—most especially of all, if you are about to part from a being so beautiful, beloved, and devoted as I then thought MATILDA SCHOUZOFF. Beautiful ! Yes ! devoted ? phoo ! Beloved ? ha, ha ! — But I am advancing matters.

We had our usual company to supper, excepting of course TUFFSKIN, who, for *very good reasons*, did not show, and drank many a friendly bumper to our Quaker friends, whose last night it was, and whose luggage lay piled in the hotel corridors, ready to be carried off to the steamer before dawn. Young DOBKINS was particularly melancholy. He has beautiful blue eyes, and a figure and an expression, as I have previously stated, singularly like my own. The young fellow's eyes I remarked began to fill with tears, and he spoke with profound emotion of the kindness which he had received from inhabitants of St. Petersburg, contrasting the splendour and elegance of the society there with the humdrum routine of Godmanchester, Bristol, and other cities whither his lot had led him, as a Quaker, a manufacturer, and a man.

I know the world pretty well, and when a young fellow begins to blush and shake, and sigh, and tremble in his voice, and hang down his head, and rub his eyes with his fist, I feel tolerably certain what is the matter. 'Hullo, my friend BROADBRIM,' says I, 'there's a woman in the case. I see that in a jiffey.'

BROADBRIM gave a heave of his chest, a squeeze to my hand, and demurely pleaded guilty to the soft impeachment; a woman there was, as beautiful! oh, as be-eu-eu-ti-ful as an angel, he gurgled out, concealing his emotions and a part of his comely young countenance (confound it!) in a frothing beaker of champagne—a woman, the loveliest being in St. Petersburg, from whom he did not know how he should tear himself away.

The loveliest being in St. Petersburg! thought I; no, no, my fine lad, *that* young person is disposed of elsewhere, naturally presuming that the young fellow had lost his heart to some girl of the English factory, some hide and tallow merchant's daughter, in his own shop-keeping, slop-selling, square-toed walk of life.

I have a feeling heart, and having been touched by love and frantic with passion many many scores of times in my life, I can feel another's woe under those painful and delicate circumstances. I consoled honest DOBKINS, therefore; I clapped him on the back, returned squeeze for squeeze of his hand, and pledged his lady love in innumerable bumpers of champagne, for which—poor satisfaction—I now console myself by thinking that the young rascal was left to pay.

As we were talking, DOBKINS's servant brought him a note, which he seized eagerly, read with glittering eyes and flushing cheeks, over which he murmured a hundred gasps and exclamations, and was about to kiss, had not my presence deterred him.

'Kiss away, my boy,' said I; 'I have osculated reams of note-paper in my time, and know full well whom that pretty little packet comes from.'

'Do thee?' says he, blushing up to the temples.

'Of course I do,' I answered with a laugh. 'Dost thou think, O bashful BROADBRIM! that the'—I protest I had here very nearly written down my name and title—'that VERAX has never been in love with a pretty girl?'

'Chief,' says he—for Chief I am, though my tribe is well-nigh extinct, and my Chieftainship a mockery—'Chief,' says he, 'dost thee know that this letter concerns thee; a great danger menaces thee—exile, chains,' and in a low whisper, so that the waiter should not hear, who was cutting the string of the sixth bottle—'*Siberia!*'

'Dost the whole town know it?' cried I; 'double-distilled donkey that I was—is my disgrace the talk even of the hemp and tallow merchants of the city?'

'My letter,' says DOBKINS, slowly, and with much agitation—

the artful young hypocrite, I should like to wring his neck—'my letter is from one who is a very good friend to thee, who fears the dreadful fate that awaits thee in the eternal snow '—the canting young humbug—'who points out the only way to avert thy evil fortune—the way to freedom, the way to escape from thy tyrant, perhaps to revenge thyself on him at some future day.'

'Ha! boy!' I exclaimed, strongly moved by the young crocodile's words, for as I never told falsehood myself I am slow to suspect it in another; 'so thou knowest the fate that menaces me, and hast found out means to avert it; speak, my friend; whatever a man of courage may do I am ready to attempt, in order to escape from a tyrant, and one day to avenge my wrong.'

'Easy, my good friend !' cries this young square-toes, this arch sly-boots. 'We Quakers are of the peaceful sort; here is no question about revenge, but about escape, and that immediately. Thee knowest that the gates of Petersburg are shut against thee, and that thee may as well hope to escape from the Autocrat as from death, when the day comes. A way, however, there is, and but one, by which thee can put thyself out of reach of the claws of this Russian Eagle; and though I shall risk myself not a little, nevertheless for thy sake, and for the sake of those who are interested in thy welfare, I will abide the peril so I may set thee free. Our steamer, the *John Bright*, sails from the Potemkin Quay at half-past two o'clock this morning, when the tide serves. The friends have given orders to be waked at one, which is now the hour. Thee must take my passports, thee must shave off thy moustaches, and put on the broadbrim and drab, which thee loves to laugh at, and so escape.'

'Generous boy !' I exclaimed, gripping his hand like a vice; 'and what will happen to you ?' I was quite confounded by the seeming nobility of the young scoundrel's self-sacrifice.

'Never thee mind that,' says BROADBRIM. 'How can I help it if a rogue makes off with my coat, my hat, and my passport ? I am a Briton, and my Ambassador will get me another.' I took him to my heart, this loyal, this gallant, this guileless, this affectionate heart, that beats with eternal tenderness for the friend who does me a kindness—that rankles with eternal revenge against the villain who betrays me !

I agreed to his proposal. To put on his great-coat and broad hat was an easy matter; though to part with my moustaches I own was difficult; can we help our little vanities ? our long bushy auburn-coloured curly vanities ? I rather would say. A more beautiful pair of moustaches never decorated the lip of man. I loved them perhaps the more because my MATILDA loved them. I went up to my chamber, and was absent a few minutes.

When I returned, DOBKINS started back. 'Gracious heavens!' said he, and looked positively quite pale. 'Gracious heavens,' says he, 'what an alteration!'

Altered I was indeed. I had taken off my splendid uniform of an unattached colonel of Russian Cavalry—yellow, with pink facings, and the Black Russian Spread Eagle embroidered tastefully on the back—and put on a snuff-coloured suit of DOBKINS'S, which I found in his room, No. 10. My face was shaved as clean as a baby's. I had a broad-brimmed hat on. I placed in the Quaker's hand an envelope, sealed with a royal 'scutcheon that once flamed in the van of Erin's battle; it contained my moustaches. I am not ashamed to own that the tear bedewed my manly cheek as I bade him deliver the packet to the PRINCESS MATILDA SCHOUZOFF.

The young villain rushed up into his room and put on my uniform, which fitted him to a nicety, and I painted him a pair of moustaches with one of the burnt champagne corks, of which a half-dozen were lying on the table; you would really have thought it was myself as you looked at him. Ah! fatal resemblance! Ah! sorrow that throws its bleak shade alike o'er my life and my woes!

Six hours afterwards the *John Bright* steamer was before Cronstadt, and it was not until we were out of reach of the guns of that fortress (which I have a certain plan for silencing) that the friends of the Peace Deputation were aware that I, and not their young companion, was on board.

I did not care, for good reasons, to go to London; but as soon as we got to Dantzig, put myself into the railroad, and betook myself to Paris, where my old friend, the EMPEROR NAPOLEON THE THIRD, received me with his usual hospitality. In several interviews with his Majesty I laid before him the fullest information regarding the military and pecuniary resources of the Russian empire which has ever yet, as I believe, found its way out of those immense dominions. What I told the French monarch (I confess myself a friend to despots, and an enemy to philosophers and praters)—what information I had the good fortune to convey to him I shall not, of course, publish here. My plans, were they followed, would burst in thunder upon the crumbling battlements of Cronstadt, and hurl into mid-air the ships and arsenals of Sebastopol. I fear other counsels than mine may be followed.

ST. ARNAUD and I had a dispute long ago, when he was in

a very different situation in life.   With the English commanders I cannot communicate, owing to my peculiar position and the Ballingarry affair.   It was that unlucky business likewise which prevented my friend, the EMPEROR OF THE FRENCH, from giving me a command over troops which were to act in conjunction with the forces of the English QUEEN.   He offered me Algeria, but I preferred active service against ROMANOFF, and the Colonel of Bashi-Bozouks has already put a shot or two into the proud wings of the Russian Eagle.

If anything was wanting to sharpen the edge of my hatred against Russia, against men and women, against Quakers especially, it was a paragraph which my kind friend, the EMPEROR NAPOLEON, showed to me one afternoon as we were sitting in the Pavillon Marsan, talking over Russia and the war.   I was translating for him—and I think I have said that I speak the language perfectly—some of the lying bulletins out of the Petersburg gazettes, in which his Majesty and his British allies are abused in a most vulgar manner, when, glancing down a column of fashionable intelligence, I came to the following paragraph :—

Conversion of an ENGLISH QUAKER TO THE ORTHODOX FAITH. A young Quaker nobleman, of the highest birth, whose family has devoted itself for some time past to commercial pursuits, whereby he has realised an immense fortune, has quitted the lamentable errors and benighted faith under which most of his countrymen labour, and has professed himself a convert to the only true and orthodox religion.   It is M. DOBKINSKI's intention to establish himself in our capital, and his Majesty has graciously awarded him the order of ST. ANDREW of the second class, the rank of Colonel, and the permission to marry MATILDA, daughter of Police President PRINCE SCHOUZOFF.

'Mick, my good fellow,' said his Majesty, the EMPEROR NAPOLEON, 'you look a little pale :' and no wonder ; I did look a little pale, though I did not inform my Imperial interlocutor of the causes of my disquiet, but you and the public now may understand in part, for my adventures are not nearly over, why it is that I am a

BASHI-BOZOUK.

IMPORTANT FROM THE SEAT OF WAR![1]

JOURNAL OF THE SIEGE OF SILISTRIA.

BY OUR OWN BASHI-BOZOUK.

I.

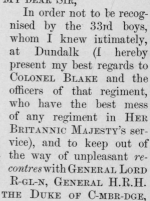

Scutari, Tuesday.

MY DEAR SIR,

In order not to be recognised by the 33rd boys, whom I knew intimately, at Dundalk (I hereby present my best regards to COLONEL BLAKE and the officers of that regiment, who have the best mess of any regiment in HER BRITANNIC MAJESTY's service), and to keep out of the way of unpleasant *recontres* with GENERAL LORD R-GL-N, GENERAL H.R.H. THE DUKE OF C-MBR-DGE, and other acquaintances of happier years, I have taken the precaution since my arrival here of dyeing my face, beard, and hands, and wearing a plaister over my nose and right eye. I use BURGESS's walnut ketchup for my face and hands in preference to India soy, which I employed at first; but for which the flies and wasps, which abound in this country, have a great liking.

Yesterday, as I was having an audience of the Sultan's mother, the dear SULTANA VALIDEH, a whacking big hornet, attracted by the confounded soy, settled close on my nose, stung me, and occasioned atrocious agonies. Of course, I had to grin as if nothing was the matter, and continue the conversation, which was *most interesting*. When the Sultana left us I could bear the pain no longer, but rubbed my nose, and tore off the plaister which covered that and my eye.

It was so swollen that the gallant and excellent English Pr-nce, who made one at our consultation, very likely *could* not recognise

[1] [July 22, 29 ; August 5, 1854.]

me. At any rate, he did not. A dancing dervish (a most holy man, and great favourite of the Sultana's) fetched some leaves out of the garden, and having chewed them, fomented my *feature*, which speedily resumed its own classic shape. Mem.—To inquire what the plant is, and send some to dear friends at home ; where a *fellow of spirit* may often get a swelled eye still, praised be luck !—at elections, fairs, and so forth.

The splendid proposals which her Highness made to me (in private) on the part of her imperial son, of course, are out of the question. The young PRINCESS NIJOONA (for those who like that style of beauty) is lovely certainly. She is but sixteen, and must weigh as many stone. Her eyebrows meet. Her complexion is very fair (though I must say I think she is painted). Her teeth are not good, owing to the quantity of sweetmeats they take. When I go to see the SULTANA VALIDEH I am half choked with the lumps of sugar-candy which I am obliged to swallow whenever I say anything witty, and that, of course, is at every other observation. It seems NIJOONA remarked me as I was riding in the Valley of the Sweet Waters (hers must have been the hand which held out the three rhododendrons and the polyanthus from behind the pink and silver curtains of that emerald-green aroba !) and was pleased with my personal appearance. NIJOONA ! thou art not the first, by long chalks, who has been charmed by this figure !

Wishing to soothe every lady's disappointment as much as possible—when a hint was given me in a certain august quarter— I told one of the few falsehoods which I have uttered in my life, and said I was married in my own country. And the upshot of this silly fib was to show how *useless* it is to lie.

The young lady's imperial grandmother did not seem to consider my previous marriage an objection. 'All that we shall require is that NIJOONA shall be the first wife : and if the second makes any objection, my dear Colonel,' the Sultan-Mother said, in her arch way, 'there is plenty of sacking in the bazaars, and the Bosphorus is very deep.'

To have the rank of Pasha, and a palace at Constantinople and at Therapia, with fifty millions of piastres down, and jewels to a still larger amount ; to divide the command with OMER PASHA ; and, at the end of the war, to have the hereditary pashalic of Syria, with palaces built for me at Jerusalem, Damascus, and Beyroot—these, I confess, were handsome offers, not to be attributed so much to my merit, no doubt, as to the passion which young NIJOONA had conceived for me : who is, as is well known, her imperial father's favourite, to whom his Highness can refuse *nothing*.

The poor thing actually tried to fascinate me by her simple accomplishments, and sang me one or two songs to her guitar. Asking me if I was also a musician, I took up the little instrument and sang, ' *Who fears to speak of Ninety-Eight?* ' (out of my friend DUFFY's paper), in a way which brought tears into the eyes of the Pr-nc-ss-s. No wonder they were affected as the poor Exile sang !

But marriage and turning Turk was quite another *paire de bottes*. When NIJOONA went weeping out of the room, led away by her maids, and her grandmother put the question to me point-blank, I was about to answer point-blank, No ! but a look from my friend, the dancing dervish, put me on my guard. ' Madam,' said I, ' I must ask your R-y-l permission to have some conversation with my reverend friend here regarding the two faiths, and if he can convince me—then, indeed ! ' She is a very warm partisan of her creed ; she gave me a couple of little tracts, *The Washerwoman of Therapia* and *The Boatman of the Bosphorus*, which, she said, had converted a great number of Poles and Hungarians, and left me after my promising to study these works !

' Unless you intend to come round, MULLIGOON,' said my friend, the dervish, ' you had better put some distance between you and the princess. She is a fiery little creature, and will have you strangled or poisoned, as sure as your name is what it is.'

So it seems there is to be no rest for me—not in Dublin, not in London, not in Petersburg, not in Constantinople ! Finding that the coach was going to Varna that afternoon (and most uncomfortable conveyances those Turkish stage-coaches are) I took a place for myself and my servant in it, with letters to the Governor of Silistria. And, by the time the clock of the Mosque of Saint Sophia struck thirteen (the hour at which the Sultana-Mother had appointed me) the next day, I had left Varna, and was on horseback on the road to Silistria.

You now understand why my death was announced on the very first day of the siege of this place ; a piece of news which put poor NIJOONA into a dreadful fury ; she was so enraged to think I had escaped her vengeance. I do not envy NOBBI PASHA, whom she has married since by order of her imperial father. NOBBI is a quiet man, and she leads him and his family the deuce's own life.

The Governor of Silistria welcomed me with that distinction which I am accustomed to receive from brave men. Having been just obliged to hang the colonel of a regiment of most refractory Bashi-Bozouks, the Pasha was pleased to offer me the vacant command, which I accepted, and when I had partaken of coffee and pipes, given my views of the affairs of Europe, the advance of the Russians, etc., to his Excellency, a person of the highest distinction, greatest bravery, and most aristocratic manners, he wrote a line by an aide-de-camp, and, mounting horses, which were provided for us, I rode down to the place by the Mosque of SULTAN SELIM, a little to the left of the Bakers' quarter of the Old Bazaar, where my Bashi-Bozouks were quartered.

A more drunken and ferocious set of vagabonds eyes never lighted upon. In the centre of the place they had stuck up their standard with a hideous Russian head, surmounted by its cocked hat on the top. The tom-toms, kettle-drums, jinjalls, and other music of the regiment were around this. The men were scattered here and there, some sleeping, some smoking, many intoxicated, and under a rude canopy sate a dozen of officers, of whom a gigantic woolly-haired mulatto seemed the chief; he had a skin of wine by his side as big as a portmanteau, and was gnawing a leg of lamb with his long fangs, holding it up with his huge fists, and glaring at me over the meat.

'Are you the Bimbashi?' says I. 'Are you, gentlemen, the Captains and Lieutenants of this pretty regiment?'

'Yes,' they replied, seasoning their answer with curses in a hundred dialects.

'Then stand up!' I roared out, 'whilst I read my commission' —and accordingly taking that document from the aide-de-camp (who, I must say, trembled like a mould of jelly), I kissed the paper, held it to my forehead three times, and then read it to the officers and men.

'Ho! ho! ho! and so *you* are the Colonel, are you?' yelled the Bimbashi, laying his leg of lamb down and springing up, rubbing the gravy off his mouth with his great brawny arm—'A stranger! and a Giaour, and you are come to be set over us, are you? Keep the gates, you sentinels! Take that Russian's head off the flag, Ensign!'

'Who sides with the Sultan, and who with the Major?' says I.

'We propose that the promotion goes with the regiment,' roared out the officers.

'Where are the non-commissioned officers?' says I. Seven or eight of them were standing apart as I saw. 'Let the men fall in!' I roared. 'Captains, go to your companies. Major!'

What I was going to say to him does not matter; for the ruffian fired a shot at me, and then sent the pistol flying at my head.

It knocked down the poor aide-de-camp who was with me—

upon which, seeing I had to do with nine ruffians, of course I produced my revolvers, one of COLT's and one of HANDCOCK's, regarding the respective merits of which there has been some question.

The practice, as I take it, is pretty equal. With the COLT I shot three captains, two lieutenants, missing No. 6, the ensign— with the HANDCOCK I potted two ensigns, a captain, a lieutenant, and finally my friend the major, sending a ball into his great mouth, and stopping his horrid language for the future towards his colonel and your

BASHI-BOZOUK.

II.

Fort of Arab Tabia, Thursday.

DEAR SIR,

I resume my pen, and continue my account of our siege. I accompany the MS. with drawings, which you will please to have copied by proper persons at home. The one I have hastily dashed off on this page represents myself just now with a little incident that happened. I give you my honour I was so tired after twenty-three hours in the saddle, or in the trenches, that I did not care to remove the shell, but let it blaze away at its leisure. It only killed nineteen men. I thought a few pictures of myself might please the girls at home; and you will take care the artist you employ makes me *handsome enough*, or if I survive this siege, woe be to him on my return home !

Friday. After dispatching that little business with the officers, I appointed the non-commissioned officers to the vacant posts : reserving the place of major for my faithful friend G——. Some disturbance may possibly take place on account of the appointments, the Pasha in command of the town naturally liking to have the patronage. If he breaks all these ill-looking scoundrels, I shall not be a whit put out of temper. My temper, when I am pleased, is often very fine.

Inspected the defunct Bimbashi's quarters, and selected out of his stock such things as suited me. The late villain appears to have had an appetite for plunder ; I have the less remorse in having suppressed him. I found in his rooms thirteen very handsome suits of clothes, of different but handsome patterns. Selected for every-day wear a pink pelisse, yellow trousers, and a shawl round my fez ; for Sundays a light blue cashmere ditto ditto, shulwars striped white and crimson, pea-green morocco boots with silver spurs, and another equally elegant dress for change—the rest I distributed among my men. Besides the clothes, I found among the villain's effects :—

A desk, marked Mr. J. T. Jones, containing £2000 of circular notes of Coutts', payable to John Thomas Jones, Esq., with the circular letter containing Mr. John Thomas Jones's signature. I warn Mr. J.'s family that they can have the desk back again, containing—

Two quires of Bath post paper.

Eighteen letters, one containing a lock of hair, and signed ' your ever ever faithful Anna Maria.'

Jones's journal and fifteen of his inn bills (it appears he kept his accounts with much regularity).

A box of Cockle's compound Antibilious Pills, of which I own to having given six one evening to one of my captains, Crummy Effendi, who was indisposed, and—

The circular letter containing Jones's signature. The notes, I am sorry to say, have been taken by some one, and were cashed by Messrs. Nephelegeretes & Co., of Pera, upon a rather clumsy forgery of Jones's signature.

In the poor major's kit I further found :—

A brace of silver-mounted pistols, and a yataghan, with a case of gold, as I first thought, covered with turquoises. If the late Bimbashi, as I have too much reason to suspect, robbed some innocent family of this yataghan, thinking it was gold, the villain was grievously disappointed, for I could only get 500 piastres for the knife when I sold it at Adrianople.

Proceeding in my perquisitions I discovered :—

A worsted stocking, containing a Russia leather pocket-book with 3673 paper roubles of Russia and a bag of 996 silver roubles, chiefly of the EMPEROR ALEXANDER'S reign, which—I mean the paper roubles— I gave to the Commandant of Silistria. The silver I thought proper to retain, and make no doubt that the scoundrel I had just exterminated had been in league with the enemy. Also I found—

A portmanteau, marked 'solid leather,' containing two dozen shirts, marked J. T. J.

Stockings, collars, and handkerchiefs with the same mark.

Six cases of brown Windsor soap ;

And a silver-mounted dressing-case—rather a handsome thing—the bottle-stoppers, etc., marked J. T. J., with a lion rampant for a crest. The maker, WEST, in St. James's Street.

But how the deuce can I tell to whom a portmanteau belongs marked only 'Warranted Solid Leather'? Of course à la guerre it is à la guerre. I found the linen most comfortable, and the stockings and slippers very pleasant for a change, when I came in wet and weary out of the trenches. That major certainly had robbed somebody and was a lawless villain, whose life was rightly sacrificed to his cupidity.

Saturday. Paraded my regiment, and gave them fourteen hours under arms. Had to chastise seven or eight of them, showing them que je n'entendais pas la plaisanterie. Confiscated a goose and a lamb, which one villain had robbed out of the bazaar, and sent the giblets back to the family. On this day we received information in Silistria that a Russian corps was advancing out of the Dobrudscha upon Rassova.

Monday. My quarters are pretty good in the house of the Greek Papa POLYPHLOESBOEOS. His wife BOOPIS must have been good-looking, his daughter RHODODACTYLOS is extremely so. Sate with them, and drank Rakee, whilst the old gentleman was at church. Sang *Who fears to speak of Ninety-Eight?* and *The Shan Van Voght* to the ladies, who were affected to tears.

After I had done singing, pretty little RHODODACTYLOS took the instrument, and improvised a plaintive ballad respecting the late events with my regiment, beginning

Μῆνιν ἄειδε, θεά, μεγαθύμου Μυλλιγανοῖο,

which my modesty forbids my translating, so really undeserved were the compliments paid to the courage, personal appearance, etc., of a certain Colonel of Bashi-Bozouks.

They produced some Cyprus wine, and we had an excellent

pilaff, over which old POLYPHLOESBOEOS found us on return from chapel. As we had polished off the rice and lamb, the old man dined on the flaps of bread which we had used for plates, and I left the old monster actually picking crumbs off the tablecloth.

Tuesday. Annoyed all night by the old Papa's snoring. Finding he has a very comfortable bed, ordered it to my room. Went out with my Bozouks to the bridge of Routschouk, where we found the advanced guard of the enemy. Charged them nine

times, but were beaten back by the Russians, with a loss of thirty-nine of ours killed and seventy-eight wounded. All things considered, however, my men behaved very well. RHODODAC-TYLOS a good deal agitated, and her mother, BOOPIS POTNIA, delighted at my return. The old Papa seemingly not very glad to see me.

16. A strong cannonade from the islands of the Danube. The enemy's advanced guard at Adikoi. A skirmish with the Bashi-Bozouks, who retired towards Arab Tabia. The rain fell very heavily from after twelve o'clock. The macintosh I took from the young officer of the Lobski Hussars of great use and comfort. Poor fellow! He too very likely had been in England! The cloak is marked Piccadilly! Such is life.

18. The enemy, who has been establishing batteries upon the islands and the left bank, opened his fire this day from noon until night. POLYPHLOESBOEOS, in great perturbation, took up his residence in the cellar, where I did not grudge the old chap fuddling himself with Cyprus wine. His comrade, the Papa DOLICOSCHIOS called—as he was talking his head knocked off by a cannon-ball—broke china in corner-cupboard; his hand still holding his beard, which was uncommonly fine, the other his large umbrella.

19. The enemy opened his trenches at about two English miles off our lines—his left towards Arab Tabia, his right on the Danube. Slept as sound as a roach on the old Papa's mattress, though the Russians never ceased firing from sunset until the morning of the 20th, when his first parallel was completed. The enemy's chasseurs, trying to establish themselves on the height opposite Arab Tabia, the Bashi-Bozouks and Albanians drove them back. Little finger carried off by a Minié ball. Gallant conduct of KARAGOOZ BEG, killed a Russian Colonel and put on his boots in the face of the enemy. Poor, poor little RHODODAC-TYLOS! Sadly put out by accident to my little finger. Two Circassian prisoners announce an attack for to-night—Bashi-Bozouks kept up in consequence.

20. The enemy's guns are uncommonly well served. Every one of their balls hit. Twenty-four pound shot knocked letter I was reading out of my hand, and plumped into the bosom of HOKIM-AGA, Commandant's Aide-de-Camp. Had order in his pocket—from a certain high quarter—to shoot me, and reward of 100,000 sequins to bring my head to Constantinople. Did not tell poor little RHODODACTYLOS for fear of alarming this timid little fluttering affectionate creature! Mem.—MRS. POLYPHLOES-BOEOS begins to look very sulky at me.

24. Provisions are growing rather scarce in my quarters, and old POLYPHLOESBOEOS begins to grumble. This evening for supper I ate the bread and the pilaff too. My appetite is excellent. MRS. P. and my little RHODODACTYLOS would only touch a little morsel. Young SPIRIDION POLYMETIS, whom I have appointed Lieutenant *vice* BORBORYGMOS, who ran away disgracefully last night, has been useful in these latter days carrying my messages to or from the Commander of the place. In the sally we made last night, SPIRIDION rode back very good-naturedly into the enemy's column for my umbrella; it was the old priest's, and not having drawn my sword, I had been constrained to use it in order to poke out a Cossack Colonel's eye who was making himself very officious in front.

Mem.—I am growing rather rich in cash. Besides thirty-nine piastres which I brought with me, I have

A portmanteau of handsome clothes as above, value say £80.

969 silver roubles.

£2000, which came to me by the laws of war.

A gold snuff-box, with the portrait of the EMPEROR set in diamonds, and the order of the Saracen's Head of the second class in brilliants also, sent by his Imperial Majesty to MAJOR-GENERAL BARON SLABBERS, whom I slew in the second attack on the 22nd.

Twelve silver-gilt candlesticks, and a couple of statues of an ecclesiastical pattern, I confess, and some gold-lace vestments of which the old Papa POLYPHLOESBOEOS has made me a present (very unwillingly) out of his church. He may have a hesitation, but I have none, in taking possession of the bullion employed in the cathedral of these schismatics.

A gold bowl, a picture-frame ditto ditto, and a silver armchair which SPIRIDION was instrumental in procuring for me from the abbot of the Armenian Convent hard by. I shall value these at even more than the bazaar price, as they were the means of saving the reverend man's life ; indeed, I should have hanged him had he not given them up.

A bag of loose diamonds, emeralds, and a silver soup-ladle of English manufacture given to me with the grateful tear of a Jewish family.

BASHI-BOZOUK.

III.

Fort of Arab Tabia, June 25.

DEAR SIR,

Some jealous scoundrels (I suspect the envious malignity of a couple of English Officers, who are making themselves very officious here) have been complaining of the plundering propensities of my Bashi-Bozouks. In an angry interview with H. E. MUSSA PASHA this morning, I repelled the accusation with scorn, and challenged both the English Officers for the honour of our corps. N.B.—The Turks do not understand the practice of civilised European gentlemen : and MUSSA PASHA said, 'Suppose CAPTAIN B. shoots you, will that prove you did not take the Jew Merchant's silver soup-ladle and diamonds? Go and shoot as many Russians as you please, MULLIGOON FERIK! but let us hear of no more plundering.' It is in vain to expect in half-educated men the refinement and delicate feelings of gentlemen with a long line of ancestry. The enemy made three attacks this evening on Arab Tabia. As I brought in a prisoner, though very much mutilated, MAJOR-GENERAL COUNT SWIGGAMOFF, who led the last attack, HIS EXCELLENCY MUSSA PASHA was pleased to compliment me, said he would send my name to the Commander-in-Chief for decoration, and look over the affair of the Jew, who was making a deuce of a disturbance.

The affair last night was very hot. My arm this morning is black and blue from lifting iron. The Russians had actually entered the redoubt and cut down our artillerymen at their guns, when the Bashi-Bozouks luckily arriving gave a different turn to affairs. We may expect a great attack in a day or two. My prisoner says that MARSHAL PASKIEWITCH was in such a rage as to kick the Major-General at the head of the column.

June 27. Three tremendous attacks upon Arab Tabia took place to-night. The first, under the command of GENERAL COUNT SLUTZ of the Alexander Regiment, was very nearly doing for us.

They came on in spite of the fire of our guns, their drums beating, their officers in the front waving their hats and cursing and swearing in the most frightful manner. The Russians actually clambered through the embrasures and over the guns. COUNT SLUTZ, a very stout man, in jack boots, was rammed up in an embrasure against a Paixhans gun, and there I confess I prodded him. After his death the survivors of the attacking column fell back in much disorder. This must have been at 10.35 by the late Count's repeater.

At 11.22 P.M. the gallant foe returned in still greater force ; they did not fire a shot until they were close upon us, and I heard a voice calling out—' Three hundred thousand silver roubles and the Order of SAINT ANNE, second class, for the man who brings in MULLIGANOFF dead or alive ! ' I thought I knew the voice. ' Ha, my boy ! ' I roared out from the bastion. ' Ha, TUFFSKIN, my boy ! How did you like the bastinado at the Hôtel d'Europe ? ' Indeed it was poor TUFFSKIN, who had arrived only that morning at the army. He will never suffer the cat-of-nine-tails more. It was the fortune of war, and now he is no more I can do justice to a gallant enemy. I gave his earrings to little RHODODACTYLOS, on my return to my quarters after.

THE THIRD ATTACK, which was the most severe of all. By this time ammunition had been luckily brought to us in the fort, and as the enemy came up we received him with a fire so murderous, that 452 men were killed, and 2706 wounded, by the first discharge. We gave them a second by the time they were up to our guns, and then, rushing out on the disordered column, my gallant Bashi-Bozouks drove the storming party back three miles through their own entrenchments and into the Danube, where, such was their impetuosity, many of my fellows were actually drowned with the Russians. I had marked and seized an old officer who had been making himself particularly conspicuous, and, having broken my sword, was pummelling him most severely with the handle about the face and ribs, when he cried out in very good French, ' *Tenez*, MULLIGANOFF ! *Je me rends. Je suis le* MARÉCHAL PRINCE PASKIE ' . . . but I heard no more, for a shot entered my shoulder and down I dropped. Provoking.

I had to walk home five miles with a bullet in my shoulder, and did not reach my quarters till 7 o'clock A.M. What a scream of delight little RHODODACTYLOS gave at beholding me. They were eating a piece of horse for breakfast, for provisions are getting scarce. I took my share of the *chivalric* meal, and then had the conical ball extracted, which had given me much annoyance. Prisoners who came in this day, the 28th, announced that PRINCE PASKIEWITCH had received some severe contusions the night before, and that PRINCE GORTSCHAKOFF had resumed the command of the siege.

30. Had some fever from my wound. The fire of the enemy was so hot that no less than twenty-nine cannon balls and four shells fell into my room, which burst there, and filled the place with smoke. I could not move, as the surgeon had forbidden me to stir, even taking away my pantaloons, so as to prevent the possibility of my quitting my apartment. In the intervals of the firing my charming RHODODACTYLOS was so attentive and kind to the *poor wounded Bashi-Bozouk,* that my heart melted towards the dear girl. I offered her my hand, on condition, of course, that she would separate from the Greek schism, and the blushing young creature gave me her own rosy fingers in reply.

July 1. The siege is raised. The Russians are in full retreat, my Bashi-Bozouks after them. I am so weak that I cannot move from my bed. Cowards and detractors have been blackening my character to SAMMI PASHA, who has now the command of SILISTRIA, and I am a *prisoner.* I who saved SILISTRIA !

2. RHODODACTYLOS was allowed to come in to me with a little calves'-foot jelly, which she had been making. I told the dear girl where I had secreted my property, viz. in a hole under the pumpkin bed in the garden of the house, where poor old POLYPHLOESBOEOS discovered me *investing* some of my property on the 23rd. I was in the hole, spade in hand, digging, and thereby saved my life ; for a round shot took off POLYPHLOESBOEOS'S head just over me ; and the poor man thus paid for his curiosity.

4. Anniversary of American Independence. I rallied this day. The sentry was taken off yesterday, and I received my order of Nisham from the English officer here, who says my conduct is overlooked—I think it *is* overlooked indeed !—in consequence of my gallantry. The house being empty, I went down to the garden, where I kept my things.

O RHODODACTYLOS ! O woman, faithless woman ! Would you believe it, I only found the desk and papers marked J. T. Jones ; every other single item of my property has been taken away, except a boot-jack, an old coat, and a pair of very old trousers, and I was told by the clerk of the Greek Chapel that RHODODACTYLOS and SPIRIDION were married yesterday morning, and that they left Silistria the same afternoon for Bulgaria, in an aroba very heavily laden. SPIRIDION was in a pink pelisse, red-striped trousers, and pea-green boots. RHODODACTYLOS, the clerk said, blazed in diamonds ; and unless you accept the bill I have drawn upon you through MESSRS. ORNITHES of this city, I am actually a penniless

BASHI-BOZOUK.

MR. PUNCH TO AN EMINENT PERSONAGE.[1]

OST EMINENT LORD,

I have scarcely congratulated our mutual friend, the British Public, on your return from Rome to Golden Square. It is an honour and pleasure to possess amongst us a Prince so illustrious—to find him busy for our welfare, and devising kind schemes for our good.

Knowing how excellent many of the customs are of the foreign cities in which it has been your good fortune to be bred, you naturally wish to benefit your province of England and your archdiocese of Westminster with importations from abroad ; and as my wife comes home with a bonnet from Paris, my son with a pair of moustaches from Germany, your Eminence brings an *Index Expurgatorius* from the Vatican and a little plan of an Inquisition from Spain. Often as I pass that modest house in that modest Golden Square I think, with a respectful wonder, that the greatest man of all the Empire lives within. *Principibus praestat et regibus*, etc., I will not continue the quotation. But so the fact is. You are the equal of the QUEEN herself, what my friend MULLIGAN calls the 'Shuparior' of Princes. Poor DR. SUMNER is not fit to kiss your honour's shoe-strings, or DR. WHATELY to hold your red hat. Say that the LORD CHANCELLOR, HIS ROYAL HIGHNESS FIELD-MARSHAL PRINCE ALBERT, and your Eminent Lordship were to visit my humble abode, I should be obliged to give you the *pas* before H.R.H. the FIELD-MARSHAL— upon my word I should—you would have to lead MRS. PUNCH into

[1] [September 16, 1854.]

dinner : the other illustrious guest, of course, would be appropriated by my mother-in-law, and as for the Chancellor, his Lordship and I would be obliged to walk in the dining-room arm-in-arm.

We should not be expected to kneel, I suppose ? I could hardly get my old knee-bones down so low ; not but that this very winter at Rome I saw scores of folks doing so, and kissing your Eminent Lordship's hand as if it were a young beauty's.

What a fine thing it is to think that a man of this Prodigious Rank (for such yours is) should be an Englishman after all, and care for us, our laws and our people ! In the late little affair of BOYLE v. WISEMAN you came into Court like any other Briton ; and after writing a libel against this poor BOYLE who vexed you (holy JOB was vexed with 'em too), how affably you took advantage of the law which nonsuited him. It is the greatest compliment which has been paid to our Courts, since PRINCE HENRY'S behaviour in that notorious affair with Chief-Justice GASCOYNE. A Cardinal by the Divine pity, a Prince of Rome, you came into an English Court to take your chance there ; you stood by the laws of your country ; that is to say, you did not exactly stand— you bolted, as the law gave you full permission to do—I can fancy the confusion of poor BOYLE losing you when he thought he had got you ; and the calm good-humour of your Eminence's face, seeming to say, ' Don't you wish you may ? '

The law business, although noble and edifying, is not, however, that which occasions these brief and respectful remarks. It is on your Eminent Lordship's appearance as an educator of all England that the Nation ought to be congratulated It's kind of you. The very thing we like is the Roman system. What we want is a good *Index Expurgatorius ;* a parental board of Inquisition to look over the books for our people, and prevent them from being poisoned by bad literature. Most pestilent lies are told by fellows who write books ; most wicked doctrines promulgated ; and it. is uncommonly good-natured in a man occupied as your Eminence is, in the affairs of your own Church ; rows and squabbles with refractory priests ; affairs of your newly-created province ; regulations of suffragans and minor clergy ; writing articles for *The Dublin Review ;* and reports to that august foreign Court and Sovereign, greatest of all Courts, Sovereign of all Sovereigns, of which, and under whom, you are yourself a most distinguished and ornamental Prince and Dignitary—I say it is exceedingly kind of one so illustrious and so busy to think about us outside Britons at all, and offer to help us in our emergency.

I had read in my favourite journal, *The Record*, a brief report of ' CARDINAL WISEMAN'S Lecture on the Home Education of the

Poor,' but waited until Sunday and my still greater favourite, *The Tablet*, arrived, with the authentic report of the Lecture. Here is the journal before me, which speaks out like a man for its own part, and saying, 'We have often thought that even to a limited philosophical point of view the Index of Prohibited Books, of all other Catholic Institutions the one scorned and hated by Protestants, is one that *commends* itself most highly to the calm view of Reason.' Here is *The Tablet* and the report of the Cardinal's Lectures. May I venture to make a respectful tonsure in the columns?

His Eminence confined himself chiefly to the general topic of the want of a suitable popular literature, reserving for his next lecture the consideration of the modes by which it might be supplied. It seems most important, said his Eminence, that the public, especially those interested in the education of the people, should know what is at present the literature which awaits the rural population on leaving school. In France this has been done, and it may be useful to know the results of the inquiry. For several hundred years the population of France was supplied with a cheap literature by the well-known system of Colportage, by means of which some eight or nine millions of small volumes and pamphlets were circulated amongst the people. But in 1852 a decree was issued by the Minister of the Police appointing a commission to examine all books sold by licensed hawkers, who were in future not to be allowed to circulate any without the Government Stamp of approbation. This very interesting report of the Commission has this year been published, from which it appears that of the books that had been examined three-fourths had been condemned. If I were in a position of political influence (said his Eminence) I should most strongly urge upon the legislature the importance of appointing a Committee of Inquiry into this matter.

Of course you would. You would do as they do at Rome. We have read about *expugnandos, comburendos, expurgandos,* and the old processes, which commend themselves, as our friend *The Tablet* says, 'most highly to the calm view of reason.' And if you were in a position of political influence, we know, dear Eminence, that you would keep your promise.

But you see you are not in a position of political influence. We don't want to go down on our knees, as they do at Rome. To kiss your hand is not to us the source of the slightest comfort. Gentlemen who choose to do so are welcome; but it appears from the Census church returns that you and your followers are but as two hundred thousand to the ten millions of the unroman English. CHADBAND has as large a flock as you have; who, had he his will, would no doubt smash the windows of your mass-houses, break your images, and bonnet your Eminence on your big hat. We give hospitality to CHADBAND and WISEMAN. Why not to other religionists? Our exemplary ally, who has stopped the Colporteurs, has stopped PUNCH too in his dominions. Can it be that if your Eminence were in a position of political influence you would go so far? Heaven help us! I fear yes. We should have a certain shop in St. Bride's shut up if that 'political influence' could but be managed, and 'calm reason' could but get its own way. You would no more let us in than in Rome, where you have political influence, you let the Thirty-nine Articles pass the

Porta del Popolo! Fancy your Eminence's faith and practice restored among us, and we should see not only FRANCIS MOORE, Physician, against whose poor old almanacs you are wrath, but CHARLES JAMES (now JAMES of London) and MR. PUNCH walking out of the city, and across the *fines patriae*, like TITYRUS and MELIBAES!

Considering that your religion is not ours, but exists here on toleration; that your journals take their fill in abusing our Church and political establishments (I have heard of DR. NEWMAN in the pulpit making admirable fun of the former); that you are free to publish your tracts, apologues, homilies, and sell them where and at what price you please, is it not a little premature in your eminent Lordship to quarrel with other folks for doing

exactly what you do ? Were you in a station of 'political
influence,' I do not say, of course, you would gag every man of us
according to the Roman mode ; but meanwhile, why should we
have a censorship for our press, on account of the hostility to
our received institutions of any writer or party of writers living
among us ? Upon my honour and conscience, I do not believe
there is any party in England so opposed to our views of right,
morals, politics, as the party of which you are the head. And
you are let to speak, to sneer, insinuate, deny, assert exactly what
you please. Say a Mormonite Gospel is an absurd and monstrous
dupery in my eyes ; so I believe is a winking statue. But the man
who advocates either is welcome to publish his belief in this
country, where the mischief is met not by persecution, but by free
discussion, and where JOE SMITH's disciples (decently attired)
have as good a right to a sea-baptism as DR. NEWMAN to wear a
hair-shirt or FATHER IGNATIUS to shave his head. How did you
win those two gentlemen over to your side ? By free discussion.
How is the conversion of all England to come about, and the day
when we shall all be down on our marrowbones in the street when
your Eminence walks it ? By more free discussion, more books,
more preaching, more pamphlets, more cuts at the Established
Church and what not. We can't have that commission of inquiry
as yet in your own particular interest ; otherwise your shop would
be shut as well as other people's, and your preachers would be as
mum as the MADIAI. In our field the wholesome literature and
the bad, the tares and the wheat, must grow up together, and,
saving your Eminent presence, that is very likely the reason why
some of the rubbish, stamped with the tiara and cross keys, and
guaranteed with a '*permissu Superiorum*,' is allowed to pass
current in the country. Mischievous works, forsooth ! pernicious
literature ! degraded superstitions ! absurd Almanacs ! A most
eminent Lord ! Don't you think for absurdity, for superstition,
for mischief and folly, there are books published by your own
people that can equal FRANCIS MOORE, the Radical press, the
Penny Novelist, or

Your obedient humble servant,

PUNCH ?

A SECOND LETTER TO AN EMINENT PERSONAGE.[1]

BSURDITY and superstition, mischief and folly, a friend cries to me on perusing my letter to your Eminence in the last number as ever was of this Miscellany. ' My good MR. PUNCH, what expressions are these to use concerning a great body of Christians, and to their chief in this country ! What is the use of hard words ? What call have you to be putting your old nose into the quarrel, and is it (the quarrel I mean) not much better carried on without your interference ?'

What right have his Eminence, NICHOLAS CARDINAL WISE-MAN, and *The Tablet* newspaper to tell the public that they would like to appoint a censorship over our literature ? My good Sir, I pay taxes in Fleet Street as well as his Eminence in Golden Square—I am *Civis Romanus* as well as the Prince of the Flaminian Gate, and have as good a right to say my say as MR. LUCAS. Nor, upon common occasions, can there be any earthly use in using such naughty words as superstition, absurdity, folly, etc., to any body of brother Englishmen.

Your Eminence does not use a hard word—you are as mild as milk—you would just like to have a little censorship over us, for the sake of the poor benighted peasantry and mechanics in these islands—just to see that lies are not told to them, and they are kept out of harm's way. Were you in a situation of political influence you would strongly urge the importance of an inquiry—that's all. What on earth is the good of being angry ?

Potztausend Donnerwetter ! Corpo di Bacco ! Mille tonnerres d'un petit bonhomme ! When you propose, ever so politely, to gag the press of this country, we intend to be in a

[1] [September 23, 1854.]

rage.   Sing, chant, shave, wear hats as broad as you like, gloves
as crimson, stockings or no stockings.   No man wants to meddle
with you.   But leave us and our liberty alone.   We will not
have it gagged or shorn in the Roman fashion, and at the
slightest hint of your desires that way we shall do our best to
awaken the wrath of our Sovereign Master the British Lion : in
the den of whose magnanimity your Eminence and followers are
welcome to rest in peace, but from whose mane, please the Fates,
you shall not shear a single hair.   Poor, decrepit, toothless old
FRANCIS MOORE !   Why should he not be let on to mumble his
old humbugs ?   The old gentleman has nearly lied himself out ;
and quakes his old prophecies to but a very very few old women.
Need we send for familiars of the Inquisition to clap a handker-
chief over his face and drag him away to the Holy Office ?   To
let him talk on is best—to let everybody speak.   He has as good
a right to preach and to frighten his congregations and to conjure
the stars and to bawl out his abracadabra, as any other professor.
And it is because you would persecute him that I am moved,
yea, feel constrained to say, ' O sir, have you not also got a
grimoire, and a wonder-book, that seems to us unbelievers no
better than friend FRANCIS's hocus-pocus ? '

I said 'absurd,' I said 'mischievous.'   I beg my son,
MASTER PUNCH, to take down from the bookshelf some amusing
volumes which I keep there, to wit, the *Essay on Development*
and the *Lives of the English Saints*, written by several clerical
gentlemen who, no doubt, have knelt long ere this at your
Eminence's feet.   I declare, on my conscience, that the credulity
which FRANCIS MOORE, Physician, would have of us is a trifle
compared to that demanded by your Doctors.   Read, my son,
from the *Essay on Development*, the proper way in which the
faithful should receive the stories regarding the Church.

MASTER PUNCH reads—

Mythical representations, at least in their better form, may be considered facts, or narratives untrue, but like the truth. . . . The same
remark may be made upon certain narratives of martyrdom or of the
details of such narratives, or of certain alleged miracles, or heroic acts
or speeches, all of which are the spontaneous produce of religious
feeling under imperfect knowledge.   If the alleged facts did not occur,
they ought to have occurred (if I may so speak) ; they are such as
might have occurred, and would have occurred under circumstances ;
and they belong to the parties to whom they are attributed potentially,
if not actually.—*Development*, 345.

Now is a doctrine like that absurd or not ? mischievous or

not? Would you have country village-folk instructed in history after this fashion, your reverences providing the details? Would our friend the Astrologer ask for better laws of evidence, and upon such might he not call upon the people to believe in his friars, FRIAR BACON and FRIAR BUNGAY? Given this, and HER MAJESTY'S Inspectors of Schools ought to examine boys in *The Seven Champions of Christendom*, and put *King Arthur* and *Jack the Giant Killer* in their place in English history. Read me my favourite little bit about SAINT GERMANUS, my dear, from *The Lives of the English Saints*. MASTER PUNCH reads—

While SAINT GERMANUS was in this country (449) the Saxons made one of their annual inroads into Britain. SAINT GERMANUS (an old soldier), upon information that the combined armies of the Saxons and Picts were approaching, at once resolved on putting himself at the head of the British forces. Having led the troops into a narrow defile, he gave orders to them what to do. When the Saxons drew near with all the confidence of men secure of victory, the holy Bishop pronounced three successive times the word ALLELUIA, which was immediately taken up by the whole British army and chanted in chorus. The sound was repeated and reverberated by the echo from the mountains, and with such violence that the rocks and even the very heavens themselves seemed to tremble. The barbarians, supposing so loud a shout must issue from an immense body of men, threw down their arms and ran away in all directions.

Now, I can beat this with a hundred extracts out of *The Golden Legend* (which is in the book-case yonder), but I will trouble your Eminence to match it out of FRANCIS MOORE. Suppose the country restored to the faith of our fathers, suppose an army under NICHOLAS of Westminster advantageously posted along Oxford Street; Holborn in possession of the enemy; and an army of Greek schismatics under NICHOLAS of Petersburg, and his son, with a battery of guns before the Marble Arch. NICHOLAS (the Czar) is about to open his fire. NICHOLAS the Cardinal orders three volleys of Alleluia along his whole line, and away goes the Calmuck horse, foot, and dragoons, leaving guns, standards, muskets, lances, knouts, etc., behind them! Would you, on your conscience as an Englishman, and 'supposing you were in an influential military position,' handle the British army in that way? Is that story not in your books? Do you believe in it, or any part of it. Ought it to have occurred? Did SAINT GERMANUS so defeat the Picts and Danes potentially? Pooh!

Now, my dear child, read me that bit about my darling Saint, SAINT GUNDLE.

SAINT GUNDLE was a king in Glamorganshire about 500 ; his wife was GLADUSA, one of the ten daughters of KING BRACHAN. One night a supernatural voice broke in on the slumbers of GUNDLE and GLADUSA, and said, ' The King of Heaven hath called me hither. . . . I will show you the straight path which you must keep, unto the heritance of God. —Lift up your minds, and for what is perishable, slight not your souls. On the river's bank is a rising ground ; and where a white steed is grazing there is thy habitation.'

The king arose in the morning ; he gave up his sovereignty to his son CADOC ; he left his house, he proceeded to the hill, and found the animal described. There he built a church, and there he began an abstinent and saintly life ; his dress a hair-cloth, his drink water, his bread of barley mixed with wood ashes. He rose at midnight and plunged into cold water, and by day he laboured for his livelihood.— *St. Gundleus,* 7.

There's a king in Glamorganshire for you ? *The King of Heaven* sent a messenger to him to leave his wife, live on a rising hill, dress in hair-cloth, mix wood ashes with his barley-bread, and jump into cold water at midnight ! In another charming passage, in the life of sweet SAINT EBBA, we are told regarding SAINT CUTHBERT that—

It is well known that SAINT CUTHBERT carried the jealousy of inter-course with women, characteristic of all Saints, to a very extraordinary pitch. . . . Yet such was the reputation of EBBA's sanctity and the spiritual wisdom of her discourse, that SAINT BEDE informs us that when she sent messengers to the man of God, he went and stopped several days in conversation with her, going out of the gates at night-fall, and spending the hours of darkness in prayer, either up to his neck in the water, or in the chilly air.—*St. Ebba,* 114.

And we may be sure the Chronicler speaks in terms poetic and respectful of ' the hair shirts and the iron girdles, and the secret spikes corroding the flesh, and the long weals of the heavy discipline, and the craving thirst, and the stone pillow and the cold vigil,' which these good souls applied to one another, and would recommend to posterity.

If Absurdity and Superstition, mischief and folly, are hard words,—as hard I own they are,—are they too hard ? But I think with all this in your calendar, your Eminence is harder still upon poor old FRANCIS MOORE'S.

Put up the precious volumes, little PUNCH, my son ! I have done. I am going to call no more hard names ; and would live in peace with every gentleman, and have him say his prayers as best likes him. Good SAINT EDMUND, as I read, 'would so spend the whole night, beating his breast, and falling with his bare knees on the floor, *in such a way as to disturb the sleep of his clerks who were lodged beneath.*' I know not if your present Eminence bumps up and down in this manner, or if you sleep over your secretaries, MONSIGNOR SEARLE and MR. GAYTHORN— in that case, it is them I would pity; not with your Lordship I would interfere. May you have a quiet life, and give us one! May all mollahs, priests, rabbis, have peace! May bishops in our native shovel-hats, or pontiffs in those more extensive tiles which roof the heads of the Roman clergy, have the respect of their flocks, and preach and practise to their edification! But prythee, my good Lord Cardinal, leave us alone, standing on our ancient Anglo-Saxon ways. Bring no Roman Sbirri to guide us. We wish to be allied with our friends in France; but we desire to keep our free press too. *The Tablet* says rightly that 'the Index of Prohibited Books is of all things the most scorned and hated of Protestants.' Yes. And we won't have it, however much, as one of the Indicators, your Eminence may recommend it. We won't have it: by SAINT GUTHLAC and SAINT GUNDLE!

PUNCH.

AUTHORS' MISERIES.

AUTHORS' MISERIES.

No. I.

PERHAPS you flatter yourself that you have made an impression on Miss Flannigan (at Worthing), and you find her asleep over your favourite Number.

No. II.

As you are conducting Lady Gotobed to her carriage from Lady Highjinks' 'Noble party,' and fancying yourself a man of fashion, you hear the servants in the hall saying one to another, 'That's him—that's Poonch!'

No. III.

HAVING corresponded with Miss Rudge, the gifted Poetess (authoress of *Floranthe, The Lovelock of Montrose, Moans of the Heart-strings*, etc.), and exchanged portraits and your own poems with her, you meet at last.

You are disappointed in her appearance and find her about forty years older than her picture; perhaps you, too, have grown rather fat and seedy since yours was taken in the year 1817.

No. IV.

As you are labouring on your great work (in a style, let us add, equal to the subject) LADY ANNA MARIA TOMNODDY'S compliments arrive, and she requests you will cast your eye over the accompanying manuscript, in six volumes, *The Mysteries of Mayfair*, correct the errors, if any, and find a publisher for the same.

N.B.—You have in your bookcase Captain Bangles's *Buffaloes and Banyan Trees* in MS. ; the Rev. Mr. Growl's *Sermons to a Congregation at Swansea*, ditto, ditto ; Miss Piminy's *Wildflower Coronal, a Wreath of Village Poesy ;* and Mr. Clapperton's six *Manuscript Tragedies ;* of all of which you are requested to give your opinion.

No. V.

THE Printer's boy is sitting in the hall; the Editor has written to say that your last contributions are not up to the mark, and that you must be more funny, if you please. MR. SNIP, the tailor, has called again that morning. You have a splitting headache, from a transaction over-night, and as you are writing an exceedingly light and humorous article, your dear ANNA MARIA wishes to know how you *dare* dine at Greenwich, and with whom you dined?

I suppose she found the bill in your coat-pocket. How changed ANNA MARIA is from what she was when you married her! and how uncommonly ill-tempered she has grown!

No. VI.

Old Gentleman. 'I am sorry to see you occupied, my dear Miss Wiggets, with that trivial paper *Punch!* A railway is not a place, in my opinion, for jokes. I never joke—never.'

Miss W. 'So I should think, sir.'

Old Gentleman. 'And besides, are you aware who are the conductors of the paper, and that they are Chartists, Deists, Antichrists, and Socialists, to a man? I have it from the best authority, that they meet together once a week in a tavern in St. Giles's, where they concoct their infamous Print. The chief part of their income is derived from threatening letters which they send to the nobility and gentry. The principal writer is a returned convict. Two have been tried at the Old Bailey; and their Artist—as for their Artist . . .

Guard. 'Swin–dun! Sta–tion!'

OLD GENTLEMAN.   MISS WIGGETS.   TWO AUTHORS.

No. VII.

MR. TIMS AND A GOOD-NATURED FRIEND.

G. N. F. 'Have you read the *Macadamiser*, Tims ? '

T. 'Hem ! no. Do people read the *Macadamiser* ? '

G. N. F. 'He, he ! I say, Tims, there's a most unjustifiable attack upon you in it. Look here.' (*He kindly takes out the* '*Macadamiser.*')

T. (*reads*) ' " This person is before us again. He is ignorant, vulgar, and a cockney. He is one of that most contemptible race of men, a professional buffoon. He is," ' etc., etc. (TIMS *reads ad libitum.*) 'Thank you, my dear fellow ; it was uncommonly good-natured of you to bring the critique.'

I. SOCIAL CUTS.

THE HAMPSTEAD ROAD.[1]

A COMEDY IN FOUR TABLEAUX.

TABLEAU I.

'THE MAGNOLIAS,' MR. SMITH'S NEAT COTTAGE IN THE
HAMPSTEAD ROAD.

NURSE (*behind the shrubbery*). O you darling tootsy pootsy.
BABY. Gllgrllwgllgelluggle.
NURSE. Baby see pooty flowers?
CLOCK (*from cottage*). Ting, ting, ting, ting, ting, ting.

[1] [July 15, 1848.]

2 E

Tableau II.

Enter Policeman X.21.

Clock goes on. Ting, ting, ting, ting, ting, ting.

X.21 (*whistles*). Whew-e-oo-o-oo !

Nurse. Come and see pooty osses in the zoad, baby.

TABLEAU III.

X.21. Well, I declare! it's Miss MARY.

NURSE. Law! Mr. Pleaceman; who ever expected to see you here!

X.21. You *do* look so——

BABY. Googleglooggrrr.

MRS. SMITH (*from window*). Well, if it isn't that good-for-nothing hussy of a nurse speaking to the policeman.

NURSE. Lor, it's Missis! }
BABY. Gloogloogrl.   }   [*Exeunt omnes.*
X.21. Blow her old hi's!   }

Tableau IV.

THE HALL OF MR. SMITH'S COTTAGE.

MRS. SMITH. Get out, you imperence. Give me my child; you pollute it, you vicious wretch, you do. Take your wages and go.

BABY. Boo-ooo-ooo-wah-wah-wah.

PAGE (*snivels*).

MARY (*with a last look at the child, exit*). [*Exeunt omnes.*

MARY becomes Mrs. X.21; at first she often walks up the Hampstead Road to look at the baby she has left. Then she has domestic cares of her own, or will have; for the truth is, I only saw the first three Tableaux of this comedy last Saturday as ever was.   SPEC.

ASSUMPTION OF ARISTOCRACY.

'Give that card to your master, and say a gentleman wants to see him.'

THE HEAVIES.[1]

I.

Captain Ragg and Cornet Famish. (*Scene—The Park.*)

R. 'See that dem Mulligan dwive by, with that dem high-stepping haws? Iwishman Mulligan—hate Iwishmen.'

F. 'I hate them because they dress so like Tigers. Hate a man who don't dress quietly.'

R. 'Dem 'em, so do Ay.'

[1] [August 15, 1846.]

THE HEAVIES.

II.

CAPTAIN RAGG DICTATING TO CORNET FAMISH.

Ragg. 'Our wedgment is awdrd abwawd.'
Famish. 'Ordered abroad?'
Ragg. 'And I cannot leave my deawest Anna Mawia.'
Famish. 'I cannot leave my dear Miss Baker.'
Ragg. 'Without a stwuggle.'
Famish. 'Without a · · · Hang it. I say, Ragg!'
Ragg. 'Whawt?'
Famish. 'How d'ye spell "struggle"? with one G or two?'
Ragg. 'O—demy—twy thwee G's, Famish, my boy.'

THE EXCITEMENT IN BELGRAVIA.

MR. BUTCHER *and* MASTER BUTCHER-BOY.

'Now, BILL, have you took the leg of mutton to 29, and the sweetbread to 24?'

'Yes, master.'

'Well, now your work is done—you'll take this bit of chalk and chalk up "No Popry." Do you ear?'

'Why, master?'

'Why, because "Popes is enemies to butcher's meat on Fridays," and Britons will have none of 'em.'   [*Exit* BILL.

THE EXCITEMENT IN BELGRAVIA.

JEAMES *and the* BUTLER.

Jeames. Aving now igsamined my satiffigite, and found my figger satasfactury, elow me to hask one question—is Sir John's a High-Church family, Mr. Brown? and do you fast, according to the rubric, hevery Friday in the year? because in this case, the place will not do for me.

Butler. MR. JEAMES, we will try and get you a dispensation.

A CARD PARTY.

THE ASCOT CUP DAY.[1]

'Why are you on the crossing, James？ Is your father Hill？'
'No. He's drove Mother down to Hascot.'

[1] [June 28, 1845.]

[This drawing was included in John Leech's *Pictures of Life and Character ;* but Mr. M. H. Spielmann, the historian of *Punch,* states 'there is no doubt that the drawing came from Thackeray, and was duly credited to him in the editorial book.']

THE STAGS. A DRAMA OF TO-DAY.

DRAMATIS PERSONAE.

Tom Stag, a Retired Thimblerigger.
Jim Stag, an Unfortunate Costermonger.

(*Tom dictates to Jim.*)

Name in full . .	'*Victor Wellesley Delancey.*'
Residence . . .	'*Staglands, Bucks.*'
Profession . . .	'*Major-General*, K.C.B., K.T.S., K.S.W.'
Reference . . .	{ '*His Grace the Duke of Wellington.* *Sir Robert Peel. Coutts and Co.*'

'That'll do. Now, Mary, a vafer ; and, Jim, I don't mind
standing a pint of alf and alf!'

MR. NEBUCHADNEZZAR AND THE WAITER.

Mr. Nebuchadnezzar. 'What is there for dinner, waiter?'
Waiter. 'Sir, a nice Leg of Pork is just come up.'

[Nebuchadnezzar sits down, and helps himself to pig, crackling, sage and onions and all.]

ONE 'WHO CAN MINISTER TO A MIND DISEASED.'

'You seem in low spirits, Jem; you really should go into Society.'

MAY DIFFERENCE OF OPINION NEVER ALTER FRIENDSHIP.

Dumpy Young Lady. 'Well, for my part, Matilda, I like long Waists and Flounces.'

A SCENE IN ST. JAMES'S PARK.

A TEA-TABLE TRAGEDY.

Miss Potts. 'Married her Uncle's black footman, as I'm a sinful woman.'

Mrs. Potts. 'No ?'

Mrs. Watts. 'O !'

Miss Watts. 'Law !!'

HALF-AN-HOUR BEFORE DINNER.

NIMINY and PIMINY staring at the ladies seated in a circle in the drawing-room.

Niminy. 'That's a fain woman in yallah.'
Piminy. 'H'm!—pooty well,'

HORRID TRAGEDY IN PRIVATE LIFE.[1]

[1] [February 6, 1847.]

['This was a drawing,' Mr. M. H. Spielmann remarks in *The History of 'Punch,'* 'representing a room in which two ladies, or a lady and a servant, are in the state of the greatest alarm. What the meaning of it all is there is nothing whatever to indicate (unless it be that something has fallen on the taller lady's dress), and on its appearance *The Man in the Moon* offered a reward of £100 and a free pardon to any one who would publish an explanation. The reward was never claimed, and Thackeray's contribution remains one of *Punch's* Prize Puzzles, unsolved, and apparently unsolvable.'

Mr. Ritchie, however, has since furnished the explanation. The room was Thackeray's study, and where his two little girls were found by him dressed up in various tablecloths and curtains. One was enacting a queen, and was ordering the rival sovereign off to instant execution, when he came home unexpectedly, and drew them then and there.]

LITERATURE AT A STAND.

'I say, Jim, vich do you give the prufferance, Eugene Shue or Halexander Dumas?'

A SIDE-BOX TALK.

Roguy. SEE THAT GIRL LOOKING AT ME, POGUY?

Poguy. DON'T I? I DECLARE SHE CAN'T KEEP HER EYES OFF YOU.

Roguy. WHAT WOMEN CARE FOR, POGUY, MY BOY, IS NOT FEATURES, BUT EXPRESSION.

[He pokes POGUY *in the waistcoat.*

DOMESTIC SCENES—SERVED WITH A WRIT.

II. MISCELLANEOUS SKETCHES.

ADVERTISEMENT TO PERSONS IN WANT OF A BROUGHAM.

RECOLLECTIONS OF THE OPERA.

THE FLYING DUKE.

PUNCH'S CONDENSED MAGAZINE.

THE LOWLY BARD TO HIS LADY LOVE.

THEATRICAL INTELLIGENCE EXTRAORDINARY.

TALES FOR THE MARINES.

PIRATICAL EXPEDITIONS.

TREATMENT OF PICTURES IN THE NATIONAL GALLERY.

THEATRICAL ASTRONOMY.

Sudden Appearance of a Star.

HOBSON'S CHOICE:[1]

OR THE PERPLEXITIES OF A GENTLEMAN IN SEARCH OF A SERVANT.

[1] [See vol. xvii. p. 359, of this edition : *Travels in London, etc.*]

THE CABINET AND COLONEL SIBTHORP.

THE GUARDS AND THE LINE.

WHITEBAIT DINNER TO SIR ROBERT PEEL.

MATRIMONIAL DICTIONARY.

THE TWO INCAPABLES.

NAVAL OPERATIONS.

A PERILOUS PRECEDENT.

THE COURT APOLLO

DEBATE ON THE NAVY.

THE FOOTMAN.

THE GOMERSAL MUSEUM.

POPULAR MOVEMENT.   MUSIC IN EBONY.

THE ASTLEY - NAPOLEON MUSEUM.

GRAND JUNCTION: OR, VALUE OF HEATH OF LIVERPOOL.

MR. MOLONY ON THE POSITION OF THE BAR AND ATTORNEYS.

'OUR HOME EXPRESSES.'

ADMIRALTY AND ASSISTANT-SURVEYORS.

THE END

Printed by R. & R. CLARK, LIMITED, *Edinburgh.*

MACMILLAN'S THREE-AND-SIXPENNY LIBRARY OF BOOKS BY POPULAR AUTHORS

Crown 8vo.

THIS SERIES comprises over four hundred volumes in various departments of Literature. Prominent among them is a new and attractive edition of The Works of Thackeray, *issued under the editorship of Mr. Lewis Melville. It contains all the Original Illustrations, and includes a great number of scattered pieces and illustrations which have not hitherto appeared in any collected edition of the works.* The Works of Charles Dickens, *reprinted from the first editions, with all the Original Illustrations, and with Introductions, Biographical and Bibliographical, by Charles Dickens the Younger, and an attractive edition of* The Novels of Charles Lever, *illustrated by Phiz and G. Cruik-*

*shank, have also a place in the Library.
The attention of book buyers may be especially directed to* The Border Edition
of the Waverley Novels, *edited by Mr.
Andrew Lang, which, with its large type
and convenient form, and its copious illustrations by well-known artists, possesses
features which place it in the forefront of
editions now obtainable of the famous novels.*
The Works of Mr. Thomas Hardy, *including the poems, have also been added
to the Three-and-Sixpenny Library.*

*Among other works by notable con-
temporary authors will be found those of*
Mr. F. Marion Crawford, Rolf Boldrewood,
Mr. H. G. Wells, Gertrude Atherton, Mr.
Egerton Castle, Mr. A. E. W. Mason,
Maarten Maartens, *and* Miss Rosa Nou-
chette Carey ; *while among the productions
of an earlier period may be mentioned the
works of* Charles Kingsley, Frederick Deni-
son Maurice, Thomas Hughes, *and* Dean
Farrar ; *and the novels and tales of* Charlotte
M. Yonge, Mrs. Craik, *and* Mrs. Oliphant.

THE

WORKS OF THACKERAY

*Reprints of the First Editions, with all the Original Illustrations,
and with Facsimiles of Wrappers, etc.*

Messrs. MACMILLAN & CO., Limited, beg leave to invite the
attention of book buyers to the Edition of THE WORKS OF
THACKERAY in their Three-and-Sixpenny Library, which is the
Completest Edition of the Author's Works that has been placed
on the market.

The Publishers have been fortunate in securing the services of
Mr. LEWIS MELVILLE, the well-known Thackeray Expert. With
his assistance they have been able to include in this Edition a
great number of scattered pieces from Thackeray's pen, and illustrations from his pencil which have not hitherto been contained in
any collected edition of the works. Mr. Melville has read all
the sheets as they passed through the press, and collated them
carefully with the original editions. He has also provided Bibliographical Introductions and occasional Footnotes.

List of the Series.

VOL.

1. Vanity Fair. With 190 Illustrations.

2. The History of Pendennis. With 180
   Illustrations.

3. The Newcomes. With 167 Illustrations

4. The History of Henry Esmond.

5. The Virginians. With 148 Illustrations.

6. Barry Lyndon and Catherine. With 4
   Illustrations.

7. The Paris and Irish Sketch Books. With
   63 Illustrations.

MACMILLAN'S
EDITION OF THACKERAY

SOME OPINIONS OF THE PRESS

EXPOSITORY TIMES.—"An edition to do credit even to this publishing house, and not likely to be surpassed until they surpass it with a cheaper and better themselves."

WHITEHALL REVIEW.—"Never before has such a cheap and excellent edition of Thackeray been seen."

ACADEMY.—"A better one-volume edition at three shillings and sixpence could not be desired."

GRAPHIC.—"In its plain but pretty blue binding is both serviceable and attractive."

DAILY GRAPHIC.—"An excellent, cheap reprint."

PALL MALL GAZETTE.—"The size of the books is handy, paper and printing are good, and the binding, which is of blue cloth, is simple but tasteful. Altogether the publishers are to be congratulated upon a reprint which ought to be popular."

GLOBE.—"The paper is thin but good, the type used is clear to read, and the binding is neat and effective."

LADY'S PICTORIAL.—"The paper is good, the type clear and large, and the binding tasteful. Messrs. Macmillan are to be thanked for so admirable and inexpensive an edition of our great satirist."

WORLD.—"Nothing could be better than the new edition."

BLACK AND WHITE.—"The more one sees of the edition the more enamoured of it he becomes. It is so good and neat, immaculate as to print, and admirably bound."

SCOTSMAN.—"This admirable edition."

LITERARY WORLD.—"The paper and printing and general get up are everything that one could desire."

ST. JAMES'S GAZETTE.—"A clear and pretty edition."

THE

WORKS OF DICKENS

Reprints of the First Editions, with all the original Illustrations,
and with Introductions, Biographical and Bibliographical,
by CHARLES DICKENS the Younger.

THE PICKWICK PAPERS. With 50 Illustrations.

OLIVER TWIST. With 27 Illustrations.

NICHOLAS NICKLEBY. With 44 Illustrations.

MARTIN CHUZZLEWIT. With 41 Illustrations.

THE OLD CURIOSITY SHOP. With 97 Illustrations.

BARNABY RUDGE. With 76 Illustrations.

DOMBEY AND SON. With 40 Illustrations.

CHRISTMAS BOOKS. With 65 Illustrations.

SKETCHES BY BOZ. With 44 Illustrations.

AMERICAN NOTES AND PICTURES FROM ITALY. With 4 Illustrations.

DAVID COPPERFIELD. With 40 Illustrations.

BLEAK HOUSE. With 43 Illustrations.

LITTLE DORRIT. With 40 Illustrations.

THE LETTERS OF CHARLES DICKENS.

A TALE OF TWO CITIES. With 15 Illustrations.

GREAT EXPECTATIONS; AND HARD TIMES.

OUR MUTUAL FRIEND. With 40 Illustrations.

MACMILLAN'S
EDITION OF DICKENS

SOME OPINIONS OF THE PRESS

ATHENÆUM.—"Handy in form, well printed, illustrated with reproductions of the original plates, introduced with bibliographical notes by the novelist's son, and above all issued at a most moderate price, this edition will appeal successfully to a large number of readers."

SPEAKER.—"We do not think there exists a better edition."

MORNING POST.—"The edition will be highly appreciated."

SCOTSMAN.—"This reprint offers peculiar attractions. Of a handy size, in one volume, of clear, good-sized print, and with its capital comic illustrations, it is a volume to be desired."

NEWCASTLE CHRONICLE.—"The most satisfactory edition of the book that has been issued."

GLASGOW HERALD.—"None of the recent editions of Dickens can be compared with that which Messrs. Macmillan inaugurate with the issue of *Pickwick.* . . . Printed in a large, clear type, very readable."

GLOBE.—"They have used an admirably clear type and good paper, and the binding is unexceptionable. . . . May be selected as the most desirable cheap edition of the immortal ' Papers ' that has ever been offered to the public."

MANCHESTER EXAMINER.—"Handy in form, well printed, illustrated with reduced reproductions of the original plates, introduced with bibliographical notes by the novelist's son, and above all issued at a moderate price, this edition will appeal successfully to a large number of readers."

THE QUEEN.—"A specially pleasant and convenient form in which to re-read Dickens."

THE STAR.—"This new ' Dickens Series,' with its reproductions of the original illustrations, is a joy to the possessor."

Complete in Twenty-four Volumes. Crown 8vo, tastefully bound in green cloth, gilt. Price 3s. 6d. each.

In special cloth binding, flat backs, gilt tops. Supplied in Sets only of 24 volumes. Price £4 4s.

Also an edition with all the 250 original etchings. In 24 volumes. Crown 8vo, gilt tops. Price 6s. each.

THE LARGE TYPE
BORDER EDITION OF THE
WAVERLEY NOVELS

EDITED WITH

INTRODUCTORY ESSAYS AND NOTES

BY

ANDREW LANG
SUPPLEMENTING THOSE OF THE AUTHOR.

With Two Hundred and Fifty New and Original Illustrations by Eminent Artists.

BY the kind permission of the Hon. Mrs. MAXWELL-SCOTT, of Abbotsford, the great-granddaughter of Sir WALTER, the MSS. and other material at Abbotsford were examined by Mr. ANDREW LANG during the preparation of his Introductory Essays and Notes to the Series, so that the BORDER EDITION may be said to contain all the results of the latest researches as to the composition of the Waverley Novels.

The Border Waverley

1. WAVERLEY. With 12 Illustrations by Sir H. RAE-
   BURN, R.A., R. W. MACBETH, A.R.A., JOHN PETTIE, R.A.,
   H. MACBETH-RAEBURN, D. HERDMAN, W. J. LEITCH,
   ROBERT HERDMAN, R.S.A., and J. ECKFORD LAUDER.

2. GUY MANNERING. With 10 Illustrations by J.
   MACWHIRTER, A.R.A., R. W. MACBETH, A.R.A., C. O.
   MURRAY, CLARK STANTON, R.S.A., GOURLAY STEELL,
   R.S.A., F. S. WALKER, R. HERDMAN, R.S.A., and J. B.
   MACDONALD, A.R.S.A.

3. THE ANTIQUARY. With 10 Illustrations by J.
   MACWHIRTER, A.R.A., SAM BOUGH, R.S.A., R. HERD-
   MAN, R.S.A., W. M'TAGGART, A.R.S.A., J. B. MAC-
   DONALD, A.R.S.A., and A. H. TOURRIER.

4. ROB ROY. With 10 Illustrations by R. W. MACBETH,
   A.R.A., and SAM BOUGH, R.S.A.

5. OLD MORTALITY. With 10 Illustrations by J. MAC-
   WHIRTER, A.R.A., R. HERDMAN, R.S.A., SAM BOUGH,
   R.S.A., M. L. GOW, D. Y. CAMERON, LOCKHART BOGLE,
   and ALFRED HARTLEY.

6. THE HEART OF MIDLOTHIAN. With 10 Illustra-
   tions by Sir J. E. MILLAIS, Bart., HUGH CAMERON, R.S.A.,
   SAM BOUGH, R.S.A., R. HERDMAN, R.S.A., and WAL.
   PAGET.

7. A LEGEND OF MONTROSE and THE BLACK DWARF.
   With 7 Illustrations by Sir GEORGE REID, P.R.S.A.,
   GEORGE HAY, R.S.A., HORATIO MACCULLOCH, R.S.A.
   W. E. LOCKHART, R.S.A., H. MACBETH-RAEBURN, and
   T. SCOTT.

8. THE BRIDE OF LAMMERMOOR. With 8 Illustrations
   by Sir J. E. MILLAIS, Bart., JOHN SMART, R.S.A., SAM
   BOUGH, R.S.A., GEORGE HAY, R.S.A., and H. MACBETH-
   RAEBURN.

9. IVANHOE. With 12 Illustrations by AD. LALAUZE.

10. THE MONASTERY. With 10 Illustrations by GOR-
    DON BROWNE.

11. THE ABBOT. With 10 Illustrations by GORDON
    BROWNE.

The Border Waverley

12. KENILWORTH. With 12 Illustrations by AD. LALAUZE.

13. THE PIRATE. With 10 Illustrations by W. E. LOCKHART, R.S.A., SAM BOUGH, R.S.A., HERBERT DICKSEE, W. STRANG, LOCKHART BOGLE, C. J. HOLMES, and F. S. WALKER.

14. THE FORTUNES OF NIGEL. With 10 Illustrations by JOHN PETTIE, R.A., and R. W. MACBETH, A.R.A.

15. PEVERIL OF THE PEAK. With 15 Illustrations by W. Q. ORCHARDSON, R.A. JOHN PETTIE, R.A., F. DADD, R.I., ARTHUR HOPKINS, A.R.W.S., and S. L. WOOD.

16 QUENTIN DURWARD. With 12 Illustrations by AD. LALAUZE.

17. ST. RONAN'S WELL. With 10 Illustrations by Sir G. REID, P.R.S.A., R. W. MACBETH, A.R.A., W. HOLE, R.S.A., and A. FORESTIER.

18. REDGAUNTLET. With 12 Illustrations by Sir JAMES D. LINTON, P.R.I., JAMES ORROCK, R.I., SAM BOUGH, R.S.A., W. HOLE, R.S.A., G. HAY, R.S.A., T. SCOTT, A.R.S.A., W. BOUCHER, and FRANK SHORT.

19. THE BETROTHED and THE TALISMAN. With 10 Illustrations by HERBERT DICKSEE, WAL. PAGET, and J. LE BLANT.

20. WOODSTOCK. With 10 Illustrations by W. HOLE, R.S.A.

21. THE FAIR MAID OF PERTH. With 10 Illustrations by Sir G. REID, P.R.S.A., JOHN PETTIE, R.A., R. W. MACBETH, A.R.A., and ROBERT HERDMAN, R.S.A.

22. ANNE OF GEIERSTEIN. With 10 Illustrations by R. DE LOS RIOS.

23. COUNT ROBERT OF PARIS and THE SURGEON'S DAUGHTER. With 10 Illustrations by W. HATHERELL, R.I., and W. B. WOLLEN, R.I.

24. CASTLE DANGEROUS, CHRONICLES OF THE CANON-GATE, ETC. With 10 Illustrations by H. MACBETH-RAE-BURN and G. D. ARMOUR.

The Border Waverley
SOME OPINIONS OF THE PRESS

TIMES.—"It would be difficult to find in these days a more competent and sympathetic editor of Scott than his countryman, the brilliant and versatile man of letters who has undertaken the task, and if any proof were wanted either of his qualifications or of his skill and discretion in displaying them, Mr. Lang has furnished it abundantly in his charming Introduction to 'Waverley.' The editor's own notes are judiciously sparing, but conspicuously to the point, and they are very discreetly separated from those of the author, Mr. Lang's laudable purpose being to illustrate and explain Scott, not to make the notes a pretext for displaying his own critical faculty and literary erudition. The illustrations by various competent hands are beautiful in themselves and beautifully executed, and, altogether, the 'Border Edition' of the Waverley Novels bids fair to become the classical edition of the great Scottish classic."

SPECTATOR.—"We trust that this fine edition of our greatest and most poetical of novelists will attain, if it has not already done so, the high popularity it deserves. To all Scott's lovers it is a pleasure to know that, despite the daily and weekly inrush of ephemeral fiction, the sale of his works is said by the booksellers to rank next below Tennyson's in poetry, and above that of everybody else in prose."

ATHENÆUM.—"The handsome 'Border Edition' has been brought to a successful conclusion. The publisher deserves to be complimented on the manner in which the edition has been printed and illustrated, and Mr. Lang on the way in which he has performed his portion of the work. His introductions have been tasteful and readable; he has not overdone his part; and, while he has supplied much useful information, he has by no means overburdened the volumes with notes."

NOTES AND QUERIES.—"This spirited and ambitious enterprise has been conducted to a safe termination, and the most ideal edition of the Waverley Novels in existence is now completed."

SATURDAY REVIEW.—"Of all the many collections of the Waverley Novels, the 'Border Edition' is incomparably the most handsome and the most desirable. . . . Type, paper, illustrations, are altogether admirable."

MAGAZINE OF ART.—"Size, type, paper, and printing, to say nothing of the excessively liberal and charming introduction of the illustrations, make this perhaps the most desirable edition of Scott ever issued on this side of the Border."

DAILY CHRONICLE.—"There is absolutely no fault to be found with it, as to paper, type, or arrangement."

THE WORKS OF
THOMAS HARDY

Collected Edition

1. TESS OF THE D'URBERVILLES.
2. FAR FROM THE MADDING CROWD.
3. THE MAYOR OF CASTERBRIDGE.
4. A PAIR OF BLUE EYES.
5. TWO ON A TOWER.
6. THE RETURN OF THE NATIVE.
7. THE WOODLANDERS.
8. JUDE THE OBSCURE.
9. THE TRUMPET-MAJOR.
10. THE HAND OF ETHELBERTA.
11. A LAODICEAN.
12. DESPERATE REMEDIES.
13. WESSEX TALES.
14. LIFE'S LITTLE IRONIES.
15. A GROUP OF NOBLE DAMES.
16. UNDER THE GREENWOOD TREE.
17. THE WELL-BELOVED.
18. WESSEX POEMS, and other Verses.
19. POEMS OF THE PAST AND THE PRESENT.

THE

WORKS OF THOMAS HARDY

SOME PRESS OPINIONS OF THE THREE-AND-SIXPENNY ISSUE

PALL MALL GAZETTE.—". . . their charming edition of the works of Thomas Hardy . . . the price asked for it . . . is absurdly cheap. . . . Any more convenient and beautiful form of presentation for these books it would be difficult to find."

ATHENÆUM.—"This edition is so comely and so moderate in price that it may well placate those who have sighed for earlier issues out of their reach. Mr. Hardy's prefaces to the volumes should not be missed, for they are models of a difficult art, whether reflective, informative, or combative."

UNIFORM EDITION OF THE

NOVELS OF CHARLES LEVER

With all the Original Illustrations.

1. HARRY LORREQUER. Illustrated by PHIZ.

2. CHARLES O'MALLEY. Illustrated by PHIZ.

3. JACK HINTON THE GUARDSMAN. Illustrated by PHIZ.

4. TOM BURKE OF OURS. Illustrated by PHIZ.

5. ARTHUR O'LEARY. Illustrated by G. CRUIK-SHANK.

6. LORD KILGOBBIN. Illustrated by LUKE FILDES.

THE NOVELS OF
F. MARION CRAWFORD

MR. ISAACS: A Tale of Modern India.

ATHENÆUM.—"A work of unusual ability. . . . It fully deserves the notice it is sure to attract."

DOCTOR CLAUDIUS: A True Story.

ATHENÆUM.—"Few recent books have been so difficult to lay down when once begun."

A ROMAN SINGER.

TIMES.—"A masterpiece of narrative. . . . Unlike any other romance in English literature."

ZOROASTER.

GUARDIAN.—"An instance of the highest and noblest form of novel. . . . Alike in the originality of its conception and the power with which it is wrought out, it stands on a level that is almost entirely its own."

MARZIO'S CRUCIFIX.

TIMES.—"A subtle compound of artistic feeling, avarice, malice. and criminal frenzy is this carver of silver chalices and crucifixes."

A TALE OF A LONELY PARISH.

GUARDIAN.—"The tale is written with all Mr. Crawford's skill."

PAUL PATOFF.

ST. JAMES'S GAZETTE.—"Those who neglect to read *Paul Patoff* will throw away a very pleasurable opportunity."

WITH THE IMMORTALS.

SPECTATOR.—"Cannot fail to please a reader who enjoys crisp, clear, vigorous writing, and thoughts that are alike original and suggestive."

GREIFENSTEIN.

SPECTATOR.—"Altogether, we like *Greifenstein* decidedly—so much so as to doubt whether it does not dislodge *A Roman Singer* from the place hitherto occupied by the latter as our favourite amongst Mr. Crawford's novels."

TAQUISARA: A Novel.

PALL MALL GAZETTE.—"Cannot fail to be read with interest and pleasure by all to whom clever characterisation and delicate drawing make appeal."

A ROSE OF YESTERDAY.

SPEAKER.—"There is something in *A Rose of Yesterday* which makes the book linger with a distinct aroma of its own in the reader's memory."

SANT' ILARIO.

ATHENÆUM.—"The plot is skilfully concocted, and the interest is sustained to the end. . . . A very clever piece of work."

A CIGARETTE-MAKER'S ROMANCE.

GLOBE.—"We are inclined to think this is the best of Mr. Marion Crawford's stories."

KHALED: A Tale of Arabia.

ANTI-JACOBIN.—"Mr. Crawford has written some stories more powerful, but none more attractive than this."

THE THREE FATES.

NATIONAL OBSERVER.—"Increases in strength and in interest even to the end."

THE WITCH OF PRAGUE.

ACADEMY.—"Is so remarkable a book as to be certain of as wide a popularity as any of its predecessors ; it is a romance of singular daring and power."

THE NOVELS OF
F. MARION CRAWFORD

MARION DARCHE: A Story without Comment.
ATHENÆUM.—"Readers in search of a good novel may be recommended to lose no time in making the acquaintance of Marion Darche, her devoted friends, and her one enemy."

KATHARINE LAUDERDALE.
PUNCH.—"Admirable in its simple pathos, its unforced humour, and, above all, in its truth to human nature."

THE CHILDREN OF THE KING.
DAILY CHRONICLE.—"Mr. Crawford has not done better than *The Children of the King* for a long time. The story itself is a simple and beautiful one."

PIETRO GHISLERI.
SPEAKER.—"Mr. Marion Crawford is an artist, and a great one, and he has been brilliantly successful in a task in which ninety-nine out of every hundred writers would have failed."

DON ORSINO.
ATHENÆUM.—"*Don Orsino* is a story with many strong points, and it is told with all the spirit we have been wont to expect from its author."

CASA BRACCIO.
GUARDIAN.—"A very powerful story and a finished work of art."

ADAM JOHNSTONE'S SON.
DAILY NEWS.—"Mr. Crawford has written stories richer in incident and more powerful in intention, but we do not think that he has handled more deftly or shown a more delicate insight into tendencies that go towards making some of the more spiritual tragedies of life."

THE RALSTONS.
ATHENÆUM.—"The present instalment of what promises to be a very voluminous family history, increasing in interest and power as it develops, turns upon the death of Robert and the disposition of his millions, which afford ample scope for the author's pleasantly ingenious talent in raising and surmounting difficulties of details."

CORLEONE: A Tale of Sicily.
PALL MALL GAZETTE.—"A splendid romance.'

VIA CRUCIS: A Romance of the Second Crusade.
GRAPHIC.—"A stirring story.'

IN THE PALACE OF THE KING: A Love Story of Old Madrid.
SPECTATOR.—"A truly thrilling tale."

CECILIA: A Story of Modern Rome.
ILLUSTRATED LONDON NEWS.—"Can only enhance Mr. Crawford's reputation. . . . Admirably treated with all the subtlety, finesse, and delicacy which are characteristic of the author at his best."

MARIETTA: A Maid of Venice.
PUNCH.—"Marion Crawford is at his very best in *Marietta, A Maid of Venice.* It is a powerfully dramatic story of Venice under 'The Ten,' told in a series of picturesque scenes described in strikingly artistic word-painting, the action being carried on by well-imagined clearly-defined characters."

THE HEART OF ROME.
PALL MALL GAZETTE.—"In freshness, delicacy, and pictorial charm, it has all the marks of its author's best work and his essential spirit."

SOPRANO: A Portrait.
ACADEMY.—"Always interesting, and told with the author's deep knowledge of human nature, and his unvarying charm."

WHOSOEVER SHALL OFFEND . . .
DAILY TELEGRAPH.—"Mr. Marion Crawford's new novel will, it is safe to say, take its place among the most successful and most widely-admired of all his stories. . . . Sure to be read by thousands, and to give pleasure and entertainment wherever it is read."

THE NOVELS OF
ROLF BOLDREWOOD

ROBBERY UNDER ARMS.
A STORY OF LIFE AND ADVENTURE IN THE BUSH AND IN THE GOLD-FIELDS OF AUSTRALIA.

GUARDIAN.—"A singularly spirited and stirring tale of Australian life, chiefly in the remoter settlements."

A MODERN BUCCANEER.
DAILY CHRONICLE.—"We do not forget *Robbery under Arms*, or any of its various successors, when we say that Rolf Boldrewood has never done anything so good as *A Modern Buccaneer*. It is good, too, in a manner which is for the author a new one."

THE MINER'S RIGHT.
A TALE OF THE AUSTRALIAN GOLD-FIELDS.

WORLD.—"Full of good passages, passages abounding in vivacity, in the colour and play of life. . . . The pith of the book lies in its singularly fresh and vivid pictures of the humours of the gold-fields—tragic humours enough they are, too, here and again."

THE SQUATTER'S DREAM.
FIELD.—"The details are filled in by a hand evidently well conversant with his subject, and everything is *ben trovato*, if not actually true. A perusal of these cheerfully-written pages will probably give a better idea of realities of Australian life than could be obtained from many more pretentious works."

A SYDNEY-SIDE SAXON.
GLASGOW HERALD.—"The interest never flags, and altogether *A Sydney-Side Saxon* is a really refreshing book."

A COLONIAL REFORMER.
ATHENÆUM.—"A series of natural and entertaining pictures of Australian life, which are, above all things, readable."

NEVERMORE.
OBSERVER.—"An exciting story of Ballarat in the 'fifties. Its hero, Lance Trevanion, is a character which for force of delineation has no equal in Rolf Boldrewood's previous novels."

PLAIN LIVING. A Bush Idyll.
ACADEMY.—"A hearty story, deriving charm from the odours of the bush and the bleating of incalculable sheep."

MY RUN HOME.
ATHENÆUM.—"Rolf Boldrewood's last story is a racy volume. It has many of the best qualities of Whyte-Melville, the breezy freshness and vigour of Frank Smedley, with the dash and something of the abandon of Lever. . . . His last volume is one of his best."

THE SEALSKIN CLOAK.
TIMES.—"A well-written story."

THE CROOKED STICK; or, Pollie's Probation.
ACADEMY.—"A charming picture of Australian station life."

OLD MELBOURNE MEMORIES.
NATIONAL OBSERVER.—"His book deserves to be read in England with as much appreciation as it has already gained in the country of its birth."

A ROMANCE OF CANVAS TOWN, and other Stories.
ATHENÆUM.—"The book is interesting for its obvious insight into life in the Australian bush."

WAR TO THE KNIFE; or, Tangata Maori.
ACADEMY.—"A stirring romance."

BABES IN THE BUSH.
OUTLOOK.—"A lively and picturesque story."
DAILY TELEGRAPH.—"Bristles with thrilling incident."

IN BAD COMPANY, and other Stories.
DAILY NEWS.—"The best work this popular author has done for some time."

By H. G. WELLS

THE PLATTNER STORY: and others.

TALES OF SPACE AND TIME.

THE STOLEN BACILLUS: and other Incidents.

THE INVISIBLE MAN. A Grotesque Romance.
Eighth Edition.

LOVE AND MR. LEWISHAM. A Story of a very
Young Couple.

WHEN THE SLEEPER WAKES.

THE FIRST MEN IN THE MOON.

TWELVE STORIES AND A DREAM.

THE FOOD OF THE GODS AND HOW IT
Came to Earth.

KIPPS: The Story of a Simple Soul.

By A. E. W. MASON

THE COURTSHIP OF MORRICE BUCKLER.

THE PHILANDERERS.

MIRANDA OF THE BALCONY.

By EGERTON CASTLE

THE BATH COMEDY.

THE PRIDE OF JENNICO. Being a Memoir of
Captain Basil Jennico.

"LA BELLA," AND OTHERS.

"YOUNG APRIL."

By MAARTEN MAARTENS

THE GREATER GLORY. A Story of High Life.

MY LADY NOBODY. A Novel.

GOD'S FOOL. A Koopstad Story.

THE SIN OF JOOST AVELINGH. A Dutch Story.

HER MEMORY.

THE NOVELS OF
ROSA N. CAREY

Nearly 700,000 of these works have been printed.

52nd Thousand.
NELLIE'S MEMORIES.
STANDARD.—"Miss Carey has the gift of writing naturally and simply, her pathos is true and unforced, and her conversations are sprightly and sharp."

38th Thousand.
WEE WIFIE.
LADY.—"Miss Carey's novels are always welcome; they are out of the common run, immaculately pure, and very high in tone."

32nd Thousand.
BARBARA HEATHCOTE'S TRIAL.
DAILY TELEGRAPH.—"A novel or a sort which it would be a real loss to miss."

25th Thousand.
ROBERT ORD'S ATONEMENT.
STANDARD.—"*Robert Ord's Atonement* is a delightful book, very quiet as to its story, but very strong in character, and instinct with that delicate pathos which is the salient point of all the writings of this author."

35th Thousand.
WOOED AND MARRIED.
STANDARD.—"There is plenty of romance in the heroine's life. But it would not be fair to tell our readers wherein that romance consists or how it ends. Let them read the book for themselves. We will undertake to promise that they will like it."

24th Thousand.
HERIOT'S CHOICE.
MORNING POST.—"Deserves to be extensively known and read. . . . Will doubtless find as many admirers as readers."

29th Thousand.
QUEENIE'S WHIM.
GUARDIAN.—"A thoroughly good and wholesome story."

38th Thousand.
NOT LIKE OTHER GIRLS.
PALL MALL GAZETTE.—"Like all the other stories we have had from the same gifted pen, this volume, *Not Like Other Girls*, takes a sane and healthy view of life and its concerns. . . . It is an excellent story to put in the hands of girls."

24th Thousand.
MARY ST. JOHN.
JOHN BULL.—"The story is a simple one, but told with much grace and unaffected pathos."

23rd Thousand.
FOR LILIAS.
VANITY FAIR.—"A simple, earnest, and withal very interesting story; well conceived, carefully worked out, and sympathetically told."

31st Thousand.
UNCLE MAX.
LADY.—"So intrinsically good that the world of novel-readers ought to be genuinely grateful."

21st Thousand.
RUE WITH A DIFFERENCE.
BOOKMAN.—"Fresh and charming. . . . A piece of distinctly good work."

23rd Thousand.
THE HIGHWAY OF FATE.
BOOKMAN.—"This pretty love story . . . is charming, sparkling, and never mawkish."

THE NOVELS OF
ROSA N. CAREY

Nearly 700,000 of these works have been printed.

34th Thousand.
ONLY THE GOVERNESS.

PALL MALL GAZETTE.—"This novel is for those who like stories with something of Jane Austen's power, but with more intensity of feeling than Jane Austen displayed, who are not inclined to call pathos twaddle, and who care to see life and human nature in their most beautiful form."

27th Thousand.
LOVER OR FRIEND?

GUARDIAN.—"The refinement of style and delicacy of thought will make *Lover or Friend?* popular with all readers who are not too deeply bitten with a desire for things improbable in their lighter literature."

21st Thousand.
BASIL LYNDHURST.

PALL MALL GAZETTE.—"We doubt whether anything has been written of late years so fresh, so pretty, so thoroughly natural and bright. The novel as a whole is charming."

25th Thousand.
SIR GODFREY'S GRAND-DAUGHTERS.

OBSERVER.—"A capital story. The interest steadily grows, and by the time one reaches the third volume the story has become enthralling."

24th Thousand.
THE OLD, OLD STORY.

DAILY NEWS.—"Miss Carey's fluent pen has not lost its power of writing fresh and wholesome fiction."

27th Thousand.
THE MISTRESS OF BRAE FARM.

PALL MALL GAZETTE.—"Miss Carey's untiring pen loses none of its power, and her latest work is as gracefully written, as full of quiet home charm, as fresh and wholesome, so to speak, as its many predecessors."

14th Thousand.
MRS. ROMNEY and "BUT MEN MUST WORK."

PALL MALL GAZETTE.—"By no means the least attractive of the works of this charming writer."

3rd Thousand.
OTHER PEOPLE'S LIVES.

BRADFORD OBSERVER.—"There is a quiet charm about this story which finds its way into the innermost shrines of life. The book is wholesome and good, and cannot fail to give pleasure to those who love beauty."

25th Thousand.
HERB OF GRACE.

WESTMINSTER GAZETTE.—"A clever delineator of character, possessed of a reserve of strength in a quiet, easy, flowing style, Miss Carey never fails to please a large class of readers. *Herb of Grace* is no exception to the rule. . . ."

22nd Thousand.
A PASSAGE PERILOUS.

TIMES.—"Told with all Miss Carey's usual charm of quiet, well-bred sentiment."

21st Thousand.
AT THE MOORINGS.

DAILY NEWS.—"Miss Carey's many admirers will undoubtedly accord the book a hearty welcome."

18th Thousand.
THE HOUSEHOLD OF PETER.

BOOKMAN.—"A safe and charming book."

THE NOVELS AND TALES OF

CHARLOTTE M. YONGE

THE HEIR OF REDCLYFFE. With Illustrations by KATE GREENAWAY.

HEARTSEASE; or, the Brother's Wife. New Edition. With Illustrations by KATE GREENAWAY.

HOPES AND FEARS; or, Scenes from the Life of a Spinster. With Illustrations by HERBERT GANDY.

DYNEVOR TERRACE; or, the Clue of Life. With Illustrations by ADRIAN STOKES.

THE DAISY CHAIN; or, Aspirations. A Family Chronicle With Illustrations by J. P. ATKINSON.

THE TRIAL: More Links of the Daisy Chain. With Illustrations by J. P. ATKINSON.

THE PILLARS OF THE HOUSE; or, Under Wode, under Rode. Two Vols. With Illustrations by HERBERT GANDY.

THE YOUNG STEPMOTHER; or, a Chronicle of Mistakes. With Illustrations by MARIAN HUXLEY.

THE CLEVER WOMAN OF THE FAMILY. With Illustrations by ADRIAN STOKES.

THE THREE BRIDES. With Illustrations by ADRIAN STOKES.

MY YOUNG ALCIDES: A Faded Photograph. With Illustrations by ADRIAN STOKES.

THE CAGED LION. With Illustrations by W. J. HENNESSY.

THE DOVE IN THE EAGLE'S NEST. With Illustrations by W. J. HENNESSY.

THE CHAPLET OF PEARLS; or, the White and Black Ribaumont. With Illustrations by W. J. HENNESSY.

LADY HESTER; or, Ursula's Narrative; and THE DANVERS PAPERS. With Illustrations by JANE E. COOK.

MAGNUM BONUM; or, Mother Carey's Brood. With Illustrations by W. J. HENNESSY.

LOVE AND LIFE: an Old Story in Eighteenth Century Costume. With Illustrations by W. J. HENNESSY.

UNKNOWN TO HISTORY. A Story of the Captivity of Mary of Scotland. With Illustrations by W. J. HENNESSY.

STRAY PEARLS. Memoirs of Margaret de Ribaumont, Viscountess of Bellaise. With Illustrations by W. J. HENNESSY.

THE NOVELS AND TALES OF
CHARLOTTE M. YONGE

THE ARMOURER'S 'PRENTICES. With Illustrations by W. J. HENNESSY.

THE TWO SIDES OF THE SHIELD. With Illustrations by W. J. HENNESSY.

NUTTIE'S FATHER. With Illustrations by W. J. HENNESSY.

SCENES AND CHARACTERS; or, Eighteen Months at Beechcroft. With Illustrations by W. J. HENNESSY.

CHANTRY HOUSE. With Illustrations by W. J. HENNESSY.

A MODERN TELEMACHUS. With Illustrations by W. J. HENNESSY.

BYWORDS. A collection of Tales new and old.

BEECHCROFT AT ROCKSTONE.

MORE BYWORDS.

A REPUTED CHANGELING; or, Three Seventh Years Two Centuries Ago.

THE LITTLE DUKE, RICHARD THE FEARLESS. With Illustrations.

THE LANCES OF LYNWOOD. With Illustrations by J. B.

THE PRINCE AND THE PAGE : A Story of the Last Crusade. With Illustrations by ADRIAN STOKES.

TWO PENNILESS PRINCESSES. With Illustrations by W. J. HENNESSY.

THAT STICK.

AN OLD WOMAN'S OUTLOOK IN A HAMPSHIRE VILLAGE.

GRISLY GRISELL; or, The Laidly Lady of Whitburn. A Tale of the Wars of the Roses.

HENRIETTA'S WISH. Second Edition.

THE LONG VACATION.

THE RELEASE; or, Caroline's French Kindred.

THE PILGRIMAGE OF THE BEN BERIAH.

THE TWO GUARDIANS; or, Home in this World. Second Edition.

COUNTESS KATE AND THE STOKESLEY SECRET.

MODERN BROODS; or, Developments Unlooked for.

STROLLING PLAYERS : A Harmony of Contrasts. By C. M. YONGE and C. R. COLERIDGE.

Works by Mrs. Craik

Olive : A Novel.   With Illustrations by G. BOWERS.

The Ogilvies : A Novel.   With Illustrations.

Agatha's Husband : A Novel.   With Illustrations by WALTER CRANE.

The Head of the Family : A Novel.   With Illustrations by WALTER CRANE.

Two Marriages.

The Laurel Bush.

King Arthur : Not a Love Story.

About Money, and other Things.

Concerning Men, and other Papers.

Works by Mrs. Oliphant

Neighbours on the Green.

Kirsteen : the Story of a Scotch Family Seventy Years Ago.

A Beleaguered City : A Story of the Seen and the Unseen.

Hester : a Story of Contemporary Life.

He that Will Not when He May.

The Railway Man and his Children.

The Marriage of Elinor.

Sir Tom.

The Heir-Presumptive and the Heir-Apparent.

A Country Gentleman and his Family.

A Son of the Soil.

The Second Son.

The Wizard's Son : A Novel.

The Curate in Charge.

Lady William. | Young Musgrave.

The Works of Dean Farrar

SEEKERS AFTER GOD. The Lives of Seneca, Epictetus, and Marcus Aurelius.

ETERNAL HOPE. Sermons preached in Westminster Abbey.

THE FALL OF MAN : and other Sermons.

THE WITNESS OF HISTORY TO CHRIST.

THE SILENCE AND VOICES OF GOD, with other Sermons.

"IN THE DAYS OF THY YOUTH." Sermons on Practical Subjects.

SAINTLY WORKERS. Five Lenten Lectures.

EPHPHATHA ; or, the Amelioration of the World.

MERCY AND JUDGMENT : a few last words on Christian Eschatology.

SERMONS & ADDRESSES DELIVERED IN AMERICA.

THE WORKS OF

Frederick Denison Maurice

SERMONS PREACHED IN LINCOLN'S INN CHAPEL. In six vols.

SERMONS PREACHED IN COUNTRY CHURCHES.

CHRISTMAS DAY: and other Sermons.

THEOLOGICAL ESSAYS.

THE PROPHETS AND KINGS OF THE OLD TESTAMENT.

THE PATRIARCHS AND LAWGIVERS OF THE OLD TESTAMENT.

THE GOSPEL OF THE KINGDOM OF HEAVEN.

THE GOSPEL OF ST. JOHN.

THE EPISTLES OF ST. JOHN.

THE FRIENDSHIP OF BOOKS: and other Lectures.

THE PRAYER BOOK AND THE LORD'S PRAYER.

THE DOCTRINE OF SACRIFICE. Deduced from the Scriptures.

THE ACTS OF THE APOSTLES.

THE KINGDOM OF CHRIST ; or, Hints to a Quaker respecting the Principles, Constitution, and Ordinances of the Catholic Church. 2 vols.

THE WORKS OF

CHARLES KINGSLEY

WESTWARD HO!

HYPATIA; or, New Foes with an old Face.

TWO YEARS AGO.

ALTON LOCKE, Tailor and Poet. An Autobiography.

HEREWARD THE WAKE, "Last of the English."

YEAST: A Problem.

POEMS: including The Saint's Tragedy, Andromeda, Songs Ballads, etc.

THE WATER-BABIES: A Fairy Tale for a Land-Baby. With Illustrations by LINLEY SAMBOURNE.

THE HEROES; or, Greek Fairy Tales for my Children. With Illustrations by the Author.

GLAUCUS; or, The Wonders of the Shore. With Illustrations.

MADAME HOW AND LADY WHY; or, First Lessons in Earth Lore for Children. With Illustrations.

AT LAST. A Christmas in the West Indies. With Illustrations.

THE HERMITS.

HISTORICAL LECTURES AND ESSAYS.

PLAYS AND PURITANS, and other Historical Essays.

THE ROMAN AND THE TEUTON.

PROSE IDYLLS, New and Old.

SCIENTIFIC LECTURES AND ESSAYS.

SANITARY AND SOCIAL LECTURES AND ESSAYS.

LITERARY AND GENERAL LECTURES AND ESSAYS.

ALL SAINTS' DAY: and other Sermons.

DISCIPLINE: and other Sermons.

THE GOOD NEWS OF GOD. Sermons.

GOSPEL OF THE PENTATEUCH.

SERMONS FOR THE TIMES.

SERMONS ON NATIONAL SUBJECTS.

VILLAGE SERMONS, AND TOWN AND COUNTRY SERMONS.

THE WATER OF LIFE: and other Sermons.

WESTMINSTER SERMONS.

ENGLISH
MEN OF LETTERS

EDITED BY JOHN MORLEY.

Arranged in 13 Volumes, each containing the Lives of three Authors.

I. **Chaucer.** By Dr. A. W. WARD. **Spenser.** By Dean CHURCH. **Dryden.** By Prof. SAINTSBURY.

II. **Milton.** By MARK PATTISON. **Goldsmith.** By W. BLACK. **Cowper.** By GOLDWIN SMITH.

III. **Byron.** By Professor NICHOL. **Shelley.** By J. A. SYMONDS. **Keats.** By SIDNEY COLVIN.

IV. **Wordsworth.** By F. W. H. MYERS. **Southey.** By Prof. DOWDEN. **Landor.** By SIDNEY COLVIN.

V. **Charles Lamb.** By Canon AINGER. **Addison.** By W. J. COURTHOPE. **Swift.** By Sir LESLIE STEPHEN, K.C.B.

VI. **Scott.** By R. H. HUTTON. **Burns.** By Principal SHAIRP. **Coleridge.** By H. D. TRAILL.

VII. **Hume.** By Prof. HUXLEY, F.R.S. **Locke.** By THOS. FOWLER. **Burke.** By JOHN MORLEY.

VIII. **Defoe.** By W. MINTO. **Sterne.** By H. D. TRAILL. **Hawthorne.** By HENRY JAMES.

IX. **Fielding.** By AUSTIN DOBSON. **Thackeray.** By ANTHONY TROLLOPE. **Dickens.** By Dr. A. W. WARD.

X. **Gibbon.** By J. C. MORISON. **Carlyle.** By Professor NICHOL. **Macaulay.** By J. C. MORISON.

XI. **Sydney.** By J. A. SYMONDS. **De Quincey.** By Prof. MASSON. **Sheridan.** By Mrs. OLIPHANT.

XII. **Pope.** By Sir LESLIE STEPHEN, K.C.B. **Johnson.** By Sir LESLIE STEPHEN, K.C.B. **Gray.** By EDMUND GOSSE.

XIII. **Bacon.** By Dean CHURCH. **Bunyan.** By J. A. FROUDE. **Bentley.** By Sir RICHARD JEBB.

By GERTRUDE ATHERTON

THE CONQUEROR.
A DAUGHTER OF THE VINE.
THE CALIFORNIANS.

By J. H. SHORTHOUSE

JOHN INGLESANT: A Romance.
SIR PERCIVAL: a Story of the Past and of the Present.
THE LITTLE SCHOOLMASTER MARK.
THE COUNTESS EVE.
A TEACHER OF THE VIOLIN.
BLANCHE, LADY FALAISE.

By HUGH CONWAY

A FAMILY AFFAIR. | LIVING OR DEAD.

By W. CLARK RUSSELL

MAROONED.

By ANNIE KEARY

A YORK AND A LANCASTER ROSE.
CASTLE DALY: the Story of an Irish Home thirty
    years ago.
JANET'S HOME. | OLDBURY.
A DOUBTING HEART.
THE NATIONS AROUND ISRAEL.

By E. WERNER

FICKLE FORTUNE.

By W. WARDE FOWLER

A YEAR WITH THE BIRDS. Illustrated.
TALES OF THE BIRDS. Illustrated.
MORE TALES OF THE BIRDS. Illustrated.
SUMMER STUDIES OF BIRDS AND BOOKS.

By FRANK BUCKLAND

CURIOSITIES OF NATURAL HISTORY. Illustrated. In four volumes :

FIRST SERIES—Rats, Serpents, Fishes, Frogs, Monkeys, etc.
SECOND SERIES—Fossils, Bears, Wolves, Cats, Eagles, Hedgehogs, Eels, Herrings, Whales.
THIRD SERIES—Wild Ducks, Fishing, Lions, Tigers, Foxes, Porpoises.
FOURTH SERIES—Giants, Mummies, Mermaids, Wonderful People, Salmon, etc.

By ARCHIBALD FORBES

BARRACKS, BIVOUACS, AND BATTLES.
SOUVENIRS OF SOME CONTINENTS.

By THOMAS HUGHES

TOM BROWN'S SCHOOLDAYS.
TOM BROWN AT OXFORD.
THE SCOURING OF THE WHITE HORSE.
ALFRED THE GREAT.

By MONTAGU WILLIAMS

LEAVES OF A LIFE. | LATER LEAVES.
ROUND LONDON.

By W. E. NORRIS

THIRLBY HALL.
A BACHELOR'S BLUNDER.

The Works of SHAKESPEARE

VICTORIA EDITION. In Three Volumes.
Vol. I. COMEDIES. Vol. II. HISTORIES. Vol. III. TRAGEDIES.

Works by Various Authors

Hogan, **M.P.**

Flitters, Tatters, and the Counsellor

The New Antigone | Memories of Father Healy

Canon ATKINSON.—The Last of the Giant Killers

—— Playhours and Half-Holidays; or, further Experiences of Two Schoolboys

Sir S. BAKER.—True Tales for my Grandsons

R. H. BARHAM.—The Ingoldsby Legends

Rev. R. H. D. BARHAM.—Life of Theodore Hook

BLENNERHASSET and SLEEMAN.—Adventures in Mashonaland

LANOE FALCONER.—Cecilia de Noel

W. FORBES-MITCHELL.—Reminiscences of the Great Mutiny

Rev. J. GILMORE.—Storm Warriors

CUTCLIFFE HYNE.—The "Paradise" Coal-Boat

MARY LINSKILL.—Tales of the North Riding

S. R. LYSAGHT.—The Marplot

—— One of the Grenvilles

M. M'LENNAN.—Muckle Jock, and other Stories

LUCAS MALET.—Mrs. Lorimer

G. MASSON.—A Compendious Dictionary of the French Language

Major GAMBIER PARRY.—The Story of Dick

E. C. PRICE.—In the Lion's Mouth

Lord REDESDALE.—Tales of Old Japan

W. C. RHOADES.—John Trevennick

MARCHESA THEODOLI.—Under Pressure

ANTHONY TROLLOPE.—The Three Clerks

Mrs. HUMPHRY WARD.—Miss Bretherton

CHARLES WHITEHEAD.—Richard Savage

THE GLOBE LIBRARY

Crown 8vo. 3s. 6d. each.

The volumes marked with an asterisk (*) are also issued in limp leather, with full gilt back and gilt edges. 5s. net each.

*Boswell's Life of Johnson. With an Introduction by MOWBRAY MORRIS.

*Burns's Complete Works. Edited from the best Printed and MS. Authorities, with Memoir and Glossarial Index. By A. SMITH.

*The Works of Geoffrey Chaucer. Edited by ALFRED W. POLLARD, H. F. HEATH, M. H. LIDDELL, and W. S. McCORMICK.

*Cowper's Poetical Works. Edited, with Biographical Introduction and Notes by W. BENHAM, B.D.

Robinson Crusoe. Edited after the original Edition, with a Biographical Introduction by HENRY KINGSLEY, F.R.G.S.

*Dryden's Poetical Works. Edited, with a Memoir, Revised Texts, and Notes, by W. D. CHRISTIE, M.A.

*The Diary of John Evelyn. With an Introduction and Notes by AUSTIN DOBSON, Hon. LL.D. Edin.

Froissart's Chronicles. Translated by Lord BERNERS. Edited by G. C. MACAULAY, M.A.

*Goldsmith's Miscellaneous Works. With Biographical Introduction by Professor MASSON.

Horace. Rendered into English Prose, with Introduction, Running Analysis, Notes, and Index. By J. LONSDALE, M.A., and S. LEE, M.A.

*The Poetical Works of John Keats. Edited, with Introduction and Notes, by WILLIAM T. ARNOLD.

Morte D'Arthur. The Book of King Arthur, and of his Noble Knights of the Round Table. The Original Edition of Caxton, revised for modern use. With Introduction, Notes, and Glossary. By Sir E. STRACHEY. [by Professor MASSON.

*Milton's Poetical Works. Edited, with Introduction,

*The Diary of Samuel Pepys. With an Introduction and Notes by G. GREGORY SMITH.

*Pope's Poetical Works. Edited, with Notes and Introductory Memoir, by Dr. A. W. WARD.

*Sir Walter Scott's Poetical Works. Edited, with Biographical and Critical Memoir, by Prof. F. T. PALGRAVE. With Introduction and Notes.

*Shakespeare's Complete Works. Edited by W. G. CLARK, M.A., and W. ALDIS WRIGHT, M.A. With Glossary.

*Spenser's Complete Works. Edited from the Original Editions and Manuscripts, with Glossary, by R. MORRIS, and a Memoir by J. W. HALES, M.A. [edges. 4s. 6d.]

*Tennyson's Poetical Works. [Also in extra cloth, gilt

Virgil. Rendered into English Prose, with Introductions, Notes Analysis, and Index. By J. LONSDALE, M.A., and S. LEE, M.A.

ILLUSTRATED
STANDARD NOVELS

Crown 8vo. Cloth Elegant, gilt edges (Peacock Edition).
3s. 6d. each.

Also issued in ornamental cloth binding. 2s. 6d. each.

By JANE AUSTEN

With Introductions by AUSTIN DOBSON, *and Illustrations by*
HUGH THOMSON *and* C. E. BROCK.

PRIDE AND PREJUDICE.	MANSFIELD PARK.
SENSE AND SENSIBILITY.	NORTHANGER ABBEY,
EMMA.	AND PERSUASION.

By J. FENIMORE COOPER

With Illustrations by C. E. BROCK *and* H. M. BROCK.

THE LAST OF THE MOHICANS. With a General Introduction by Mowbray Morris.

THE DEERSLAYER.	THE PIONEERS.
THE PATHFINDER.	THE PRAIRIE.

By MARIA EDGEWORTH

With Introductions by ANNE THACKERAY RITCHIE, *and Illustrations by* CHRIS HAMMOND *and* CARL SCHLOESSER.

ORMOND.	HELEN.
CASTLE RACKRENT, AND	BELINDA.
THE ABSENTEE.	PARENT'S ASSISTANT.
POPULAR TALES.	

By CAPTAIN MARRYAT

With Introductions by DAVID HANNAY, *and Illustrations by*
H. M. BROCK, J. AYTON SYMINGTON, FRED PEGRAM, F. H.
TOWNSEND, H. R. MILLAR, *and* E. J. SULLIVAN.

JAPHET IN SEARCH OF	JACOB FAITHFUL.
A FATHER.	PETER SIMPLE.

ILLUSTRATED
STANDARD NOVELS

By CAPTAIN MARRYAT—*continued*.

MIDSHIPMAN EASY.
THE KING'S OWN.
THE PHANTOM SHIP.
SNARLEY-YOW.
POOR JACK.

THE PIRATE, AND THE
 THREE CUTTERS.
MASTERMAN READY.
FRANK MILDMAY.
NEWTON FORSTER.

By THOMAS LOVE PEACOCK

With Introductions by GEORGE SAINTSBURY, *and Illustrations
by* H. R. MILLAR *and* F. H. TOWNSEND.

HEADLONG HALL, AND
 NIGHTMARE ABBEY.
MAID MARIAN, AND
 CROTCHET CASTLE.

GRYLL GRANGE.
MELINCOURT.
MISFORTUNES OF ELPHIN
 AND RHODODAPHNE.

BY VARIOUS AUTHORS

WESTWARD HO! By CHARLES KINGSLEY. Illustrated
by C. E. Brock.

HANDY ANDY. By SAMUEL LOVER. Illustrated by
H. M. Brock. With Introduction by Charles Whibley.

TOM CRINGLE'S LOG. By MICHAEL SCOTT. Illustrated by J. Ayton Symington. With Introduction by Mowbray Morris.

ANNALS OF THE PARISH. By JOHN GALT. Illustrated
By C. E. Brock. With Introduction by Alfred Ainger.

SYBIL, OR THE TWO NATIONS, ETC. By BENJAMIN
DISRAELI. Illustrated by F. Pegram. With Introduction by
H. D. Traill.

LAVENGRO. By GEORGE BORROW. Illustrated by
E. J. Sullivan. With Introduction by Augustine Birrell, K.C.

ADVENTURES OF HAJJI BABA OF ISPAHAN. By JAMES
MORIER. Illustrated by H. R. Millar. With Introduction by
Lord Curzon.

THE NEW CRANFORD SERIES

Crown 8vo, Cloth Elegant, Gilt Edges, 3s. 6d. per volume.

Cranford. By Mrs. GASKELL. With Preface by Anne Thackeray Ritchie and 100 Illustrations by Hugh Thomson.

The Vicar of Wakefield. With 182 Illustrations by Hugh Thomson, and Preface by Austin Dobson.

Our Village. By MARY RUSSELL MITFORD. Introduction by Anne Thackeray Ritchie, and 100 Illustrations by Hugh Thomson.

Gulliver's Travels. With Introduction by Sir Henry Craik, K.C.B., and 100 Illustrations by C. E. Brock.

The Humorous Poems of Thomas Hood. With Preface by Alfred Ainger, and 130 Illustrations by C. E. Brock.

Sheridan's The School for Scandal and The Rivals. Illustrated by E. J. Sullivan. With Introduction by A. Birrell.

Household Stories. By the Brothers GRIMM. Translated by Lucy Crane. With Pictures by Walter Crane.

Reynard the Fox. Edited by J. JACOBS. With Illustrations by W. Frank Calderon.

Coaching Days and Coaching Ways. By W. OUTRAM TRISTRAM. With Illustrations by H. Railton and Hugh Thomson.

Coridon's Song; and other Verses. With Introduction by Austin Dobson and Illustrations by Hugh Thomson.

The Fables of Æsop. Selected by JOSEPH JACOBS. Illustrated by R. Heighway.

Old Christmas. By WASHINGTON IRVING. With Illustrations by R. Caldecott.

Bracebridge Hall. With Illustrations by R. CALDECOTT.

Rip Van Winkle and the Legend of Sleepy Hollow. With 50 Illustrations and a Preface by George H. Boughton, A.R.A.

The Alhambra. With Illustrations by J. Pennell and Introduction by E. R. Pennell.

MACMILLAN & CO., LTD., LONDON.

J. PALMER, PRINTER, CAMBRIDGE. 20 . 4 . 0